*Southern Literary Studies*
FRED HOBSON, EDITOR

# A Talent for Living

JOSEPHINE PINCKNEY
AND THE CHARLESTON LITERARY
TRADITION

*Barbara L. Bellows*

LOUISIANA STATE UNIVERSITY PRESS

BATON ROUGE

Published by Louisiana State University Press
Copyright © 2006 by Louisiana State University Press
All rights reserved
Manufactured in the United States of America


DESIGNER: Amanda McDonald Scallan
TYPEFACE: Whitman


Library of Congress Cataloging-in-Publication Data

Bellows, Barbara L.
A talent for living : Josephine Pinckney and the Charleston literary tradition / Barabara L. Bellows
    p. cm. — (Southern literary studies)
    Includes bibliographical references and index.
    ISBN 978-0-8071-3163-3 (cloth)
    1. Pinckney, Josephine, 1895–1957. 2. Novelists, American — 20th century — Biography.
    I. Title. II. Series.
    PS3531.I7Z56 2006
    813'.52 — dc22

2005030876

*To the memory of my parents, Mary Louise and George Bellows*

# Contents

Preface | xi

Introduction | 1

1. The Last Aristocrat | 12

2. The Education of a Young Poet | 23

3. "My Heart Is Still My Own" | 38

4. Inventing a Southern Literature | 57

5. A Grave for Love | 77

6. Sea-Drinking Cities | 91

7. Thirty-six Chalmers Street | 111

8. Speaking for the South | 132

9. Farewell to First Love | 153

10. Willkie and War | 164

11. American Fantasy | 177

12. Great Mischief | 194

13. "Death, My Son and Foe" | 212

Notes | 231
Bibliography | 267
Index | 281

# Illustrations

*Following page 90*

Valentine House at 900 Capitol Street, Richmond

Camilla Pinckney, ca. 1897

Eldorado, the Pinckney family plantation

*Mrs. Motte Directing the Generals Marion and Lee to Burn Her Mansion to Dislodge the British*

*Charles Cotesworth Pinckney in His Sixth Year (1789–1865)*

Captain Thomas Pinckney, ca. 1908

C. Cotesworth Pinckney with his aunt Lucy Stewart

Pinckney family home, 21 King Street, Charleston, ca. 1935

Josephine Lyons Scott Pinckney, 1898

Josephine Pinckney, ca. 1907

Josephine Pinckney, ca. 1912

Pinckney in the Eliza Lucas Pinckney dress, 1923

DuBose Heyward and Dorothy Heyward, ca. 1925

Amy Lowell, ca. 1920

Richard Bowditch Wigglesworth, ca. 1918

Hervey Allen, 1930

Henry Seidel Canby, ca. 1925

*A Charleston Residence,* Pinckney's home at 36 Chalmers Street

Dining room at 36 Chalmers Street

Prentiss Taylor, 1932

Samuel Gaillard Stoney Jr., 1936

Harriet Porcher (Stoney) Simons, ca. 1927

Josephine Pinckney and DuBose Heyward, ca. 1935

Wendell Willkie and Mary Pickford, 1940

Pinckney, Albert Simons, Harold Mouzon, and George C. Rogers Sr., 1950

Pinckney at a concert given by the Society for the Preservation of
    Spirituals, 1955

Joseph Hergesheimer, ca. 1930

*A Portrait of Miss Josephine Pinckney,* by A.E. (George William Russell), 1931

Dust jacket for *Great Mischief,* 1948

Josephine Pinckney, 1945

# Preface

I wrote this book to solve a mystery. Why had the award-winning author Josephine Pinckney fallen into oblivion after a lifetime of achievement? The story of the Charleston woman who wrote essays, short stories, reviews, a noted book of evocative poetry, and five beautifully crafted novels drew me in while I was doing research for a new introduction to her most celebrated novel, *Three O'Clock Dinner* (1945), for the Southern Classics series of the University of South Carolina Press. Although I knew little about Pinckney when I set out, as a historian I was well acquainted with the heroes and heroines of her legendary family. Pinckney belonged to the sixth American generation of a family boasting jurists, war heroes, statesmen, governors, diplomats, and presidential candidates. The family's imprint on the politics, culture, and economics of the Low Country was so profound that Charleston's golden era during the years between 1730 and 1830 has been dubbed the "Age of the Pinckneys."[1]

My first clue about Pinckney came from accounts of the Poetry Society of South Carolina, a seminal organization started in 1920 that promoted the cultural revival often called the Charleston Renaissance. At twenty-five years of age, the "brilliant" Pinckney was the youngest among the founders. When I started this project in 1999, Pinckney's role (as well as that of other women) in the society had been neglected. All of the existing literature on the group accepts author John Bennett's claim that he and poets DuBose Heyward and Hervey Allen were the engines behind its inception and, by implication, the Charleston Literary Movement. As I dug around in the primary sources, a variety of founding narratives emerged, including one suggesting that the society actually first coalesced under the Lady Banksia roses bedecking the piazza of Josephine Pinckney's family mansion at 21 King Street.[2]

I have to confess that I had hoped to find Pinckney involved with something more exciting during the Roaring Twenties than the founding of a poetry society. I wanted fast cars, fast living, and bootleg liquor in hip flasks. Actually I was not entirely disappointed, for Pinckney blossomed into a young woman intensely alive to the excitement of the modern era. Although Charleston always remained her spiritual home, as an adult she came to know Rome and Paris as well as she knew

Boston and New York. And, in its early days, the Poetry Society possessed a certain drama of its own. Pinckney joined Allen and Heyward in their attempted plot to hijack the slow-moving train of sentimental southern literature. In their most ambitious dreams, they had also hoped to soften racial attitudes and to "re-set the switch" directing the literary trends away from the region's postwar "perfervid bunk" and toward writing that reflected the true heart of the South.[3]

I found Josephine Pinckney's papers in the South Carolina Historical Society in Charleston. After a cursory survey of the collection, I surmised, with the innocence that precedes every writing project, that I could finish the research in a few months. Of course, I was wrong. Years have passed as I tracked down her letters and correspondence in libraries and archives from Charleston to Boston. But it has been a pleasurable search. I still agree with one of Pinckney's eulogists that "no one was ever bored in her presence."[4]

The range of Pinckney's correspondence hints at the many dimensions of her life, especially her interest in music, art, literature, historic preservation, local politics, and international events. She had both men and women among her close friends. Letters from DuBose Heyward and Hervey Allen were expected. So were those from other southern authors, such as Donald Davidson and Ellen Glasgow. Wall Street lawyer and presidential hopeful Wendell Willkie was a surprise. So was Lincoln Kirstein, founder of the American Ballet Company. After further probing, I realized that Pinckney had skillfully parlayed the connections made through the Poetry Society with professors, publishers, and poets into a web of influential friends, contacts, and advisers. Although she took the Carolina Low Country as a subject in her poetry, and as the setting in most of her novels, Pinckney was clearly determined from the beginning of her career to find fame in a much larger world.

The perimeters of the peninsula city could not contain Pinckney's curiosity to know, to experience, to feel. Pinckney honed her talent for living, long a hallmark of southern life, and gave rein to her lust for travel, good food, fine wine, and informed (sometimes combative) conversation. Far from the moss-backed literary-lady, Pinckney was restless all her life. Enjoying an independent income, she led a migratory existence—winter and spring in Charleston, summer and fall in New York, New England, or Europe. She moved between worlds as different as those of a songbird winging back and forth from the Arctic tundra to Caribbean beaches. The only real variable in the patterns of her life was the speed at which she annually left Charleston—first by steamer, then train, automobile, jet.

I took vicarious pleasure in mapping out Pinckney's travels. In the first years of the 1920s alone, Pinckney appears having cocktails in Bernard Berenson's

Italian villa, picnicking in East Gloucester (the summer playground for Boston intellectuals), ruminating at the devastated battlefields of France, sharing lobster cutlets with Brahmin poet Amy Lowell at midnight, and paddling Harvard professor John Livingston Lowes through a swamp near her family plantation on the Santee River delta. Pinckney never embraced the jaded nihilism of the flapper, but she enjoyed the new freedoms that had even worked their way into the austere Charleston society that never danced "the charleston" (or ever capitalized its name). She smoked in public, served Manhattans to debutantes, and reciprocated the many and ardent attentions of men smitten with her powerful philter of Old South romance and modern sophistication. She often confused her admirers with mixed signals of hauteur and come hither.

At some point during this research, my interest in Pinckney made the leap from academic to personal. Even though I write these last words in the Upper East Side of Manhattan and have spent the last twenty years on my own extended peregrination around the Northeast, I should confess that I, too, am Charleston-born and share with Pinckney the affection of the native daughter for the old city. And, like Pinckney, it seems that I can never comfortably settle there, nor can I ever quite escape the powerful magnetic field that draws me back.

Pinckney and I are separated by slightly more than a half-century, not so very long in Charleston time. We were christened in the same Episcopal church. We walked the same oak-shaded streets, developed the same inexplicable affection for the poisonous oleander and the rank pluff mud, and could still be struck dumb by the harbor-side beauty off the Battery. We both experienced the exhilaration of threatening hurricanes, as well as the perverse pleasure of steamy August nights. We also shared a fondness for shrimp pie. She thought my favorite recipe (with bread crumbs) "inferior" to her receipt (with rice).[5] Until I went to college, my family—like hers—still had "dinner" in the middle of the day, although at two o'clock, not the three of older times, and a supper at night. We buried our parents in Charleston's Magnolia Cemetery, where Pinckney now rests.

In a sense, Pinckney has edited her own biography. She left firm instructions that her personal notebooks be burned upon her death. Fortunately, numerous pages escaped the flames, tucked in books, stuffed in the corner of boxes, overlooked. When I first began rifling through her papers, I felt I was violating the privacy of a woman who kept her heart locked tight. As I came to know Pinckney better, I realized she understood the allure of the high wall or drawn shutter. She wanted her story told and hoped somehow that her life might enhance her family's august reputation. She even left crumbs of explanatory notes that helped me find my way. On one of her notebook's surviving pages, she instructed herself:

"Believe in things. My own life. My autobiography would be interesting to write not because I am remarkable, but because it would be the stuff of which other people are made. My failures, my successes would echo theirs. The human heart is the stuff of literature. Write a candid autobiography . . . and lay it aside as clay to make poems and novels of." With Pinckney, the story was always the thing.

Josephine Pinckney was still alive when I was born, so in typical Charleston style I know people who knew people whom she had known. The usual lonely life of the working historian burrowed in silent library stacks and darkened microfilm rooms was transformed into an unusually social undertaking for me by the generosity of the many people who were willing to reach back into their memories, sift through their scrapbooks, and reach high up on their bookshelves for information about Pinckney and her times. I now recollect the interviews that I did with Pinckney's friends and relatives over tea, lunch, picnics, cocktails, and dinner with intense pleasure. I am honored that some of her friends are now my friends too.

With his contagious enthusiasm for intellectual pursuit and wide-ranging curiosity, prolific author Anthony H. Harrigan Jr. has been my mainstay through the long course of this project, reading drafts, offering advice, and sharing his own work with me. Elizabeth Ravenel Harrigan too has shared her deep understanding of Low Country history and helped me with Gullah translations. Professor George W. Williams and Harriet P. Williams, resident scholars at One Tradd Street, have challenged my assumptions and stimulated my thinking. I have treasured our conversations about so many subjects, and I appreciate their willingness to read early drafts and the graceful way they have saved me from many errors. As both Charleston natives and longtime residents of New England, Elizabeth Elliott Sass Phillips and I have developed a particular affinity. She too has been generous in reading draft chapters and sharing her unique perspective on Charleston's cultural past. Anne Whaley Sinkler LeClercq has been exceptionally generous with her time, and in sharing letters with me from her personal collection.

Elise Pinckney, the reigning expert on Pinckney family history, and Robert Cuthbert have both shared their research and expansive knowledge of South Carolina's history with me. They also gave me one of the most pleasant days I can remember when they included me on one of their "expeditions" up to the South Santee district north of Charleston and led me through the woods to the ruins of Eldorado, the Pinckney family plantation.

Other members of the Pinckney family, Pie Pinckney Friendly, Betsey Pinckney Apple, Isabella Breckinridge, Anne Pinckney Gay, and Jane Pinckney Hanahan were gracious in sharing books, family lore and photographs. Through their charm and wit I believe I have caught a glimpse of their Great Aunt Jo. Landon W. and Anne Garland, Pinckney's cousins from her mother's side, kindly introduced me to other members of the Scott family, including Tazewell Ellet and Mary Blair Valentine. Judge James Keith, Elizabeth Burden, Charles Duell, Bradford H. Walker, and Lisa Sutphin also helped me understand Camilla Scott Pinckney's influence on her daughter.

Others who have helped shaped my understanding of Pinckney and her world are Anne Baker Leland Bridges, J. Palmer Gaillard, Susan Street Gaillard, Virginia Gourdin, Harriott Means Johnson, the late Serena Simons Leonhardt, Baroness Eleanor Stone Perenyi, Roderick Quiroz, Harriet Popham MacDougal Rigney, S. Stoney Simons, Sidney Lockwood Tynan, Elizabeth Williams, Roy Williams III, and John Zeigler.

My work in libraries and archives was also pleasurable because of the dedicated professionals who facilitated my research and helped me locate photographs. Dr. Eric Emerson of the South Carolina Historical Society and his staff, especially Pat Kruger, Mike Coker, and Dr. Nicholas Butler (now Research Archivist at the Charleston County Library), were always helpful and patient with my many requests over the years. My thanks also go to Catherine Sadler and the staff at the Charleston Library Society; Jane Yates, archivist at The Citadel; Barbara Doyle at the Middleton Place Archives; and Jonathan Poston and Karen Emmons at Historic Charleston Foundation. I very much appreciate the help I received from Elizabeth Dunn of the Duke University Library; Alycia Vivona and Raymond Teichman, archivists of the Eleanor Roosevelt Papers at Hyde Park; Ernest J. Emrich, Manuscript Reference Librarian at the Library of Congress; Danielle Rougeau of the Abernathy Collection at Middlebury College; and Sue Presnell of the Lilly Library at Indiana University. Phyllis Scott did some very helpful research for me in the court records of Warrenton, Virginia.

This biography of Josephine Pinckney is but a link in the chain of scholarship that has been recovering the importance of Charleston's "Lost Generation" of writers and artists over the last decade. I am particularly indebted to Harlan M. Greene, biographer of John Bennett and project archivist at the Avery Institute. Both scholar and novelist, he has freely shared his expansive knowledge of the history and literature of the Charleston Renaissance as well as his shrewd understanding of human nature and motivation.

I was fortunate to have the best possible readers for this manuscript. Professor Fred Hobson, editor of Louisiana State University Press's Southern Literature Studies series, gallantly first read my manuscript when it was double its final length and then, after revisions, read it again. My second reader, Heyward scholar Professor James M. Hutchisson of the English Department of The Citadel, made helpful comments drawing from his deep storehouse of knowledge of the Charleston Renaissance. I am grateful to Candis LaPrade, formerly acquisitions editor at LSU Press, for shepherding this project through the first hurdles toward publication, and to executive editor John Easterly and senior editor George Roupe for seeing it through to the end. Glenn Perkins copyedited my manuscript with accuracy, patience, and good humor.

Claire E. Wilson has gallantly provided invaluable long-distance assistance with this manuscript. I am indebted to her for her careful work, astute observations, assiduity in tracking down photographs, good cheer, and for so many things over many years.

A special note of appreciation goes to George and Patricia Bellows for their many acts of kindness, including turning over "the blue room" to me when I first began my research in Charleston.

My husband Steven C. Rockefeller, innocent of the power that "home" exerts on a southerner, never dreamed that his life would be turned upside down by a book project and that he would be living (at least part-time) in Charleston. He has been a wonderful sport through it all and, perhaps touched a bit by the old city's magic, has been cultivating his own talent for living. I hope he knows how deeply grateful I am.

*A Talent for Living*

# Introduction

"Immortality works at random," wrote Josephine Pinckney in 1945, the year she became a best-selling novelist and won international fame. "It perpetuates often the wrong person and misses the right ones."[1] Pinckney proved prescient, even though *Three O'Clock Dinner*, her most successful of five novels, was released that year by Viking Press with a great deal of "ballyhoo." A Literary Guild selection, the novel took off "with atomic speed." Against "a thousand to one odds," Metro-Goldwyn-Mayer studio bought the screen rights to her Charleston story for the unprecedented amount of $125,000. Critical and popular reaction was overwhelmingly positive. *Three O'Clock Dinner* was soon entertaining readers in seven different languages. Pinckney joined Thomas Wolfe and Ellen Glasgow as winners of the Southern Authors Award given annually for the best book on a southern subject. The American Library Association included *Three O'Clock Dinner* on its list of the "Fifty Most Outstanding Books" of 1945, along with Richard Wright's *Black Boy* and John Steinbeck's *Cannery Row*.[2]

Already enjoying a substantial reputation in the literary circles of the South for her poetry and prose, as well as for her active role in the promotion of southern letters, Pinckney earned national and international fame. Her editor at Viking Press, Marshall A. Best, also worked with James Joyce and Rebecca West, but he remembered Pinckney "more warmly" than any other of the distinguished writers of that time. Best particularly appreciated the "charm and grace of her character, the intelligence of her insights into people, the delights of her Charleston ambiance tempered by her cosmopolitan ways and her irony."[3] Since her death in 1957, however, she has disappeared from the canon of southern authors.

Born in 1895, Josephine Pinckney grew to maturity in a world on the cusp of change. She began awakening to the potential of her own life at the same time that many Charlestonians felt they were rising from a long, dreamless sleep. Trapped for so long in the South's winter of defeat and poverty after the Civil War and burdened by feelings of resentment and bitterness following Reconstruction, Charleston and its people began to come alive again when the blessings of economic prosperity began to be lightly showered upon the region during World War I. Pinckney's own journey of self-discovery paralleled Charleston's rediscovery of itself as a half-century of isolation ebbed away.

The coming of the modern age in the South resembled the subtle shifts in light that herald the beginning of the southern spring. Imperceptibly longer days beckon the shy narcissus; its white bloom stands bravely above the winter sere, alerting the unwary, lest they be blinded by the explosion of the subtropical color and fragrance, heat and light soon to come. The transformation of the landscape is so dramatic that it seems to mark not a mere shift in the tilt of the Earth but the dawn of an entirely different universe. Or so it seemed to many as the South edged cautiously into the modern era that remade America.

Although evidence of a quickening of interest in the arts could be detected in Charleston by 1915, the years immediately after World War I were the most productive. Sensing the transformation at work in their world, Charlestonians grew passionately interested in the Low Country's unique folkways, just as they were in the process of leaving them behind. Much of the energy fueling the twenty-five-year period often referred to as the Charleston Renaissance, came from civic leaders, writers, and artists intensely occupied with sorting out which of the elements of southern culture should be preserved into the twentieth century and which should be eulogized and cast away.[4]

Pinckney's gifts did not approach those of the stars of modern southern literature; she belonged to the supporting cast of writers who contributed to the richness of American fiction during its most exciting era. Pinckney's words rang with wit and wisdom. She could be enormously funny in the way of Virginia authors Ellen Glasgow and James Branch Cabell, who both mastered the "urbane fantasy." Charleston and Richmond were among the few places left in America after World War I where a story could still be woven around a recognizable code of manners. Pinckney's efforts to write realistic dramas of class conflict of the sort that literary critics praised during the 1930s always seemed to collapse into social comedies. Pinckney could never avoid seeing some humor in even the most wrenching human situation. At her best, for example in *Three O'Clock Dinner,* she could rival the charm of Glasgow's comedy *They Stooped to Folly.*[5]

Just as Charleston does not fit comfortably into most generalizations about the South, Pinckney's writing does not fit easily into the larger scheme of southern literature. Thought "peculiar," Pinckney admitted, even in its own region, Charleston was born of an aristocrat's dream, the "darling" of Lord Proprietor Sir Anthony Ashley Cooper. By the time of the American Revolution, Charleston was a major port city with links throughout the Atlantic world. Its culture reflected a strong English and Anglican heritage enriched by diverse groups, from French Puritan Huguenots to Sephardic Jews, Irish Catholic immigrants, and African Americans with centuries-old roots in the Low Country.[6]

Pinckney was the mistress of a small world. In her writing she captured the genius loci, the spirit, of Charleston. Praising her essay on southern society in *Culture in the South* (1934), Nashville poet Donald Davidson lauded her ability to describe "what folks are like . . . Who else could have done it so well? Nobody, only Josephine Pinckney." Pinckney took the advice of another of the Vanderbilt writers, John Crowe Ransom, who believed in 1932 that Charleston would remain "irrelevant" to the larger southern movement unless its writers focused on the social landscape that lay before them: "The beautiful houses are still there, so are the fine manners, and the conversation in the ample drawing rooms and dining-rooms."[7] Pinckney wrote with humor, irony, impatience, and tenderness about her own people who lived in those decaying houses. With the insights of the social historian, Pinckney chronicled the disintegrating southern idea of the formal society. In her stories, the last of the fine Madeira is poured and the ancestral dishes are smashed on the floor.

If Pinckney's plots were sometimes thin, her characterizations were always memorable. She had a shrewd ability to penetrate into the heart of human motivation. Her writing style offers moments of pure pleasure for the reader and reflects her origins as a poet. She wrote with the unblinking eye of the skeptic and the steady hand of the etcher. The truth of Pinckney's words cost her popularity at home, for the die-hards of Charleston brooked no criticism of their closed society. Pinckney paid no homage at "the altar of Dixie" and rejected the romantic primitivism that attracted other southern writers (and worried her writing was not "Confederate" enough for popular success). Pinckney thought the Carolina Low Country unique and never considered the South to be a mystical, organic whole. She also avoided the temptation to copy successful trends in American literature along the lines of "Scott Fitzgerald Drinks Bourbon with the Last Confederate Veteran."

As she matured as a writer, Pinckney increasingly concerned herself with characters who displayed the universal traits of love, jealousy, envy, and forgiveness ("the same old Adam"), rather than the canned attributes of southerners. During the 1940s and 1950s, reviewers compared her with Isak Dinesen or Daphne DuMaurier for her story-telling ability and with Jane Austen and Edith Wharton for her penetrating social analysis, but seldom other southerners. "I am not Hemingway," Pinckney wrote in her notebook. "I am Woolf."[8]

Pinckney always marveled over the static quality of Charleston society even during periods of dizzying transformation in other parts of America. Although "the dark reaper" may take up this person or that, she observed, the Ravenels, the Middletons, and Rutledges, with their genetic predisposition against change, persisted. She concluded that the Low Country had somehow slipped through Darwin's web of evolution, perhaps because society there was organized around families, not individuals.[9] In no instance was this observation more accurate than in her own family.

The most powerful force shaping Josephine's early life was her knowledge that she was part of a clan; "blood of the blood, bone of the bone" of South Carolina's oldest families. The Pinckneys rank among the founding families of America. The clan's swashbuckling founder, Thomas Pinckney of County Durham, England, first made landfall in Charleston in 1692. He was one of the English privateers known in legend as the "Red Sea Men" for their wide ranging adventures against French merchant vessels. Two of South Carolina's signers of the Constitution were Pinckneys; the other two were related by marriage. Over the generations, the Pinckneys intermarried with their political allies and other prominent local families so exclusively that double and even triple first cousins were common. And then those cousins married. Before the Civil War, Charlestonians also formed alliances with equally distinguished families in New York, Philadelphia, or Newport and became part of "one of the exclusive, self-limiting circles of America," as Pinckney phrased it.[10] She belonged to that tiny American aristocracy that survived from the colonial period to the modern age.

In contrast to the experience of older writers such as Edith Wharton or Ellen Glasgow, though, Pinckney found encouragement for her literary ambitions. Her celebrated family's history actually pressed her to make something extraordinary of her own fortunate life. Her biggest challenge, in fact, was to feel worthy of her heritage. The founding matriarchs of her line, her great-great-grandmothers Eliza Lucas Pinckney and Rebecca Brewton Motte, were placed on pedestals by historians of the early republic who were striving to create an American pantheon of heroes and heroines.

Eliza Lucas Pinckney was an eighteenth-century Demeter who oversaw three plantations when a very young woman, helped promote indigo as an export commodity, read widely, kept a letter book of exquisite beauty, followed London theater, loved music, and married Chief Justice Charles Pinckney (the son of the adventurer ). After her husband died in 1758, she raised a daughter and two sons (Charles Cotesworth and Thomas) whom she relentlessly exhorted to do their duty to God, their country, and their family. The devout, Oxford-educated Pinckneys emerged as heroes of the American Revolution and leaders of the new nation. They wreathed their family in glory. Thomas (Josephine's great-grandfather) was elected South Carolina's second governor. Charles Cotesworth, a brevetted general during the war, was a signer of the Constitution. They moved in high-powered Federalist circles close to George Washington and Alexander Hamilton, were founders of the Society of the Cincinnati, and enjoyed a standing that might best be described as peers of the realm. The Pinckneys, both social conservatives and defenders of states' rights, were also the only brothers to run for the presidency of the United States, Thomas in 1796 and Charles Cotesworth in 1804 and 1808.

In 1945, the year of Josephine's own great success as a novelist, the *Encyclopedia Britannica* invited her to write an entry for Eliza Lucas Pinckney. The exercise humbled her as earlier generations also had been humbled by the reputation of this pious and venerated paragon. As an older cousin, Harriott Horry Rutledge Ravenel, had written in 1896 about this girl-planter and mother of heroes, "When will any 'New Woman' do more for her country?"[11]

The other pillar of Josephine's famous family, Rebecca Brewton Motte, was the sister and heir of the fabulously wealthy merchant Miles Brewton, widow of Jacob Motte and the mother of Governor Thomas Pinckney's two wives (he married Frances Motte Middleton after the death of his first wife, Elizabeth).[12] She was hailed as an American Athena for her early support of the American Revolution in 1775, as well as for her fortitude protecting her daughters in the face of British occupation of both her city mansion and her plantation. When Francis Marion asked her permission to burn down her Congaree River plantation house in May 1781 so he might capture the British officers quartered within, she not only agreed but even provided the fire arrows, or so the story goes.[13] The South Carolina Chapter of the Daughters of the American Revolution named their first chapter after Motte. A large marble tablet (made from the top of one of her pier tables) dedicated to her memory hangs near that of Revolutionary hero General William Moultrie in Charleston's St. Phillip's Episcopal Church.

The two eighteenth-century rice plantations on the South Santee River so intimately associated with the Pinckney family, Fairfield and Eldorado, belonged first to Rebecca Motte.[14] She profited from the rich delta lands, produced a fortune in "Carolina Gold," and paid off all her debts incurred during the Revolution. After Rebecca Motte grew too feeble to live alone, she bought several tracts of land nearby Fairfield Plantation where Governor Pinckney and his second wife, Frances Motte Middleton, together built Eldorado, a high-ceiled, wide-corridored mansion, out of a tangle of maritime forest. The Pinckney family seat was locally referred to as "Mrs. Motte's home." When she died, Rebecca Motte, who always held the legal title, left Eldorado to her daughter Frances.[15]

The tendency of the Pinckney men to marry women of beauty and fortune allowed them the economic freedom to pursue statecraft while continuing to live the life of a lord, but it also endowed their wives with power within the relationship. One of the recurring themes in Josephine Pinckney's writing revolves around the elements of conflict that often arise in a marriage when the wife owns the family home. The burdensome past, especially in the form of huge houses and worthless property weighing on subsequent generations of diminished means, is a theme in several of her novels, especially *Three O'Clock Dinner* (1945) and *Splendid in Ashes* (1958). In 1930, when agrarianism began to influence southern writers, Pinckney wrote a short story about the connection between land and family. In "They Shall Return as Strangers," a young man who has moved to New York reflects on the meaning of his family's island off the coast of South Carolina: "There is something about the ground your family has walked back and forth on that gives you a kind of sense of them. I am not talking about family pride—it's a kind of feeling. . . . It's a sort of refuge between individual egotism and being obliterated in the mass. It isn't that I think so much of the Fairfields, . . . they are just a good county family, but I like that feeling of being a part of a tribe—and of course you are, whether you like it or not."[16]

Pinckney's past endowed her with a complex legacy. Her name, and its connection with the founding of the American republic, gave her a certain cachet in the North as well as the South. Boston even had a Pinckney Street honoring one of her ancestors. The psychic burden, though, of the aristocratic credo of honor—the Code, as Pinckney called it—proved weighty and alienating and made demands on southern women as well as men. Older and much more tenacious than the rules of Victorian behavior, the Code trapped its adherents in a web of kinship, duty, and mutual obligation. Its rules defining honor, gentility, and chivalry had bound southern society together for over a century. The foundation stone of the Code was an almost tribal attachment to one's own: family, friends, home, church, and even political party. "We don't criticize our families to outsiders," Pinckney wrote. "We keep up disintegrating friendships, we cling to the party label Democratic."[17]

Violation of the Code meant falling outside of the kinship protection of the family, the source of southern identity. To be estranged from one's family was to suffer a social death in the South tantamount to being outside the church in colonial Massachusetts Bay. The ruin of a southerner's public reputation bore no less opprobrium than being excluded from the company of the elect did to the Puritan. In the end, it will be remembered, even the rapscallion Rhett Butler returned to Charleston in hopes of once again being "received" by his family.

Over the generations, the legacies of the past were used to teach young Pinckneys, both boys and girls, about their responsibilities for the future. Even after the Civil War, the Code maintained a powerful hold. Family elders would march little children in to gaze upon the symbols of their glorious past. Those youth born into the poverty of the post–Civil War world gasped at Governor Pinckney's elaborate white court suit worn to bow before the King of England when he served as America's first ambassador to the Court of St. James. They struggled with the weight of his ivory-handled sword with its silver scabbard given to him by his brothers-in-arms of the Society of the Cincinnati.[18]

Josephine Pinckney's older cousin, poet Archibald Rutledge, remembered his formidable grandmother opening a great chest full of these wonders for him during the 1890s. At the time, his family was so poor that they had to grow string beans in the grand expanse of lawns of Hampton Plantation where George Washington once breakfasted. Rather than feeling uplifted and capable of personal glory himself, Rutledge, a tall rangy youth in patched clothes, shrank with shame. The great, unbridgeable gulf between the governor and himself felt like a slap from the grave, "a secret reprimand."[19]

For Josephine Pinckney, born later and into more prosperous circumstances, the impact of the past was empowering instead of paralyzing. Even as a young woman, she felt entirely equal to donning a dress reputed to be that of Eliza Lucas Pinckney's. She wore it in a 1923 pageant celebrating the founding of the Charleston Museum 150 years earlier. When the time came for her to choose the heirlooms she wanted, Josephine picked the governor's sword. She enjoyed telling friends how her great-grandfather had summarily slashed down a mutineer during the American Revolution.[20]

If Pinckney had written the famous scene in a Harvard dorm room from Faulkner's *Absalom, Absalom!* when the Canadian Shreve McCannon asked "just one thing more" of his roommate Quentin, she would have changed that devastating question "Why do you hate the South?" She would have had McCannon ask, "Why do you hate your family, the Compsons?" Quentin would have had to say with equal vehemence, "I don't hate them." In Pinckney's world, this admission, the voluntary separation from one's source of identity would have been the equally self-destroying thought. "The family, its generations," Pinckney once wrote, "is life itself."[21]

Pinckney, nevertheless, spent much of her life struggling to break loose from the hoary grasp of the Code. From childhood, her behavior was judged by her family and community against the standard of "what a Pinckney should do." In her adult life, the hectoring voice came from within. Depression stalked her off and on throughout her life. She took on the burden of family honor with an earnestness more often observed in oldest sons than youngest daughters. If she had lived in different times, Pinckney would surely have gone into politics, her obsession. As it was, the heroic aspects of an artist's life attracted her to writing.[22]

Reserved, thoughtful, and introspective, Pinckney developed a hypersensitivity to flaws or weaknesses in herself and others. She was excessively vulnerable to censure or rejection. The withering criticism she sometimes leveled at her friends and associates paled in comparison to the intense scrutiny she directed inward. The responsibilities of duty, participation in civic affairs, and the perpetuation of institutions long associated with the Pinckneys, however, distracted her and siphoned off her energies. The Code more or less "rode" Pinckney all her life, like the night "hags" of Gullah lore that she wrote about to such magical effect in her fantasy *Great Mischief* (1948). Pinckney resisted the temptation of entitlement and gave herself over to public service. Deeply involved in the cultural renaissance of Charleston in the 1920s, Pinckney played a key role in aspects of civic life from historic preservation to civil rights. Her life reflected her philosophy that citizens "should enrich the place they live in by putting their lives into it, and they should be enriched by it in return."[23]

The Code held the strings to Pinckney's conscience, but her mind was free to pursue the modes of modern thought. Pinckney belonged to the generation that came to adulthood in the confluence of dangerous currents and riptides where the nineteenth and twentieth centuries flowed together. Of all the Charleston writers who embarked on the risky voyage across these waters into the modern world, only Josephine Pinckney made it safely to shore and developed a sensibility in harmony with her times.

As Pinckney tried to accommodate herself to the disjuncture between the simple certainties of her youth and the discontinuities of the modern world, she lost faith in the comfortable words of the Episcopal prayer book, although their poetry stayed with her always. She did not entirely abandon the notions of sin or redemption but came to understand them more in the context of the ancient Stoics. She accepted the tragic dimension of life, that man's fate was to suffer and sacrifice, and expect no heaven at the end of the long and twisting road. The only true human freedom was deciding how to cope with what life dealt out. Her intellectual wrestling with the relationship of character and fate, and the nature of good and evil, elevates her novels beyond much of the tepid popular fiction of her day.

Pinckney was conversant about Marx, accepting of Darwin, and fascinated by Freud. She obviously read widely about human psychology, how deeply is not clear. She may have undergone psychoanalysis, possibly during a long stay in Switzerland in 1925, but would have been characteristically reluctant to reveal this experience if she had. Pinckney also would have been familiar with the work of Karen Horney through her psychoanalyst friend Caroline Newton, daughter of the famous book collector A. Edward Newton. Newton, who was psychoanalyzed by Freud in 1922, also did consultations with Horney. Horney differed from Freud in her belief that some human neuroses have origins in fears, prejudices, and social values of a particular culture, ideas that later show up in Pinckney's references to the southern "inferiority complexes" and Charlestonians' "fatal desire to please."[24]

Pinckney understood that the inexorable force of modern democracy would level society and elevate the many at the expense of the few. She knew this was how it must be, should be. She took an early, behind-the-scenes lead in the civil rights movement with Charletson's Inter-racial Commission formed during the 1920s. She was a quiet player in the drive to open the Democratic Party primary to South Carolina blacks during the 1940s and for school integration during the 1950s. Her politics were advanced for Charleston, but still conservative (she abandoned the Democratic Party during Roosevelt's Second New Deal). A feminist in deed, she was not in name. Dressed in white gloves and camellia corsages, Pinckney understood the power of femininity in southern society and moved quietly and deliberately to change her world.

Pinckney's liberalism was that of the patrician: realistic, but still wistful for the lost "kingliness" of the old planter society. She clung to the belief that if the enlightened upper classes had retained political power in the old Confederate states, they could have remedied many of the ancient vices of southern society on their own. With a Turgenevian understanding that good people were often caught in the web of a bad system not of their creation, Pinckney rejected the sociological school's penchant for making symbols of people. Instead, she berated the last of the aristocrats, those of her generation, for not fulfilling their duties as "the upper crust" and for making their demise a matter of such little consequence. Pinckney had hoped during the 1930s that the "spiritual heritage" of the aristocratic class might survive in the South. She imagined that their conservatism, veneration of tradition, and deep connection to the values of the agricultural world might somehow provide a bulwark, "a long gray line," against the crass commercialism and standardization that she thought was sickening the soul of modern America.[25] Pinckney's goal in her life and in her art was preserving the most humane nonmaterialistic aspects of southern living.

Pinckney claimed a "talent for friendship" and formed lifelong bonds with forward-thinking, socially liberal women.[26] Some were friends of her youth, such as Harriet Porcher Stoney Simons and Caroline Sidney Sinkler Lockwood, who defied the stereotypes of upper-class southern ladies. Pinckney also found friends among the hard-hitting female powerhouses who shaped the American mind after

World War I. Some were popular writers she met in New York, but most worked behind the scenes as publishers or editors. Pinckney fell in with the circle surrounding Ellen Glasgow's great friend, Irita Van Doren, powerful editor of the *New York Herald Tribune* book review section and originator of the best-seller list. Van Doren and her frequently venomous reviewer Isabel Paterson had the ability to make or break reputations of emerging authors, such as Sinclair Lewis or John Steinbeck. Pinckney was coached in the often acrimonious politics that raged among literary women by her close friend (and frequent competitor) Grace Stone, a popular novelist best remembered for *The Bitter Tea of General Yen* (1933).

During the 1930s, Pinckney inched away from the literary niche of "southern writer." She found a more comfortable place in the universe of the popular modernists—magazine writers, novelists, newspaper editors, and publishers—based primarily in New York. They were willing to entertain as well as educate "middlebrow" American readers during the turbulent decades of the 1920s and 1930s. Graceful, intelligent, and dignified, Pinckney presented an important counterweight to the prevailing stereotypes of southerners drawn from corrupt race-baiting politicians, such as South Carolina's senator Cole Blease or the townfolk of Dayton, Tennessee, who wanted to close their minds to Darwin and all modern challenges to their narrow vision.

Pinckney fretted about the katzenjammer world bequeathed to her generation by the Great War, but she also found her times utterly fascinating. She gravitated toward talented men and women who suspected that the world was indeed going to hell in a hand basket but had decided to enjoy the ride. The decades between the wars were filled with as much laughter as anguish, as much Ring Lardner as Scott Fitzgerald. Pinckney with her quick, sometimes biting, wit joined the chorus. For her dalliance in the middlebrow world outside of the university (meaning Chapel Hill or Vanderbilt), for her novels being published by book clubs, and for having poems in magazines that ran cartoons, Pinckney lost the interest of later scholars who dismissed her with the damning epithet "popular."[27]

One of the most profound influences on Pinckney was Henry Seidel Canby, the Yale professor who in 1924 founded the *Saturday Review of Literature*, the fountainhead of popular modernism. Among the foremost American tastemakers during the years between the world wars, Canby set the tone for the Book-of-the-Month Club by being its first judge.[28] Canby, who sought to stimulate a truly American literature, became Pinckney's mentor and opened the pages of his influential magazine to other young southern writers when few national journals would consider their submissions. Without Canby, the Southern Renaissance would not have unfolded in quite the way that it did.

Some of Pinckney's ineffable qualities captured the public imagination and distinguished her from the scores of popular women novelists. Part of her appeal derived from the merger of her professional identity with the public reputation of Charleston. Her rise to popularity had paralleled the establishment of the city as a fashionable tourist destination. When Charleston's standing declined during the 1950s as national concerns about southern segregation intensified, interest in Pinckney's work followed the same trajectory. During the height of her popularity immediately after World War II, though, Pinckney emerged as a cultural icon, the last southern aristocrat, perhaps the last "lady." Charleston, a down-at-the-heels city at the time, enjoyed the blush of her reflected glamour. Perhaps Charlestonians saw something in Pinckney—of the past living comfortably with the present—that reminded them of their highest aspirations for their future.

Although intensely private, Pinckney projected a public image that reinforced her professional reputation. She created the ideal setting, living among her family antiques in a restored nineteenth-century lavender-stuccoed house on cobblestoned Chalmers Street. She entertained extensively and ran a salon where the most intellectually curious among the local population mingled with the most interesting among the Low Country's wealthy northern colony, as well as with famed visitors from the many worlds in which Pinckney moved. At the time of her death in 1957, Pinckney was widely regarded as "the leading lady of America's hardest-to-please city."[29]

# 1

# The Last Aristocrat

Josephine Lyons Scott Pinckney was born in a time and in a place where the dead exercised uncommon power over the living. The time was January 29, 1895, and the place Charleston, South Carolina. Her father, Captain Thomas Pinckney, a Confederate veteran from one of South Carolina's most renowned families, was sixty-six years old when she was born. Her mother, Camilla Scott, who hailed from the Virginia gentry, married Captain Pinckney in 1892 when she was nearly forty. She had come within a whisker's breadth of joining the legions of Richmond spinsters in black. The birth of their daughter three years later had the aura of the miraculous about it. The smiling circle gathered around the baptismal font at Josephine's christening suggests how strongly the past survived in the present among the Pinckney family. The eighty-three-year-old rector of Charleston's Grace Episcopal Church, the Reverend Charles Cotesworth Pinckney, was Captain Tom's brother. He also stood as Josephine's godfather. Time seemed to have doubled back on itself. On the same day, the elderly minister christened his little niece and his own grandson. One of Josephine's godmothers was Mrs. Charles Bennett, the wife of Charleston's last rice miller, the end of a long line; just as Captain Pinckney was among the last of the rice planters.[1]

Josephine Pinckney thus began her life between two worlds, one dying and the other just being born. She was the last of a vestigial plantation aristocracy (America's first) based on family, agriculture, land, and republican ideals. But she was born at the time when the second American aristocracy, the product of exuberant industrial wealth, self-made men, and rugged individualism, was asserting itself and reshaping the values of the nation. By the time she reached adulthood during World War I, the modern age was transforming American life in disturbing, but also exhilarating, ways.

Pinckney spent her first years at 29 Legaré Street in a spacious four-story white clapboard house built about 1835 on one of the largest lots in the city.[2] As a child, Josephine played amongst a clutter of desks, cupboards, trunks, and bureaus overflowing with wonderful treasures. For her, history was concrete, something to be held in the hand, not just a memory. The Pinckneys venerated the relics of their ancestors—ivory miniatures, dishes, and clothes—like the bones of saints. Almost every furnishing in Josephine's childhood world had a story that was as highly polished as fine mahogany. Through many repetitions of these tales, Josephine learned her place in the universe of the family: what it meant to be a Pinckney and the last of the Low Country aristocrats.

The judging eyes of gallant soldiers, honored statesmen, and elegant, accomplished ladies gazed down on the young Josephine from portraits lining the walls. French damask curtains that once hung in the eighteenth-century East Bay mansion of Chief Justice Charles and Eliza Lucas Pinckney survived to grace the windows of Josephine's own house. Josephine Pinckney's father, Captain Thomas Pinckney CSA, studied his accounts at the same desk that his grandfather, the Governor Thomas Pinckney, used in London during his tenure as America's first ambassador to Great Britain. Captain Tom casually tucked his grandfather's important state papers away in a cabinet.[3]

One of the family's prized possessions was an elaborate Recamier sofa, part of a massive collection of japanned furniture believed to have been purchased by General Charles Cotesworth Pinckney on his unsuccessful diplomatic mission to the revolutionary government in France during what became known as the XYZ affair, for the three French agents who demanded bribes to promote trade relations between the countries.[4] Since General Pinckney had three daughters who gave him no heirs, many of his personal treasures, such as beautifully decorative Sèvres china, fell into the inheritance stream of his brother. In her own home, Josephine would prominently display a commanding portrait by James Earle of the general in full military dress. Josephine's family felt a particular responsibility for upholding the memory and reputation of their ancestor. In 1911, an "inquisitive Yankee" from the National Portrait Gallery pestered Captain Tom by asking him to confirm that the general did indeed utter his famous retort to the notorious French agents: "Millions for Defense, but not one cent for tribute." Captain Tom knew the truth, that General Pinckney had actually sputtered in anger, "No, No, not a sixpence." Hesitant to point his correspondent to revealing sources, Captain Tom joked that he might just "call this Yankee down and ask to know his reasons for asking these particulars of an honored member of our family."[5]

Captain Tom had been born in 1828, a few months after the death of his noted grandfather, Governor Thomas Pinckney. This year, the same year that Tennessean Andrew Jackson's landmark presidential victory inaugurated the Age of the Common Man in national politics, also marked the end of the Age of the Pinckneys. Mourned by conservative intellectual Hugh S. Legaré as "the most delightful specimen of our old Carolina gentlemen," the patrician Pinckney was among the last of the founding generation. Their passing coincided with the decline in South

Carolina's plantation economy and its reputation within the larger nation.[6]

Reflecting on the experience of her own family, Josephine Pinckney wrote in 1930 that "At one period in our history it looked as though the South, given enough time, would furnish an American aristocracy comparable to the European." But, she observed, "The spirit of the age is against aristocracy, the world is committed to democracy." The aristocrats in the South, Pinckney observed, were "once a small class with wide political power; their descendants are a small class with no more power than their numbers warrant." The "money power—that mud in which the most refined flower of civilization must, alas, have its roots—has gone elsewhere."[7]

Through a series of unexpected events, Governor Thomas Pinckney's second son and Josephine's grandfather, Cotesworth Pinckney, inherited Eldorado, the family seat on the South Santee River.[8] Although Cotesworth Pinckney prevailed in his 1832 run for lieutenant governor on the pro-nullification platform, the dignified, Harvard-educated lawyer had little interest in the hurly-burly, glad-handing of the hustings required of office seekers in the transformed political climate. A man of old-fashioned gravity, Pinckney preferred the life of the rice planter, with its happy mix of field and forest, blooded horses and hunting, leather-bound books before the fire, and the companionship of congenial friends. In 1811, he married the beautiful Caroline Phoebe Elliott, whose father, Sea Island cotton baron William Elliott II of Beaufort, possessed one of the greatest fortunes in the state.

During the 1830s, the Pinckneys were swept up in the religious fervor of the Second Great Awakening, a widespread religious revival, and focused great energy on the moral training of their five children.[9] The high-minded Cotesworth Pinckney dedicated himself to piety and the public demonstrations of Christian charity that became during that period almost as important in the reputation of southern gentlemen as affability and hospitality had once been. Even though his fellow planters thought him crazy, Cotesworth Pinckney listened to his conscience and was the first among them to hire a Methodist missionary to bring Christianity to his slaves. Pinckney's elder son, Cotesworth Jr., was also so touched by the evangelical spirit that he abandoned his law practice and studied for the Episcopal priesthood. It was he who christened baby Josephine in 1895.[10]

Tom Pinckney, the easy-going youngest son, accepted the traditional tenets of faith and family with little questioning. From his earliest boyhood, he had determined to be a planter, but as a teenager he obeyed his father's wishes first to acquire professional training. In 1846, Pinckney attended the University of Virginia then took a degree at the Medical College at Charleston. He did advanced work at the College of Physicians and Surgeons in New York but never established a practice. At the first opportunity he returned to the land he loved, borrowed money to buy slaves, and set out to work the lands his parents gave him from Rebecca Motte's estate. And then the war came.[11]

Waving away a doctor's deferment, Pinckney joined the young paladins defending the South Santee from Federal invasion and was voted captain of the local militia, which was later attached to Company D of the 4th South Carolina Calvary. He was captured in 1864 at the hellish battle of Hawes Store, north of Richmond, where most of his boyhood friends were killed. He suffered cruelly in several Union prisons and was among the "Immortal Six Hundred," prisoners used as human shields directly in the line of fire by Federal troops to prevent a Confederate offensive against their position at Fort Johnson, just south of Charleston. Eventually, he was exchanged in Charleston harbor in December 1864.[12] Neither of his parents survived the war.

The house at Eldorado remained standing, under the supervision of an English overseer, but according to Pinckney's memoirs, he found his plantation "in a shocking condition" with "the very devil to pay." The former slaves had laid claim to the plantation believing all that had been the Pinckneys was now theirs.[13] For the next five years, Captain Tom Pinckney remained a bachelor living in near-frontier conditions, hunting for a living and trying to get his rice fields back in production. Captain Tom made a pillowed landing in 1870. He married Mary Amanda Stewart, daughter of a wealthy Scottish tobacco broker, and one of the few southern women whose patrimony remained intact after the war. The bride was thirty years old; Pinckney was forty-two. Largesse from Stewart's brother Dan had kept the Richmond, Virginia, family flourishing after the war wiped out much of their wealth. Unlike so many of her friends, Mary Amanda Stewart had an elaborate wedding at her family's Brook Hill estate and the "grand tour" for her honeymoon.[14]

Pinckney finally felt poised to realize his dream of living the independent life of the planter.[15] His wife brought capital into the marriage for major improvements; the labor force was stabilized through the use of annual contracts. But even the removal of Federal troops and the return of Democratic Party rule in South Carolina in 1877 could do nothing to restore the flagging rice culture of the Santee delta. Nature was relentless. Hurricanes destroyed diking. Freshets from upriver deluged fields. Prices declined with foreign competition. The humid days and miasmic nights along the Santee marshlands eroded Mary Stewart's delicate health and proved toxic to her babies. By 1881, only one child survived of the six she had borne.[16] Fearing the loss of his wife and his sole surviving child, six-year-old Charles Cotesworth, Captain Tom abandoned Fairfield in 1887. After the third

straight year of crop-destroying floods, the Pinckneys moved more or less permanently to the Stewarts' splendid home at Brook Hill, where his mother-in-law,
Mary Williamson Stewart, and her two unmarried daughters still resided.[17]

In 1889, Mary Stewart Pinckney died. Her family collapsed in grief. A memorial pamphlet printed in Richmond described her as that "highest type of woman-
hood—the Christ-like child, daughter, wife, and mother." She was buried in the
oak-shaded graveyard at Emmanuel Church near Brook Hill. Encircling her graceful monument are the tiny tablets of her dead children. Captain Tom and his son,
fourteen-year-old Cotesworth, stayed on with the Stewarts.[18]

In the latter months of 1890, the estimable Captain Tom Pinckney (at age
sixty-two, elderly by the standards of the time) became grist for the Richmond
gossip mill. With his sainted wife dead scarcely a year, he could be seen walking with another woman on East Franklin Street. Almost twenty years his junior,
Camilla Scott was a cousin of the Stewarts and frequently visited the unmarried
sisters Lucy and Annie. By March 1891, the Scott sisters had also begun whispering among themselves: "Mr. Pinckney has declared his 'devotions' to Camilla." To
her sisters' surprise, the strong-minded spinster accepted those "devotions," and
they agreed to marry. When Captain Tom went to his mother-in-law and confided
his plans, she was stricken by his haste and begged him to wait. Even Captain
Tom's own kin raised their eyebrows. His cousin Lise Rutledge Ravenel expressed
her shock at the news of her "no longer young" cousin taking another wife. How
could he, she wondered, violate the memory of Mary Pinckney, that "charming,
clever, and altogether delightful woman?"[19]

And what was not said, or not publicly said, was that Camilla, who was undeni-
ably clever ("smart as hell" a cousin remembered), had a bristly personality. Born
in 1854 into the comfort of Oakwood, a Greek revival showplace near Warrenton,
Virginia, in Fauquier County, Scott had nevertheless suffered tragically as a child.
The first act of her life had been to disappoint her mother who hoped her second
child might be a boy. Camilla could project a pleasant side, but she also kept a
poison quiver poised close at hand. Never pretty in the style of the Virginia belle,
Camilla's most tactful relatives occasionally referred to her as "handsome." Long
before her postponed wedding in 1892, a low-key affair at her half brother's won-
derfully rambling home in Warrenton, Camilla Scott had drawn about her a chilly
mantle, more befitting a White Russian princess in exile than a daughter of the
South. Her teenaged stepson Cotesworth Pinckney began to refer to her in private
as "the Madame," a woman who delivered her not-to-be questioned opinions in a
strong voice with the broad "a" of the Virginia gentry. In contrast to Captain Tom,
who worried that he had not lived up to all the obligations that life demanded of a

Pinckney, Camilla Scott believed that life had not fulfilled its duty to her. Instead of making Camilla Pinckney more compassionate and understanding, her early trials made her bitter and jealous, a woman of tight-corseted fury.

The Stewart family more or less recovered from their disappointment over Captain Tom's remarriage. Camilla Scott was, after all, kin; her parents and grandparents all well known in Virginia. Her father, Robert Eden Scott, had been a respected Fauquier County lawyer of "inflexible integrity" with a reputation as an "intellectual Hercules." He wore his gray hair long in the old-fashioned style, swept straight back from his face. Deeply involved in state politics, Scott belonged to the "Old Line Whig" faction in Virginia politics, the conservative heirs of the Federalist Party. The first of the Scott family arrived in Virginia from Scotland about 1710. Hailing from the scholarly, sober, middle class, they had nothing of the fabled swaggering Virginia cavalier about them. The first generations were Anglican ministers giving moral instruction to the rising gentry. Abstemious living, wealthy brides, and some savvy land speculation boosted the Scott family fortunes. Starting with Camilla's grandfather, the Scotts took up the law.[20] A hint of the old self-righteousness, however, always lingered among them, and a melancholy, too.

The older Stewarts also remembered Camilla's mother, Heningham Watkins Lyons, once a Richmond fashion plate with an "intellectual face." "Hennie" was a lively young woman who loved reading, politics, and the social life around the Virginia capital. Her own mother had died when she was a child. Heningham Lyons was much younger than Scott and was his third wife.[21] Camilla's grandfather, the elegant and shrewd lawyer James Lyons was also a state politician and entertained lavishly at his home Laburnum, near Brook Hill. Before the Civil War, dignitaries such as William Seward enjoyed his hospitality, and during the conflict, members of Lee's high command and Davis's cabinet frequently called.[22]

Of course, the Stewarts all agreed, Camilla Scott had none of the incandescent grace of their Mary Amanda. In fact, they detected a bit of the brashness like those New Women who were changing Virginia with their ideas about the role of women, even advocating suffrage and equal rights. When Camilla Pinckney's cousin, Katherine I. Keith, died in 1895, the local Virginia newspaper regretted that her sort of modest, cultured lady was fast becoming extinct in the South, "for one does not find that type in the women of today."[23]

Said (usually in an uncomplimentary fashion) to have the "mind of a man," Camilla often pulled her chair from the ladies' table and sat with the men, freely interjecting her thoughts about woman's suffrage, politics, or the economy into their conversations. Still, she was family. Young Cotesworth Pinckney's decision to stay in the loving circle of the Stewarts at Brook Hill when Captain Tom and his new wife returned to Fairfield somewhat assuaged their pain. When Josephine was born in 1892, a surprising dividend in Captain Tom's old age, the extended Stewart family wrapped her into the warm embrace of their kinship. She enjoyed a dual citizenship, being as much at home in Richmond as in Charleston. Both towns would influence her development, but in very different ways.

The very name of her child—Josephine Lyons Scott Pinckney—signaled a triumph for Camilla. Breaking away from the inevitable Elizas, Marias, Harriotts, or Carolines peppered through the Pinckney genealogy, Captain Tom agreed that their baby could be named for Camilla's recently lamented sister. For Josephine, bearing this name would add more weight to the yoke of the sorrowful past. Unlike the Pinckneys who seemed to have some exceptional rejuvenating power about them, the suffering of Camilla's family—the Lyons of Richmond and the Scotts of Warrenton—was breathtakingly tragic in its magnitude, with war, murder, fire, and hunger, all taking their toll.[24]

After her marriage, Camilla Pinckney took particular pleasure in flaunting her recent good fortune to her own less fortunate relatives. She loathed the heat of Charleston and in the summers used to take an overdressed little Josephine to visit the Scott family still living in the highlands of Warrenton. Like the fairy tale stepsister wreaking revenge, Camilla lorded her new status over her more popular sisters when she chose. She usually stayed in the Winchester Street home of Taylor and Fanny Carter Scott where she had been married. Camilla snored like a "wild animal" and always kept the whole house awake, but no one, of course, ever dared say a word.[25]

Any question about "who was whom" in Virginia could be answered by the many years of memory gathered on Winchester Street. Soft voices punctuated still cool evenings in the piedmont and blended into the crickets' chorus, the squeaking cadence of rusting chains on porch swings, and the back-and-forth of rocking chairs in need of paint. Aunt Lizzie Scott Rives in her dime store steel-rim glasses bobbed her head while she did intricate crochet and recounted tales of all the changes in the family fortunes. Sometimes she sang snatches of old folk tunes learned from her Scottish grandmother. Although the Scotts had played important roles in the history of their state, porch talk on Winchester Street was much more likely to dwell on family gossip, delicious tales of fratricidal jealousy, murder and feuds, suspiciously timed births and "tainted" blood, impassioned duels and midnight escapes from the law.

The Scotts' stories criss-crossed generations, even centuries. With the wide span of ages of the porch-sitters, someone could always recall a relative who had met Lafayette, knew some tittle-tattle about George Washington's mother, identify which babies had been held by General Robert E. Lee, or recount how Cousin Fanny Scott, the mistress of the Winchester Street house, had coolly hid Confederate daredevil John Mosby from his blue-coated pursuers. A question might be raised about who now had the pike seized by great-uncle John Scott when he led the Black Horse troop against John Brown and his band at Harper's Ferry. Unlike the Pinckneys, the Scotts had few souvenirs of their distinguished past. Before they lost the family plantation, the showplace Oakwood out on Waterloo Road, Taylor Scott had dug up some of the boxwoods from the famous gardens and planted them around his own modest house. Often the porch commentaries would end on a sour note, with a bitter comment about Yankees, Republicans, or Free Silver.[26]

At some point during family gatherings, though, as the evening wore on and the laughter thinned, the porch would fall silent. The conversation would take a more sober tone. Josephine, who perhaps was only half-listening to the chatter, would be able to feel the solemn force of history descend upon this family. Eyes would slightly lose their focus as they looked into the dark. Thoughts turned involuntarily to how things might have been different, about how all that was once theirs was now gone. Oh Lost! All vanished save honor, of course. Through the stories told on Winchester Street, Josephine learned the many ways of being a heroine. Success could be measured not so much in achieving as in forbearing with grace, and finding strength in Christian fortitude. Beneath the anger in the South of Pinckney's childhood lay an unfathomable sadness.

The shattering event of Camilla Scott's life, indeed the lives of all the Scotts, had been the murder of her father in May 1862 by two Union soldiers. She was eight years old, the seventh of his ten children from three marriages, when a wagon lumbered up the steep hill to Oakwood bearing his body.[27] Robert Eden Scott had held strong Unionist sentiments. His abiding fear that the beautiful rolling hills of northern Virginia would become the "cockpit" of the war was realized. Within a year of secession, the land around Warrenton had become known as "disputed territory" because it had changed hands so many times. In the spring of 1862, the Union forces had control. The roads of Fauquier County were thick with Union pickets and also with deserters and stragglers. When he heard of the rape of two women in his neighborhood, Scott moved quickly to organize a posse of other local men also too old for the army. He tried to apprehend a pair of deserters from a brigade of Wisconsin volunteers hiding among slaves on the Winchester Road, but one shot him dead at point blank, broke Scott's own gun over his body, and fled away.[28]

Even prior to the war and the death of Robert Eden Scott, Camilla Scott's large extended family, including her dictatorial grandmother and scheming aunt, had not lived very happily together at Oakwood. Their tenuous bonds disintegrated into a tangle of accusations and threats when it was discovered that Camilla's father inexplicably had left no will. Before his estate could be probated, "the Public Enemy" descended upon Oakwood and burned everything they could not carry away. The adult women of the household fled, leaving all the children alone with Camilla's mother, who was pregnant with her fifth child. Trapped behind enemy lines, the children went hungry. "Starvation is the consequence of Civil War," Union general Ambrose Burnside snapped when local citizens pleaded on Scott's behalf. Throughout this and all the trials of her life, Heningham Scott tried to accept her fate, believing that Providence had been pleased to "exercise His own will, not mine."[29]

Eventually, during a lull in the fighting just before the Battle of Fredericksburg in December 1862, Heningham's father, James Lyons, pulled diplomatic strings and got the family the necessary clearances. His son fetched Heningham and her children to the safety of Laburnum. They lived there in a little cottage among a grove of trees. Camilla played with her Stewart cousins at nearby Brook Hill. In 1864, a black arsonist vengefully torched Judge Lyons's house, burning it to the ground. South Carolina diarist Mary Boykin Chesnut, whose husband was serving in the Confederate congress, and other concerned friends rode out to help but found only "a pitiful sight." In April 1865, all of Richmond was in flames as the Confederate army made its last retreat. Camilla's mother fell into a "deep eclipse."[30]

Not until 1868 and the settlement of Robert Eden Scott's estate did Camilla's family begin to creep beyond the reach of actual want. After living in Fauquier County for a few years, where Camilla enjoyed only the most rudimentary education at Warrenton's Female Institute, Heningham Scott relocated to Richmond. She rented a barracks-like mansion, a former dry goods emporium at 900 Capitol Street, and opened a boarding house (an acceptable alternative for gentle southern ladies in straitened circumstances). The building consumed much of a city block and lacked any pleasing architectural detail whatsoever. Heningham called her establishment "Valentine House" after the original owner, Mann S. Valentine, who had made a postwar fortune with his beef extract formula. Fearful she would sink again into hateful dependency, Heningham Scott became obsessed with saving money. Whenever a competing boarding house opened or a room lay vacant, Scott panicked. She counted every penny and practiced a joyless self-denial.[31] Her children, who had been born to expect other things from their lives, performed all the household activities from shopping and changing beds to washing dirty windows and cleaning mottled spittoons. Even in the destitution that swept over the South, even among her own kin, Camilla Scott was heartbreakingly deprived. She suffered terribly during the boarding-house years, her pride hurting even more than her lye-soap-roughened hands.

Young Camilla's deprivation proved all the more bitter by the revival of the ideal of the "belle" in the first years after the Civil War. When she was thirteen, the famous White Sulphur Springs resort nestled in the Alleghenies near Greenbrier, Virginia, reopened for business. "The White" had been the most famous of the numerous spas in the Old Dominion where the antebellum aristocracy from North and South had set up a marriage mart to insure that like married like. The first belles after the war, Mary Triplett and Mary Ould, enjoyed an adoration known only to screen stars of later generations. At a time when a brilliant marriage presented the only possible escape from her gritty life at the boarding house with its sour smells and soiled antimacassars, Camilla seldom had callers. A cloud seemed to hang over this poor Cinderella. Young Richmond men of good families, themselves in reduced circumstances as well, fluttered around the door of the Valentine House, but they asked for the other sisters, Josephine or Imogene, who had the determined ability to find a bit of sunshine despite their dismal situation. Even when Camilla received an invitation, she had nothing to wear. The Scott girls depended on hand-me-downs from their only slightly more prosperous cousins and had to take turns going out because they all drew from the same pool of washed-out, mended clothes. A sixteen-year-old Camilla "received little joy from her outing," a house party in Alexandria, her tight-fisted mother reported in 1870, and had returned home in tears, having been shamed before the other girls by her ill-fitting homemade frocks.[32]

In April 1886, Heningham Lyons Scott died, convinced she would bear "no spot upon me in eternity."[33] She left enough money that Camilla and her youngest sister Imogene, the child born six weeks after her father's murder, could escape Valentine House forever. They moved to the neat row house on East Franklin Street where Captain Pinckney came to call.

One spring evening in 1897, when Josephine was two years old, a startling message was delivered to 29 Legaré Street. Eldorado, where her Seabrook cousins were living, had burned to the ground. The fault lay in a damaged chimney. Presumably, the devastating earthquake of 1886 had caused an undetected crack. The fire spread rapidly, fueled by the old wood siding cut and planed under General Thomas Pinckney's watchful eye. Help came too late. The Pinckney family seat disappeared in a fury of flame and crashing timbers. Only the four chimneys, the brick foundations in the English basement, and the front steps remained, shrouded by smoke from burning embers. The onlookers suffered agonies as they remembered how much of the past was disappearing before their eyes. When she was able to speak, the first thing Mamie Seabrook uttered was "The books." Those well-loved volumes that had survived revolution and civil war—Mills and LePages atlases, the family Bible, along with the other family treasures and "mementos of those loved and lost" were all gone.[34]

The maritime forest soon reclaimed Eldorado. Vines and brambles covered the jagged brick piers breaking through the trees in protest. In 1915, when Captain Tom died, Eldorado passed to Josephine, an heiress to ruin.

## 2

## *The Education of a Young Poet*

Josephine Pinckney grew into a honey-haired child with a mass of artfully twirled ringlets. Large sad-looking eyes of a type once called "soulful" dominated her round face. Dressed in laces with chubby feet squeezed into Mary Janes, she was Captain Tom's delight. He wrapped her in an envelope of affluence remote to the experiences of most young southerners of her generation. Tours of Europe, summers at New England resorts, camp in the New Hampshire woods, beautiful bespoke clothes all set her apart from friends and even family members. During the Christmas season of 1902, seven-year-old Josephine reported to a motherless Virginia cousin whose own holiday was probably rather meager, "I received so many xmas presents that I had a tree of my own."[1]

Camilla Pinckney's desires had been honed by deprivation; her taste, by her years in Richmond, a town rebuilt from wartime ruin in the Victorian style, brownstone and massive. None of the several houses in Charleston that Captain Tom rented after they left Fairfield suited her. In 1907, he agreed to buy 21 King Street. Pinckney moved his family of three into the most arrogantly Victorian house in the city, a four-story Italianate palazzo whose brownstone exterior was set off by wide Charleston porches. Carved shells and other marine motifs decorated the window surrounds of the second floor. Built about 1856, 21 King Street towered over its neighbors. At the time the Pinckneys moved in, some old-time Charlestonians still called the mansion "O'Donnell's Folly," an unkind jest at the nouveau riche Irish contractor who lost his ladylove to another while building this over-elaborate love offering.[2]

The interior of the Pinckney home was as extravagant as the exterior. On the first floor, two large, paneled drawing rooms ran en suite, illuminated by huge chandeliers hanging from fourteen-foot high ceilings. The dining room and library could both be opened for parties. Large plaster decorations with classical motifs adorned the walls; ceiling medallions bore the image of popular songstress Jenny Lind who once visited Charleston. Since the expansive rooms dwarfed the Pinckney's delicate Federal-era antiques, Captain Tom bought Camilla the more up-to-date heavy mahogany furniture she coveted while on a trip to Chicago.[3] Elderly Captain Tom installed Charleston's first elevator in a private home.

Sparkling fresh paint and energetically polished brass lamps made the house even more conspicuous in a town well known during this era as "too poor to paint and too proud to whitewash." To stroll the narrow streets and alleyways of Charleston during Josephine Pinckney's childhood was to feel like a tourist at Pompeii, to be made witness to a great calamity. The mummified remains of past splendor, a "somber and shadowy magnificence," loomed over the city and invited names such as "Death on the Atlantic."[4] During the first decade of the twentieth century, many of the old Low Country families finally hit bottom after years of depression, boll weevil, and bad cotton weather. They sadly pulled the shutters on their ancestral plantations and crowded in with relatives in their moldering houses in town. Camilla offended local sensibilities by flaunting her wealth. The most notable aspect of the aristocratic code was the aversion to "talking rich or poor," as one of Charleston's social arbiters, Louisa McCord Stoney, explained to her own daughter in 1915. "This is the greatest test of your gentility—that good old-fashioned self-respecting courtesy that we Southerners and old fashioned Northerners still cherish."[5]

Josephine developed into an acute little observer of adults and their foibles. She could fathom drama even in a Sunday dinner. "When I was growing up," she recollected, "family dinners were the chief form of entertainment in the South. Not that anyone regarded them as social or as necessarily entertaining."[6] Living as the only child in her forbidding house, and in such different circumstances from most of her playmates, left young Josephine with feelings of isolation and profound loneliness which haunted her all her life. As an adult, she would refer to her emotional seclusion as her "ivory tower." Over time, the ivory tower would become her personal metaphor for the distance she always felt even from her closest friends. She believed that members of her social circle treated her differently, deferentially, with less familiarity and less candor, than they did one another. In her own mind, she rationalized their behavior as a response to her aristocratic birth, her wealth, and her fame as a novelist. In her last novel, *Splendid in Ashes* (1958), Pinckney has two characters touring an august Charleston mansion. One visitor comments enviously on the spaciousness of the elegant rooms, the elaborate decorations, and richness of the furnishings. The other whispers, "You wouldn't want to live in a mausoleum like this."[7]

Camilla Pinckney presided over her "cabbage rose" of a house with stiff restraint. She adopted the Victorian style of shaming and never hesitated to criticize or correct her willful daughter in public, at least after Captain Tom's death. Even when Josephine was an adult with her own friends ringed around the formal dinner table, the ever-present Camilla would often interrupt her mid-sentence with a "Now, Josephine," followed either by an addition, correction, or directive. In response, Pinckney would visibly shrink a little.[8] At the first opportunity, she would flee to her own room where very early on she learned to imagine another world.

The towering 21 King Street offered Josephine one great advantage over the traditional eighteenth-century Charleston houses huddled together in rows with shuttered windows and walled gardens. The view from the fourth floor offered her a perspective on the world enjoyed by few Charlestonians, whose preoccupation with keeping prying eyes out also limited their vision. Below her, the dense live oaks and broad-leafed magnolias that canopied the old city formed a green carpet, a verdant pathway to the shimmering, slow-moving currents at work at the peninsula's tip where local legend claims the Ashley and Cooper Rivers swirl together and spawn the Atlantic Ocean. Josephine studied art and music but was particularly attracted to the orderliness, and the control, of a world on paper. Small child-sized bound notebooks crammed with her schoolgirl jottings, pencil drawings, and poetry survive among her papers. Slips of paper tucked inside carry warnings in a firm adult hand to future inquiring biographers: "Juvenilia—Never to be published."

Josephine Pinckney would have developed into a very different sort of person had there not been another world within the universe of 21 King Street. To escape the cool, formal house where Camilla held stiff-spined sway, Josephine found an alternative reality in the cozy kitchen of bubbling pots and soft singing where Victoria Rutledge set the rules. The child of slaves, "Vic" was born in 1875, probably in the freedmen settlements along the Santee River. She never learned to write, but she could sign her name with a regal "Victoria R." Possessing a Rabelaisian wit, and a figure to match, she frequently threw her head back in laughter to reveal a solitary front tooth. A lover of all God's creatures, animals and human, Vic had many friends who streamed through the Pinckney kitchen, visiting and exchanging gossip.[9] When Josephine matured into a young poet, she would draw from the colorful sights and sounds of the backyard commonplaces she watched from her window, the yard man raking in the heat, the "vegetubble lady with basket on 'he head."

Rutledge believed that the Pinckneys' social standing rubbed off on her, and she regaled in the big parties she helped orchestrate. She bragged to her friends that Captain Tom lacked "just one quarter of having 80 million Dollars." Rutledge had her own strong sense of propriety, a "snobbishness" toward those, black and white, who did not meet her unyielding standards of behavior. She particularly resented patronizing northern visitors who violated the well-established etiquette of race and acted "conciliatory" toward her.[10]

Victoria Rutledge was already part of the Pinckney household when Josephine was born in 1895. She lived in backyard servants' quarters with her husband, William Rutledge, a literate drayman who drove the family carriages. The infant Josephine came under Vic's particular care, and they formed an extraordinary bond. One of Josephine's earliest childhood memories was of waking abruptly from a feverish sleep while she was sick and being frightened. Then, a powerful sense of calm and well-being blanketed her when she realized that Victoria sat quietly on the piazza, humming outside her room ready to attend her every need.[11]

Because little Jo cared so deeply for her, and truly needed her, Victoria had great power over the child and could upset her easily when displeased. When Josephine got older, she was irritated by Victoria's always choosing "the stream of least resistance." She even hid food from her to try to hold her exploding waistline in check. They disagreed and quarreled from time to time over their many years together; feelings were often hurt. After much pouting and tooth-sucking on both sides, they always made up. In sharp contrast to her treatment at the hands of the relentlessly critical Camilla, Josephine grew up secure in Victoria's "unquestioning devotion." One night, when the two of them were alone, Victoria thought she heard an intruder. She overcame her own fears of the dark to storm down to the lower hall with a smoky kerosene lantern in one hand and an ax in the other, ready to defend Miss Josie.[12]

More than just a caregiver, Victoria also appealed to Josephine's sense of wonder and excited her freewheeling imagination. To venture down to Victoria's kitchen was to pass into a world spiced with magic. Victoria still wore the traditional African-style turban, told her stories in the musical Gullah dialect, and interpreted daily events through the gauze of ancient superstition. Rutledge believed with all her soul that Evil was afoot in the world. She slept with the light on, for "hags ruled the night." Every calamity known to mankind, she firmly believed, could be addressed by a vast repertoire of spells and curses. Most could be ameliorated, if not defeated, by some potion from her kitchen which included exotic ingredients never listed in Fanny Farmer's New England cookbook.

Often swept away by her "love of the sensational," Victoria would tell the rapt little Josephine elaborate stories about life in "lamp oil times" and explain the cosmology of the underworld. In one of her early poems, "Hag!" Josephine drew upon the memories of those afternoons of sitting with Victoria who picked shrimp with brown paper bag fashioned as a cap on her head:

Hags is human people,
En' dey kin ketch a ol' black cat en' boil it
En' take a bone en' hol' it in dey mout',
Den dy kin go troo any key-hole livin'.

Victoria's tall tales about the red-bodied hags slipping into people's bedrooms through keyholes differed from the morally instructive fairy tales that were standard fare in the Victorian nursery. Not only were the stories in Victoria's world unique, but the rhythm and cadence of the language, the melodic intonations of Low Country Gullah as she spun out her macabre tales, also contrasted with the standard line and verse of the poets so enjoyed during the literary evenings Captain Tom and Camilla held. Upstairs all poetry was measured by the lock-step iambic pentameter of Alfred Lord Tennyson. Victoria's kitchen was filled with the free-form chant of the Gullah song or spiritual with a syntax and grammar all its own.

Rutledge spun out a world view that provided Josephine with a context for her experiences in the plantation environment of Fairfield and Eldorado. Although she probably never lived at Fairfield for any length of time, Josephine visited with relatives all around the Santee district. The pampered city child came to life in the yellow sands and overgrown wilderness garden that had been so much a part of her family's past. Palmetto and live oak, wood duck and alligator, heron rookeries and black-water cypress swamp all wedged themselves into her imagination, competing with the highly civilized constructs of her youth: the Grand Hotel of Rome, staterooms on ocean liners, suites at New York's Mayfair Hotel, and the parlors of 21 King Street. Always, the spectral remains of lost Eldorado and the dark brooding waters of the Santee's Washoe Reserve challenged the pervasive Victorian certainty of progress.

Pinckney's early formal education began at a "dame school" run by her father's cousins, Rebecca Motte Frost ("Rebe") and her sister Mary, when they lived at 4 Logan Street. She later spent a few years at the Confederate College, a "female seminary" originally founded in 1867 to shelter the widows of Confederate veterans and educate their daughters. In 1909, a new school for girls opened in Charleston. Mary Vardine McBee, a transplanted northerner, founded Ashley Hall in a converted mansion on Rutledge Avenue. She planned to offer a curriculum designed to prepare Charleston girls for topnotch northern women's colleges. Camilla Pinckney rushed to enroll Josephine as its first student. From Camilla Pinckney's point of view, equally important as the educational opportunity was that Ashley Hall offered boarding for students. With a teenaged Josephine (who was growing more willful every day) safely tucked away, Camilla could indulge her passion for travel.

In her senior year, Josephine helped launch Ashley Hall's literary magazine *Cerberus*. Already displaying the hallmarks of her literary persona, she was in charge of the humor and poetry sections. With her work on *Cerberus*, she learned the importance of a patron. Sputtering at first, attracting little interest and few contributions, *Cerberus* had languished until Josephine's cousin Herbert Ravenel Sass kindly gave the girls' efforts a serious and positive review in the *Charleston News and Courier*. After this bit of promotion, the magazine soared in local prestige.[13] In 1913, Josephine graduated amid a flurry of white dresses and red roses.

Josephine's interest in books and writing was not only encouraged at home but more or less expected. The Pinckney family had historically been involved in many dimensions of cultural life of Charleston, including the founding of both the Charleston Library Society in 1748, the first social library organized in the South (the third in America), and the Charleston Museum in 1773 (first in the New World). Even during the years that are sometimes viewed as the city's dark ages around the turn of the century, the talk at 21 King Street was of literature and books. The chivalric novels of Sir Walter Scott were still favorites with Captain Tom. Harriet Beecher Stowe's *Uncle Tom's Cabin* was banned in the Pinckney household but so was Mary Boykin Chesnut's *Diary from Dixie*. According to the Stewart aunts who had ripped up their petticoats for the Cause and nursed the sick, Chesnut, who enjoyed her luxuries, had not sufficiently sacrificed during the siege of Richmond.[14]

In fact, Pinckney's relatives constituted a literary circle all their own. Josephine's great-grandfather William Elliott wrote the classic *Carolina Sports by Land and Water* (1846) and had belonged to novelist William Gilmore Simms's circle that had tried to establish a southern literary tradition in the nineteenth century. Her great-great grandmother Eliza Lucas Pinckney, whose own writings were first published in 1850 by a granddaughter (more than a half century after her death), deserves fame as the founding mother of Charleston literature as much as for her achievements in agriculture. Every generation produced writers. Politics occupied the Pinckneys during the decades before the Civil War. General Charles Cotesworth Pinckney's strong-minded daughter Maria Henrietta, anonymously published a pro-nullification screed in 1832. Henry Laurens Pinckney edited the states' rights organ, the *Charleston Mercury*.

After the Civil War, the Pinckneys spent their intellectual energies reflecting on the glories of the past. Captain Tom Pinckney had kept a diary during the Civil War and Reconstruction which he later turned into a narrative that one appreciative reader concluded was "quite as good as a tale by Kipling or O. Henry." One of his anecdotes described the fate of Governor Thomas Pinckney's notable library. During the Civil War, the Pinckney family moved thousands of volumes from Eldorado to Hampton Plantation for safety. After the war was over, the illiterate freed slaves fell upon the boxed volumes with inexplicable vengeance. What they did not tear up, they scattered around the circumference of the house like stepping stones. One of the vandals later explained that although they could not read, they had reasoned that the whites' power over them had come from the magic contained in the heavy volumes; destroy the books, destroy the power. In 1906, his prospective publisher wanted him to expand his story by at least two-thirds, but at seventy-eight years old, he was reluctant to spend much more time on this project. He passed his memoirs on to Myrta Lockett Avary who was collecting stories for her book *Dixie after the War* (1906). She took his account as representative of the experience of Low Country planters and chronicled his story in a chapter called "The Devil on the Santee."[15]

In 1895, Captain Tom's brother the Reverend Charles Cotesworth Pinckney Jr., wrote a laudatory biography of his grandfather Governor Thomas Pinckney. One cousin, Gustavus Memminger Pinckney, published *The Life of John C. Calhoun* in 1903. A Pinckney cousin from the Motte side, Elizabeth Allston Pringle, told her postwar story of struggle in *A Woman Rice Planter* in 1913. Captain Tom's "Cousin Hat," Harriott Horry Rutledge Ravenel, was the historian of her generation, writing biographies of Eliza Lucas Pinckney and kinsman Congressman William Lowndes, as well as a history of Charleston. Ravenel's son Frank married Charlestonian Beatrice Witte who had already begun her career as a poet during her years at Radcliffe College. Harriott Ravenel's daughter, Anna Eliza, married lawyer George Herbert Sass. Writing under the name of "Barton Grey," Sass won prizes for his patriotic poetry during the Civil War and was widely considered the successor to South Carolina's Henry Timrod, poet laureate of the Confederacy. Sass encouraged interest in the arts among Charlestonians through a weekly column in the *Charleston News and Courier*. In 1904, the New York firm of George P. Putnam published his collected poetry as *The Heart's Quest*. His son and Josephine's cousin, Herbert Ravenel Sass, was a naturalist as well as a writer, working first as a newspaper editor and then in 1925 boldly striking out to write full time. Through his nature stories, more poetry than polemic, published in popular magazines such as the *Saturday Evening Post*, he became the first modern Charleston writer to win national attention. Another of Josephine's generation, Archibald Rutledge, who as a boy had been so intimidated by Governor Pinckney's court suit and sword, began writing poetry even before his graduation from college in 1904 and eventually became the state's first poet laureate.[16]

Captain Tom also kept well connected to Virginia writers. His former brother-in-law, Joseph Bryan, had gained control of Richmond's two leading newspapers by 1908. When southern writers would come to town, the Pinckneys often held evening parties for them. They frequently included their former neighbor on Legaré Street, John Bennett, who had won youthful celebrity in 1895 for the classic children's book *Master Skylark*.

Josephine Pinckney embarked on a course of "education through travel" after her graduation from Ashley Hall and followed her parents on their peregrinations. Years before, Captain Tom Pinckney had leased out his unproductive acres to a group of southern-born businessmen living in New York who still craved shooting ducks over the old rice fields. The house at Fairfield fell into disrepair.[17] Living off his "own income" of blue chip bonds and industrial stocks, as he explained to the census takers of 1910, Pinckney was free to spend as much time as he pleased in Richmond, where his only son had settled after graduating from the University of Virginia. Cotesworth Pinckney married Elsie Morris and began a family, eventually having three children, Morton Morris, Thomas, and Frances. Taking a position in a Richmond bank, Cotesworth Pinckney benefited from the improved business environment in Richmond, but he resented the coarseness that came along with the new money that flowed into the city. He continued to believe in the old southern practice of business as a series of personal transactions among gentlemen and rejected the modern corporate models that invaded the South along with northern capital.[18]

Twenty years older than Josephine, and as relaxed and genial as his sister was intense, he cultivated the persona of the "wit," roughly the male equivalent of a "belle" (but with a longer shelf life). Known at the Westmoreland Club for his brilliant repartee, he won local fame for his quips, such as his warning to friends that mixing sugar in their bourbon would "knick" their kidneys. He lived an easy, uncomplicated life in the fashionable district of Ginter Park, with his manservant Richard Jones close at hand to do his bidding. Jones picked up the nickname of "Bear" because he enjoyed wearing a great fur coat that Pinckney had bought for him in Russia. One typical request from Pinckney, when spotting an intruder while lounging in his garden with a drink in his hand, might be "Bear, go throw a rock at that rabbit."[19]

Whenever Josephine's friends wanted to watch her bristle, they called her a "mongrel" of mixed ancestry; her aristocratic Low Country blood being mingled with that of the Tidewater. Pinckney's Richmond connections did introduce her to a broader range of experience. In contrast to languid Charleston where the scent of loquat and wisteria continued to fill the air, in Richmond the smell of tobacco permeated every sector of the city. The whiff of bright leaf smelled like money to the investors of the nation's largest cigarette and cigar factories that had located there. From fertilizer to blotting paper, the old Confederate capital's manufacturing plant hummed. Insurance and banking thrived.[20] Obsession with the Lost Cause that characterized the years that Camilla Pinckney had lived there gradually gave way to a preoccupation with progress. In contrast to Charleston, where the slumbering economy drove out the most energetic and forward-looking, prosperity brought new people and new ideas to Richmond.

Virtually the only haggard remnant of Richmond's antebellum tradition of culture, of past ideals of literature and leisure that survived into Josephine's youth, was the cult of beauty that had put poor Camilla to such disadvantage. The idealized belle lived a life of self-gratification while trying to snag a rich husband. That their empty-headedness and frivolity only heightened the popular appeal of the beauties suggests the degree to which Virginians, and perhaps most southerners, had simply given up. Lacking the heart to compete in the new industrial order, they gave themselves over to the romance of tragic decline.[21]

In 1890, Camilla probably joined Richmond's preoccupation with its native daughter, Irene Langhorne of Virginia. The last of the Virginia belles, she was the first southern girl to be invited north for the debutante season. Men of great fortunes—from well-born Princeton undergraduates to Gilded Age millionaires—fell at her feet. By the time Josephine was born, all of Virginia, and much of the nation, waited with bated breath to learn which proposal Irene Langhorne would accept of the sixty-nine she had received. She made a surprising choice. In a love match, she married New York illustrator Charles Dana Gibson, the well-known and popular artist who transformed the concept of the American beauty from round-cheeked and wan to slim and athletic. The Gibson Girl, who cast off the bustle and train for sports clothes convenient for cycling, tennis, or croquet, could also be a great deal of fun and very independent. She abandoned the bicycle built for two to travel under her own power. This was the model that Camilla Pinckney embraced for her own daughter. She loved to relate the story of how, while sitting at the water's edge during a vacation, she noticed a particularly daring diver among the young people. As she paused to watch the diver surface, she was amazed when the exultant face of her daughter—that daredevil Josephine—emerged from the cold, clear water, an all-American girl of the twentieth century.[22]

As Josephine entered her teenaged years, she adopted the *belle dame sans merci* attitude suggested by the aloof Gibson Girl—not the pose of the jaded, worldly woman of the European Decadents' fascination, but one of independence, innocence, and hopeful optimism. Josephine's closest friends knew her to be fun, engaging, and ironic, but she also gained a reputation early on for fickleness and arms-lengths relationships as Charleston's own "Hard Hearted Hannah." Boyfriends often had the feeling expressed in "The Tennessee Waltz," the old cotillion favorite of her youth, "you are a part of me now, but where is your heart?" Whenever a relationship got too "mushy," Josephine retreated.[23]

With few models either in Charleston or Richmond, that matched her ambitions for herself, Josephine drew many of her ideas about life and love from magazines, such as the popular Philadelphia-based *Ladies' Home Journal.* Wedged in between recipes for Jell-O salads and new fashions were subtle messages about the role of women in a changing world. Some articles encouraged women to participate in the nation's public life ("Why Mrs. Elliott's Civic League Went to Pieces: And How She Pulled It Together Again") or probed questions of equal rights ("Should a Woman Get a Man's Pay?"). Stories of adventure entertained at the same time they incited women to consider broader horizons beyond domestic life ("The Romance of a Girl Who Was Bent on 'Doing Something': And She Certainly Did It!"). Young women set on marriage were encouraged to take the initiative in affairs of the heart, as did the heroine in "The Cat That Got the Bird: The Cat Being a Girl, the Bird Being a Young Man." Even the advertisements carried their own subtle messages. "Lady Sealpax Athletic Underwear" was said to be designed in such a way that every woman might feel "Just as Comfortable as Brother."

Madison Avenue also reinforced Josephine's passion for driving. Ads for the elegant Franklin automobile, the make Camilla favored, showed an updated Gibson girl at the wheel. The concept of a woman driving herself in an automobile was so foreign to Charlestonians during the 1920s that neighbor children were shocked at seeing Miss Josephine slipping into the front seat of the Pinckneys' long black car, usually the province of a dignified chauffeur, and speeding away from the curb.[24]

In November 1915, just as Josephine was in a fit of preparation for the winter social season punctuated with debutante parties and culminating with the St. Cecilia Ball, Captain Tom died. Always resilient, despite his many griefs and disappointments, Pinckney had possessed a gracious, easy-going nature of the sort that his daughter would describe as "sitting loosely in the saddle of life." Courtly with women and honest with men, Captain Tom had "never cared to be brilliant," one friend remembered, " but he had a sound judgment, which aided by a strong sense of humor, guided him to the right road."[25]

All the new frocks, tweeds for country parties, and silk ball gowns hung despondently in her closet while she donned black for the long, traditional grieving period. Camilla Pinckney seized center stage and threw herself into mourning with the morbid enthusiasm of Queen Victoria herself. She traded her outrageous and unbecoming hats (mausoleums of feathers from untold numbers of now-extinct birds) for yards of heavy black veil. After all those early years of begging, borrowing, wearing out, and making do, Camilla had engaged in an orgy of high fashion garb that few Charleston matrons, who generally leaned toward the subdued and understated anyway, could afford. Basic black was a pleasant relief for all involved.[26]

Captain Tom's poor state of health had restricted Camilla's travel considerably toward the end of his life, but after his death she fled Charleston—too hot in the summer, too chill and damp in the winter—with increased frequency. She expected Josephine to be her traveling companion and felt no compunction about disrupting the usual social activities of a young woman of twenty-one. In January 1916, Camilla Pinckney booked them on a transatlantic cruise for two to Europe. That the Great War raged and German U-boats prowled beneath the sea did little to thwart her determination. With Paris too dangerous for her to attend the Sorbonne as she had hoped, Josephine enrolled in summer school at Columbia University when they returned. She took two courses in English and a class in physical education, and she developed a passion for the freedom of New York City. Stuck at home after America joined the war in 1917, with rationing of gas and trains crowded with servicemen making travel difficult, Josephine impatiently waited for her life to begin. She participated with her friends in the city's mobilization to defeat the Huns, rolled some bandages, sold some war bonds, but she mostly lived the unfocused life of the well-to-do southern girl languishing in the netherworld between school and marriage.[27]

Pinckney tried to dodge the inevitable question about her future. In Charleston, like the English parishes of Jane Austen's day, society revolved around the intrigues of courtship and marriage, dowries and legacies. Most of this small circle was concerned with maintaining the aristocratic fabric of Charleston society by knotting the generations of the same families together through marriage. When Josephine became an heiress, rich in both property and capital upon the death of Captain Tom, the town buzzed with interest about which of the scions of the impoverished ancient families she might choose. Hawk-eyed Camilla homed in on the bony wrists protruding below worn coat sleeves and short pant cuffs exposing darned socks. Many of these men had land, good names, and fine manners but little income and few prospects.

Some young men found jobs related to their lost world, brokered cotton, or tried real estate, selling off bits and pieces of friends' plantations to wealthy, winter-weary northerners searching for vacation homes and shooting clubs. For a while a shimmering mirage of prosperity surrounded the profitable mining of phosphates on idle acres that once benefited the Pinckneys and many others. Planters' sons were teased into thinking that once again the earth might deliver them. But the phosphate boom lasted less than a generation, leaving many who had bet on digging their fortune out of the ground not only disappointed but deeply in debt, mortgaged to their hopes.

To call on Miss Jo required a young man to screw up his courage, climb a steep set of brownstone steps, and knock on the massive entry door of 21 King Street. One young suitor who waited hopefully for admittance to the Pinckney inner sanctum with startled brown eyes and a sweet tentative smile penetrated Josephine's heart as few ever would. A poorly educated insurance salesman named DuBose Heyward, ten years her senior, began paying serious court to Josephine around the time of Captain Tom's death. Pinckney gravitated toward the gentle dreamy young man with no prospects. Her mother became concerned.

DuBose descended from a bloodline equally as distinguished as the Pinckneys. The Heywards were also seventeenth-century founders of South Carolina. Reaping the same great fortunes from rice as the Pinckneys had before the Civil War, Heyward's family, unlike Captain Tom's, had no safety net of Virginia money and experienced a breathtaking decline. Even during a time in Charleston when poverty was the norm, Heyward's childhood had been notably tragic. He barely escaped death as an infant when bricks crashed into his crib during the earthquake of 1886. Not long after, his father died, leaving his mother to support the family by writing stories of the South and giving public recitations in Gullah, the language of the Sea Island blacks. Heyward and his sister sometimes went to bed hungry. His education was spotty. A victim of polio at eighteen years old, he suffered bad health throughout his early manhood. Grasping Heyward's hand felt like taking hold of a delicate bird, even though he could muster a surprisingly muscular handshake. The Heywards lived in a cramped, century-old Church Street house with brick walls as thick as a jail's, made even smaller by their need to take in boarders.[28]

Yet DuBose Heyward possessed "memorable charm," as Pinckney recalled. The "engaging contrasts in his personality" first attracted her. His natural sweetness was ballasted by his quick wit: "unaffectedly courteous manners disguised a good head for business and practical affairs." Romantic by nature, Heyward conjured one "wild air castle" after another. They shared a love of simple pleasures in the woodlands and the beaches, swimming and keeping midnight vigils for sea turtles laying their eggs in the soft sand. At the Heywards' little cottage on Sullivan's Island, "Bo" would carry on such playful dinner table banter as he wielded the hominy spoon that those gathered enjoyed their humble fish supper as much as any feast. In the evening, the young people would move out to the beach, roast marshmallows, and dreamily sing old plantation songs.[29]

Most important, Heyward shared Pinckney's interest in literature. After his daily grind, Heyward kept late hours struggling to write poetry and stories. "Have you read anything of Tagaré's," he asked Josephine in 1915. "Great, the most poetic stuff that I have ever read. I suppose I think so for the very simple reason that he found out my innermost little dreams and then sending them back to me as his own, he's made me realize how beautiful they are anyway." DuBose and Josephine collaborated on a poem when mutual friends became engaged, but the verse gave no hint of their future fame:

> A rustic youth, beside the maid, adored
> And on the evening air his rapture poured
> And as I paused I heard the swain exclaim
> "Elope with me—for I possess a FORD!!"[30]

Their friendship had developed through the "Brothers and Sisters Club," a group of young single Charlestonians who socialized together and found what simple fun the quiet old town had to offer. The group also engaged in "little literary evenings" and liked to imagine that perhaps Robert Browning and his circle might have started this way. In 1916, Heyward addressed Pinckney as his "comrade in letters" when he announced he had sold a poem, "Love and Passion," to *Snappy Stories*. Heyward also belonged to the Brotherhood of Galahad. Writing to make a date with Pinckney after an absence of two months, Heyward promised: "I still test out 100% Galahadian." In their ritual, which bore not a little hostility to the fair sex, the Galahadians swore "To love God, fear woman, and elude the net of matrimony." In answer to the question "Where can you find an honest woman?" the group answered in unison: "In Magnolia Cemetery."[31]

Despite their protests of abjuring women, DuBose actually found a great deal of competition among the Galahadians for Josephine's attention. George Lamb Buist, a young Charleston lawyer, pursued her for decades, always making himself available when she needed an escort or a driver. He never married until very late in his life. Gordon Miller, another lawyer with a literary bent, was also her frequent companion. He once scribbled a little ditty to her.

> Were I a poet like DuBose
> I'd find some graceful way

To woo you with a winning verse
On Valentine his day . . .
But I am just prosaic me
And write to let you know
A valentine is in my heart
Addressed to you, dear Jo.[32]

With America's entry into World War I in 1917, questions about marriage suddenly pressed with greater urgency among Josephine's own friends in Charleston. The Galahads of Charleston enlisted and implored their girlfriends to make quick decisions before they clambered aboard the trains on their way to France. Author John Bennett sympathized with a young woman hesitant to do her patriotic duty, "shrinking away from the end of her freedom . . . which marriage seems, and so much is, to a girl."[33]

By 1917, most of Josephine's strapping young admirers were "over there" headed for the front; only DuBose remained of the old crowd. Too frail to fight, his left side weakened from polio, he remained at home with his mother, selling insurance, doing some local war work, and writing martial poems—a tragic, yet manly figure, some thought.[34] Likely this was the juncture when Camilla feared that DuBose might win the day with Josephine through the process of elimination, and she stepped in. A marriage with DuBose Heyward was impossible, unthinkable, forbidden. Heyward clearly had no future. Also, after her years of nursing Captain Tom, who was decades older than she, Pinckney probably did not want Josephine to experience the dark side of being an older man's darling.

One of Heningham Scott's mantras had been that marrying into a family of "good people . . . is almost everything."[35] In full agreement with her mother, Camilla Pinckney had already developed some very particular ideas of her own about Josephine's matrimonial future. She could not have been less interested in having her daughter weave one more Heyward, Rutledge, or Elliott through the Pinckney family tapestry. Camilla's intense scrutiny of the young men of Charleston who began circling around the forbidding façade of 21 King Street hoping for a glimpse of the blossoming daughter of the house convinced her of the need to expose Josephine to another pool of suitors, wealthy Ivy League men, such as had come courting the Langhorne sisters.

Savannah author Harry Hervey observed the domineering Camilla Pinckney at work in her daughter's life while he was living in Charleston during the early 1920s. He even modeled a character after her in his bitter novel *The Damned Don't Cry* about his hometown of Savannah, Georgia, portraying the fictional Camilla

Habersham as "a belligerent, bigoted, unhappy old lady" who ultimately destroys her nephew's happiness.[36]

The romance between Josephine Pinckney and DuBose Heyward ultimately flickered, but their friendship remained profound and survived as a touchstone in both their lives. One bond was their shared understanding of the Code that men and women from their class historically lived by. From time to time, until Heyward's death, little waves of gossip about them would surface around Charleston, but then be gone with the next tide.

In January 1919, Josephine went to college. In 1918, after fifteen years of agitation by local women's clubs, President Harrison Randolph announced that due to "a world of new conditions" with the nation at war, the College of Charleston would embark on the radical experiment of coeducation. Rather than undertake a full course of study at age twenty-four, Pinckney registered as a special student, taking only two English courses. However, she relished the opportunity to work on the *College of Charleston Magazine*. With few upperclassmen on campus, she moved right into the role of associate editor. In her one semester at the college, she had several poems and a short story published in the school magazine.[37]

Influenced by the rising national interest in poetry, Pinckney began writing verse with greater seriousness and discipline. While searching for a diversion, she had found her true love. In September 1919, she experienced the thrill of seeing her name in print in a national literary magazine. After Pinckney's poem "Nuptial" first appeared in *Contemporary Verse,* she was smitten for life.

# 3

## "My Heart Is Still My Own"

By 1918, other young Charleston women were also awakening to the power of poetry. Josephine Pinckney began meeting with Elizabeth Miles (who later married one of the Galahads, Fred Horlbeck) and Helen von Kolnitz (who, as Helen Hyer, became poet laureate of South Carolina) to read one another's verse and explore new trends in literature under the tutelage of Laura M. Bragg. Bragg, the middle-aged director of the Charleston Museum, organized regular sessions at the Gibbes Street home of Belle Heyward where she boarded. The centerpiece of their conversations was often the latest issue of *Poetry*, a Chicago-based publication promoting the revolutionary "new poetry" that was breaking free from the tyranny of traditional poetic forms. Pinckney and her friends huddled over dog-eared copies of *Poetry* and were amused, shocked, and intrigued by the radical poems of Robert Frost, Vachel Lindsay, Carl Sandburg, and Ezra Pound. Accustomed to rhyming iambic pentameter, they puzzled over vers libre, Imagism, and polyphonic prose. They frankly wondered if these unconventional verses using colloquial language were indeed poetry at all. In one issue, Pinckney came upon four poems by the "girl-poet" Edna St. Vincent Millay. Millay had won youthful fame with the long, ethereal "Renascence," but these poems were different. One in particular, "First Fig" struck a chord with Pinckney, as it did with legions of young people who were attracted like moths to the image of the "lovely light" thrown by a candle burning at both ends. By 1920, a Millay biographer has speculated, few English-speaking people under thirty could not quote a few lines of her verse.[1]

Millay dared to write, and *Poetry* editor Harriet Monroe dared to publish, poetry that was more sexually liberating than morally uplifting. Pinckney, who had already developed her lifelong dislike of Emily Dickinson, found that Millay shared her own evolving philosophy: life was short; it might as well be fun. Millay's poetry, sentimental and sexual at the same time, provided "symbolic access to modernity" for young Americans. Whether or not she accepted the idea that free love went hand in hand with free verse, as some argued, Pinckney could conceptualize modernism as an intellectual counterweight to the Code and her mother's thick-stocking pieties. In Millay, she found a woman whose hair was quite as unruly and figure as boyish as her own, yet men swooned at her feet.

Millay stooped to conquer by the irresistible combination of her passionate verse and her own unique persona (both crafted with equal care and deliberation). Literary critic Edmund Wilson, who joined the battalions intoxicated by her charms, claimed that falling in love with Millay was simply the inevitable result of knowing her.[2] More than a few men along the Atlantic seaboard would say the same thing about Pinckney.

During World War I, Americans searching for a way to express their hopes and fears came to believe that within the potent economical line of verse dwelled the essence of the time-spirit, the zeitgeist, of the modern age. Through a shared passion, Pinckney and the younger Charleston poets began to feel a bond with the other youth of America, a generation not yet given its own name by F. Scott Fitzgerald, as the transmitters of the modern, pilgrims trudging along the ragged edge of history. Millay had proclaimed, "The younger generation forms a country of its own. It has no geographical borders." Across the globe, the generation that came to age during the Great War "are going to do things. They are going to change things."[3]

The glorification of youth presented a departure for young southerners who had lived their entire lives haunted by the larger-than-life Confederate generation. For the first time, Pinckney's generation recognized itself in print. Pinckney, whose life was burdened by centuries of ancestral greatness, referred in a poem to her own postwar generation as "the children of the later days": "Our own age rings with faint satirical laughter, / We nourish a distrust / . . . There is no simple heart . . ."[4]

In 1919, Pinckney heard a rumor that a young veteran who had recently moved to Charleston had actually met Edna Millay. She sought out the tall young stranger from Pittsburgh who had taken a position teaching English at Porter Military Academy, a private Episcopal school. DuBose Heyward had already become acquainted with William Hervey Allen at the Legaré Street home of writer John Bennett, whose son was one of Allen's students. Bill Allen (who now wanted to be called "Hervey") shared their interest in poetry and had already self-published a volume of verse. Allen projected an easygoing bonhomie calling his friends "old man" while dragging on his pipe. All arms and legs, he would rock back tenuously in his chair and tell stories of his encounters with famous literary folk during his recent session at Harvard summer school.[5] In 1919, Boston was basking in its last days as the nation's literary capital. One of Allen's best friends was the young drama student Sidney Coe Howard whose many later accomplishments would include the screenplay for *Gone with the Wind*. He had also met Edwin Arlington Robinson, the most acclaimed poet of the day, and the colorful Amy Lowell, a major literary power broker whose entrepreneurial approach to poetry rivaled that of Harriet Monroe.[6]

Bennett began hosting Heyward and Allen for regular Wednesday suppers and "fangfests" critiquing one another's work. Heyward wrapped Allen into his wide circle of friends, which of course included Pinckney, and even won him a coveted bid to join the St. Cecilia Society. Before long, Allen could be seen knocking at the door of 21 King Street. Even the hypercritical Camilla Pinckney enjoyed the young man's visits to read poetry with Josephine. Standing 6' 4," the twenty-seven-year-old Allen still had the physique of the collegiate athlete he had been. The slow-moving, slow-talking poet conveyed the impression of great physical power held gently in reserve. He had chosen Charleston as a pleasant place to recover from horrific wounds to his legs in France. His limp gave him the panache of a man of the world, one who had been to hell and back. At the same time, something in his sensitive face, in his blue eyes, often obscured behind thick-lensed, military-issue glasses, spoke of tragic romance buried within. Allen attracted Pinckney with his "shoot-the-moon," "let's go for broke" approach to life and art. In an early poem, his own anthem for the postwar generation, Allen had proclaimed, "We have a rendezvous with life." He beckoned his southern friends to get back in the game of living and quit sulking in their tents like the defeated Achilles.[7]

This "Norse giant" took Pinckney's literary aspirations seriously and encouraged her to act on her dreams. Self-confident and comfortable with women poets, Allen adopted a "parental interest" in her writing. He advised her "in the meerschaum pipe sort of way" and directed her reading toward the weighty theoretical tomes he had studied during his Harvard summers.[8] After Allen leased a little wood frame house at 19 Savage Street, Pinckney, Heyward, and the other writers began gravitating to his cozy poet's corner. Propriety forbade young single Charlestonians from living on their own, had they been able to afford the luxury of escaping their families' oversight. Allen found that even on a beginning teacher's salary, he could hire a turbaned cook and a man to keep him in firewood and polish floors. He decorated the interior with rugs scattered over the gleaming floors, bright copper pots, and old shawls over his worn furniture. A large bust of Augustus rested on the mantle over a wide fireplace; books lined the walls. Allen, whose appetites matched his size, had probably already started the tradition (for which he would become famous in New York) of fried chicken and beer breakfasts, with some waffles on the side for traditionalists.[9]

Laura Bragg and Bennett frequently joined the young and provided chaperonage of a sort, but this bit of freedom let Pinckney and the others imagine for a few candlelit hours the bohemian life of the fabled poets of Greenwich Village, the world of Millay and Floyd Dell, where art mattered most of all and the relationships between men and women were equal and free from all restraints. More than twenty years later, Hervey Allen reflected on the "terrific and variegated experiences" during the Charleston Renaissance, which "ran the entire gamut of every kind of interest, biological, financial, political, and purely humanly personal." Both men and women shared in the drama and adventure of the time: "it was complete friendship in the entire round and scale," he remembered.[10]

At first, when Laura Bragg had suggested the Legaré Street poets have a joint session with the Gibbes Street "girls," John Bennett and his wife became suspicious. Bennett had no interest at all in women as writers and looked askance at Bragg's "adorable Flappers." He saw them as seductresses who read poetry of very "dubious taste" waiting to lure the Two Genii (as he called Allen and Heyward) away from his "middle aged society." Bennett also thought that becoming too closely associated in the public mind with women writers was a bad idea for male poets. Sensitive to the stigma of literature as a feminine occupation, he constantly urged Heyward and Allen to produce "virile poetry."[11] His wife Susan Bennett, who had two young daughters of her own, feared that the controlling Bragg (an inveterate matchmaker) was trying to marry off Josephine to the talented Allen.[12]

At some point during the early months of 1920, the Gibbes Street and Legaré Street contingents combined forces to form the Poetry Society of South Carolina along the institutional lines of the Poetry Society of America. By April, plans were "well underway." Accounts differ on the exact details of the creation story, but through some alchemy—the friction between Bragg and Bennett, the attraction between the male and female poets, the ambitions of Heyward and Allen, the seismic shift from the Victorian South to the modern South—a noteworthy organization emerged.

The goal of its founders—Heyward, Allen, Bennett, Pinckney, Bragg—was not to encourage the professional writing of poetry but to meet the needs of the entire "word-using" community and thus build a constituency for literature. When Hervey Allen described events in Charleston to Harriet Monroe, he wrote: "This may be no small thing we are fostering." Allen served on the executive committee of the Poetry Society but hovered mostly in the background, Machiavelli among the poets. In retrospect, Allen played a role reminiscent of the soldier in the children's story "Stone Soup." In the fable, a soldier wanders into a town paralyzed by famine. Quickly sizing up the situation, he claims to have a magic stone that will produce a tasty, nutritious soup if the town can but supply a pot of water. One is found. This soup would be enhanced, he then tells them, if somehow he just had a few onions, maybe a potato, a little salt pork. Miraculously, the townspeople come forth with concealed bits of food that when put together with a little of the soldier's "magic" produce the most nourishing soup in anyone's memory.

As in this fable, Charleston was a community that felt itself culturally starved at the same time that a storehouse of resources lay close at hand. And Hervey Allen did have a bit of the sorcerer about him. His confirmation that the Carolina Low Country provided a treasure trove of literary possibility gave confidence to the Charleston poets that they could write about the land they loved without falling into the artistic trap of sentimentality or provinciality. Without their ever knowing it, Allen used his growing influence in publishing circles to smooth the way for Bennett, Heyward, and Pinckney to find the initial success they craved in the larger world of literature. He also gave crucial behind-the-scenes help to Beatrice Ravenel, a poet in her late forties trying to recover her lost art but who despaired that she could not compete with "the horrible cleverness of the younger generation, who are treading down the older writers in the true Keatsian manner."[13]

As its "treasurer—and treasure, too" Josephine Pinckney lent her youthful, lighthearted insouciance to the enterprise that "gaily began its career as the propagandist of Southern poetry." She described the Poetry Society as operating as both "a forum and a studio," offering programs to interest the dues-payer who enjoyed dressing up, hearing a speaker, and having a glass of punch, as well as the practicing poets. The study groups generally met in private homes where from four to twelve amateur poets would gather to have a "cosy time in real Bohemian fashion" over crackers, cheese, and a modest homebrew, or cakes and Cokes. The sessions led by Allen, who according to Pinckney, would draw from his pipe and "puff smoke and poetic doctrine into the air" tended to be like academic seminars. Pinckney's, on the other hand, tended to end "with much hilarity."[14]

The activities of the society became the talk of the town. Two hundred and fifty townspeople, mostly from Pinckney's upper circle, joined. Few Charlestonians had even heard of Carl Sandburg before the Poetry Society took the daring step of inviting him to give its inaugural lecture. Prior to his arrival in Charleston, Pinckney, Heyward, Bragg and others gathered at 7 Gibbes Street "to talk Sandburg exclusively" and debate his "radical" approach. After his performance, during which Sandburg played his guitar, some were still skeptical, but a dialogue about the elements of poetry had begun which involved the larger community and would continue for a decade.[15] Exactly when the accelerated pulse of culture in Charleston reached the point when talk began of a "renaissance" is not clear, but local people embraced the term in a nod to the nineteenth-century flurry of literary activity that had been snuffed out by sectional politics and then the Civil War. Of perhaps greater significance was the national recognition that something of importance was happening in the South, especially in Charleston.

In 1921, an editorial in the *Charleston News and Courier* reflected upon the new local energy for the arts: "This is a finer city and a better city to live in than many of us realized." The Poetry Society of South Carolina would give form and substance to the first glimmerings of a cultural revival across the entire South and would provide a model for poetry societies in Georgia, Florida, Texas, and Maryland. Within four years, more than two thousand southerners had joined poetry societies. By 1923, eight literary publications were produced in the South, including the *Yearbook of the Poetry Society of South Carolina,* an annual collection of poems and summary of cultural events that provided a barometer of the blossoming "renaissance."[16] More than thirty Charleston writers would publish books of verse with trade presses by 1930. The Poetry Society was also the vehicle upon which Allen, Heyward, and Pinckney would all ride out beyond the limits of a small southern town and into the larger world of literature.

Interest in poetry was part of a much broader national trend. In Charleston, as in much of America "taste," the ability to discern aesthetic quality, became a factor in social standing, especially among women who dominated the Poetry Society. The popularity of an organization, such as the Poetry Society of South Carolina, derived in part from the guidance it provided to the average citizen anxious to be au courant.[17]

The program committee of the Poetry Society ranged widely in their search for speakers and did not necessarily seek to reinforce local values. When Millay won the Pulitzer Prize in 1923, DuBose Heyward wrote Allen that he had to use all his influence to recruit Millay. "The Society must have a woman, and are wild for Edna," he insisted, even though Amy Lowell had warned that compared to Millay, "Sappho is a model of virtue and propriety."[18] John Bennett told University of South Carolina professor Yates Snowden that one of the society's aims was "to fetch Harriet Monroe, Vachel Lindsay and other such *rarae aves* and pater nosters down this-a-way."[19] In March 1921, Harriet Monroe agreed to visit Charleston on her cultural fact-finding tour, seeking to evaluate the creative explosion rumored to be sweeping the South. Her schedule brought her to the city at a time when both Allen and Heyward were away. Pinckney seized the opportunity to invite Monroe to stay at 21 King Street. Monroe ended up being pleasantly surprised with Charleston and with Pinckney.

Although this "spinster on fire" was passionate in her determination to awaken Americans to the excitement of the New Poetry, Monroe gave a dry, singsong lecture. But ever polite, the substantial crowd gathered at South Carolina Society Hall applauded heartily. After Pinckney gave her the insider's tour of the city, Monroe understood the multiple dimensions of the cultural revival and the regional values expressed by the writers as well as architects and artists who considered the city as a whole a work of art. Camilla Pinckney had likely explained her own role in founding the Southern States Art League in 1921 an organization that encouraged southern artists to take the South as their subject, to render "on canvas and in bronze those hidden qualities of the heart, those traditions of neighborly life, those relations to the soil that have made us what we are."[20] At the Gibbes Art Gallery, Monroe saw the luminous work of Charleston artists, such as Alice Ravenel Huger Smith and Elizabeth O'Neill Verner, and perceived the driving force at work in Charleston was an attempt both to recover a lost tradition of culture and to produce a unique, autochthonous art.

Although Monroe personally favored "red light" poetry, fervent calls to strike down child labor, and odes to women's rights, she had returned to Chicago convinced that something of importance was brewing in the South. Native southerners possessed more ambition than she had imagined. Through Pinckney, she sensed excited energy rather than the expected enervation and stagnation of mind. The younger generation of Charlestonians, she wrote, was quite capable of loving their past without being "enslaved" by it. At the same time, after a night at 21 King Street, she also detected a "desperate fluttering of some free spirit beating its wings against ancient barriers."[21]

Pinckney had thrust a sheaf of poems into Monroe's hands before the editor left Charleston and waited anxiously for the verdict. Monroe soon sent word that she wanted to publish four of Pinckney's poems in the vaunted pages of *Poetry*. One of them, "In the Barn," employed the lyrical Gullah language of the plantation blacks that had been used to great effect by DuBose Heyward. This poem won the first Caroline Sinkler Prize awarded by the Poetry Society and was included in William Stanley Braithwaite's annual *Anthology of Best Magazine Poetry*, an accolade that often signaled a young poet's career was on its way. "Ain't that grand?" Pinckney wrote Laura Bragg when she heard the news.[22]

Pinckney's work once again appeared in *Poetry* in April 1922. Monroe agreed to Hervey Allen's request made the previous September that he and Heyward serve as guest editors of a special "southern number" of her magazine to celebrate "the present poetic stir in the South." He also wanted her to endorse the Charleston Literary Movement. After three hundred years, Monroe declared in her introductory essay (taken verbatim from Allen's suggestion), the romance of the South's early history and legend involving "three strongly contrasted races" in the context of the plantation, the sea, and the city had found their interpreters in the poets of the Carolina Low Country.[23]

Monroe suspected correctly that Heyward and Allen planned to showcase their own work primarily. She expressed no concern that they ignored the aspiring poets of Nashville, Richmond, or New Orleans, but she did worry that the Charleston men would ignore southern women. "And perhaps Miss Pinckney and others of your group have some poems we could use," Monroe suggested.[24] In April 1922, Pinckney's "Spring Makes Me Wonder" appeared in the "Southern Number" of *Poetry*.

This success whetted Pinckney's growing ambition. As she glimpsed the possibility of a vocation as a poet, she also had to acknowledge the inadequacy of her own training. Hervey Allen helped her understand that poetry was a technical skill as well as the product of emotion and intelligence. She clearly needed a much firmer foundation in composition, criticism, and literary history. Camilla Pinckney pressed Josephine to study at the Sorbonne after their planned European tour in the summer of 1921, so they might have an extended stay in Paris. But this time Pinckney dug in her heels and "declared there was no place like Boston to educate a girl." She insisted on enrolling for a semester in Radcliffe College where she could work with the same Harvard professors who had trained Allen. As the time to leave approached, however, Pinckney began to fret that an extended absence from Charleston would diminish her influence in the newly formed Poetry Society. Allen promised to keep "the lamp lit in front of your niche at the PSSC. Count on it!"[25]

In June 1921, Pinckney passed off her duties as treasurer of the Poetry Society to Laura Bragg. She expected to be gone from Charleston for almost a year. Before beginning her Radcliffe studies, she had to accommodate Camilla's desire for a summer tour of Europe, their first since the Great War tore the continent apart. Pinckney dreaded the prospect. She also deeply resented the fact that Allen had wrangled a spot for DuBose Heyward at the MacDowell Colony, where they planned to summer in the "company of select spirits."[26] While she dutifully trudged after her mother who had an inexhaustible zeal for dusty museums and damp castles, the "genii" shared a cabin in the lovely cool of the New Hampshire woods and collaborated on a book of poetry with the Carolina Low Country as its unifying theme.

London, Pinckney's first stop, "failed to be thrilling from a literary point of view," she complained to Bragg. When she arrived, Pinckney made straight for Bloomsbury to seek out Harold Munro's Poetry Book Shop, a mecca for a circle that called themselves the Georgian poets. During the boredom of her Atlantic crossing, Pinckney had perhaps conjured an image of herself strolling over to the Devonshire Street store and being hailed as a comrade in poetry. Possibly, in the narrow aisles she might bump elbows with T. S. Eliot, whose Criterion Club met there regularly. In her most ambitious daydream, Eliot would even ask her, as a founder of the Poetry Society, to sit in on the conversation. Twice Pinckney navigated the warren of London streets from her hotel to the Poetry Book Shop and tried in her most charming southern manner to engage the brusque Munro in conversation. On both occasions, he rebuffed her. She even tried bribery, buying several books for the Poetry Society shelves, but he refused to "unbend." Munro's slight disappointed her mightily. She dismissed him as "too British for any use, stiff and unforthcoming to a degree." Pinckney had hoped to have some stories of literary encounters of her own when she next saw Allen and Heyward, but the whole episode was a "fizzle."[27]

Stymied in her pursuit of high culture, Pinckney shrugged and gave herself over to pleasure. She linked up with a number of southern friends vacationing in London, then made the crossing with her mother to Paris. Pinckney strolled the boulevards and winding alleys of the Left Bank and imbibed the delicious flavor of the city where young American expatriate writers crowded sidewalk cafés, sipped strong coffee, and talked excitedly about a revolution in literature. Josephine's spirits sagged when Camilla insisted they explore the châteaux district around Tours. Her days blended one into another in a fog of French history, topiary gardens, dusty tapestries, and gilded period furniture. The exhausting cycle of rail schedules, organized tours, and checking in and out of hotels had left Josephine little time to write even a line of poetry during the summer. Visions of Allen and Heyward giving themselves over to their muse every day bedeviled her. When city grit clung to Pinckney and her feet ached, she grew "green with envy." Her boredom gave rise to a jealousy as malignant as the harpies or gargoyles glaring at her from the vaulted cathedral. She tuned out the drone of tour guides and the prattle of Camilla and envisioned Allen and Heyward "chewing the cud" with Stephen Vincent Benét and Max Bodenheim and becoming "thick as thieves" with popular Irish poet Padraic Colum.[28]

Pinckney feared that Allen and Heyward would seize all the credit for the incipient Charleston Literary Movement for themselves. In his frequent letters, Allen protested this was not the case and that he had been showing her poems around the MacDowell Colony. Edwin Arlington Robinson, America's most highly regarded poet, reportedly praised her four poems from *Poetry*. Pinckney pressed Allen for details, Robinson's exact words, good and bad, since "Good adverse criticism is the hardest thing to get in Charleston."[29]

Allen had dragged himself back to the classroom by the time Josephine's ship landed in New York in late September 1921. He had switched jobs, now teaching at the public high school of Charleston, but he continued to wear his military gear, his brass-buckled Sam Browne belt and a big hat he claimed saw service on the

Mexican border. Heyward had settled himself at his desk in the insurance office. Already running late for registration, Pinckney frantically dashed to Cambridge and her lodgings at 41 Concord Avenue. As soon as Camilla returned home to Charleston, Josephine's spirits rose dramatically. She made plans to burn her candle at both ends after months of her mother's stifling oversight. Cambridge promised to be "stacks of fun," she wrote Allen. In contrast to the past several months, "I'm liking my life very much at the moment." In her typical backhanded way, she congratulated Allen on *Wampum and Old Gold* (1921), his new book of poems published by the distinguished Younger Poets series of Yale University Press. "I warn you not to push me too far by being too successful," Pinckney threatened, "or my present respectful admiration will be turned to jealous rage and then there is no knowing what will happen."[30]

Pinckney arrived at the Radcliffe College registrar's office feeling "quite lost" as she tried to navigate the unfamiliar waters of academic registration. Her confusion turned to outrage when the "miserable Radcliffe people" refused to allow her mid-year admission into Harvard professor John Livingston Lowes's two-semester course on nineteenth-century poets. Allen had insisted a course with Lowes was a must. Determined, Pinckney laid siege both to the administration and Lowes himself, vowing "to eaves-drop if nothing else can be arranged." At last, she finagled a seat in English 35a as well as English 72, "Composition."[31]

Her third course, English 5 taught by the legendary Professor Charles T. Copeland, presented a different sort of challenge. Pinckney had apparently met Copeland during a vacation at the Walpole Inn in New Hampshire and had written him for advanced permission to take his criticism course. His reply did little to inflate her confidence. He welcomed her to "join his little course" but added that he considered it "my duty to tell you that I think you will not lead the class. I couldn't say that to a real old 'before the war' girl of high degree, but when a girl of high degree is as terrifically modern and sensible as you are, she will like to know how things look." In her earlier correspondence with the Radcliffe registrar, she noted "Professor Copeland has written me a letter which, I think, means that he has a place for me."[32]

Pinckney began her studies in Cambridge just as the antifeminine reaction in the literary community was hardening. Harvard philosopher George Santayana probably coined the damning phrase "the feminization of American culture" in a 1902 lecture, but he was by no means the first to blame the sentimentalization of American literature on female writers and female readers who kept the popular pulp magazines in business. The power of Yale professor Herbert Spencer's perversion of Darwin's theory, in which he argued that women were less highly developed than men and thus incapable of original thought, found a ready audience in the Ivy League. Copeland started his career as part of a new movement on campus that included philosopher William James and dramatist George Pierce Baker who related their courses to issues in contemporary life. His comments to the "terrifically modern" Pinckney suggest how blind even the most enlightened of the Harvard faculty were on the subject of women's achievement.[33]

For many men wanting a career in the arts, the promise of the modern age was liberation from the dominance of women that had theoretically characterized the Victorian era. In 1927, Harold E. Stearns would alert readers of *Civilization in the United States* that never before in human history had art, music, literature, and education, "the things of the mind and the spirit," been relegated almost exclusively to women, whose taste was almost uniformly sentimental and conventional. Ezra Pound, who had a bitter falling out with Amy Lowell over the interpretation of Imagism, crowed in 1922 that T. S. Eliot's masterwork, *The Waste Land*, which painted a bleak postwar landscape, "ends [the] idea of poetry for ladies." The twentieth century was destined to be the century of the masculine in literature, Pound predicted. All that was female would be passé. Novelist Joseph Hergesheimer, whose own enormous popularity had begun to ebb during the 1920s, also blamed women's influence for the decline in literary standards. He urged male writers to "wipe the sachet powder from their eyes" and create a literature "universal to the heart." Hergesheimer called for the rekindling of men's emotional life that had been stripped away by women.[34]

In the classroom, Pinckney found her courses excruciatingly difficult. Her instructors were brutal, and her grades embarrassingly poor. Pinckney insisted that she learned a great deal at Radcliffe and from "the point of view of enjoyment," she judged her time in Cambridge "a great success." Laura Bragg hounded her for details of her love life, bluntly asking Pinckney if she had committed herself to any one man yet. "I am not engaged," Pinckney replied. "I have met some very promising Bostonians, and of course there is always one who is nicer than the others." She hastened to add, "my heart is still my own."[35]

The nicest of the Bostonians from Josephine's perspective was Richard Bowditch Wigglesworth. He was also her mother's favorite. Dick Wigglesworth could not have been more perfect in Camilla's estimate had she ordered him straight from central casting as a mate for her daughter (excepting, of course, his Unitarian affiliation). Four years older than Josephine and still unmarried at thirty-one, a former All-American quarterback and hockey star, Dick was a seventh-generation Harvard graduate, the first being the Massachusetts divine, Michael Wigglesworth, famous for his chilling "Day of Doom" sermon. One of Josephine's

Virginia cousins remembered collapsing in peals of laughter when as a tiny boy he heard the odd, Yankee-sounding Wigglesworth name so proudly intoned by Camilla around the dinner table in Warrenton as a person perhaps destined to play a major role in her daughter's future.[36]

Wigglesworth's family lived in Milton, Massachusetts, where his father, George, was a lawyer, textile magnate, and prominent leader in Boston's civic circles. Dick's mother, Mary Dixwell Wigglesworth, also traced her New England lineage back many generations. One of her grandfathers, Nathaniel I. Bowditch, wrote the classic mariners' bible, *The New American Practical Navigator*. Her brother-in-law was Oliver Wendell Holmes. After undergraduate school at Harvard, Dick Wigglesworth traveled around the world and briefly served as private secretary to W. Cameron Forbes, governor general of the Philippine Islands, before beginning Harvard Law School. He graduated in 1916 and served in France during World War I. When he met Pinckney, he was just beginning a job in Washington as legal adviser to the U.S. assistant secretary of the Treasury in charge of foreign loans.[37]

As the term drew to a close in January, Pinckney regretted leaving Cambridge, where "every minute has been full of interesting things." At the same time, she keenly felt that the world was spinning rapidly around her while she remained at a standstill. Allen and Heyward's book *Carolina Chansons* was scheduled for publication in 1922. Heyward, in particular, was all atwitter, believing more completely than ever that his dreams might come true—had come true, actually to a larger extent than anyone would ever have anticipated. Pinckney missed their big moment when they read selections to the Poetry Society amiably assembled in South Carolina Hall and eager to be pleased by the first fruit of the Charleston Literary Movement.[38]

Pinckney's mock-wrath flared up at Allen when she learned he had come north during Christmas and had not called her. Her first impulse, she wrote the offending poet, "was to seize a pen and scratch you off my list for good and all . . . But after vigil and prayer, I have decided to write you a letter anyway, if only to show that I don't give a d—." Trying to make amends, Allen agreed to one of Pinckney's most persistent demands. She was desperate to meet the influential Amy Lowell and had been badgering him for an introduction. The summer after their idyll at the MacDowell Colony, Allen had taken Heyward to a "wonderful" dinner with Lowell at her Brookline home and afterward he "fair rippled and bubbled" about the whole affair. She had earlier coaxed him, "It should be a simple matter to vamp Amy into asking you up for a little visit. We poetesses do dote upon you poets and are always eager to have them about."[39]

Allen hesitated to grant Pinckney's boon because Lowell had not only already written an endorsement of the first Poetry Society *Yearbook* but also agreed to judge the first annual Blindman Prize competition—eight pounds of poems, 360 entries.[40] Understanding Allen's "aversion to riding the old girl to death," Pinckney offered to let him off the hook.[41] In the end, though, the soft-hearted Allen capitulated. He risked asking one more favor of Lowell who kept a close tab on her accounts receivable. Knowing Lowell well, her innate snobbery, dread of tiresome people, and respect for accomplishment, he framed Josephine in the most desirable light possible. He described her as a young Charleston lady from "the old Coatsworth [sic] Pinckney folks" and "really delightful." She is writing some "good stuff," has appeared in Braithwaite's anthology, and is the treasurer of the Poetry Society in Charleston. "She would like to know you and you will not be bored I can promise you."[42]

With equal parts curiosity and courtesy, Lowell obliged Allen and issued the long-sought invitation to Josephine (and the unshakable Camilla) for dinner at "Sevenels." Lowell's father, the industrialist Augustus Lowell, had named his expansive home for the seven Lowells who lived there. Allen thoroughly prepared Pinckney for the possibility of an unorthodox evening. Depending on her mood, Lowell occasionally took perverse joy in scaring her guests, especially if she thought them overreaching. By the time the Pinckneys arrived at the gates of Sevenels, guarded by two white marble lions in front and real-life snarling dogs behind, they were ready for anything.

Lowell worked all night and slept during the day. Josephine knew this, so the Pinckneys were not surprised that she was nowhere in sight when they arrived. A servant answered the gate and invited them into the dark-paneled receiving hall. Two exquisite Chinese vases rested on a long teak table. Mrs. Ada Russell, a former actress whose quiet dignity provided a foil for Lowell's intensity, acted as hostess and greeted arriving guests. After her father died, Lowell had redecorated the formal house to her own taste, combining family antiques with Asian art. Heavy draperies shut out the daylight while she slept. She brought her own sunshine into the music room with shimmering saffron satin on the walls, blond wood furniture, the warm colors of a Monet painting, and a grand piano polished to a high sheen. The many remaining Victorian trappings would have appealed to Camilla: massive furniture and thick oriental rugs. Every doorknob was silver.

Integrating her private life and her work, Lowell tore down the partitions between the sitting room and library of twelve thousand volumes to create one great oak-paneled room, a noble chamber for the woman who considered herself "the last of the barons." Lowell's reputation as a discerning collector of books and autograph manuscripts exceeded her standing as a poet. Enthralled with John Keats's work since her girlhood, she possessed an extensive collection of his papers and was laboring on a mammoth biography of the poet at the time she first met the Pinckneys. Love of books was their first tie. Pinckney had already begun her own collection of first editions and later became deeply interested in the "book collecting game," which reached its height of popularity in America between 1910 and 1930.[43]

During her renovation of Sevenels, Lowell had a special humidity-controlled storeroom built exclusively for her cigars. Much has made been made over her unconventional habit, but cigar smoking made perfect sense for a writer. She found cigarettes burned down too quickly; all the snuffing out and the relighting distracted her. Pipes proved too much trouble altogether. A chewing wad was not to be considered; snuff, too messy. After much experimentation, she hit on mild, light-colored Manila cigars that were so enjoyable she incorporated them into the ritual around her writing. Fearing German U-boats during World War I might cut off her supply, she had imported ten thousand.[44]

At some point in the evening, usually during the meal—it could be the soup, it could be the nuts—Lowell would dramatically descend the sweeping staircase elegantly carpeted in crimson silk made to her order. The adventure would then begin. The first encounter with Lowell could be startling. The poet, an expansive beauty-seeking soul, had become cruelly trapped in an overblown, almost grotesque, body by a glandular disorder that had set in during her adolescence. She carried almost 250 pounds on a delicate five-foot frame that her brave little pompadour failed to enhance. Lowell's passion for "high-collared dresses sprinkled with beads and lavishly trimmed with passementerie" did little to underplay her bulk. Some jibed that her tight-fitting clothes made her look upholstered, like a small sofa. "Lord," she once exclaimed, "I'm a walking side-show."[45]

The shock of Amy Lowell's appearance only lasted a moment. On second glance, her fine features—lovely small hands, delicate feet, great care and neatness in her dress—overshadowed her flaws. Never a beauty, she became a personality and set a stage around herself replete with lovely things and interesting people. Glimmering silver, crystal goblets brimming with fine wine, baskets of flowers, well-prepared food served with precision, and fast-paced conversation elevated evenings at Sevenels to sheer magic.[46]

Most visitors to Sevenels wanted something. Young poets hoped for patronage. Older, established poets often wanted money to shore up rickety "little magazines." Lowell also had responsibilities outside the literary world to various family philanthropies, so directors of this and chairmen of that often came calling. When meeting people for the first time, Lowell stared hard and did a quick appraisal of motives. Her brilliant blue eyes were penetrating, but not unkind.[47] When Lowell focused on Pinckney's eager-to-be-agreeable face, she saw something familiar. Lowell recognized Pinckney's ambitions and yearning for fame, and she understood what drove her.

Outwardly, two individuals could scarcely have been more different: one a young southern lady, thin and angular, still very much an amateur poetess; the other a stout, almost swollen, middle-aged New Englander who had created herself into an international literary phenomenon. They recognized each other, however, as the last of a breed, the survivors of a hereditary American aristocracy that had been forged even before the American Revolution. They even both had relatives who had represented the United States at the Spanish court and at the Court of Saint James. Lowell grieved that hers was the last generation. Her siblings had no children to carry on.[48]

Amy Lowell was, like Josephine Pinckney, more than just a product of the distinguished bloodlines. Being a Lowell had made her what she was, the same way that being a Pinckney had indelibly shaped Josephine. Lowell was as thoroughgoing a Bostonian as Pinckney was a Charlestonian; for each, family history and personal history melded together. Puritanism and perfectionism molded the personality of one; Anglicanism and duty shaped the personality of the other. At a time when regional distinctions had begun melting away and American diversity was giving way to a mass culture, Pinckney and Lowell both cultivated and exploited their historic and unique identities, but were also limited by them.

The friendship that developed between Lowell and Pinckney echoed the national reconciliation at work during the twenties. Unlike his scholarly abolitionist half-brother poet James Russell Lowell, Amy Lowell's father Augustus swore allegiance to the hardheaded, tough-minded Yankee branch that gave its name to the gritty textile-mill town. The Lowells, like many other prominent Boston families, had profited first from the slave trade and then from cotton mills fed by southern plantations.[49]

Although the Lowells' living came from flywheels and spewing smokestacks, love of the earth, their *own* earth, suffused both them and the Pinckneys. Both created magnificent gardens. Both were ancient families, as far as American families went, and had exercised a great deal of energy taming the wilderness they found. Both were accustomed to the almost staggering abundance that America bestowed on the fortunate and took it as their due. Augustus Lowell was known to have cut a thousand roses in one day from the Sevenels garden.[50]

The Lowells and the Pinckneys felt the heavy responsibilities that their positions had pressed on them. Having money was like having elected office. Neither Lowell nor Pinckney would be able to fully dedicate herself entirely to her own pursuit of literature, because noblesse oblige compelled each to contribute part of her time, as well as part of her wealth, in service to others. Born late in their mothers' lives, separated from their siblings by many years, Pinckney and Lowell both had solitary childhoods behind walled gardens. They found their earliest companions in books. Even though both were clearly bright and their families valued learning, their formal educations bordered on the desultory. To compensate, both became autodidacts, learning by picking up this book then that, prowling around in the family libraries. As Lowell put it, "there is no playing truant to the schooling one gives oneself."[51]

Utterly secure in their social standing, neither Lowell nor Pinckney ever felt entirely confident about her intellect. Relentlessly self-critical, both held themselves to the high standards set by the men of their families. Both ultimately rejected the boring life of the society woman with her clubs, garden parties, and polite chatter; both would become exceptionally hard workers at their writing. Their wealth always colored the opinion of critics in a negative way, inspiring accusations of dilettantism. Their personalities came to overshadow their literary accomplishments. The most common criticism of both would be that they kept their emotions in safe harbor. Unwilling to reveal their deepest feelings even in their poetry, they preferred to relate to others through their minds, but not their hearts. Alfred Kreymborg criticized Lowell for guarding her heart "like an aristocrat."[52]

Their first meeting in 1922 planted the seed of a friendship that took a great deal of nurturing but ultimately flourished by the time of Lowell's premature death in 1925. What started out as Pinckney's hope of finding a mentor for her poetry, or at very least an introduction to a magazine publisher, evolved into a relationship of mutual admiration. Lowell's theories, particularly Imagism, definitely influenced the young writer, who came to think of writing as creating word pictures.

After the publication of *Carolina Chansons* in 1923, Lowell considered Hervey Allen the brightest star among the young male poets of his generation. (She thought Millay and Wylie the best.) She took him on as her special pet and tried to involve herself in all aspects of his life, even suggesting that he pursue a romantic relationship with Pinckney. Pinckney did occasionally act the part of the youthful flibbertigibbet, but Lowell thought Allen judged her too harshly and dismissed her too readily as a lightweight, little more than an amusing dinner partner. Admitting that Pinckney would probably never "shine" as one of America's great poets, she pronounced the young Charlestonian "one of the fine creatures of this world."

Lowell asserted, "I think Josephine is of a type which if there were any call for heroism, would discover herself to be a first class heroine."[53]

Pinckney returned to Charleston in early March 1922 with Dick Wigglesworth not far behind. He led the procession of springtime guests at 21 King Street, alive once again now that Josephine was home. She had scarcely caught her breath before preparations began for Amy Lowell's arrival at the end of the month. The special challenge of entertaining Lowell reaped rich rewards for the Poetry Society. On the evening of March 30, the ballroom of the South Carolina Society Hall overflowed with proud Charlestonians and poetry lovers from several states who had come to pay homage to the woman who had done so much for her craft. As she made her entrance, the audience spontaneously stood in her honor. Lowell, whose life was crowded equally with disappointments as well as privileges, was deeply moved. She made a powerful connection with her audience as she discussed the recent trends in poetry and read some of her own poems in her well-tempered patrician voice.

Touched by Josephine's attentions, Lowell invited Pinckney and her mother to visit her in New England during the summer of 1922. They accepted immediately and began planning their vacation. They booked rooms in the Hawthorne Inn on the harbor at East Gloucester Harbor, Massachusetts. East Gloucester offered multiple attractions, not the least of which was proximity to the Wigglesworth's summer establishment at exclusive Manchester-by-the-Sea. Like the White Sulphur Springs of Camilla's day, the Hawthorne Inn had enjoyed a reputation as a marriage mart ever since its founding in 1891. Attracted by the inn's genteel entertainments such as tea dances, concerts, plays, tennis, golf, and boating, prominent New England families encouraged their older children to look for potential mates among those of similar background and balance sheet. A local quip even had it that in New England, "matches were not made in heaven, but at the Hawthorne Inn."[54]

The Pinckneys found life at the Hawthorne Inn so congenial that they made it an annual summer destination and often stayed from late July until frost flecked the lawns on October mornings. Caroline Sidney Sinkler, the aunt of one of Josephine's lifelong friends, Carrie Sinkler, owned a summer home, Wrong Roof, on a nearby private spit of land called Eastern Point. Born in 1860 at Belvidere Plantation north of Charleston, Sinkler retained her charming southern ways, her lovely habit of stretching out her "oo"s, long after she emerged as the "Enchantress of Philadelphia." Through the generosity of her very wealthy widowed sister, Elizabeth Sinkler Coxe, "Aunt Cad" lived a life of luxury and travel. She was well known by art collectors in Rome and jewelry merchants on Bond Street. Vivacious and intelligent, she surrounded herself with amusing talented people. One of her friends, Owen Wister, author of *Lady Baltimore* (1906), likely used her as the model for his memorable character Eliza Le Heu, the honorable, humorous plantation girl who personified the best type of southerner after the Civil War. With no pressing financial need to marry, Sinkler waved aside all suitors until in the summer of her life she met a man who rivaled her in charm and passion for life. Just before their wedding, he died falling through the ice while skating on the Schuylkill River. After a suitable interval in black, she embarked on "a festive mourning" of lavender, which became her trademark in wardrobe, interior design, and even her stationery. A whiff of lilac always lingered as she passed.[55]

Pinckney thrived on the energy that swirled around "Aunt Cad." Sinkler was the oldest member of a select little colony of the clever, self-absorbed, articulate, and accomplished. Her portion of Eastern Point was sometimes referred to as the "she shore"; the residents were either were independent single women or unmarried men: Joanna Davidge operated a New York City girls' school; Cecilia Beaux and Lucy Taggart were both artists.[56] With no children to amuse, Sinkler's friends concentrated on amusing themselves.

Another positive aspect of East Gloucester was its proximity to Peterborough and Boston. Pinckney could take her Ford, a friend, and (properly chaperoned, of course) buzz over to the MacDowell Colony to check in on Heyward or to see Allen, who was studying at the Harvard summer school. Whereas the summer before she was obsessed over the young men's proximity to the influential male poets at the colony, this summer she was spinning over their access to the famous "girl poets," especially the slinky and seductive Elinor Wylie. Pinckney fretted that Heyward would succumb to the charms of this "poetic vamp." She rumored that the troubled Wylie as "an advocate of free love who is about to take unto herself her third affinity and has a deserted child and a suicidal husband on what would be her conscience if she had one." On the other hand, Pinckney admitted, perhaps this uninhibited, highly charged woman was exactly what Heyward needed.[57]

Heyward had found romance but wisely not with the overwrought Wylie. Instead of the great scenes of passion Pinckney imagined, Heyward was actually taking long moonlight walks around the colony with Dorothy Kuhns, an attractive playwright from Ohio and a member of the Baker Workshop 47 at Harvard. Small, fragile, of uncertain health, gazing at the world with startled dark eyes, Dorothy looked so much like Heyward that they could pass for twins. Hardworking and determined to succeed in a very competitive business, Dorothy also had a delightfully madcap side, an "inadvertent Gracie Allen, asking cockeyed questions," as she described herself.[58] Smart, funny, strong-minded, attractive, Dorothy Kuhns had many of the same qualities as the inaccessible and unattainable Josephine Pinckney.

At the heart of Pinckney's querulous state was her own frustration over the slow-moving romance with Dick Wigglesworth. She remarked sourly to Laura Bragg that at Gloucester she was "seeing a lot of my idealistic Boston friend, but we don't seem to be getting on very fast."[59] "The Idealist," a poem written in the early 1920s, bears a distinct similarity to the preoccupied Mr. Wigglesworth sitting on the New England shore so focused on the problems of world peace that he could not see the treasure before him.

> The tide ran out,
> Lost interest, lay slack,
> And left him on the bare beach
> Weighing imponderables.

Pinckney was back at home for New Year's Eve of 1922. She and Hervey Allen broke away from a party at Laura Bragg's retreat. Allen wrote Lowell of their memorable evening: "I spent New Years at Snug Harbor . . . Joe Pinckney and I walked late at night to see an ancient house that stared out across the marsh like a blind face from a lace cap of mosses and live oaks." They talked of poetry and, no doubt, their dreams of their futures. Both were restive. Allen had begun to weary of being a "southern poet." After he captured the city's magic and romance in *Carolina Chansons*, Charleston began to lose some of its magic for him. Inspired by the broad night sky, Allen probably told Pinckney about his new project, a counter to T. S. Eliot's bleak vision, in which he planned to write about the Low Country, "not simply as Carolina, but as a part of the cosmos."[60] Pinckney, less sure about her own plans, knew only that she craved the cosmopolitan life outside of Carolina.

# 4

## *Inventing a Southern Literature*

In mid-January 1923, Josephine Pinckney awakened "much talk" in Charleston. She and DuBose Heyward had hopped the train to New York (unchaperoned) for a "huge lark" at the annual Poetry Society of America dinner. Hervey Allen discreetly followed on a later run, not wanting to appear to "tag" along with them. For Pinckney, waltzing into the festivities at the Roof Garden of Manhattan's Hotel Astor with Hervey on one arm and DuBose on the other was every bit as thrilling as if she, like the Langhorne sisters of an earlier generation, had been asked to take her bow before the Four Hundred of New York society. Attending the gala event was indeed a debut for her into the world of literature. She beamed when she was recognized from the podium as a founder of the Poetry Society of South Carolina.[1]

Professor John Erskine of Columbia University welcomed the Charleston contingent and praised the Poetry Society for preserving "the spirit of the South." Erskine paid tribute to the city of Charleston for remaining "so individual, so patrician, so pervaded with a feeling of having achieved inward peace." After Erskine spoke, Heyward rose to make the case for southern literature as a unique genre in American letters. Pinckney, never reconciled to Heyward's monopoly of the spotlight, had earlier wisecracked to Amy Lowell that in preparation for his big moment, "DuBose is sitting up nights preparing to tell them all about poetry, with particular reference to that certain member of the PS of SC."[2]

Southern poets sing a different song from T. S. Eliot and the modernists, Heyward proclaimed. "The people of the South love their soil. They are not submerged in huge cities bewailing their fate; they are not preoccupied with psychoanalysis. They love the old homes where they have lived for generations. They love the old landscapes . . . They have traveled. They have read, but they will not write foreign poetry in the English language and they will probably prefer to use the old classic forms of verse. They have nature, history, folklore, legend, tradition; they will express their old homeland about them with its long roots reaching into the past."[3] In Heyward and Pinckney, leaders of the nation's poetry establishment glimpsed the faces of the Charleston Literary Movement: men and women, aristocratic and attractive, forward thinking yet dubious about modernism. They liked what they saw.

The conservative mood of the nation after the costly idealism of World War I created a receptive environment for southern writers. Only a month before the New York gala, Charles Stork, poet and New York-based editor of *Contemporary Verse,* had warned, "Traditional culture has its back up against the wall." Commercial publishers pandered to "mob taste" for "cheap excitement," and foreign-born writers corrupted American literature with their sexually deviant, proletarian, and coarse urban themes. But all was not lost, Stork believed, as long as "the old English stock" remained "well to the fore." Seeking to promote the aspects of American literature that conveyed the nation's "aristocratic spirit" and "close to the earth" qualities, Stork was willing to publish unknown southern writers. In fact, he claimed considerable personal credit for the Charleston Renaissance, boasting that he had "discovered" DuBose Heyward, "introduced" Hervey Allen, and published the first cycle of poems by Beatrice Ravenel and the first lyric of Josephine L. S. Pinckney ("Nuptial" in 1919). Stork proclaimed Charleston, "the Literary Capital of the South."[4]

Still, many northern critics viewed the idea of southern literature with skepticism. Even southern writers feared that promoting a regional literature would only open the sluice gates for local color and treacly sentiment. Sectional antagonism also lingered, north and south. As late as 1938, a Massachusetts newspaper ran an article on Pinckney, Bennett, and Heyward as founders of Charleston Literary Movement under the headline, "Charleston, Which Started Civil War, Also Started Southern Literary Renaissance."[5] In the decades before the Civil War, southern literature had served as the hand maiden of pro-slavery ideologues. Immediately after Appomattox, much southern writing festered into an angry, self-exculpatory defense of the Lost Cause. During the 1880s, southern apologists (mostly Virginians, such as Thomas Nelson Page, a writer much admired in the Pinckney household) denied ever supporting slavery. At the same time that they claimed to be the heart and soul of the Confederacy, they disavowed secession and blamed South Carolina hotspurs for igniting the cruel war. The architects of Lost Cause literature tapped into the American desire for romance. Northern publishers cranked out novels of plantations, chivalry, and happy darkies. Their urban audience, caught in a vortex of change wrought by the hurricane of an industrializing economy and the storm surge of immigration, lapped up the happy stories of romantic reunion between North and South.[6]

To flourish in the literary environment of the 1920s, Charleston writers well understood that resorting to special pleadings, filiopietism, or the old deceptions would be fatal. Truth-telling, in fact, was the mantra of modernism: facts, alone, the "acid" test of value. Pinckney and her cohorts believed that truth would indeed set them free from the mannered, apologetic writing of an earlier generation. What made the quest of the Charleston Literary Movement distinct from the modernist search for truth was the underlying assumption that shining a light beneath the layered falsehood of southern fluffery—the moonlight, the magnolias, ol' massa— would not necessarily reveal a world of unmitigated horrors. Pinckney's cousin, naturalist and writer Herbert Ravenel Sass acknowledged that Charlestonians who once looked at their past through "rose-tinted lights" had to cast aside their "policy of dignified evasion." Sass did not believe realism perforce meant ugliness. "We have nothing to fear from a candid exposition of the facts," Sass wrote to editor Thomas R. Waring.[7]

The recognition of the Charleston Literary Movement by organizations such as the Poetry Society of America brought an era of isolation, long decades of cultural reconstruction, to a close. Reunion promised a unified national narrative and a step toward creating a genuine American literature, itself still a lowly province in English departments across the country. Just as the poets of Chicago had added a new perspective to the traditional canon of New England writing during their own "renaissance" around 1912, Charlestonians thought they too had a story to tell. In 1921, British author W. L. George described the way the nation had broken free of the cultural dominance of New England: "New York was the microcosm of the new civilization of America, of which the Middle West is the basis and the South, the memory."[8]

Regionalism as expressed by artists, writers, scholars, and public-policy-makers was a force touching all aspects of American life in the 1920s and 1930s. Southerners were not alone in touting their unique way of life that emphasized tradition, individualism, family, intimacy with the land, harmony with the built environment, and higher appreciation for matters of the spirit over material wealth. Regionalists argued that this bundle of virtues presented an important roadblock to the wrecking ball of change and local folkways a better prescription for the good life.[9] Writers across America promoted a "literary localism" to stem the tide of abstraction and discontinuity dominating the modern elements in literature. As even personality became more standardized, Charlestonians offered a last glimpse of an example of the "idiosyncratic American self." National interest in the work of Pinckney and Heyward stemmed in part from their ability to authentically portray the last "Carolina aristocrats" before they too went the way of the Connecticut Yankee, the New York Knickerbocker, and the Pennsylvania Dutch. Hervey Allen enticed his acquaintances—scholars, authors, and critics— southward to lecture at the Poetry Society by promising a modest stipend and a glimpse into the cloistered world of "the Brahmins" of the Low Country.[10]

Critics would of course argue that that the "elite" artists and writers of the Charleston Renaissance loved their home too much, were too deeply invested in using a distorted presentation of the past to bolster their own standing, and thus lacked the creative tension, even alienation from their surroundings, to see the truth.[11] But what was the truth about the South? Was there anything distinctive about it in the twentieth century, except a shared history of defeat and poverty? Were the distinctive features that remained all negative: one-horse farms, one-party politics, one-gallused politicians, one-crop agriculture, one-room schoolhouses, one dominant race? Was there anything between sentimentality and the lynching bee, the jessamine and the boll weevil? Did some metaphysical or spiritual power still resonate from the region even in face of the great homogenizing forces of industrial capitalism? Was there a usable past to guide the future, or had southern traditions all been discredited by history's chastening hand? Could the truth be told?

Pinckney, who insisted that "few people realize how much courage it takes in a community like ours to ignore the established tabus," joined others of the Charleston Literary Movement who would break the code of silence by using irony and realism to admit the fatal flaws of the old Low Country aristocracy. She insisted, however, as did Sass and Heyward and others, that the beauty the oligarchs bequeathed to the future generations—their houses, their furniture, their paintings, their gardens, their talent for living—should all be considered as mitigating factors in the harsh tribunal of modern public opinion.[12]

In 1924, Randolph-Macon College historian Francis Butler Simkins praised the Charleston poets for continuing the tradition of beauty in literature. He had feared that after the myths of the Old South were dispelled, the region would give itself over completely to the hurried New South mentality that focused exclusively on the race for "the material and progress through standardization." Instead, he believed that through the Charleston Literary Movement, better educated and more prosperous southerners would come to appreciate the beautiful, the good, and the true, all qualities in short supply in the South of the 1920s.[13]

The initial primacy of the Charleston Literary Movement did not go unchallenged. The "Southern Number" of *Poetry* in 1922 with Harriet Monroe's endorsement caused a near riot on Whitland Avenue, the Nashville home of James Frank, where a circle of men—Vanderbilt faculty and undergraduates, businessmen-amateurs, and a dilettante or two—had been gathering for a number of years to discuss poetry. The most talented (those who would become known as the "Fugitive poets") were young English professors John Crowe Ransom and Donald

Davidson and their exceptional students, Allen Tate, Robert Penn Warren, and Merrill Moore. The first issue of their own poetry magazine, *The Fugitive*, had nearly crossed in the mail with the "Southern Number." Tate and Davidson fired off outraged letters to "Aunt Harriet" so full of invective that she slammed shut the pages of *Poetry* to them for a decade, much to the Charlestonians' delight.[14]

Josephine Pinckney was safely in Europe when the war between Nashville and Charleston broke out, but she suffered guilt by association. The Fugitives saw her name and immediately associated her with the supercilious gentility. They dismissed the aristocratic interpretation of the southern past laid down by the "effete" Charlestonians and the "old snobs" of Virginia. "The picturesque charm of the Carolina Lowcountry was one thing," Donald Davidson argued, "but the pugnaciousness of the western South, still 'half-horse, half-alligator' and ready to fight all comers, was another thing." The Tennesseans held themselves up as the spiritual heirs of the Democratic tradition, of Andrew Jackson and his virile band of sharpshooting, ear-biting, eye-gouging frontiersmen. At the end of his life, Donald Davidson contended that one of the major points distinguishing the hardworking Fugitives of anonymous pedigrees (who actually used pseudonyms in the first issues of their magazine) from the "gallant" Poetry Society of South Carolina was its membership roster that boasted "the great names of Charleston: I mean the Heywards, Hugers, Manigaults, Middletons, Pinckneys, Ravenels, Stoneys, Warings, and others."[15]

The Fugitives sought their primary identity in art, striving to be poets from the South, as opposed to the Charlestonians who saw themselves first and foremost as southern poets. Dedicated to the modernist search for the universal and concentrating on aesthetics and technique, the early work of the Nashville poets was influenced by their close study of modernists T. S. Eliot and Ezra Pound. The best of the Fugitive poets experimented with verse that wove in themes of metaphysics, psychoanalysis, and fantasy.[16]

One source of the young Fugitive's rage was their frustrated struggle to reconcile their identities as southerners and scholars, an oxymoronic situation at a time when 25 percent of all southerners could not even read. All born in dusty little farm towns of Tennessee or Kentucky, the Fugitives' robust intellects set them apart from their families and communities. In his excellent study of Allen Tate's early life, Thomas Underwood describes the young poet's "spiritual loneliness" and painful relationship with his "terrible family." Tate felt himself "an orphan of the South," the region where individual identity was so intimately tied to kinship. To some degree, Ransom and Davidson shared his feelings of disconnection as well. The *Fugitive* magazine, in fact, drew its name from a poem by one of its members that dealt with an outcast and a loner. This loneliness only fueled their resentment toward those Charlestonians who could claim continuity with a notable past and who appeared supremely confident that they and they alone, could speak for the South. Neither did the Fugitives feel truly at home in the narrow micro-universe of the academy because Vanderbilt University and the surrounding town of Nashville with its ersatz Parthenon were in thrall to the commercial values of the New South. As Daniel J. Singal has argued, for Ransom, Tate, and Davidson, at least, their ties to the "brethren" of the Fugitive group was their most "secure tie to the South."[17]

Pinckney, so deeply rooted in the soil of the Carolina Low Country, compared the Fugitive poets to "air plants, delicate and strange, floating through the ether from which they are evoked, confined by no garden close." She admired their "unusual intelligence," but believed their poetry "too elliptical for even the agile mind." Pinckney, who accepted the limits of her vision and admitted her own provincialism, chided the self-conscious young men for being so afraid of appearing "obvious and parochial." They painfully avoided all "local allusions" to the countryside surrounding Nashville, she observed, choosing instead to animate their poetry with dragons, naiads, and deep limpid pools.[18]

Professionally trained and steeped in the great poetic traditions, the Fugitives were the closest the South came to "Highbrows," but they also retained some of the prejudices of their narrow upbringing. They bitterly resented the authority of powerful, reputation-making or breaking women such as Harriet Monroe and Amy Lowell. Allen Tate and Donald Davidson, particularly, disparaged rival poets as effeminate, noting "the bray of Midwestern jackasses and the girlish hip-movements of the Yale-Harvard-Princeton pretty boys." In a 1925 essay in *The Nation* slamming the anti-intellectualism of the Old South "bookish culture" that existed in Charleston and Richmond, Allen Tate employed an allegorical figure he called the "Charming Lady" to represent the uncritical sentimentality of the past.[19] Davidson and Tate swore a vendetta against Allen and Heyward and criticized the Charleston Literary Movement as a whole for focusing on the "sham stuff" of southern life: "magnolias, niggers, and cotton." Davidson criticized DuBose Heyward's sympathetic rendering of Charleston blacks as "taking New York's point of view on the negro."[20] Davidson and Tate particularly deplored the democratization of American culture and denied any responsibility to engage and uplift the South with its "damnably barbaric mind."[21]

North Carolina journalist Gerald W. Johnson, who believed that the vast majority of southerners needed the intellectual equivalents of "brogans and homespun," wrote Pinckney that the only real problem with Tate, Davidson and the other Fugitive poets was that "they had shut themselves too long in the Vanderbilt University library, and had forgotten what the South looks like."[22]

John Crowe Ransom found his first visit to Charleston in 1928 illuminating and confusing. He wrote Pinckney that he was not even sure Charleston was "southern" or even "American." "I find no analogies in the whole American scene," he wrote. "I have to think of Europe, but this is not Europe, but America as it might be if Americans were Europeans and not the pioneering frontiering folk they were." The Charleston tradition, he thought, harked back to "(early) 18th Century London, only with a French slant, and another slant which is its own and no other." The Tennessee tradition, "loath as I am to confess it," he surmised, "must be a degenerate form of the Virginia tradition. . . . which is 18th century rural England." In a convoluted way, Ransom makes an important point. Pinckney's poetry, and that of the Charleston Literary Movement, is not a modern poetry of ideas but, with its veneration of nature and place, has more in common with the English pastoral tradition. She considered her style "Wordsworthian."[23] In her youth, Pinckney believed that nature, rather than human love, provided the inspiration for the most powerful poetry. In a very early poem, *The Harbor*, Pinckney described dawn walkers on Charleston's High Battery watching a sunrise on a sultry June morning, when all of a sudden, they "Can bear it no longer, They stir and turn homeward / clinging together, Refugees from too great beauty."

The efforts of Pinckney and the poets of her circle to reinterpret a shared past of poverty and defeat also parallels those of twentieth-century Irish writers trying to find meaning in their own tragic history. Around 1904, a literary circle formed at the Dublin home of A.E. (George William Russell), mystic, poet, journalist, and artist, which formed the wellspring of an Irish literary renaissance.[24] Among the regulars at the Rathgar Street house were James Joyce, John Synge, and Padraic Colum. Their readings were spiced with politics, for their goal of reasserting the Irish cultural identity paralleled the underground movement for liberation from British domination. The late-night talk ran high in A.E.'s smoky den. Young Colum, swept away by the dream of Ireland, joined the Irish Volunteers in 1907, and then Sein Fein. The ensuing "troubles" after the Easter Rebellion of 1916 sent Colum and his rapier-tongued wife Mary to seek asylum in New York.[25]

Hervey Allen had met Colum at the MacDowell Colony and invited him twice to Charleston. Colum had endorsed the Charleston Literary Movement, praising the Poetry Society for introducing a welcome diversity to American letters: "The birds of the south are different—should not the poets be different too?" The importance of the South, he observed, is that it has memory, "showing itself through landscape and character" and "that is better for poetry than anything else except that which is poetry itself—desire."[26] On his first visit in 1921, Pinckney was away, but on the second in 1924, Colum stayed at 21 King Street. With an admiring crowd at his feet, Colum often held forth until the wee hours about the Irish determination to reassert the Gaelic language and its folk tales and myths as part of their resistance to the "the conquest."

Colum, who was brooding and merry by turns, used 21 King Street as home base for nearly a month as he toured around the South on speaking engagements. By the time he left for the train station, Camilla Pinckney had taken to her bed, but Josephine was exhilarated. Colum dazzled her with stories of the heady days in Dublin when he helped William Butler Yeats, Lady Isabella Augusta Gregory, and A.E. plan the Irish National Theatre, an enterprise inspired by both artistic and patriotic motives. After he told her about the efforts being made by Chicago native Dan Reed and his wife Isabelle to establish the Town Theatre in Columbia, Pinckney, who could imagine herself like Lady Gregory as playwright and patron, volunteered to help and tried to cajole Allen and Heyward into assisting her in finding them a "hay loft" for a permanent home. She also was a moving force behind the Poetry Society's establishment of a "drama committee" that would perform John Milington Synge's version of the classic Irish tragedy *Deirdre of the Sorrows* in 1922 and George Bernard Shaw's *Candida* with Pinckney in the lead the next year.[27]

While spending time in Charleston and learning more about its own dispossessed aristocracy and more than a decade of Federal occupation after the Civil War, Colum began to see similarities between Charleston and Dublin, two nibbled-away old cities brought to their knees by history. Yet, they both still stood, unrepentant, unreconstructed, unforgiven; survivors shunned by progress, broken and bent. Cracked Georgian fanlights characterized one; sagging broad piazzas, the other. Just as success shaped the character of smug Victorians in England and New England, hardship also molded the losers, the Irish and the Southron. Their Anglo-Saxon detractors thought them fey and quixotic. Only a native sardonic humor and a tragic sensibility elevated them from the dead weight of self-pity. Despite everything, Dubliners, like Charlestonians, tended toward kindliness and sociability. Charm and graceful manners persisted as habits from better times. Eccentricity was tolerated and even cultivated. The southern love of oratory, which Josephine Pinckney observed could take on the characteristic of "a machine gun fire of misdirected vitality," rivaled that of the Irish, who Oscar Wilde asserted were "the greatest talkers since the Greeks."[28]

Dublin and Charleston treasured raconteurs, but not intellectuals. James Joyce called the Emerald Isle, "This lovely land that always sent / Her writers and artists to banishment." Not so eloquent, but equally poignant, was Gerald W. Johnson's assertion in 1923 that while New Englanders could flourish in New England, and even Kansans in Kansas, the South possessed some mysterious centrifugal force "that hurls artists across her borders like stones from a sling." Charleston native Percy C. Whaley, who moved to Washington, lamented that creative writers could not do their best work in Charleston because it was "a sort of lotus land" where the people are complacent in their ignorance. But "damn it all, they have some of the most lovable people on this whole earth down there. They can make you madder than any other people on earth. They do the craziest things of any people on earth. And yet, in some respects, they are the finest people on earth."[29]

A little smaller in area than the Palmetto State, Ireland too could comfortably be accommodated into the apt quip by James Louis Petigru that South Carolina was "too small for a republic and too big for an insane asylum." Where citizens had experienced disenfranchisement, politics was life itself; the whiff of treason filled the air. Contrariness and resistance to national conformity found in both Dublin and Charleston was summed up best by the trenchant comment of the Anglo-Irish philosopher George Berkeley, "We Irishmen think otherwise."[30]

Another connection between the Irish renaissance and the Charleston Renaissance was the importance of language as a means of resistance to the modern forces of standardization. One area of life in which the homogenization of culture was most obvious was in the campaign for uniformity of language ("de-Babelization") that had a revival following World War I. The dream of discovering the single universal logic that underlay all language dates back to the Enlightenment. Twentieth-century European philosophers such as Ludwig Wittgenstein dreamed of an "unmediated language." T. S. Eliot ended *The Waste Land,* the icon of modernist poetry, with DA, the Sanskrit root word and symbol of the unity of all languages.[31]

Language, not mere accent, had long been considered one of the South's defining cultural traits. In 1853, Louisa Susannah McCord criticized Harriet Beecher Stowe, author of *Uncle Tom's Cabin,* on many counts including her tendency to make "her Southern ladies and gentlemen talk rather vulgar Yankee-English." During the Civil War, Confederate printers ran off thousands of southern language dictionaries. When Pinckney was growing up in Charleston, questions of correct pronunciation were settled by heaving off the shelf worn copies of English dictionaries scarcely revised since the eighteenth century. Noah Webster's "American," or as they saw it, New England dictionary, was unwelcome even in the local Charleston Library Society, where the only concession to modernity was the *Oxford English Dictionary*.[32] Even during the 1920s, southerners were still differentiated by their accents. One New York reviewer commented that Josephine Pinckney's Low Country accent corrupted her rhyming technique. Babette Deutsch had first thought Pinckney was attempting near-rhymes with her use of "fear" and "there" in a poem, until she realized on reading further that the Charleston poet was attempting an "honest rhyme" in the "soft, slurred speech of the South."[33]

The Low Country's most powerful counter to standardized English was Gullah, a Creole language unique to the Carolina and Georgia rice coast. Gullah evolved as a result of the slave trade when captive Africans who spoke as many as forty different dialects were all thrown together for seasoning in the West Indies and had to communicate not only among themselves but also with the English. Once considered only the gibberish of the uneducated, by the 1920s enough research had been done by John and Susan Bennett, Samuel Gaillard Stoney Jr., and others to assert that Gullah had all the qualities of a distinct language. The Low Country blacks who lived in the remote plantation districts and sea islands were actually conservators of seventeenth-century speech, much like the isolated mountaineers of the Appalachians who spoke an English common in Shakespeare's day.[34]

Like jazz, which also gained popularity during the twenties, Gullah enjoys a freedom from form, and has its own grammar that perverts traditional syntax with a vocabulary that blends African idiom and old English. Gullah became a language almost indecipherable to the uninitiated. In 1922, when Ambrose E. Gonzales published his pathbreaking collection of Gullah stories, *The Black Border*, he had to include a glossary so the general reader could make sense of the folk tales. No existing encyclopedia or dictionary included entries relative to the Gullah Negroes or their dialect.[35]

Although the Fugitive poets had criticized the incorporation of African American themes in the work of Charlestonians, John Crowe Ransom was impressed by his first encounter with "the most perfect specimen" of the Low Country Gullah when he visited Charleston in 1928. He wrote Pinckney with great excitement about the "delicious" difficulty he had communicating with the black porter at the train station. "Our darkies here in Tennessee are just the black editions of our more illiterate selves," Ransom complained, but "your Gullahs are quite different; they are distinctly another race, and as stubborn in their particularity as you are in yours; which is as it should be."[36]

Formerly dismissed as the language of the field and the slave quarters inappropriate for polite company, by the time of the Charleston Renaissance, the ability to speak Gullah was like a shibboleth that separated the authentic plantation aristocrats from pretenders, as once the Gileadites were distinguished from the Ephraimites. Gullah, the language of the slave was perforce also the language of the master. Even among Josephine Pinckney's generation, Gullah was often the first language of the former master class, learned in the nursery from their black nurses or "dahs."

Well-versed in the idiom from her childhood with Victoria Rutledge, Pinckney, like Heyward, seized upon Gullah life and folk legend to express her own uniqueness in the world of American letters. Other regionalist writers, such as Willa Cather speaking for the West and Dorothy Canfield Fisher for New England, also used local dialects as a means of praising traditional values within their richly nuanced novels. Pinckney's award-winning poem "In the Barn" begins with "Scipio" singing an authentic Gullah spiritual during his labors. As the sun is setting, he hopes to keep away the "evil eye."

> You kin dig my grabe
> Wid a silber spade—
> Eb'rybody who is libin' Got to die.

Her macabre "Gulla' Lullaby" was published in *Bookman* in 1925: "Long eyed Buzzard sleeks his feathers with his beak,— / 'Death will be a-coming either this week or next week . . .' / *Go to sleep my little baby.*"[37]

As Pinckney tried to break away from the formal conventions and subjects of Victorian poetry, Gullah presented her with rhythmic language with which to describe the commonplaces of everyday life. The streets of Charleston were flooded with the chants of the black street hucksters advertising "Schwimpy— raw—raw—raw . . . " Pinckney called the purveyors of seafood and seasonal produce "featherless songsters" and admired their unique verses and individualistic singing styles "bursting forth in the fragmentary tunes, the elaborate inflections, the spoken calls, and the translation of the commonest vegetables into symbols of profound mystery."[38]

Pinckney believed that the hucksters intuitively grasped the most basic principle of poetry, certainly the one that informed her own verse. A poem could just "be" and did not need a "meaning," she always argued. She was drawn to Lowell's Imagism , which valued words for their beauty and music, over the dense symbolism of Eliot and the moderns. "With many a fine poem the music of the syllables carries one along, although the meaning may be obscure," she wrote to an admirer of her work. "It is my opinion that poetry is primarily a matter of *feeling* not of intellect; therefore musical words that stir in the hearer a sense of beauty, words that make pictures and colors in his mind, are the important thing and the meaning is secondary." In an article for *Town and Country* magazine, Pinckney described her interaction with Joe Hodges, a street vendor who unwittingly confirmed her theory. Standing by his runty, cream-colored ox, whose neck was wreathed in sweet smelling lavender wisteria, he swung into his song:

> See me now
> Fresh and fine, Wegetubble of all kin',
> I got yuh green pea, snabbean, I come all de way f'um Mount Pleasant
> Wid muh little sprawny oxis.
> Peace declay [declare] de rabbit lay.

She asked him the meaning of the "cabalistic" last line. He explained, "Dat ain' mean nuttin', Missis . . . He jus' make a nice sound."[39]

After World War I, the Low Country plantation culture that perpetuated the Gullah language and traditions began to disintegrate rapidly with the dying off of the "old time Negro" and with the younger blacks heading for town or for great opportunities in the North. Preserving the old spirituals and folktales became a matter of "genuine importance" among the whites who felt a deep connection to Gullah culture. As standardized hymn sheets were becoming popular in the black urban churches and young blacks began regarding the Gullah language like the head turban, as one more symbol of their slave past to be cast away, traditional Low Country spirituals that were passed orally down the generations were clearly in danger of being lost.

Pinckney was studying in Cambridge in 1922 when members of the Folklore Committee of the Poetry Society organized "a unique civic musical innovation," perhaps the first ever in the South. The committee invited white and black singers, from the city and the countryside, to a gathering for the purpose of teaching one another Gullah songs. Many of the songs had variations unique to a particular plantation or community. The resulting concert attracted a large crowd and was considered "an inspiring success" both for the demonstration of racial cooperation and for its cultural significance.[40]

In that same year, the Society for the Preservation of Spirituals was formed. Heyward was a founding member. Pinckney joined as soon as she returned to the city. Although Charlestonians had limited interest in academic poetry, they loved to sing. Gathering around a parlor piano was one of the most popular occupations in the Charleston of Pinckney's youth, when few families had resources for more elaborate entertainments. The Gullah songs stirred the homesick among the old plantation families forced off the land and into town "not only because of their beauty, but also because of their associations and the memories they evoked." A shared sentiment that the spirituals and other songs of the land should be preserved coalesced among friends of Pinckney's cousin May Elliott Hutson. The Hutsons had moved to Charleston from Tomotley Plantation in Beaufort County about 1916. Those who frequently gathered at their home formed an informal social organization dedicated to systematically collecting and preserving the spirituals of the "old time negro." Membership was limited to those "plantation-bred, or plantation-broken," with good, but not professionally trained, voices. Over time, Pinckney believed that the Spirituals Society, last bastion of the old planter aristocracy, became an even more exclusive association than the St. Cecilia Society.[41]

If the Poetry Society of South Carolina might be considered the "mind" of the Charleston Renaissance, the Spirituals Society qualifies as its "soul," for that group recognized the shared heritage of white and black in the Carolina Low Country. M. DeWolfe Howe, a journalist who wrote an article on the society for the *Atlantic* magazine in 1930, believed it represented a tacit acknowledgment of centuries of interdependence between the two races. The whites, he noted with approval, were "singing those songs in a spirit of sympathy, reverence, and devotion which are themselves survivals from a less cynical age." Thus, Howe observed, came the unique "song of Charleston" that sprung "as inevitably from Charleston soil as the seaward-looking houses that could be found nowhere else."[42]

The Spirituals Society linked Pinckney's interest in language, music, and the heritage of the Low Country. She volunteered for the Committee on Research and Preservation, which was charged with creating the authoritative text of each spiritual for permanent preservation. The committee took an academic approach to their task, seeking to place each spiritual in its own context by determining as far as possible its history and locality of origin. Since Gullah was strictly an oral language, getting proper inflection and cadence was critical. DuBose Heyward had warned that anyone hoping to transcribe Gullah had to be "letter perfect." Pinckney brought to the transcriptions, which were later praised by professional folklorists, the same attention to detail she lavished on her own poetry. She sang with the Spirituals Society for over thirty years until her death and gained a reputation among the second-generation members as an absolute stickler for correct pronunciation and nuance in Gullah.[43]

Pinckney also joined the Committee on Expeditions, an assignment that suggested pith helmets, khaki puttees, and travel in foreign parts like the archaeologists who discovered King Tut's tomb in 1922. Pinckney helped locate

African American churches in outlying areas where society members could go to hear "old time negroes" sing. The experience was riveting. On the appointed Sunday, she and her friends would career in thin-tired Model A's down remote unmarked dirt roads to their destination. They slipped into little pine-slab churches with sashless windows and quietly found a bench, rickety on its four peg legs. Thick kerosene lamp smoke filled the room. Palmetto hand fans worked overtime to stir the air. Garish calendars from local undertakers decorated the walls. Usually, neither the minister nor the congregation was literate. The services followed a certain form, but the remarks and prayers were extemporaneous and often ran as long as breath held out. The minister did not present himself and his flock as humble supplicants before the Lord but made long harangues, often fiery and vehement.[44]

As the congregation fell into the preacher's rhythm, murmurs of assent and cries of encouragement frequently interrupted the preacher's words. At some point, as he approached his crescendo, the Spirit would move someone to sing. Feet commenced to tap, hands to clap, bodies to "shout"—moving in time to the rhythm. The little structure resting unevenly on concrete blocks began to rock and the door precariously hanging by one hinge began to sway.[45]

In contrast to the spontaneity of the African American worshippers who gave themselves over to the rhythm and to the moment, Pinckney and other society scribes crouched over pen and pad painstakingly writing down the words and the "airs" of the tunes. They assumed the role of anthropologists rather than voyeurs; ethnographers rather than philologists. Back at home, Pinckney, along with Caroline Rutledge and Katherine Hutson, devised a system, rather like a drum score, by which they indicated the various "pattings" of the feet, hand claps, and "shouting," above and below the line. They did this with some reluctance fearing that "regularizing" the songs on paper might rob them of their "flavor."[46]

The Spiritual Society's rush to capture the very old with the very new, ironically, reflects the essence of modernism. In fact, until the first automobiles became affordable and roads into the country slightly improved, the old plantation districts had been inaccessible for decades. Charleston's cultural revival was stimulated by the city dwellers' ability to actually return to the old abandoned plantation houses—to the past, as it were. Many structures had been spared the expected looting because the descendants of the slaves who still resided in the area thought the old houses were haunted; in some respects they were. To capture authentic voices of the Gullah singers in remote locations, skillful song-seekers would jack up the rear wheels of their car and attach a pulley mechanism to operate a very primitive turntable. When the accelerator was pressed, the pulley rotated a turntable while cactus needles scratched the ancient sounds of the black singers onto modern metal plates. Recording machines were actually first marketed as scrapbooks of sound, as a means to preserve the voices of the elderly. In 1930, one of the inaugural broadcasts of WCSC, Charleston's first radio station, was a performance of the Spirituals Society patting, clapping, and sending through the airways heartfelt songs almost unintelligible to the majority of the listening audience, thus turning one of the most potent engines of homogeneity of language into the voice of Babel.[47]

Low Country aristocrats also recognized that they too were a dying breed. Just as the anthropologist and the artifact define one another, so too did the "old time negro," with an agreeable face and a nodding head, describe the white Charlestonians of old who drew their identity from this deference.[48] The fear of becoming disconnected from the past was common among most Americans during the 1920s and was played out in different ways across the nation. The various preservation activities at work in the city, one northern journalist observed— the old houses, the old gardens, the old songs, the "old time negroes," the last remnants of the plantation aristocracy—were "all fruits of the same vanishing civilization." Noting that tourists and antique dealers were still picking over the bleached bones of the seat of secession, toting away family heirlooms and ripping moldings off walls and Adam mantles away from hearths, Howe of the *Atlantic Monthly* understood that Charlestonians sought some legacy that could not be carted off. Too poor to build bronze monuments to their noble past or even to save their magnificent old buildings from the wrecking ball, Charlestonians almost accidentally had come upon a "spiritual monument—a monument literally to the spirit—of Charleston in the past" in the African American spirituals.[49]

In the preservation effort, literacy was the enemy. Education robbed singers of their spontaneity. This was not to say that Pinckney and the other members of the society were discouraging the rural blacks from receiving educations, but they did acknowledge that with the standardization of common school texts and printed song sheets in churches, that the blacks, like the Irish, would lose an important part of their past, their traditional language, religious practice, and the wisdom of stories and proverbs.

No amount of nostalgia for the old times could blind those on countryside expeditions to the shocking realities of rural life. The poverty and disease lurking inside the picturesque cabins rendered in bucolic simplicity by artists such as Elizabeth O'Neill Verner shocked Pinckney who was already becoming interested in helping improve interracial comity in the city. DuBose Heyward and Harriet P. Simons, both active members of the Spirituals Society, also developed a deep revulsion at the centuries of social injustice. By 1924, general agreement reigned that since the Spirituals Society benefited from the cultural treasures of the African Americans, it had a responsibility toward those still in the country too old or infirm to help themselves. In 1927, the official mission of the society was expanded to include relief of "the distress of the old time negro and his people." A charity committee was formed, stimulated by lingering noblesse oblige but nevertheless delivering much-needed assistance to black patients at the Pinehaven tuberculosis sanitarium, victims of flood waters along the Santee River, fifty old ex-slaves living in poverty on James Island, and fire victims on Edisto Island, who were all visited personally by Society members.[50]

The Charleston elite resonated toward the spiritual songs of the "old-time negro" with the same fervor that other southerners fell in with the rhythms of the "old-time religion" of the evangelist Billy Sunday or biblical fundamentalist William Jennings Bryan. African American spirituality with its roots in nature, many believed, had within it a regenerative power, an antidote to the nihilism of the modern age. In her last novel, Josephine Pinckney has a character observe that the African American's religious animism "may be the Negro's contribution . . . to our frayed, overwhelmed society." Society president Alfred Huger declared his conviction that "The religious philosophy of our beautiful Negro Spirituals [will] be proven, in their original, unregimented form to be the real and eternal spirit of Truth."[51]

During the 1830s, the Methodist and Baptist preachers hired by Low Country planters, such as Josephine's grandfather Cotesworth Pinckney, to introduce Christianity into the quarters taught slaves the rousing hymns of the camp meeting revivals. Gullahs of the Sea Island plantations made these songs their own, putting them into their own language, shaping the message to their own religious beliefs, and embracing an expansive concept of the sacred that did not restrict worship to one day and one place. Their religious songs helped boatmen move their oars in time and lightened the dawn-to-dusk hours of field work. Spirituals often broke the air spontaneously when a moment of danger, such as a hurricane, had passed.

The ineffable otherworldliness of the spiritual flowed from the singers' complete abandonment to their faith. The African American interpretations of the Bible stories that are expressed in songs such as "Mary Weep and Martha Moan" possessed "a quality of sadness in them that is part of earth itself."[52] Spirituals were the earnest, nature-inspired prayers of the faithful designed to be sung under moonlit skies where the "weird chants" with their "eerie, fantastic beauty" were offered up to Heaven. Many of the songs took death as their theme. When a white transcriber asked an old black woman to differentiate between a spiritual and a hymn, she couldn't understand the question. But when asked to sing one of the old songs, like "Silber Spade," she replied, "she couldn't sing that in the daylight—it was a spiritual."[53]

In their efforts to recreate the passion and joy of the spirituals, the white singers permitted themselves to lay aside critical reason and skepticism, if only for a few hours, and take on the Gullah's wholehearted simple devotion and "supposed superstitions."[54] The music of the Africans was free of the mathematical formulas of time and rhythms, coming instead from the joyful noises of nature, from the rush of the winds, the moving tides, rustle of weeds, the songs of birds. When they sang, their bodies moved as if blown by a breeze. The early gatherings of the society were often set according to the full moon and held outdoors on the members' plantations, such as Caroline Rutledge's Hampton at Santee or the Grimball's Wapoolah Plantation on Edisto Island.[55]

By 1923, the mists of religious doubt had already begun to settle in on Pinckney. Her interest in the teachings of Freud gradually transformed her view of the nature of ultimate reality. The absolute certainty with which her parents had regarded the creed of the Episcopal Church eluded her. When she forced herself to abandon Victorian sentimentality for a life based on reason and logic, religious doubt also crept in. In literary circles, during the 1920s, poetry emerged as "the secular twin" of religion, a form of modern "spiritual realism" in contrast to traditional "spiritual idealism." Toward the end of her life, she wrote in her notebook of the longing for a faith lost in the currents of modernist thought: "If we could only go daily, in the still mornings to an altar and draw strength. If we could only believe in God and believe in ourselves." Perhaps even Pinckney, the "little Agnostic" as one of her admirers nicknamed her, could suspend disbelief for a few hours during moonlit evenings and intuit Truth among the shadows of ancient oaks.[56]

As Pinckney matured and joined in the intellectual probing of the era, the "psyche" began to replace the "soul" in her thinking about human motivation, suggesting not just the influence of the moderns but also the ancients. The nights of uninhibited singing and dancing in the outdoors, with spirits boosted by a handy jug of bootleg corn liquor reminded Pinckney of a time centuries before when the Greeks relinquished all restraint in celebration of Dionysus, god of wine and fertile crops. In the revelry of the African American rituals, she believed she could see the two much-contested traditions of Christ-worship and Dionysus-worship meld together. And the whites too fell into the dark mystery of the night. In March 1927, her close friends Harriet P. Simons and her brother Sam Stoney invited more than seventy people for a party at their family's country place, Back River. They lit a "huge bonfire, then sang spirituals and while [they] were singing Ned Jennings in costume came out and did several dances with the moonlight and firelight playing on him."[57] In her poem "Still Life" (1932), Pinckney cleverly set up the dualism between the Christian and the pagan by having a black servant innocently make an arrangement that included the purple passion flower, "the Very Vine," a symbol of Christ, with the blood red pomegranate, "the living vermilion," associated with Dionysus. In one unthinking act, Pinckney argues, "Ages of challenge converge" from this "Descant of Christ and Dionysus."

Against the advice of purists in the society who believed that spirituals lost their power in stuffy auditoriums, the Spirituals Society held its first public concert in December 1923 at South Carolina Society Hall. The moonlight dancer, Edward I. R. "Ned" Jennings, one of "Miss Bragg's boys" who worked at the Charleston Museum, designed their costumes to suggest nineteenth-century plantation wear. The ladies wore simple organdy dresses with "old-fashioned berthas." The men wore their own formal clothes with stocks. Pinckney helped decorate the stage with homely arrangements of smilax and Spanish moss.[58]

The society members knew they ran the risk of appearing ridiculous and, worse, of mocking the black worshippers. Some years later, Augustine T. Smythe explained to an audience that aspects of "shouting" could be amusing, "if you cared to be amused." The Spirituals Society singers, he assured them, were not. "We have no idea of taking our colored friends and caricaturing them for your amusement. We are endeavoring, respectfully, to reproduce for you as well as our limited abilities make possible, the singing that we used to hear in the churches in the country."[59]

When the curtain was drawn, all the singers were seated. With no musical accompaniment, one singer launched the melody, as was the custom in the black churches, and the others joined in, rising, swaying, sitting, trance-like, as the spirit moved them. Even the most dignified gray-haired matron (even the reserved Miss Pinckney) might lift the skirt of her gown and dance a cakewalk. As emotions rose, the tempo increased, usually concluding in "an ecstasy of rhythm, rapid movement, and choral mass." Since spirituals originated in a community of believers as part of their joint worship, no soloists were featured; no conductor bowed. The "singers and hearers seemed joined in that unity of stage and house which is the ultimate test of the power of song and action," one observer noted.[60] Concerts traditionally ended with the singers moving around the stage, embracing one another or shaking hands singing the refrain from a Drayton Hall spiritual "Sistuh/Bruddah—I'm uh goin' to leab' you en duh hand Ob un kin' Sabeyuh" ["Sister/Brother—I'm going to leave you in the hands of the kind Saviour"].

The revival of interest in the Gullah spirituals coincided with the rage over African American culture during the Harlem Renaissance of the Twenties. The concerts by the Spirituals Society became an important part of the Charleston experience. Two things stuck in the mind of Chicago poet Edgar Lee Masters when he visited Pinckney in Charleston: the huge glistening chandeliers illuminating 21 King Street and a Spirituals Society concert. He was so taken by the poetic potential of Gullah, he even tried his hand at the dialect himself. In 1927, he sent Pinckney a copy of "Jes Give Me De Crumbs Ob De Bread" with the suggestion: "Maybe you can sing this."[61] In 1933, when Pinckney organized a concert at Eldorado including singing and dancing by about a hundred "darkies" in the moonlight, Harriet P. Simons reported "there were so many celebrities in the audience you could have sunk a ship with them."[62]

In contrast to the Manhattan audiences who took the "A train" to Harlem for an evening of primitive escapist fantasy in a world so different from their own, though, Low Country whites were drawn to the familiarity of the Gullah culture. The agrarian life, the simplicities of the countryside, the closeness to the earth, the soft voices in the evening had all been part of their shared southern past. Requests for the Spirituals Society to do benefit performances (they took no money for themselves beyond travel expenses) came from all over the state, as well as from Savannah.

Zora Neale Hurston, a leader of the Harlem Renaissance, objected to the wooden style and formal dress that black performers had begun adopting in New York when they performed before the largely white audiences. She complained that most sang solos in their highly trained voices, instead of the "harmony and disharmony, shifting keys and broken time" in which the authentic spirituals flowed. The white singers of Charleston, in contrast, reveled in "ecstatic and rhythmic motions" and gave themselves over to the music and the mood with an abandon rarely seen among black performers of spirituals on the Broadway stage. Despite the concern of a conservative member of the Spirituals Society who worried that the "uninitiated" in the audience were perhaps not quite ready for this display, the others vigorously asserted their "right to shake, rattle and roll, when they got good and ready."[63]

The difference in these two styles of presentation goes to the heart of the meaning of the Spirituals Society, and perhaps the Charleston Renaissance. The self-conscious African Americans performing before the critical New York or European audience felt compelled to prove they could duplicate the same mannered, well-modulated style of white singers. For the Charleston group, however, the goal was to assert—to shout and shriek and dance—their difference from the homogenizing forces of modern American cultural life. The Spirituals Society actually turned Victorian values on their head. In the case of the spirituals, the "uncivilized," the unlettered country blacks, were the teachers and the "civilized," the white elite, the struggling students. While "civilized" behavior was the goal of the Victorians, the moderns saw it was artificial, even destructive. When Walter J. Damrosch, conductor of the NBC radio orchestra known for his efforts to bring classical music to the masses, attended a Spirituals Society concert he commented, "There is something very touching in this brave effort on behalf of a cultured community," he wrote, "to preserve the religious musical outpourings of the African race, transplanted to our soil, where, however, it is languishing owning to the terribly disintegrating influences of white civilization on the colored people."[64]

Phillip Hewitt-Myring, a London journalist traveling the South, had frequently heard black touring troupes popular in Europe. After attending a concert by the Spirituals Society, he realized how far the commercial groups had departed from the original tradition. Their typical concert offered popular crowd-pleasers such as "Swing Low, Sweet Chariot" rendered "not as darkies on a plantation but as paid performers on a stage." In contrast, the white singers of the Spiritual Society had a policy against special requests since they only sang songs they had actually heard among the Gullah. Eschewing slick professional arrangements, they performed their songs with an "artlessness that is the height of art." At the same time, Myring observed, "the ebb and swell of their harmonies and their superb rhythmic discipline produce effects that could not be obtained by the most highly paid professional artists." The real difference between the commercial stage performance and the "clarion calls to the spirit," he concluded, was that the Charlestonians reproduced their songs "with knowledge and understanding." Most important of all, they sang "with love."[65]

5

## A Grave for Love

Whenever Josephine would become deeply involved in the local cultural affairs of Charleston, Camilla Pinckney would plan another trip. In the late summer of 1923, the Pinckneys returned to East Gloucester. Almost immediately, they became embroiled in a scandal that reverberated up and down the Atlantic seaboard. It all began innocently enough. Camilla wanted to attend the dedication of an old colonial church in Peterborough. Dreading the waste of a Sunday afternoon, Pinckney asked Allen if they could meet while Camilla was occupied. Her timing was excellent. Allen responded that the influential critic from the *Boston Evening Transcript,* William Stanley Braithwaite, was coming to the MacDowell Colony on publishing business and had agreed to stop by Allen's studio for tea. Would she join them? Nothing short of a national emergency or a fearsome act of God could have prevented Pinckney from hobnobbing with this "kingmaker," even though his mother had been a West Indian mulatto.[1]

The afternoon was perfect. About twenty of the colonists, including Padraic Colum, Louise Driscoll, Herbert Gorman, and Max Bodenheim sipped tea and shared the fruits of their summer work. A tall dignified gentleman, Braithwaite had an exotic look with his drooping mustache and pale, gold-toned skin. In Braithwaite's party was Mary Sinton Leitch, head of the Poetry Society of Virginia. Apparently, "the Olympian company gave her swimming in the head," according to Pinckney, for as soon as Leitch returned home she typed out an account transforming a casual gathering into a "grand event" and naming all the tea-drinkers. She sent her news flash to Addison Hibbard. Hibbard, a professor of English at the University of North Carolina, wrote a syndicated weekly literary column about contemporary southern literature that was equal parts news, criticism, and gossip. In early September 1923, the story splashed across forty southern newspapers, insinuating that the much-vaunted Pinckney ladies had been subjected to the almost unthinkable horror of breaking bread with a presumptuous Negro man in a New England hotbed of bohemian libertinism. The man responsible for this heinous violation of a sacred code was Hervey Allen.[2]

A storm of outrage ensued. Pinckney found the whole episode hilarious; her mother was livid. Allen politely, but vigorously, denied that Braithwaite had received any nourishment whatsoever on the grounds of MacDowell Colony. "Can't you see us all assembled around the candles with the colored brother as the guest of honor?" he replied to Louisa Stoney who had sent him a scathing letter. Pinckney wrote to Amy Lowell with glee, explaining "the cream of the joke is that Mother—whose views on the colour question are pronounced to put it mildly—wasn't even at the Colony, having gone to Peterborough for the dedication of a church and flocked exclusively with the pure in heart, such as Mr. Cram and the bishops congregated for the ceremony. It is unnecessary to describe her reaction."[3]

Not long after the tea-party fiasco, DuBose Heyward arrived in East Glouces-ter. He stunned Pinckney with the news that he had fallen hopelessly in love with Dorothy Kuhns and planned to marry her as soon as possible. Pinckney reeled at this revelation. She had of course given Heyward no reason to hope that she would ever accept him. (He would remind her years later that "that my scalp was dangling around within your easy reach for a not inconsiderable space of time.") Still, Heyward had been a comforting and undemanding presence in her life for nearly a decade. And the disapproving Camilla could not live forever.[4]

In September 1923, DuBose Heyward and Dorothy Kuhns married quietly in a Manhattan chapel.[5] Pinckney declined to join the small group of well-wishers pleading a prior commitment. She sent one of her dearest friends a telegram from Keeseville, New York: "Dreadfully sorry impossible to be with you for the great occasion . . . Mother sends best wishes." Seizing a chance to flee her pain, or was it embarrassment, she had accepted when her sometime boyfriend Gordon Miller and his sister, Marguerite, asked if they could pick her up as they drove from Charleston to Canada. While Heyward was pledging himself to Dorothy, Pinckney and the Millers cut a northward loop "through four kinds of mountains and six kinds of drinks" with prohibition-free Quebec the "zenith of the arc."[6]

When the travelers stopped at the Equinox Inn in Manchester, Vermont, Pinckney wrote Hervey Allen to discuss the precipitous action of their mutual friend. "What a topsey turvey old world . . . No tongue can tell a woman's sensa-tions on giving her best and oldest friend over to another," Pinckney lamented, "so you will not get a peep into the inner room of the feminine mind herewith." She then pleaded with him not to abandon her as well "for some MacDowell Colony chit—at least not this year. Give me time to catch my breath . . . I feel as if I had lost one lung." With Allen presumably being the other half of her life support, she instructed him, I "expect you to comfort me in the current crisis." She admitted that she had been "a stinker" for leaving him with Poetry Society drudgery while she skipped off for the summer and begged his forgiveness.[7]

When she returned to East Gloucester, Pinckney went to Sevenels to pour out her unhappiness about Heyward to Amy Lowell. The two poets stayed up until dawn eating lobster cutlets, talking about love and life. Lowell wrote Allen straight away assuring him the coast was now clear and he should pursue Pinckney right away. In their earlier conversations, when Lowell had probed Allen about his feelings for Pinckney, he had dismissed the young poet as merely an "amusing dinner partner." Lowell thought he protested too much.[8]

The Pinckneys lingered in East Gloucester longer than usual. Josephine dreaded returning to Charleston. The city buzzed with gossip about Heyward's mutiny into marriage as tattlers exchanged details of how he had at long last tossed over the proud Miss Pinckney. She was in a foul mood when they pulled into the drive of her brother's Seminary Street home in Richmond. Cotesworth Pinckney, always looking on the sunny side, tried to cheer her. He had suggested to Emily Tapscott Clark that she should call Josephine. Clark, a founder of *The Reviewer*, a "little magazine" with large ambitions, just published one of her poems in the July edition. Clark invited Pinckney to a party, and despite her dark mood, she accepted. Clark's soirees were famous for free-flowing corn liquor and free-living litterateurs such as Hunter Stagg, another of the magazine's founders, who had a penchant for the avant-garde and had even privately entertained black poet Langston Hughes.[9]

Around 1920, quite independent of the activity in Charleston or Nashville, another front of the southern renaissance had opened in Richmond. A small group of writers, "not terribly old or inordinately serious" and burdened by their "cumbrous past," undertook the "radical thing" of launching their own literary magazine. Clark, the well-connected daughter of an Episcopal priest, took responsibility as editor, although most of her past experience had involved editing the society page and writing book reviews for a recently defunct newspaper. With no financial backing, they expected to pay for the printing through advertisements and planned to ask authors to donate their essays, poems, or stories for the love of art. Since Lost Cause author Thomas Nelson Page still lived in Richmond, remaining as "Confederate" as ever, and set the tone for local literary taste, the *Reviewer* staff had to accept many contributions that they hated.[10]

Yet *The Reviewer* benefited enormously from a deeper pool of experienced local talent than the Poetry Society of South Carolina had enjoyed. "Richmond-in-Virginia," as James Branch Cabell deemed the literary blossoming in his hometown, had earlier emerged as a center of southern literature. Cabell and Ellen Glasgow contributed time, advice, essays, and pressed their wide circle of friends to support this bold initiative. Popular novelist Mary Johnston volunteered to write the lead essay in the first issue of *The Reviewer*. She presciently outlined the direction that the best, most original writing of the southern renaissance would take. She urged writers to look to their own home for inspiration. Within the borders of Richmond, she argued, one could construct the "whole Comedie Humaine": "the new springing up from the old, the old carried on with the new, the provincial and local melting into the general and universal." Writers in the modern age, Johnston suggested, should look beyond the cavaliers and belles to write the story of "the Richmond that labors" and "the life of the coloured folk."[11]

Clark convinced Pinckney to join the Richmond writers at play by promising to introduce her to one of America's most popular novelists Joseph Hergesheimer, a comrade and drinking companion of Henry L. Mencken. Hergesheimer, in Richmond doing research for a historical novel, had proved critical in launching *The Reviewer*. He gave Clark advice, cajoled his friends such as Carl Van Vechten and Eleanor Wylie into contributing their work, and introduced her to Mencken, who had initially been highly critical of the Richmond literary effort. In 1921, he had panned the first issues of *The Reviewer* for their provinciality and held up a competing magazine in New Orleans, the *Double-Dealer,* as the model of a sophisticated southern undertaking. The New Orleans founders of the *Double-Dealer* (Albert Goldstein, Julius Weiss Friend, John McClure, and Basil Thompson) had well-heeled backers anxious to transform the image of the South. They published experimental pieces by new authors such as Sherwood Anderson and Hart Crane, and an occasional piece by Allen Tate.

Hergesheimer advised the upset Clark to write Mencken. Rather than attacking Mencken, she threw herself upon his mercy. "*The Reviewer* admires and fears you enormously," she wrote. Brassy and bold, much like the fast-paced materialistic New South city Richmond had become, Clark protested that the Double-Dealers were not really southerners; they "are Jews and are not really a product of New Orleans." To prove her point, she insisted that the well-financed *Double-Dealer* was run like a "sane and reasonable magazine," one that paid its staff and contributors. "At *The Reviewer*, we are neither sane nor reasonable, for we are Confederates instead of Hebrews," Clark declared. "We are running with no money at all. And it is a gorgeous experience for us, if not an edifying spectacle for the rest of the nation."[12]

At Mencken's suggestion, Clark contacted John Bennett, soliciting manuscripts from the young Charleston writers. DuBose Heyward published his first prose and Julia Peterkin her first plantation piece in *The Reviewer*. Pinckney and her brother sent in poems.[13] *The Reviewer,* which Mencken later called a "violet" in the "Sahara of the Bozart," found its identity by teaming the most promising southerners with more established northern writers.[14] In the July 1923 issue, *The Reviewer* seemed to have hit its stride. Pinckney's "Idealist" was included, as was an Allen Tate poem; one of Gerald W. Johnson's best essays, "The Congo, Mr. Mencken," which disputed the Sahara metaphor; and another Peterkin sketch that began "God knows where the flies came from."

Emily Clark took a calculated risk by inviting Pinckney to meet Joseph Hergesheimer. Although married, Hergesheimer was a notorious womanizer. Hergesheimer bragged to Mencken about how he operated at social events, such as debutante balls in Virginia: "I lurk on the outskirts and drag the luscious swiftly into the cover of night. This in Richmond is adventurous." Clark was not concerned about Pinckney's honor. She worried about competition. Clark wanted exclusive access to Hergesheimer and his influence, but she had to produce attractive women to keep him within her orbit. Clark paid a high cost for Hergesheimer's patronage. She could not have been unaware of his opinion that she was "the ugliest girl I ever saw," or that he only dined with her because she had the best cook in Richmond. Clark's one redeeming feature, he told Mencken, was her ability at entertaining conversation.[15]

Nevertheless, Clark fawned over the writer, and watched him like a hawk whenever other ambitious women drew near. Rivalry for male patrons took on the same intensity among southern women writers as competition for gentlemen callers did among an earlier generation. South Carolina writer Julia Peterkin, for example, once stalked Hergesheimer in the Jefferson Hotel during a Richmond authors meeting. Peterkin's letters to Mencken, who published her first piece in *Smart Set*, were heavy with sexual innuendo.[16]

Hergesheimer was in the last throes of writing his novel *Balisand* when he met Pinckney in October 1923 at Emily Clark's party. The savvy Hergesheimer well understood Clark's possessive nature and claimed after meeting Pinckney that he "could not endure" that Charleston woman. Clark should have guessed Hergesheimer would be attracted to the reserved, refined Pinckney. She had lost the dew of youth but retained the charming manner of an earlier age. A man at war with his times, Hergesheimer held particular contempt for modern women and painted them in harsh dark tones in *Linda Condon* (1919) and *Cytherea* (1922). Hergesheimer, perhaps the last true believer in Virginia's cult of beauty, wanted his ladies in crinolines. Having become a "Tory of the Extreme Wing," Hergesheimer immersed himself in the eighteenth century. Vowing to Mencken than he wanted "enormously" to write "an aristocratic book," the Pennsylvania native turned to the South, the land he imagined as the last bastion of grace and civilization, of pale-handed ladies in brocade gowns and gallant men in silk coats. The action of

*Balisand* takes place in Tidewater Virginia during the critical years of the Federalist ascendancy during the presidencies of Washington and Adams from 1784 to 1800. Hergesheimer casts his hero, Richard Bales, as a Federalist, four generations removed from the founding Cavaliers. The character of Bales could have been modeled after Governor Thomas Pinckney, a Federalist Party leader who disputed Thomas Jefferson's liberal concept of the republic. After the "Revolution of 1800" and the democratic ascendancy, Bales, like Hergesheimer, believed the world was becoming unbearably common, with beauty and moral purpose being shoved out by democratic vulgarity and opportunism.[17]

In January, a jubilant Joseph Hergesheimer wrote Pinckney to announce that *Balisand,* the "longest book I have ever written or perhaps ever shall write," was near completion and to ask a favor. After writing 96,000 words in thirty-six days, he believed, "I shall have earned almost anything" and was plotting a spring spree, "pearl studs and Scotch whiskey." He planned to begin his "mildly mad course" in Charleston. Could she give him some advice? "Are there still, down by the old brick warehouses, little corner stores where I can buy limeades in perfection? Will there be any Banksia or Cherokee roses? . . . Are there, in Charleston, small dinners at once formal and informal, high drawing rooms with crystal chandeliers, the delicate and charming voices of the past made a little weary and a little wiser, and doubly appealing, by the impending disaster to all charm in the present?"[18] Pinckney suggested a suite at the elegant Villa Margharita on South Battery, only a few blocks from 21 King Street.

As the winter deepened in the Pennsylvania countryside, Hergesheimer began to fantasize about Charleston in the spring . . . and about Pinckney. "I wish I were at Charleston bringing you at the *old* Cosmopolitan—shrimp and Egyptian peas . . . flower in my buttonhole and at your sash. I hope you will have one. White." Later he asked for another "act of high-minded magnanimity." Could she let him know when the azaleas bloomed. "It will be—as they liked to say in the Ark—a sign between us."[19]

Finally, fresh from a gathering of literati in Richmond, Hergesheimer breezed into Charleston with the spring. When Clark learned of Hergesheimer's Easter plan "to bask among the palms and azaleas" in Charleston with Josephine Pinckney, she was incensed. She dashed off a sarcastic letter to the bemused Mencken, criticizing Hergesheimer's inveterate philandering. Clark compared Hergesheimer, who held that American men were all "natural polygamists," to offbeat novelist Ronald Firbanks Habarruk, "a man of many needs." Unlike Habarruk, she clarified, they are "all of one sex." She closed with the insincere "hope he is behaving himself in Charleston because this is Holy Week, and the haut monde to which this lady belongs divides its time between St. Michael's [Episcopal Church] and eating fish behind closed doors at home."[20]

Hergesheimer's expectations were fully realized, at least about the charm of the old city. He reveled in the subtle, often unexpected beauty, which caught him off guard. Unlike modern southern writers, who avoided references to moonlight at all costs, Hergesheimer had no such inhibition. Watching silvery beams shine through the oaks, reflecting on water or glancing off old carved stone, Hergesheimer felt "this glamour of all the hope and longing, the whimper of all the desire, of infinities of past men and women." He later wrote Pinckney of the powerful feelings that his time in Charleston had generated in him, of how he felt an almost overwhelmingly powerful connection with past generations when he was there. He even proposed a book about Charleston, "I mean, really, about magic: the Battery with a steamer's siren blowing in the early morning and a mockingbird singing." His trip home into the early spring bleakness of Pennsylvania was "like growing old or finding, in a sudden turn of wind and leaves that summer has gone."[21]

Pinckney agreed to meet Hergesheimer again in May. Since she already had a trip mapped out to Richmond, Philadelphia, and Washington, she accepted an invitation to stay in West Chester, which was quite near to the country residences of Caroline Sinkler and book collector A. Edward Newton. At Dower House, an exquisite eighteenth-century reproduction of his own design, Hergesheimer lived a "lordly life" financed by his prodigious productivity. He pressed her to stay on for a showing of the film version of his novel, *Cytherea,* but she had promised to join Laura Bragg at the American Association of Museums meeting Washington. He later wrote that he "was sorry I hadn't made a nuisance of myself and attempted to keep you here for Sunday. *Cytherea,* in spite of the disappointed lookers for sensationalism, was splendid. I had a supper party afterward at the Country Club and when that was done [some friends] came back to Dower House where we had champagne and I missed you."[22]

Pinckney returned home feeling depressed. Compared to her friends, she had little to show for her life. Hergesheimer's literary output was staggering—novels, essays, now a film. Laura Bragg enjoyed a national reputation for her educational work at the Charleston Museum. DuBose Heyward had completed his second book of poems, *Skylines and Horizons,* and was preparing for a two-month lecture tour. His new wife, Dorothy, seemed to have it all; marriage to Heyward, while commuting back and forth from Charleston to New York. Her play, *Nancy Ann,* was in production as a result of the Belmont Prize she had won at Harvard.[23] All the novels of the day had suggested that marriage and career did not mix, but

DuBose's willingness to give his wife such freedom may have made Pinckney wonder if she had not made a miscalculation.

Pinckney's gloom deepened when she learned that Hervey Allen had left Charleston for good, without leaving her a word of explanation. Learning that his aunt May Allen was still in town packing his things, Pinckney grabbed a friend and made a beeline for his house. As she maneuvered her Ford around the odd forty-five degree angle corner where Savage Street intersects with Broad, a wave of despair swept the car. Allen's little frame house with the weeping willow in the yard was empty; his books and furniture, even his statue of Augustus, all crated. "How could you," Pinckney wrote Hervey when she learned his New York address. "My heart simply cracked wide open . . . "What am I going to do now for an ear in which to pour my confidences? There isn't anyone else who enjoyed my wild oats with me as you did. And who will tell me when my poetry is bad?—and much more . . . "[24]

All Charleston buzzed with curiosity over Allen's hasty departure. The official word was that he had taken an appointment in the English department at Columbia University. But what was the hurry? Friends at the Poetry Society particularly let down after they had embraced him so completely. Pinckney wrote Allen that at the society's last meeting of the year, President Thomas R. Waring "pronounced a beautiful obituary over you . . . amid sobs from the ladies." She later joked about wearing a sprig of willow as his "literary relict."[25]

"Gossiping Charleston," wrote Susan Bennett (an authority on this aspect of city life) to Hervey at the end of May, "has decided that the reason you left so unexpectedly to them was because [Pinckney] would not marry you. Now do remember to live up to it and be the blighted being . . . I shall have to take Josephine to task." Just to be sure that Hervey washed his hands of Pinckney, Bennett never missed an opportunity to keep Allen posted of all her gadding about Charleston, always on the arm of a different beau. In June, Susan Bennett volunteered that she had seen nothing of Pinckney whom, she understood, was "on Folly Beach at a house party with George Buist and others."[26]

In early June, Pinckney turned to Amy Lowell. I "must pour out my heart about Hervey's departure. You are one of the few who will understand what his *loss* means to us." Lowell knew of Allen's growing dissatisfaction with Charleston and his search for another position, but she also believed Pinckney was at the heart of his unhappiness. Lowell's first intuition when she learned of his precipitous move came from "way down in the bottom of my soul with no hint whatsoever to guide me, merely my own romantic point of view." Allen had written Lowell in early January 1924 that Pinckney had "paid quite a visit" to his home in

Pittsburgh during the past Christmas season and "some of my folks gave her quite a tea." He also confided, "We hope to have a place out in the country where we can have house parties later on and a general good time. Some of the old houses are for rent for nothing and it will be a jolly adventure. This is a secret, of course . . ." Lowell believed that Hervey finally became impossibly frustrated standing "on the other side of the fence from the rainbow, year after year, and never succeeding in climbing over."[27]

When Allen left, he took two secrets with him. Both of them devastated Pinckney when the truth came out. The first concerned DuBose Heyward. He was leaving the insurance business and Charleston for the North Carolina mountains, where he planned to write a daring new sort of story about a crippled black man. Pinckney condemned his precipitous action to Amy Lowell as "novel recklessness."[28]

The word of Allen's departure spread quickly. Joseph Hergesheimer once again homed in on Pinckney when he heard the news. In the spring of 1924, film producer Jesse Laski had agreed to make "an elaborate moving picture" of his novel *Three Black Pennys* starring Lillian Gish, and he was riding high when he again invited her for a visit to Dower House. Instead of staying at home fretting, he instructed her to "observe the Madonna lily . . . this isn't new advice." Pinckney declined but agreed to a rendezvous in Manhattan. In his eye-catching tweed suits and Charvat ties, Hergesheimer squired her around Manhattan. His usual haunts included Poglani's, a dark little Italian restaurant on West Forty-Seventh Street, and the Oak Bar of the Algonquin Hotel. He invited Pinckney to a series of "high brow parties." Sipping illicit gin with the literati cast her into wide-eyed wonder. Pinckney adored having witty late-night conversations with celebrities and dropping their newsworthy names at lunch the next day. At one of their stops, Hergesheimer introduced her to the slightly-built editor Henry Seidel Canby and his much more substantial wife, Marion, always known to her crowd as "Lady." As it happened, Josephine had met the Canbys the year before when he gave a lecture to the Poetry Society. At the time of Pinckney's New York visit, Henry Canby had just embarked on a venture that would establish him as the chief moderator of the exuberant energies of literary America during the 1920s. As the editor and guiding intelligence of a new magazine, *The Saturday Review of Literature*, that was devoted to good books, good writing, and good reading, he had become in Amy Lowell's opinion *the* man for a young poet to know in New York. Pinckney got along famously with the Canbys, who invited her to spend the night at their West Cornwall, Connecticut, home on her way north to New England in July.[29]

Several years would pass before Pinckney would understand that her life had reached a turning point that evening. In the spring of 1924, the loss of Hervey and DuBose weighed on her and make her more desperate than ever to nail down an understanding with Dick Wigglesworth, who was earnestly at work in his position as secretary of the World War Foreign Debt Commission in Washington. Worried about Pinckney's melancholy, Amy Lowell invited her to Sevenels. Pinckney had somehow had tapped into Lowell's deeply buried, but nonetheless wide, vein of sympathy. They talked as two women talk; their conversation centered on their personal feelings, not just about the business of writing. They spoke of unrequited love, of Hervey Allen and his apparent emotional immaturity or "arrested development" that Lowell thought might be the product of "shell shock in Europe." Lowell spoke of the ethereal Italian actress Eleonora Duse, an international stage actress of unrivaled magnitude, whose beauty and grace inspired her first adult poem in 1902. Despite Lowell's overtures, they never met. Lowell sent some of her poems in praise of the actress to Sara Teasdale who also had dedicated poems to Eleonora Duse. Teasdale declared that she had "never read finer praise of one woman to another," with the exception of Sappho's praise of Anactoria, which (and Teasdale was very clear about this) was "a wholly different sort of thing."[30]

As Lowell concluded her long story with Duse's funeral mass, Pinckney sat speechless. Stunned by Lowell sharing such an intimate story with her, she only found her voice when she returned to Gloucester. She wrote a "bread-and-butter note" that was really wanted "to be a love-letter." "All the words I know are peaked from over work and can't possibly explain my utter inner feelings," Pinckney explained. Perhaps, she suggested to Lowell, "while inventing new poetic forms you will invent a new language of love so that people can say the things that are in their hearts for which there are no words present." Pinckney wrote Laura Bragg that Lowell was "more adorable and sweet than I dreamed she could be."[31]

Arriving back at Hawthorne Inn with her chin held high and a new outlook on life, Pinckney experienced another shock. Hervey's second secret had come to light. While Pinckney was away, Camilla had received news from Charleston about their close friend. It was not good. The details were sketchy, but the essential message revealed the reason for his hasty departure from Charleston. Allen had been accused of crossing the line of propriety with a young boy, not a student but one of the neighborhood kids who was drawn to the charismatic teacher. Allen had retained his boyish ways and won quite a following with his irreverent joking and imaginative banter. A little gang who gathered around his Savage Street home had approached Allen to help them create a ritual for a club they were forming. According to Pinckney's understanding of what transpired, one of these boys to whom he had been particularly attentive reported to his father that Hervey had told a "dirty story" to him. (The story, in Pinckney's later estimation, was "not so dirty as all that.") Scandalized, the father apparently went to the trustees of the High School of Charleston where Allen taught. All the boys involved were brought in for questioning before some key trustees; "the tale-teller stuck to his story." Allen could propose no motive for the boy to lie. Allen, Pinckney explained to Amy Lowell, "was stuck." If he chose to retain his position at the high school, a full investigation would begin. At the end, it would only be his word against the unrepentant local boy's. After consulting with a lawyer, Allen "left abruptly without a letter of recommendation." "Poor Hervey," Pinckney empathized, "was in a terrible state about it."[32]

When the story broke, DuBose and Dorothy drove over to East Gloucester from Peterborough to compare notes with Pinckney. Could the accusation possibly be true? They concluded that in light of all the time they spent together, at MacDowell Colony, on house parties, if Hervey did indeed suffer from some perversion, the women would have sensed it; DuBose, surely, would have "seen some sign." They decided Hervey was innocent, but Camilla was less sure. She went into high gear to protect her daughter's reputation. She consulted the leading men of Charleston about what course to follow. Thomas R. Waring, Poetry Society president and one of the most estimable men of the city, urged Pinckney to say nothing about the incident involving their "friend-in-common." Camilla also consulted their minister, the Reverend William Way of Grace Episcopal Church. Way informed her that Allen was indeed guilty, although he would never reveal his source. Way uncharitably advised that "the offending eye should be plucked out" and that Pinckney should cut off all communication with Allen.[33] Josephine refused.

Pinckney decided it was now or never with Dick Wigglesworth. In mid-August, Pinckney anxiously waited for him "to pop up" at the Hawthorne Inn on a visit to his family's home at nearby Manchester-by-the-Sea. Her one reservation was that the earnest Wigglesworth lacked the soul of an artist. Wigglesworth's brother, Frank, who was married to a charming and accomplished musician, had decided to chuck family expectations and take up sculpting. With this precedent, she confided to Laura Bragg, "I may make a poet of RBW yet."[34]

When Wigglesworth arrived, he brought more unwanted news. He had the opportunity for a new position with the postwar reparations commission in Berlin and had to decide soon. Pinckney panicked. On an "almost perfect day" in early September, Pinckney saw her opportunity. During a seaside picnic, when Wigglesworth suggested a canoe ride on the sparkling water, she made her move. They had really just set out and steadied the little craft, when Pinckney "took an early and good opening to explain to the young man the havoc he had wrought with

[her] heart." With all the melodrama in her young poet's soul, she blurted out that they should simply elope. But, "he was too moral for that," Pinckney wrote Amy Lowell. Astounded at her frankness, the reticent Wigglesworth, still a prisoner of Victorian respectability, had to catch his breath. He replied with glimmers of tears in his eyes "that he had suspected—feared it, for some time." Assuring Pinckney she "was first in his affections," he admitted he had not been able "to screw up enough enthusiasm for anything so irrevocable as marriage" to her.[35]

The whole incident was "quite heartbreaking," Pinckney admitted to Lowell, the only person she thought truly understood her. "Mother is horrified at my performance, poor dear." Camilla, so concerned with appearances, began contriving stories about how she personally put the quietus on the Wigglesworth affair because of insanity in his family (an aunt was reputedly "completely bughouse") and then, too, the unthinkable idea of changing the venerated, musical name of Pinckney for the harsh sounding Puritan one. "I can't tell what the psychological effects of this will be; I should say bad, from what I felt on Sunday," Pinckney wrote Lowell. Still she clung to the chance he might reconsider. "Hope sounds romantic in poetry," but she found it "rather a hard bedfellow" and "a terrific nervous and physical strain." After her ordeal she offered her sympathy to Lowell who still labored on the second volume of her Keats biography; "This concentration on the sole gentleman takes it out of one, eh?"[36]

That fall, Dick Wigglesworth left for his new job in Berlin where he quickly gained a reputation as "a confirmed bachelor." Well," Pinckney surmised when she heard he had left for Europe, "it's a complex world."[37] Soon plans were in the works for the Pinckneys' own winter cruise to the continent.

When the breeze off Gloucester Harbor turned chill, Pinckney and Camilla again headed south. They arrived at Cotesworth's home in time for Josephine to attend a large book fair in Richmond. She found an invitation from Emily Clark to a Halloween party. Among the ghoulies and ghosties, Clark promised, would be Henry Mencken. Joseph Hergesheimer later showed up to accompany Pinckney to the many other events in the city and countryside. After the meeting, Hervey Allen ran into Hergesheimer in New York, who bragged about the "grand time" he had given Pinckney in Richmond. "The usual number of men were said to be engaged to Joe," Allen reported to Lowell, "but the lady says nothing."[38]

All this attention did little to cheer Pinckney. Deeply depressed and discouraged, she withdrew into a "long orgy of reading, writing, and talking to myself" during the winter of 1924. She came out of this bleak period by finally making the long deferred commitment to a career in writing. Determined to harness all the emotion that had been stirred by her personal disappointments, she set out to write a book of poems. Word that John Farrar, a young publisher friend of Hervey Allen's, was scheduled to speak to the Poetry Society in November buoyed her spirits. Camilla lobbied successfully to have Farrar stay at 21 King Street.[39]

The Pinckneys had already met the energetic editor of the literary magazine *Bookman* at Sevenels. Also the acquisitions editor at George Doran, Farrar ranked, even in Henry Mencken's jaundiced eyes, as "one of the really fabulous characters of the early 20's." Slender, graceful, blond, he had "the peaches and cream complexion of a young girl not yet condemned to night work," Mencken recollected.[40] Farrar hailed from Vermont where his mother was a librarian and his father an advertising executive; his career blended the talents of both. He belonged to the cadre of ambitious young men with Ivy League educations, such as Random House's Bennett Cerf and Viking's Marshall A. Best, who transformed America's stodgy publishing industry during the 1920s with their understanding of the new sciences of marketing and advertising. Rather than wait for starving artists to make their way to New York, the ambitious Farrar drove the unmapped back roads and rode the rails in search of isolated writers who had not been signed with the old established firms. When Farrar spotted talent in the rough, he signed the author and waited for their promise to mature like a blue-chip bond. He possessed sincere interest in the personal life of his writers, encouraging, cajoling, passing a crying towel, or nursing a hangover. Farrar's visit to Charleston proved a critical moment in his own career, as well as in the nationalization of the Charleston Literary Movement.

Even though Farrar arrived too early at 21 King Street and caught Pinckney unprepared, with her unruly hair flying every which way, and then gave perhaps the dullest address of the season, his visit proved a great success from every other perspective. He was a brilliant house guest who praised Pinckney's work and left her "quite cheered up by his high spirits." Farrar, of course, went home with an envelope of Pinckney's latest poems and later agreed to publish "Gulla' Lullaby" in the *Bookman*. Also tucked in Farrar's suitcase was "Porgo," DuBose Heyward's manuscript about Charleston's black demimonde which John Bennett slipped to him.[41]

Inspired by Farrar's visit, Pinckney reported to Hervey Allen in late November 1924 that her book of poetry was proceeding "pretty fast."[42] The fruit of her long discontented winter spent watching the chilling rain make tracks down the long windows of 21 King Street was the hard-won realization that her future was not as the wife of a poet, dabbling in the background, sitting in on stimulating conversations about literature, passing hors d'oeuvres to fascinating people. After the humiliation of her breakup with Wigglesworth, Pinckney came finally to the harsh realization that she was going to have to submit to the discipline of being a poet herself. In a reversal of the famous Sherwood Anderson short story "The Man Who Became a Woman," about the horse trainer who developed all of the nurturing ways that he had looked for, but could not find, in a spouse, Pinckney ultimately resolved to become the poet she had always wanted to marry.

Valentine House at 900 Capitol Street, Richmond, was operated as a boarding house by Pinckney's grandmother Heningham Lyons Scott from 1876 to 1889. By 1908, about the time this photograph was taken, the old Mann S. Valentine residence was being used as a hotel.

*Courtesy Valentine/Richmond History Center, Richmond, Va.*

Camilla Scott Pinckney, Josephine Pinckney's mother. This is her identification photo from the Charleston and West Indian Exposition of 1897.

*Courtesy Charleston County Public Library*

Eldorado, the Pinckney family plantation. Charcoal drawing by Alice Ravenel Huger Smith.

*Courtesy South Carolina Historical Society*

*Mrs. Motte Directing the Generals Marion and Lee to Burn Her Mansion to Dislodge the British.* Rebecca Motte was Pinckney's great-great-grandmother, here painted in the heroic mode by John Blake White (ca. 1836).

*Courtesy United States Senate Collection (33.00001)*

The Little Grandfather. *Charles Cotes-worth Pinckney in His Sixth Year (1789–1865)*, pastel on paper, artist unknown. *Courtesy Gibbes Museum of Art/Carolina Art Association (1957.29.02)*

Captain Thomas Pinckney, father of Josephine Pinckney, ca. 1908. *Courtesy South Carolina Historical Association*

C. Cotesworth Pinckney, Josephine
Pinckney's half brother, with his aunt
Lucy Stewart.
*Courtesy Jane Pinckney Hanahan*

Pinckney family home, 21 King Street,
Charleston, ca. 1935.
*Courtesy South Carolina Historical Society*

Josephine Lyons Scott Pinckney, 1898.
*Courtesy Landon W. Garland*

Josephine Pinckney, ca. 1907.
*Courtesy South Carolina Historical Society*

Josephine Pinckney, ca. 1912.
*Courtesy South Carolina Historical Society*

Pinckney in the Eliza Lucas Pinckney dress, 1923.
*Courtesy Jane Pinckney Hanahan*

DuBose Heyward and Dorothy
Heyward, ca.1925.
*Courtesy South Carolina Historical Society*

Amy Lowell, ca. 1920.
*Courtesy Houghton Library, Harvard University*
*(bMS Am 2088)*

Richard Bowditch Wigglesworth, ca. 1918.

*Courtesy Bailey-Howe Library, University of Vermont*

Hervey Allen, 1930. This snapshot was taken by Bernard De Voto at the Bread Loaf Writers' Conference in Ripton, Vt.

*Courtesy Special Collections, Middlebury College Library, from the College Archives*

Henry Seidel Canby, ca. 1925.

*Courtesy Beinecke Rare Book and Manuscript Library, Yale University, from the Henry Seidel Canby Papers in the Yale Collection of American Literature*

*A Charleston Residence,* Pinckney's home at 36 Chalmers Street, drawn by Elizabeth O'Neill Verner.
*Courtesy David V. Hamilton, Verner Gallery, Middleburg, Va.*

Dining room at 36 Chalmers Street, with portrait of General Charles Cotesworth Pinckney by James Earle.
*Courtesy South Carolina Historical Society*

Prentiss Taylor, 1932. Photograph by Carl Van Vechten.
*Courtesy of the Carl Van Vechten Trust and the Beinecke Rare Book and Manuscript Library, Yale University*

Samuel Gaillard Stoney Jr. at the
opening night of Charleston's first
exhibition of modern art, 1936.
*Courtesy South Carolina Historical Society*

Harriet Porcher (Stoney) Simons, ca. 1927.
*Courtesy Harriet P. Williams*

Josephine Pinckney and DuBose Heyward, ca. 1935.
*Courtesy South Carolina Historical Society*

Presidential candidate Wendell Willkie charms actress Mary Pickford, 1940.
*Courtesy Lilly Library, Indiana University*

Pinckney at the Dock Street Theatre with Albert Simons, Harold Mouzon, and George C. Rogers Sr. in 1950.
*Courtesy South Carolina Historical Society*

Pinckney in her garden at 36 Chalmers Street, 1952.
*Courtesy Harlan M. Greene*

Joseph Hergesheimer, ca. 1930. Photograph by Nickolas Muray.
*Courtesy George Eastman House, copyright Nickolas Muray Photo Archives*

*A Portrait of Miss Josephine Pinckney,* a
sketch by Irish poet A.E. (George William
Russell) drawn while he was visiting at 36
Chalmers Street in 1931.
*Courtesy Historic Charleston Foundation*

Dust jacket for *Great Mischief,* by Prentiss Taylor, 1948. Photograph by Todd
Merrick.

Josephine Pinckney in 1945. This photograph
was used as the author photo on the jacket of
*Three O'Clock Dinner.*

# 6

## *Sea-Drinking Cities*

In January 1925 Camilla and Josephine left Charleston in a great flurry of steamer trunks and suitcases bound for Italy aboard the *Conte Russo*. The unbounded vista on the high seas, salt spray, and new faces pulled Pinckney out of her depression. A shipboard romance restored her confidence a bit after her recent disappointing "affaires du coeur." She could now joke with Hervey Allen about the "charming creature" who foolishly left the ship "and me—at Gibraltar in spite of my trying on him all the wiles I've learned in a long life. This was ashes in my mouth, of course." "While it is a traveler's banality to say to one at home 'I've wished for you,'" she wrote Allen, "I shall say so since you already know how commonplace I really am."[1]

The Pinckneys enjoyed a brief excursion into Spain, stopping for a day at Madeira where the sight of lavender houses wreathed with red bougainvilleas made a lasting impression upon her. At Algiers, Josephine bought a "swell costume" of blue and gold Turkish trousers at the market. Her excursion with her mother into the "smelly" Arab and Jewish quarters was less successful. At a mosque, Camilla, the steadfast pillar of the Episcopal establishment, unwittingly "stepped on an old Arab's prayer mat with her shoes *on* and got cursed out for an irreligious woman by the irate owner," giving Josephine "great joy." Next, Josephine convinced their party that they must see another custom of the country, the belly dancers. After a long wait and "much red tape and large sums of money," they entered the tent and saw the show. "The dancers weren't naked," she complained. "Very disappointing."[2]

In Sicily she began her study of Italian, which, she complained, "I was misled into thinking was an easy language to learn."[3] In the afternoons she read the classics (Theocritus's *Idylls* was a favorite) in English and worked fitfully on her own poetry. Later, in Maiori, on the Amalfi coast, Pinckney took up painting, "the most fun of anything I ever did." There, they met up with Isabella Wigglesworth, a "rebel Bostonese" painter and sister-in-law of Dick. Isabella, whose childhood nickname "Baby" had to be changed to "Bay" after the birth of a younger sister, shared Pinckney's enthusiasm for life and her sense of humor. Pinckney thought her "quite a peach" and "the member of the clan whose charm has lasted best for me." On their scenic side trips to Ravello, Pompeii, and Sorrento, Pinckney no doubt made discreet but probing inquiries about a certain young lawyer now posted in Berlin. But mostly they focused their attentions on the landscape as they struggled to capture the evanescent loveliness of the seaside in watercolors. The whole experience "went right to our heads," she wrote Allen.[4]

In early April 1925, the Pinckney party successfully negotiated the rock of the Cyclops, Scylla, and Charybdis, and settled into Rome. Pinckney awaited word from Amy Lowell who planned a celebratory trip to Europe upon completion of her Keats biography. Keats, most of Lowell's closest friends believed, was "retrospectively" the real love of her life. When Pinckney learned that *John Keats* had been released, she promised Lowell she would head right for his grave in the Protestant cemetery where "I shall lay Orestes-like upon his tomb, a curl of severed hair—in your especial honor."[5]

In Rome, Pinckney spent as much time "cogitating" as writing. After all the masterpieces of painting she had seen throughout Italy, she was wrestling with the relationship of art and poetry. Her time in Florence had been a total joy; she even developed a crush on poet and novelist Robert Nathans. Among the other intriguing people she met in Florence was art critic Bernard Berenson. Pinckney was invited to a party at his home, probably with Caroline Sidney Sinkler who was a friend of Berenson's patron Isabella Gardner Stewart. At the Villa I Tatti, she was dazzled by his "pictures" and intrigued by the stimulating talk.[6]

When Pinckney caught up with her mail, she learned that after three years the *North American Review* had finally published her poem "Dark Water." Rather than enjoying her success, she brooded over the published lines, picked the poem apart, and rewrote it. She also found letters from Hervey Allen. They had kept up a lively transatlantic correspondence wrangling over theories of poetry. From time to time, Allen cast "bon-bouches" of gossip about their literary friends, which she "gobbled up with the greatest relish."[7]

Other news, shocking news, also reached her. Amy Lowell had died quite unexpectedly from a stroke on May 12, 1925. She was only fifty-one years old. Boxes of prewar cigars were still stacked in her storeroom. Pinckney was "crushed" and grieved for her friend. She would find on her return to America that the great poetry "bubble" had popped almost simultaneously with the death of Lowell, who had made poetry fashionable. In her pose as entrepreneur and showman, Lowell had extravagantly promised more than any art form could deliver, and when she was gone, as poet Margaret Widdemer observed, "the essential values were shaken."[8]

Still reeling from this shock, Pinckney suddenly faced another crisis.

Camilla Pinckney fell critically ill with acute appendicitis and had to be taken to a sanatorium in Interlaken, Switzerland. While Camilla took her treatments and recuperated in the bracing air, Josephine turned her attention to DuBose Heyward's novel *Porgy*, recently published by John Farrar. Pinckney found fault. "DuBose will sentimentalize; it's a great pity, because he has a real natural gift for writing, I think. His think-tank appears to be undisciplined," she complained to Allen. "That prefatory poem, for instance seems to me a heinous offence against taste, and poor as poetry." Still, she had to admit that "the book is vivid and parts are brilliant." In a backhanded compliment, betraying her own desires, she concluded, "I hope it makes lots of money; it has the elements of a best seller."[9]

Once Camilla recovered, they returned to Josephine's "beloved Rome" for Christmas and set sail from Naples in January 1926.[10] When Pinckney descended the gangplank in New York after more than a year abroad, she carried a completed manuscript with her. The exotic settings had stimulated her imagination: "Sea-drinking cities have a moon-struck air." The ancient Mediterranean towns that shared the maritime essence with Charleston inspired the poem that would give her collection its title: *Sea-Drinking Cities*.

After her long European journey, Pinckney returned gratefully to the unchanging environment that had inspired many of her poems, the Carolina Low Country of misty purple lit marshes, cool green pine forests, great domed oaks strewn with lilac moss. She found, however, the literary landscape quite transformed. Even before she left for Europe, Pinckney quipped that the Poetry Society had begun to "have a dead feeling when you poked it."[11] Now it was on the verge of rigor mortis. The old stalwarts, DuBose Heyward and Hervey Allen, had drifted away from poetry. Heyward was working on a second novel *Mamba's Daughters*. Allen, now teaching at Vassar, was finishing a new biography, *Israfel: The Life and Times of Edgar Allan Poe*, which John Farrar had also secured for George Doran.

Throughout the South, the "renaissance" faltered as well. The *Double-Dealer*, the eclectic New Orleans journal, had closed shop. Emily Clark stepped down as editor of *The Reviewer* when she married Edwin Balch and moved to Philadelphia. Paul Green, a playwright at the University of North Carolina, tried to keep *The Reviewer* going in Chapel Hill where another aspect of the southern renaissance was incubating, but it failed after a year. As the last issue of the *Fugitive* had come off the press in 1925, the close communion among the Nashville poets also slipped away. John Crowe Ransom had retreated into a book on aesthetics. Allen Tate vainly sought intellectual community in New York. Donald Davidson tried to keep the Fugitive spirit alive by compiling an anthology of their poetry. Charlottesville was the one bright spot on the southern scene with the advent of the *Virginia Quarterly Review* in 1925.

Somewhere in Josephine Pinckney's many years of churchgoing, she had no doubt heard that one door seldom closes without another opening. With a newly minted manuscript, no publisher in sight, and her old network of acquaintances in disarray, Pinckney was fortunate in her acquaintance with Henry Seidel Canby, the Yale English professor turned editor. In 1924, when Pinckney first visited the Canby home in West Cornwall, Connecticut, he was on the eve of leaving his position at the *New York Post* and becoming the founding editor of the *Saturday Review of Literature*. Balding and bespectacled, Canby looked deceptively like the stereotypical absent-minded professor, but he possessed amazing wells of passionate energy, constantly primed by his intense interest in the events swirling around him. Publisher John Farrar dubbed the hyperkinetic Canby the Scarlet Pimpernel of literature who "flutters here and flutters there" with ten different projects going on at once.[12]

Over the next decade, the *Saturday Review* would become America's leading weekly. Canby assembled a distinguisted staff that included William Rose Benét and Christopher Morley. Within the covers of the *Saturday Review*, the general reader found serious criticism of recent books, biographical sketches of authors, and reflections on the course of modern literature. A sprinkling of cartoons, flecks of insider gossip about authors, and occasional good-natured caricature lightened this heavy going. For his efforts to bring good writing to a broad audience, Canby was denounced by his academic colleagues as "middlebrow" and "bourgeois" by his neighbors in Greenwich Village. Only the middlebrow, the common wisdom had it, was interested in education; the highbrow did not need it and the lowbrow did not want it.[13]

Canby, however, appeared to have hit upon the perfect formula for the times. He later reflected, "It would seem that those earliest 1920s were by some literary astrology the right time for a corporate literary personality to be born." Neither the *Saturday Review* nor the *New Yorker*, which had been started three years earlier, would have found an audience in 1910, but they both benefited from the prevailing enthusiasm for literature. "Whatever the cause," Canby surmised, "an editor who wished to give new books a chance to be read by the right people in the right way got plenty of support of the kind that cannot be bought."[14]

An Aquarius, Pinckney's astrology put her in the right place at the right time with her opportunity to cultivate a friendship with Canby, who was named the first judge of the savvy marketing innovation, the Book-of-the-Month Club in 1926, and was elected president of the Poetry Society of America in 1927. Visits to Yelping Hill had become part of the Pinckneys' summer ritual. Canby kept cottages for friends, writers, and academics near his own eighteenth-century house. Spread out, literally at her feet, were the farms and hideaways of the most powerful arbiters of reading taste in America. In the meadow below the Canby house, Joseph Wood Krutch, literary critic and dramatic reviewer for *The Nation,* despaired over the fate of the modern world. Down in Cornwall Hollow, Columbia University poet Mark Van Doren lived close to Chard Powers Smith, novelist and poet. In North Cornwall, Carl Van Doren, the Pulitzer Prize–winning historian, was hard at work. In a time when history was still considered part of the belletristic tradition, Van Doren also served as the literary editor of *The Nation.* Irita Van Doren, his Alabama-born wife, held the same position with the *New York Herald Tribune* in 1926. Small and dark with a head of wild frizzy hair, she was as attractive as she was clever, as charming as she was steel-willed. Van Doren pioneered the idea of a national "best-seller list," a measurement of popularity scorned by the New York intelligentsia. Her colleague who wrote the daily reviews at the "Trib," Lewis Gannett, also had a weekend place in Cornwall.[15]

Canby, like Lowell, recognized something in Pinckney that he found appealing. Although Canby was almost twenty years older, they had both come out of the same vanishing world of privilege and responsibility, of Victorian certainty and Episcopal verities. With ancestors who arrived with William Penn, he shared Pinckney's subtle sense of ownership in the American enterprise. Always dignified and controlled, Canby earned a reputation for unshakable moral integrity, tolerance, and fairness to others in a business that was populated by the cynical and self-promoting. Forward thinking and embracing democratic change in theory, Canby recoiled at the crassness and vulgarity that penetrated American popular culture. Canby felt particularly uncomfortable with the tone set by the young Jazz Age writers like F. Scott Fitzgerald, Ernest Hemingway, and William Faulkner, who all betrayed the modernist tendency to focus on the imperfect and neurotic elements of human nature, he believed. Canby denounced Ezra Pound and T. S. Eliot as "wild men" and criticized the avant-garde for its preoccupation with personal gratification and flaunting of conventional morality. He found little of interest or importance in the proletarian novels by immigrants such as Anzia Yezierska.[16]

When he compared Pinckney to the freethinking, free-loving image of the aging "girl-poets," Canby perhaps saw her as the "anti-Millay." After a decade, Millay's indiscriminate candle-burning had caught up with her. Her life became more of a cautionary tale than an inspiration. Pinckney sported Worth originals from Paris and evinced a sophisticated air, but she could still speak about "chaperones" with a straight face. About 1923, when Hervey Allen suggested she drive from East Gloucester to visit him in Cambridge, she fired back that such a trip unchaperoned was unthinkable: "Never ever at the peak of my modernity have I ever sought gilded youth in its college diggings, though I know it's done in Scott Fitzgerald's novels." Even into her thirties, Pinckney retained an aura of innocence. In 1928, an Atlanta journalist observed that Pinckney provided a "distinct pleasant refutation" of the stereotypical "lady poets" as persons "of indeterminate age, ancestry, with eccentric habits and funny hair." In the article, "Miss Pinckney Refuses to Succumb to Eccentricity," he praised the Charleston poet, as a lady of aristocratic birth and bearing.[17]

The bond that linked Henry Seidel Canby with Josephine Pinckney was their mutual desire to engage the complexities of the post–World War I world rather than withdraw from them. Although Canby found much about the modern scene—its fragmentation and potential for chaos—that deeply troubled him, he was also fascinated by the times in which he lived. He experimented with the idea of finding a literature adequate for the unprecedented needs of the modern moment. For every alienated member of the Lost Generation, for every cynical cultural debunker, or for every pessimistic literary realist, there were actually many more, like Canby and Pinckney, who felt a deep commitment to the modern world and experienced a meaningful connection with their times.[18] Brooding and self-destructive behavior set the tone in some quarters during the 1920s, but America during this decade also rang with great peals of laughter, often with a slight ironic edge, inspired by Robert Benchley, Ring Lardner, and Dorothy Parker. Henry Seidel Canby always sought the sunny side of the street during the "Jazz Age" and, like Pinckney, was eager to make his rendezvous with life.

When Canby folded Josephine Pinckney into his world, she found herself very much at home. For all her attraction to the "high brow" environment, Pinckney felt most comfortable in the middling terrain of "popular modernism" reflected in the editorial philosophy of the *Saturday Review*. As opposed to the mind-centered, inaccessible modernism of T. S. Eliot, for example, the underpinnings of popular modernism were reflected in the more ephemeral literature of the day, such as magazines and newspapers that helped intelligent Americans come to terms with their new twentieth-century identity. As Americans liberated their repressed Victorian selves, a competing modern style evolved, an urbane way of viewing the world that balanced irony with humor.[19]

Pinckney's summers at Yelping Hill among the architects of popular modernism would provide a launching pad for her, much as the MacDowell Colony had propelled Heyward's career. In Henry Seidel Canby, Pinckney would find a literary guardian like Hervey Allen had in Amy Lowell, except he never expected yard work from her in return. Canby used to claim that given the number of editors and critics living near his Connecticut compound, "It is not too much to say that for some years at least the fate of a new book of importance was more dependent upon the hills of Cornwall than upon anything else except its own merits."[20]

As Pinckney mingled more frequently with poets and writers of national reputation and national concerns, she began to cultivate her own unique public persona—southern aristocrat abroad, poet, and plantation owner. Not that Pinckney feigned an identity; rather, she played to her strengths, in contrast to other aspiring writers in New York who downplayed their small town origins. She distinguished herself from all others by her charm and authenticity coming from a world that so many in the North were beginning to see in a new light.

After World War I, Charleston had blossomed into a tourist mecca. Florida-bound travelers often stopped en route and lingered in the charming old city. When changes in shotgun technology made the hunting of small birds, such as quail and dove, more rewarding, wealthy northerners began spending the entire winter in the Low Country where they enjoyed shooting and riding. "Lord send us a wealthy Yankee!!" became a mantra among the local plantation folk desperate for cash. Names such as Legendre, Guggenheim, and Doubleday began appearing in the society pages of Charleston newspapers. They generated "society," in fact, with their horse shows and hunt balls. Places such as Goose Creek, Mount Pleasant, Edisto Island, and Beaufort became subjects of Manhattan dinner party conversations, in the same way that Fishers Island, Northeast Harbor, or "the Vineyard" had long been staples of upper-crust chitchat. In 1921, Ellery Sedgwick, Boston Brahmin editor of the *Atlantic Monthly*, built a summer house in Beverly, Massachusetts, to resemble a Charleston home of the Federal period using beautiful interiors stripped from the Ball family home. Mrs. Harry Payne Whitney commissioned a replica of the "Charleston room" exhibited in the Antiques and Decorators Show at the Grand Central Palace for her Long Island garden at Westbury.[21]

Josephine Pinckney so resembled what northerners had come to expect of a Charleston lady by way of attractiveness, manner, and breeding that the city and the citizen often merged in people's minds. To some extent, Pinckney probably began presenting herself in light of their expectations. At 21 King Street, letters of introduction flooded her mail from northern acquaintances who told their south-traveling friends that they had not seen Charleston until they had seen Pinckney. Young architect Eric "Tuppy" Gugler wrote her a note from New York's fashionable

Drake Hotel saying he had just had lunch "with a man who says Charleston doesn't exist as such, but only as the place you live . . . Every man in the world who has ever met you [thinks] you are out of this world for looks, genius, glory and every man's dream."[22]

Pinckney's position as one of the last southern aristocrats also made her an object of interest among New Yorkers. With a Confederate officer as a father, she seemed closer than most to the drama surrounding the end of the southern raj. During the 1920s, the concept of New York as melting pot began to recede among intellectuals, to be replaced with the idea of a mosaic of subcultures sharing the same geography. Being a southerner with an identifiable accent and a history separate from the American story of material success gave Pinckney ethnic cachet. New Yorkers' fascination with all aspects of African American life during the Harlem Renaissance of the 1920s also translated into an interest in the South in general. DuBose Heyward, whose novel *Porgy* was perfectly timed to mesh with the Harlem Renaissance, remarked in 1924 that "in the current world of letters it is almost as chic to be a Southerner as to be a Negro."[23]

Although presenting oneself as a "southern" writer might be read as playing on nostalgia and sentimentality, claiming an ethnicity was, ironically, a quintessentially modern move. With a dual identity, Pinckney could be an insider to the world of the Low Country plantation aristocracy at the same time that she was an outsider to the mainstream middle-class culture. Women found this dual citizenship particularly useful as they sought simultaneously to be accepted as equals and to stand out as unique. An imaginative woman such as Josephine Pinckney could create a mystique around herself that was hers alone.[24]

Pinckney's friendship with the Canbys was not a one-way street. She reciprocated their summer and fall hospitality with winter and spring invitations to 21 King Street. Henry Seidel Canby fell under Charleston's spell, calling it "a rose and violet city seated between two rivers and looking out to sea, like a Platonic ideal of New York." His wife even wrote an ode to the Low Country, "Sea Marsh: South Carolina." The Carolina Low Country, Canby surmised in 1931, a time when the viability of capitalism was coming into doubt, was an unspoiled and "spacious country, once the seat of an aristocratic society, happier and more truly successful than anything we can show as the result of wage slavery."[25] Canby shared Pinckney's interest in trying to perpetuate some of the best qualities of the old aristocratic class while letting its worst qualities—its prejudices and closed-mindedness—wither away. Her cadre of friends convinced him that the South had an important contribution to make to the debate over the nation's future.

Encouraged by Pinckney, Henry Seidel Canby emerged as one of the great unsung forces of the southern literary renaissance. He generously published and promoted southern writers when few national journals, especially those with a liberal bent, would consider their work. Canby encouraged southern writers to write from their hearts and drop their deference to the narrow northeastern cultural elite. Hailing from the border state of Delaware, Canby claimed to be able to see both sides of sectional issues and hoped to serve as a bridge to mutual understanding. His interest in southern writers also stemmed from his crusade, started during his Yale teaching days, to establish an authentic American literature with roots in local themes and native idiom. Southern literature, he felt strongly, was an integral part of the American narrative and a worthy topic for serious writing. The *Saturday Review* gave voice to the full southern chorus, from James Branch Cabell to William Faulkner. Josephine Pinckney became Canby's unofficial advisor on the southern literary scene and wrote reviews on southern books for the *Saturday Review.*[26]

The Fugitives of Nashville, who always told themselves that a vast left-wing conspiracy kept their work out of the mainstream press, rushed to submit essays and poems to Canby. In May 1926, Canby published Donald Davidson's "The Artist as Southerner," an article that marked a turning point in Davidson's life, and perhaps in Pinckney's as well. The process of committing to paper all the obstacles faced by serious writers trying to pursue their vocation in the South had brought Davidson to an important moment, "a spiritual 'Secession.'" Unhappy because he failed to get a position at Columbia University and frustrated by his lack of success in finding publications that would accept his poetry, Davidson "seceded" from his early modernist tendencies and began searching for his artistic identity closer to home through a study of his family history in Tennessee. Davidson hailed from Scotch-Irish rovers who crossed the mountains from Virginia "in pioneer times" about 1800 and settled on the farms and in the small towns of Middle Tennessee. Davidson's father had been a schoolteacher who, like his rolling stone relatives, moved his family from one dusty town in the Volunteer State to another. In his essay, Davidson argued that aspiring writers should give "full play" to "Southern qualities" in their work.[27] Canby agreed. So did Pinckney.

Initially, Tate and Ransom were appalled at Davidson's defection to localism. Pinckney, overlooking the Tennessean's attack on the authenticity of DuBose Heyward's work, praised Davidson in the Poetry Society's 1926 *Yearbook*. She reiterated Davidson's caveat to all poets seized with a passion for local color. She emphasized the need for "heart searching" in sorting out the meaning of locale; "don't mistake the scenery for the play." Pinckney's unsigned essay disarmed Davidson, who later praised the Poetry Society for its "fine disinterested zeal."[28]

Davidson had also won the Poetry Society's "Southern Prize" that year for "Fire on Belmont Street," part of his *Tall Men* collection that glorified the sharp-shooting, eye-gouging, ear-biting world of his fathers on the southern frontier. With the exception of an award from a Georgia poetry society, it was the only prize he ever won for his poems.

Although they had never met, Pinckney had corresponded with Davidson for several years. In 1923, John Crowe Ransom won the Southern Prize and Davidson received honorable mention. "A pretty serious mess" enveloped the whole Poetry Society when a couple of valued members objected to Ransom's poem "Armageddon" as sacrilegious and threatened to resign if it was published in the *Yearbook* that bore their names. While Heyward tried to figure out how to deal with the "gassing squad" and still maintain the society's intellectual integrity, he assigned Pinckney the task of smoothing the ruffled feathers of Davidson, who was pressing them for a publication date. She proved so skillful that the "over-the-mountain man" eventually ended up as her warm friend. "I had the pleasant task of reading *Avalon* to the Poetry Society, and I fell in love with it," she wrote Davidson with unfeigned enthusiasm. "'Pounding the casks of Christendom' is a wonderful line to read, and I for one will never ask what it means." She also asked for a subscription to *The Fugitive*, on credit.[29]

Feeling ever more kindly toward the Poetry Society, Davidson agreed to judge the Southern Prize contest in 1927. He narrowed the field to two but had to disqualify himself because he recognized one as being in the unique sonnet style of his fellow Fugitive Merrill Moore. The other entry, Pinckney's *Island Boy,* he deemed a "very fine series of pictures or moods representing a life which one likes to see a Southern poet interpret in verse." His one reservation concerned the restrained voice of this poet who seemed to be "more eyes and ears than heart." The second judge gave the prize to Pinckney.[30]

When Henry Canby turned his attentions to Pinckney's manuscript of *Sea-Drinking Cities*, he suggested some revisions and then recommended she send her collection to the new, highly praised poetry editor at Harper Brothers, Eugene Saxton. If unsuccessful there, she could always turn to her friend John Farrar, who was establishing his own imprint with two of his former associates at George H. Doran, Stanley H. and Ted Rinehart. Saxton, one of the most respected poetry editors in America, had just been hired by Harpers to reinvigorate their musty, old-fashioned operation. For decades the firm had been living off its distinguished backlist, which included works by Sir Arthur Conan Doyle, Owen Wister, and John Dewey. In 1880, Harpers had made history with the largest book order ever, shipping out one million copies of Lew Wallace's *Ben-Hur* for Sears and Roebuck, but it had not kept up with the newer strategies of the times. The first thing Saxton did was to recruit America's most popular women poets, Elinor Wylie and Edna St. Vincent Millay. He also signed James Thurber and Aldous Huxley.[31]

Pinckney put her manuscript of forty-two poems in the mail to Saxton and began making preparations to leave once again for Europe in mid-June 1927. She and Camilla planned to meet the Canbys for a swing through France by automobile. Also on her itinerary was a rendezvous with the Heywards and the ever-faithful Gordon Miller for a blowout reunion in the City of Lights. After monitoring the mail for six weeks, Pinckney cracked under the pressure of uncertainty. On the verge of dark despair, she swallowed her pride and wrote Hervey Allen for help. Could he contact his friend Saxton "immediately" and learn the fate of her manuscript? She swore this would be the last time she would impose on their friendship in this way. A substantial book of poems by a good press "ought to put me on my feet where I can row my own boat in future," Pinckney promised, and "not bother my kind friends any further."[32]

Pinckney's appeal could not have reached Allen at a worse time. With the spring term drawing to a close, final exams and term papers spilled across his desk. As Josephine well knew from a "rumbling in the air," Allen, now thirty-seven years old, planned to be married in a few weeks time to one of his Vassar students, Ann Andrews. Of course, Josephine's trip prevented her from attending the festivities in Cazenovia, New York, but she wished him "All happiness and that eternité promised by our ever-living Poet."[33]

In the spirit of auld lang syne, the weary Allen called Saxton. Saxton explained his dilemma. Books of poetry simply did not sell in quantities any longer. Hired to erase the red ink on Harper Brothers' ledgers, he needed assurance that Josephine would follow up *Sea-Drinking Cities* with some prose book "of prospective profit." Allen assured Saxton that Pinckney could do an excellent popular book of "plantation tales" as her next project. The day after his conversation with Allen, Saxton dictated the long-awaited letter. Saxton praised Pinckney's poems as "very genuine and [of] moving quality." He offered her a generous contract and the promise to make a fine book of her collection of poems. Josephine flung suits and shoes into her suitcases in a trance of complete happiness. Poetry Society secretary Helen Williman noted that Pinckney "trotted off to Europe wearing her laurels very becomingly tilted over her fortunate head."[34]

Pinckney made straight for New England at the end of her European sojourn but returned to Charleston earlier than usual for the opportunity to meet Donald Davidson, who had agreed to address the Poetry Society in October 1927. Davidson approached his trip to Charleston with the foreboding of a foray into enemy territory. He had passed through the old aristocratic town on his way to France in World War I but had never been in the place that had occupied such villainous place in his imagination, for Davidson, who had perhaps only really felt at home among the Fugitive circle, possessed the wary, suspicious nature of the perennial outsider. He felt unappreciated at Vanderbilt. He never forgot or forgave slights and still bore a grudge against Hervey Allen and DuBose Heyward for their attempt to usurp the southern literature revival. He was wary too of Pinckney. In the abstract, she represented the upper-class, privileged aspects of southern society he both envied and disdained. He had no use for lady versifiers either.

Pinckney's warm welcome, however, immediately conquered Davidson's defensiveness. She could be coolly remote to the overreaching parvenu but greeted the Fugitive poet as a kinsman in the aristocracy of talent. He enjoyed her ironic sense of humor, admired her intelligence, and shared her seriousness of purpose. They found common ground in their mutual preoccupation with the fate of the South in a rapidly changing world. Pinckney treated Davidson to an intimate view of the Low Country, including a trip to Middleton Gardens, owned by her cousin's husband, J. J. Pringle Smith. He entered the shuttered private houses of her most interesting friends, and, of course, she entertained him at 21 King Street. The ability of a southern aristocrat to awe and exact deference from the yeomanry had not entirely disappeared over the generations.

At the Poetry Society meeting, he spoke to a large and appreciative crowd on the topic of "Poetry and Progress," his further meditation on the role of the artist in the modern world. He bemoaned the ever-quickening tempo of life and the fact that "progress" had taken on an almost exclusively material context. He encouraged the writers in the audience to find their own unique identity by interpreting "the life and the ideals" of their own region. In the South, Davidson contended, "We need the spiritual salvation (and you might say conversion) that only poetry can give."[35]

For Davidson, who later confessed to Pinckney that he felt out of place in "society," having little opportunity in his life to "mix and mingle at large," the gracious reception by the local elite converted him to "a worshipper of Charleston for life." "The country, the charm, and also, may I say, the unpretentiousness of the all the people captured me—and also made me humble," Davidson wrote Pinckney after his return to Nashville, "for I felt I had not nearly as much to give Charleston as Charleston had given me." Back at Vanderbilt, Davidson regaled his colleagues with so many stories and observations about Pinckney—her charm, her house, her town, her ancestry, her antiques, her plantation, her poetry—that Merrill Moore felt he had come to know her personally.[36]

Davidson's visit was a great success and marked a belated rapprochement between the two southern literary centers after the years of tension inspired by Monroe's "Southern Number" of *Poetry* magazine. Davidson sent a letter of appreciation to the Poetry Society for their invitation and generous hospitality, which Pinckney reported was read aloud to "cheers and hand-clappings and loud purrings." She personally declared his words were like "judgments from the Lord— making wise the simple, rejoicing the heart, enlightening the eyes. We must have them again." Pinckney, who always mocked the rage for the masculine among Charleston's male poets and felt no need to be bellicose to defend her career as a poet, seized the moment to make a welcomed overture of collegial friendship. "For years I have been wanting to bridge the distance between the Fugitives and the P.S. of S.C.," she wrote Davidson after they became acquainted, "and I'm so glad you were the bridge." At a loss after the unraveling of the close-knit Fugitive circle, Davidson clearly felt Pinckney represented an understanding and perhaps kindred spirit. When Pinckney had confided her deep anxieties about the critical reception of the soon-to-be-released *Sea-Drinking Cities*, Davidson gallantly offered to "do all I can for the book hereabouts."[37]

By the end of November 1927, a special Christmas limited edition of *Sea-Drinking Cities* was in the mail to 21 King Street. Pinckney had fretfully followed her manuscript through its metamorphosis into a book. She had insisted on the special edition as a marketing ploy and bombarded Eugene Saxton, constantly fussing about the price, pressing him about the timetable, pushing him about the advertising, and quizzing him about how many free copies she might expect.[38]

Pinckney's collection quickly won recognition as a book of authentic poetry by a serious poet. Addison Hibbard of the University of North Carolina requested poems from Pinckney for his new anthology, *The Lyric South*. A few reviewers suggested that her studies of Charleston and the coast rivaled, or even surpassed, those of Heyward and Allen. Clear-eyed in her vision of the South, the foibles and frailties, the little pretensions of its people, Pinckney screened her hard truths with the gauze of affection, but not romance. Sympathetic to the pain of decline and loss, she was nevertheless impatient with stubborn clinging to archaic ways of life. Her quasi-love poems reflect her mastery of the emotional near-miss, the solitary questioning of the young woman wondering why romance could never climb the walls of her "ivory tower." "Always my love for you was an escaping thing . . . Why was it never joy," she wrote in "Spring Makes Me Wonder."

*Sea-Drinking Cities* was alive with a diversity of forms as Pinckney experimented with free verse, sonnets, short and long lyrics, off-rhyme, internal rhyme, and dialect. Never satisfied with her efforts, she scratched out infelicitous words, edited, and reworked previously published poems. Deploring the "Farmer-Laborites" faction that shanghaied American literature during the 1920s, she was determined to chronicle "the disappearing aristocratic quality in the South."[39] In "Wounded Woman," a once grand lady watches from her balcony as her dark-skinned gardener rakes leaves "With long deliberate strokes, as one who knows / The foolishness of haste and of rebellion, / Since none can change the turning of the earth." She then wills "the gardener's spade / To bury her days with his in nerveless earth." Pinckney is skeptical about the impact of revolutionary change as she probes the impact of the great transformation of the South for ex-slaves in "The Old Women":

> The old women puff and mutter about the ways
> Of life since freedom came. One says the master
> Would give her burial.
>
> The other looking sixty years away
> To dancing crowds of dizzy negroes, mumbles,
> "Free as frogs . . . "

Pinckney's genre poems were among her best. "The Misses Poar Drive to Church," first published in *The Reviewer* in 1923, was a favorite of many critics. She drew on the eccentricities of two real-life sisters, the Misses Doar, friends of Captain Tom's from the Santee District, and a true experience of her uncle, the Reverend C. C. Pinckney, in 1865.[40] She lightheartedly tells the story of two dedicated churchwomen who after the Confederate surrender insist on attending church in their once fine carriage, even though the Yankees had stolen their horses. They order their faithful old driver ("The negro coachman in beaver hat, / Slightly nibbled by moth and rat") to hitch a yoke of aged oxen to the carriage, and they ride with heads high and not the slightest idea of the amusing sight they create:

> Neatly darned are their black silk mitts
> And straight each stately sister sits.
> Out from the tall plantation gate
> Issue the Misses Poar in state.

At Grace Church, the only one open to whites at the time, "the youthful parson" finds himself confronted by the military commander of the Union forces occupying Charleston, who orders him to lead his congregation in a prayer for the president of the United States. Legend has it that Pinckney replied that he would be happy to obey since "I know of no one who needs praying for more than the President of the United States." Worried that the minister would slip in a bit of treason, armed Union soldiers stood at attention in the center aisle until the prayer had been offered.[41]

> For the Misses Poar, this heresy was too much:
> They bury their noses' patrician hook
> In dear great-grandpapa's Prayer-book
> Wherein are found urbane petitions
> To guard the Crown against seditions,
> And rest King Charles the Martyr's soul.
> Not that they hold King Charles so dear,
> Although their blood is Cavalier,
> But it suits their piety, on the whole,
> Better to pray for the Restoration
> Than the overseer of a patch-work Nation.[42]

In "On the Shelf" Pinckney conveys the feeling that the planter families had for their books by drawing on the true experience of a Santee River rice planter driven to bankruptcy. As a child, she had heard the tale of poor John Julius Pringle who had to sell off his treasured collection of Sir Walter Scott novels to feed the great crush of relations relentlessly imposing on his hospitality during the starving years after the Civil War. To "Mr. Skirling," his books were old friends, almost members of the family, frequently quoted and consulted for reference. The leather-bound books with their gold lettering, fine calf covers, and creamy vellum were also objects of commerce, merely another commodity in the modern world, where Mr. Skirling's class in their faded finery was so out of place. As the source of much of the South's romantic inspiration was lost to commerce, Pinckney subtly suggests the coming change as the Old South gives way to the New.

> The dark shop of the book-seller was sweet
> To Mr. Skirling, coming from the glare
> Of traffic-jangled streets. He slowly fingered
> His way along familiar shelves; the glow

Of scaling gold on soft dun backs in rows,—
The watered end-papers delighted him.
He priced a volume in red levant, felt
It with appraising fingers, to deceive
Himself rather than anybody else.
His voice boomed through the little shop,—a voice
Tuned to commanding negroes from a horse;
His vowels rolled and rang that never could
Be muted to the oily tones of trade.
Then out came Peveril in an off-hand way . . .

A decade after first reading Edna St. Vincent Millay in *Poetry,* Josephine Pinckney eagerly flipped through the magazine's pages to find "Young Charleston," Harriet Monroe's review of her own book. *Sea-Drinking Cities,* Monroe proclaimed, was "the true stuff of poetry" with lyrics from a writer of "impassioned sincerity." Acknowledging that Pinckney was still an apprentice to her craft, Monroe confirmed that she "knows her Charleston: the sharply varied aspects of its life— blue blood and common red, white-skinned and black—are her deep ancestral inheritance; and she presents them with a sympathy intimate and tender, whether her mood be serious or humorous."[43]

The Carolina critics focused on the modern aspects of Pinckney's writing and were cautious in praising this as a positive trend. George Armstrong Wauchope, a professor of English from the University of South Carolina, noted the influence of Lowell and the Imagists in her "pen paintings." Pinckney's "very modern" use of irregular cadence made selections such as "Lonesome Grabeya'ad" ("Dragging heavy-footed / Through scuffing sand some / Negroes came in a bullock- / Led procession") more closely resemble "beautifully chiseled prose" than traditional poetry, "a transcript of life" rather than a self-conscious imitation. Wauchope also praised Pinckney's emphasis that was "ever on truthfulness." The moralizing sentimentality of the Victorian and "the New England ethical note," Wauchope observed approvingly, was refreshingly absent.[44]

Pinckney's slim volume commanded national attention. The New York critics treated Pinckney fairly. The *Times* reviewer credited Pinckney with "fluency" but felt her too much the debutante trying overly hard to please. Babette Deutsch's estimate in the *Herald-Tribune* identified the importance of "place" in Pinckney's poetry and commented appreciatively of the "margeless leisure" and "feeling for sky and garden, drawing-room and library." She detected a similarity between Pinckney and the Sitwells, the "same feeling for all that belongs to an ancient, generous, somehow quaint, somehow pathetic tradition," absent their "long-lidded sophistication."[45]

In an interview with an Atlanta newspaper, Pinckney confirmed her belief in the importance of "place" in the best poetry. *Sea-Drinking Cities* was her rebuttal of the "open road" school of poetry made so popular in the early decades of the twentieth century by Richard Hovey's three-volume *Songs of Vagabondia*. She argued against the belief that the "nomadic life" produced good poetry. Pinckney confessed that her own hometown stirred her more than the exotic sights marveled over by travelers. Good poetry doesn't have to be about the soil, per se, but should "draw its vitamins from it." Poets should "stay at home and be themselves," she thought, for "when a people gets to pulling up its roots and drifting about," something important was lost.[46]

A man of his word, Donald Davidson's review was the first to appear. He worked over his Christmas vacation on a thoughtful and generous critique that ran as a featured "extra" in his "Spyglass" column in January 1928. Pinckney's poetic "glance," he wrote, "goes out spontaneously to the physical and spiritual life of old Charleston and coastal South Carolina, whose ways she knows and has inherited." When Allen Tate read his fulsome review, he could not resist chiding Davidson, "Miss Pinckney does pretty well."[47]

Then, editor Thomas R. Waring, anxious that Pinckney receive a good notice in her hometown, asked Davidson to do double-duty and submit another review to the *Charleston Evening Post*. Davidson agreed, praising Pinckney's "luxuriance of phrase," as well as her Wordsworthian ability to capture "natural magic" by making everyday life seem wondrous through the powers of her imagination. Davidson recognized Pinckney as a product of the Charleston Literary Movement and intimated that she had transcended the mere picturesque of Charleston poets with her sun-washed imagery, "richness of sound and color and rhythm, a subdued grace and ease." Like so many others, Davidson merged his reaction to Pinckney as a person with his judgment of Pinckney as a poet, intimating that she shared the "mystique" of a place "that has insisted on remaining itself in a time when cities conform to the national rule of monotony and no character." The poetry of Charleston was neither sentimental nor aloof, as "ignorant" people may expect from the town's reputation for insularity, he wrote, or limited by the "hauteur and aloofness" that "we outsiders" connect with Charlestonians. Instead, Pinckney's writing conveyed "the simple joys of an old, gracious life in an old beautiful city that has learned how to live." In Pinckney's approach to poetry, Davidson detected some "pain," "some withholding of self, as if for fear that too much or the wrong thing might be said," which made him think of the long Anglo-Saxon tradition that you must not be caught in the impolite act of expressing emotion but must like the soldier make a joke to cover the horror of war. "Her lyric gift is great," Davidson concluded, as he expressed desire that she would set her goal higher in the future.[48]

Another old friend from the first days of the Charleston Literary Movement stepped up to endorse both Pinckney and promote southern literature. Howard Mumford Jones, professor of English at the University of North Carolina, wrote an "enthusiastic" review for the *Chicago Daily News*. In a personal letter, he observed that she had both roses and "cabbages" in her collection, but overall "Your book seems to me the most important and interesting book of verse by a southern poet since John Crowe Ransom arrived over the hill; and I congratulate you upon your etcher's technique, your intelligence, and your subtlety." Praising her also for not flickering "an eyelash in the direction of the UDC," Jones urged her not to rest on her laurels but "always keep your lean, intelligent edge."[49]

Not all of her literary friends were as accommodating as Davidson and Jones. *Sea-Drinking Cities* drove Joseph Hergesheimer to drink. During the Christmas season of 1927, he had eagerly opened the envelope engraved with the familiar return address of 21 King Street. After a long silence, Josephine had finally written him a "charming letter," delighting Hergesheimer with its "hospitable" tone and references to "the pleasantness of the past." The following day, he was disheartened to receive a newly minted book of poetry from the same address. Pinckney's enclosure expressed her hope he might give the book some publicity. "This gets to be discouraging," Hergesheimer wrote to Henry Mencken, who disdained most poetry. A coincidence perhaps, but Hergesheimer then went on a rip-roaring binge beginning with a sip of sherry on Christmas Eve and concluding with a gallon of spiked eggnog on the 26th. Mencken, who found the news of Pinckney's poetic efforts "really appalling," consoled his friend, "Luckily, you don't have to read it on the water-wagon."[50]

After a month, Hergesheimer pulled himself together and wrote Pinckney a letter thanking her for all the nice things she had said to him. "My most public and elaborate opinion of *Sea-Drinking Cities* is that I like it." Hergesheimer reported he had just completed a great deal of writing himself and was headed to Bermuda. "There, it is my intention to hire an old barouche and a nigger with a stovepipe hat and drive around and around those circumscribed sunny roads leaving a trail of smoke from British and unthoughtful cigarettes. The water is blue and so am I, and this has nothing to do with violets or roses . . . Nor is it concerned with our always interrupted affair. It describes a state of mind."[51]

Despite positive reviews, Pinckney slipped into one of her dark moods over the slow sales of *Sea-Drinking Cities*. A January visit from DuBose Heyward, flush with *Porgy's* success and a second, almost-completed, novel, *Mamba's Daughters*, did little to cheer her. He drove into town behind the wheel of a shiny new car, resplendent in a finely tailored English suit and beige spats, swinging a Malacca cane.[52] In June, when she offered to do some entertaining if he and Dorothy came for a Charleston vacation, Heyward brushed her off. "I am by way of being dirty rich these days, dear old Joey—so in making plans there is no reason why *Sea Drinking Cities* should expect to throw parties for *Porgy* and *Mamba*."[53]

Pinckney sulked. She too wanted a flashy new car, and she wanted to be in the driver's seat. She wanted the world beating a path to her door. She wanted to be on a pedestal and stand above the mass. She radiated toward the light of fame and cursed the shadows of obscurity. She held Saxton and Harpers responsible for the tiny royalty checks she received. In April 1928, Saxton wrote, "I have an idea that you are cross with me and I hope it is not true."[54]

Thomas R. Waring, the former head of the Poetry Society and the Pinckney family's longtime adviser, hated to see Pinckney so downcast. He tried to cheer this "shining sun" among the Charleston poets. When Waring learned that bohemian poet Alfred Kreymborg was teaching a course on the Southern Renaissance at the New School for Social Research in New York (with a whole session on DuBose Heyward and the Charleston Literary Movement), he sent him a copy of *Sea-Drinking Cities*, along with Davidson's review and a note suggesting that he might want to include a word on Pinckney, who was also a founder of the Poetry Society. Kreymborg was quite amenable to promoting Pinckney. A decade before when he was a member of Greenwich Village's notorious Liberal Club, he had asserted, "It is time woman played troubadour." He judged Pinckney less mature than Allen and Heyward in her writing but thought she had crafted "a finer impression of Charleston" than they did in *Carolina Chansons*. He included a brief note on her in his survey, *Our Singing Strength*, along with a passage from "The Misses Poar."[55]

Pushing his luck, Waring asked Kreymborg to judge the Poetry Society's Caroline Sinkler Award for the best book of poetry published in 1928. As hoped, Kreymborg chose *Sea-Drinking Cities* over Donald Davidson's *Tall Men* and Cale Young Rice's *Stygian Freight*. After relaying his decision, Kreymborg closed with a flourish, "I . . . doff my old slouch hat," the poet wrote Waring, "with the respect and love I feel for the South and its artists."[56]

With her dedication of *Sea-Drinking Cities* to the memory of Captain Tom, Pinckney was, in a sense, laying a wreath on the grave of her past. Most of the entries were paeans to old times in the Low Country, now a rapidly vanishing world that he had known and taught her to love. As one reviewer noted, Pinckney gave the impression of being in haste "to catch some of these fleeting things and souls before they fade entirely in the twilight that was yesterday, and will not be tomorrow or any more on earth."[57]

Captain Tom had been much on Pinckney's mind in 1927. Continuing a family tradition she agreed to join the board of the Charleston Museum and began her term in January 1928. After years of debate on how best to honor Captain Tom, the Pinckney family established a memorial at the Charleston Museum. Hoping to boost the cause of the museum and promote historic preservation, the Pinckneys had an interior from a doomed plantation house rebuilt in the cavernous museum building, which been built to host a Confederate reunion in 1899. Filled with appropriate period furnishings, many from their family, "The Chippendale Room" was dedicated on April 9, 1928. At the last minute, engineers concluded that the structure, hastily built on reclaimed marsh on upper Ashley Avenue, could not support the large crowd expected for the event. In a compromise solution, the room was enclosed and visitors peeped in through cut-out windows "as if a crime had been committed there," John Bennett quipped.[58]

In the summer, Pinckney dutifully accompanied her mother back to Gloucester. Camilla Pinckney's health was fragile. During their four-month stay, from July to October, Josephine frequently took her to consult with a doctor in Boston's Back Bay. Camilla's mind continued to be alert, however, and she closely followed the superheated stock market from the veranda of the Hawthorne House.[59] Despite doctor's caution, the seventy-four-year-old Camilla insisted on attending a family wedding in Dedham, Massachusetts. She collapsed during their trip and was rushed to a private hospital in Boston, but she died during an emergency operation. Josephine arranged for her mother's body to be shipped in a highly polished chestnut coffin back to Charleston.

On the day of Camilla Pinckney's funeral, the Gibbes Art Gallery closed at noon to honor her service to the Carolina Art Association. Eight limousines lined Wentworth Street waiting to take the family—the Pinckneys, Scotts, and Lyons—on the long procession up to Magnolia Cemetery where Camilla would be buried next to Captain Tom.[60]

# 7

## Thirty-six Chalmers Street

After the death of Camilla Pinckney, Josephine fled the overblown mausoleum of her past at 21 King Street. "I shall have to have a less exigent establishment if I am to do any writing," she wrote Hervey Allen. She explained her plans to first rent and then sell the looming mansion that had taken on the characteristics of her mother: formal, forbidding, and very high maintenance.[1]

In 1929, Pinckney spent August in Charleston for the first time in her life. The late summer that year was "mercifully cool"; she loved it. The sensual pleasures of the steamy Low Country more than compensated for the cool breezes of the grudging New England summers. "The earth fairly bursts with a profusion of good things," she reported to Allen, with "oleanders and musk-melons, crepe-myrtle and turtle-eggs, figs, and shrimp. I live like a lord and take my diversions on the beaches, surf-bathing and turtle-egg hunting." She also took some trips out to Eldorado and Fairfield, where she thrilled to find the yellow lotus blooming in the rice fields "like an opium dream." Life continued "chaotic in a minor way" while Pinckney made the transition to life without her mother. She started some new poems and submitted a few book reviews to Henry Seidel Canby's *Saturday Review of Literature*.[2]

Pinckney had earlier accepted the invitation of her brother Cotesworth and his nearly grown son Tom to link up with them in Chicago for a quick trip through Canada and the West. All during her vacation, Pinckney conducted negotiations by wire for a new house. She had fallen in love with a rather disreputable shambles at 36 Chalmers Street. In June, she paid $6,000 in cash to the estate of Benjamin McInnes for a near wreck of a rundown tenement that had been built about 1836 by Jane Wightman, a free woman of color. Pinckney scarcely had time to relax and contemplate her future before she received a telegram that Victoria Rutledge had been diagnosed with cancer. She returned to Charleston "post haste," fearful that she might lose her two mothers within a year. Although Rutledge's doctors were encouraging about her chance for recovery, Pinckney found this episode "a disturbing business." Victoria, Pinckney explained to Hervey Allen, "is as much a part of my life as the walls of my room, especially now that I am living alone."[3]

Before Pinckney left on her trip, she and Rutledge had quarreled about her moving out of 21 King Street. "Unshakable for style," Rutledge was incensed at Pinckney's insensitivity to the importance of maintaining appearances; Charlestonians drew social standing from their names and their addresses. In their heated interchanges, Pinckney recalled that Rutledge had been "uncompromising" and brutally pointed out "that I lack the courage for grandeur." She later admitted Victoria was probably right.[4]

A number of Pinckney's friends sided with Rutledge and were aghast at her decision to live in such a run-down part of town. The crumbling, old three-story masonry structure sat flush with the broken sidewalk on a side street that still had its eighteenth-century cobblestones, then a sign of neglect rather than charm. The house had more of a past than a history. At the time Pinckney paid her first visit, three families were squeezed in cheek-to-jowl, spilling out onto the side porches.[5] To make matters worse, the rear of the property abutted the parcel at 112 Meeting Street belonging to Standard Oil of New Jersey, and the company planned to tear down three Federal-era buildings to erect a filling station.

Pinckney's passion for the preservation of Charleston's unique architecture explains in part her determination to buy the Chalmers Street house. One of the first books to herald a new self-consciousness of Charleston's past had been Alice R. Huger Smith and D. E. Huger Smith's *Dwelling Houses of Charleston* (1917). In April 1920, about the same time that plans for the Poetry Society were just beginning to congeal, other Charlestonians, led by Pinckney's cousin Susan Pringle Frost, a suffragist who became the city's first female real estate agent, were holding the organizational meeting of the Society for the Preservation of Old Dwellings. "Let us keep to the things that have stood the test of centuries" was the principle expressed at the second meeting. No one section of the city or class of building was to be privileged over another. The goal was not only to promote "preservation" of the old but also "upbuilding" of the new in a way that would contribute to a harmonious whole.[6]

Pinckney and architect Albert Simons had a "beautiful time" poring over his skillfully drafted plans for her new home.[7] Once naysayers toured the shambles with Pinckney and Simons, they too could envision a world of possibilities. Simons was one of the most effective advocates for saving Charleston's architectural treasurers from both the wrecking ball and northern plunderer. Pinckney would point to remnants of fine molding and a nice mantle hidden in the warren of rooms on the second floor and invite skeptics to see a spacious, elegant living room, that is, once the flimsy partitions were ripped away. Simons could never detect the location of the original stairs but would enthusiastically explain his concept of a circular staircase traveling gracefully from the first floor receiving room up to the third story where he could tuck a guest room and a study for Pinckney. "Look at the light," she would instruct visitors to the south-facing room where she would write her five novels. This room had more than a view, she stressed; it had an "outlook." From her study window, Pinckney could see Robert Mills's Fireproof Building, Gabriel Manigault's City Hall, Washington Park, and the spire of St. Michael's Church.[8]

Curious Charlestonians who regularly strolled down Chalmers Street to check on the progress at number 36 were taken aback when they saw painters making the first broad brush stokes across the gray stucco. Pinckney, still savoring the memory of pastel houses set off with scarlet bougainvillea in Madeira, made a bold gesture and painted her house a delicate shade of heliotrope with pale green shutters. She reluctantly abandoned her desire for a Mediterranean-style red tile roof in a bow to architectural integrity; "you can't have everything," she reasoned. Simons salvaged a romantic wrought-iron balcony from one of the Meeting Street demolitions and made it accessible from Pinckney's second floor living room by transforming a window into French doors. Morning glories and bougainvilleas soon languidly spilled over from their pots. Pinckney's choice of a nonhistorical paint color for her house actually predates Dorothy Legge's decision to paint in bright hues the East Bay Street tenements she bought in 1931 that now make "Rainbow Row" a Charleston landmark.[9]

Thirty-six Chalmers also had another feature to recommend it. Its large lot encompassed the width of the whole block so that Pinckney's walk-through garage faced Queen Street. On the other side was the side entrance to the *Charleston Evening Post*'s offices, which fronted on Meeting Street. No one knows exactly when it happened, when Josephine Pinckney began to look at Thomas R. Waring, the middle-aged newspaper editor, with different eyes. While touring through France in the summer of 1927, she had carried a little notebook. In it, she kept a strict account of expenses—how much she spent for stockings and notepaper, how much her mother owed her for train tickets or taxis. She doodled as people do, when their minds wander; a sketch of a castle, the layout of the living room at 21 King Street, and the initials TRW.[10]

And no one knows when Waring began looking back. Perhaps the poet would answer that the ways of the heart are unfathomable. Reflecting on the evanescent nature of love, Pinckney once wrote of the "nearly impossible task of capturing delicate states of soul and body in words" and wondered if "perhaps love should be a private and personal thing, not to be revealed," even in poetry.[11]

After DuBose Heyward married and Hervey Allen left town, Pinckney had no one to escort her to little intimate evenings held by the inner circle of the Poetry

Society. Laura Witte Waring, the editor's wife of many years and sister of the poet Beatrice Witte Ravenel, had grown deaf and did not enjoy going out in public. Also, her haute Victorian upbringing made her uncomfortable with the changing social mores and habits evident even in a staid place such as Charleston.[12] With his Lamboll Street home just around the corner from the Pinckney mansion, it seemed sensible that Waring, president of the society and a frequent adviser to Camilla, might walk Josephine over to the Heyward's house on Church Street when poet Sara Teasdale was visiting, or offer to drive her across the Cooper River to a dinner meeting at the Isle of Palms where much of the town retreated in the summer.

Born in 1871, during Charleston's darkest days, to a family of equal antiquity as the Pinckneys (eight generations in the city), Waring was named editor of the newly launched *Charleston Evening Post* in 1897 and continued in that position for over thirty years. Tom Waring belonged to a nearly extinct breed, like the sole surviving Carolina paroquet, as one of city's last nineteenth-century men of letters. Waring's whole life revolved around language. Although his workaday occupation forced him to craft stories in the lowest common denominator of English, Waring enjoyed a reputation for his excellent taste in literature. His life had been one "heroic stream of self-effacement" and sacrifice for his family and community. By the time he was sixty years old, he could not remember ever being young. Waring once confided to Hervey Allen, "Life has not been one grand sweet song" and after all the years of hard work "some of the foolish ideas of youth, . . . are the only valuable possessions I have." "I want to be a poet," he confessed, "and with the poets stand."[13]

Waring and Pinckney also shared a devotion to the city of Charleston, which they considered a work of art in its totality. Few individuals provided such consistent, quiet support for civic and cultural advancement of the city as did Waring. A generous, talented, and modest man, he lent the columns of his paper to the promotion of other writers' careers. He performed the unglamorous work involved with organizing and fundraising to support the arts that was so crucial to the success of the Charleston Renaissance. Waring helped craft a zoning ordinance that would create the nation's first historic district. While serving on the innovative Board of Architectural Review, Waring monitored all new construction to promote aesthetic continuity in the old city.

With their mutual interest in the Poetry Society well known about town, no one thought twice about Pinckney stopping by the *Evening Post* offices. Whenever Pinckney appeared at the door, the aging editor must have felt that she illuminated not only all the dark corners of his cluttered office but also the hooded places of his soul. Her fashionable clothes contrasted with his traditional suits. Breezy, slim, and youthful (even though she had turned thirty in 1925), a hint of "It" still lingered about her. Waring's vest buttons, however, were strained by a slight paunch. Her freshness and energy breathed new life into the dreams that had not entirely deserted the aging editor. Pinckney's most striking characteristic, thought Charlestonian Warrington Dawson when he saw her in Versailles during her 1927 French tour, was not just her "wide-awake" mind and senses but that she was "awake all over."[14]

The passion Waring and Pinckney both felt for poetry and literature spilled over into their everyday lives and found expression in their attraction to one another. She began spending more time with him just as her interest in a man from her own set, her old acquaintance and off-again, on-again beau John B. Grimball, began to cool. Pinckney saved a clutch of Grimball's letters written in early 1927 which chronicle the petering out of their relationship—first their rendezvous at the "Dodo's Nest [Eldorado]," her fall into "hateful taciturnity," his complaints of the expense of "keeping you in dogs and gin," and finally his query, "Has another Hero been delivered yet?"

In Waring, Pinckney found a highly cultivated man with a first-rate mind who also knew and understood something of the world she craved. Perhaps most important, Waring could be supportive and promote her career wholeheartedly because he was at the end of his. Pinckney knew from watching other literary couples that a pedestal only has standing room for one and realized that marriage to the sort of powerful man to whom she was attracted would reduce her to a silhouette. With Waring, who clearly adored her and gloried in her success, marriage was safely out of the question. In the new front gate of 36 Chalmers Street, Pinckney had her own initials woven into the design wrought in iron and immutable to change. Over the years, Cherokee roses climbed that fence and grew into a fragrant bower.

Even Susan Bennett, who did not distribute compliments with abandon, wrote Hervey Allen in 1929 that Pinckney had lost her past "rigidity" and looked "prettier than I ever believed she could, with her whole manner relaxed and gentle." Without the constant prodding, belittling, and piercing diatribes of Camilla Pinckney, and with her career successfully launched with *Sea-Drinking Cities*, the adoration of one special man, and the attentions of many, the former diffidence softened a bit. When Pinckney learned of the birth of Hervey Allen's first child she wrote him, "Shall I wish for [her] to be a poet? I think so, on the whole. This is not to wish [her] happiness exactly, unless of an indirect kind, but perhaps this dubious happiness is the most satisfying in the long run, and in that belief I commend your child to the care of the Muses."[15]

Thirty-six Chalmers was choreographed as much as restored. Pinckney blended the traditional and the unusual to create the ideal backdrop for herself. Just as Amy Lowell had transformed Sevenels into a stage for her performance as a grand dame of American letters, so too did Pinckney design a set that presented her as *the* interpreter of the Charleston literary tradition for the modern era. In time, when visitors called on Pinckney they came away with the impression that they had been in the presence of "the perfect lady in a perfect Southern ode." She had established herself in a romantic setting with an "eloquently lovely house" and a small secluded garden. But the bold wash of color, invoking Charleston's passionate Caribbean past, intimated that another side of Miss Pinckney stirred beneath the "air of quiet, almost inhibited reserve" that she showed in Charleston.[16]

Visitors to Pinckney's home passed through the two exterior doors typical of Charleston single houses, which were one room wide, two or three stories high, and typically had side porches and presented their gable side to the street. The first door gives entry to the piazza with its dark green joggling board; the second, to the right, to the entrance hall. Victoria Rutledge, who ultimately made her peace with change, would open the door and invite guests to wait in a tiny pale blue reception area with its exquisite Madame Recamier sofa. A beaded rooster, a souvenir from a trip to France, perched in the window and relieved the room of some of its formality. A gilt cabinet displayed delicate old family treasures that had been passed down to Pinckney: Miles Brewton's silver skewers, Rebecca Motte's chocolate pot, Eliza Lucas's tea cup, and the opal knee buckles of her mother's great-great grandfather Peter Lyons. Governor Thomas Pinckney's court clothes and christening robe were tucked in a drawer; his sword from the Cincinnati lay atop the cabinet. At just the right moment, Pinckney would sweep down the stairs in a black velvet dinner dress adorned with a collar of old lace, looking "like her house, just as she should." After a gracious welcome, guests followed her up the narrow stairs through a pale green hallway and into the inner sanctum, a beautifully proportioned drawing room set off by white woodwork and bay windows.[17]

As Pinckney's fame grew, interest in her house expanded from curiosity about the heirlooms from her famous family to how her living space related to her art. An article in *Arts and Decoration* magazine praised Pinckney's renovation of this very elegant but not very large house as evidence of Charlestonians' ability to retain elegance while adjusting to the changing economic realities of the time; "no other people have known so well how to create and establish the same beauty of living in an abbreviated form." A writer for *Antiques* concluded after a visit to 36 Chalmers that living with beauty, with "Sevres and Sheraton, Chippendale and Sully," had actually "sensitized" rather than "stifled" Pinckney's perceptions.[18] Deprivation was not necessary, after all, for artistic juices to flow. Few knew, however, how much living every day among the reminders of family greatness pressed Pinckney to make herself worthy of all she had been given.

When Josephine Pinckney entertained, visitors forgot about the depressed economic times that plagued the country after the stock market crash of 1929 and felt transported in time back to Charleston's golden age. A glimmering chandelier illuminated old silver glowing with the soft patina of age; delicately etched crystal goblets held well-chosen wine. The "Pinckney china" completed the picture. Only the uninitiated ever reached for the silver salt and pepper shakers; Pinckney believed her cook so expert in the preparation of Low Country specialties that she never bothered to fill them. Her carefully orchestrated dinners always included the most amusing and erudite Charlestonians along with distinguished visitors to the city.

Pinckney's reputation as a hostess began to surpass her reputation as a poet during the 1930s. The vast network of acquaintances she had cultivated in the northeast not only angled for invitations when they vacationed in Charleston, but they sent letters of introduction for their friends. Carl Van Vechten asked Pinckney to entertain Marc Chadbourne because "He wants to see the best of Charleston." Another friend referred British author Harold Nicholson to 36 Chalmers. Nicholson perceived immediately that the charm and attractiveness of Pinckney stemmed from her perfect fit with her surroundings. In an age of such confusion over cultural identity, Nicholson was delighted to find in Charleston "a place where people were certain of their own background and not straining to discover another."[19]

The cocktails, the candlelight, a breeze wafting through French doors, the scent of loquat aloft, and Pinckney beautifully dressed, presiding at the head of the table, often confused her male guests. The next morning, they could not remember if it was Charleston or Josephine with whom they had fallen in love. Poet Robert Hillyer wrote Pinckney from the steamer taking him back to New York, thanking her for "two of the happiest days of my life" but also apologizing for his "uncourtliness" toward her after too many drinks ("At least I now know why it is called *Mule*"). "I AM NEVER GOING TO LET IT HAPPEN AGAIN," he promised and invited her to visit in New York.[20]

Gerald W. Johnson, a North Carolina–born journalist with the *Baltimore Evening Sun,* who enjoyed his well-deserved reputation for dynamiting tradition, was swept off his feet at a dinner at Pinckney's house in 1932 during a gathering of southern writers. "The sparkle has died out a bit, but the mellow glow remains," Johnson recollected when he wrote to thank her. "That charming old house, the lovely things in it, the admirable good cheer afforded, and a hostess worthy of so marvelous a setting—how could a Tar Heel fail to be enraptured and convinced that he had entered Charleston through a gracious gate reserved for the fortunate."[21] In such a setting, even a crusading southerner could forget for just one evening that there had ever been such a thing as that terrible war, its terrible losses, terrible poverty, the terrible injustices and even think that the aristocrats were not so terrible after all.

What Johnson did not tell her then was that the morning after, he awoke with feelings about Pinckney that had "disturbed" him. He dismissed his unfamiliar emotions blaming the seductiveness of the city, the high spirits of the company, and the free flow of liquor. But when Johnson saw her in 1935, when they both received honorary degrees from the College of Charleston, he felt once again that an undeniable "spark had passed" between them that he must acknowledge. "Upon my soul," the crusty newspaper editor wrote, "I have fallen in love with you." Quickly the married editor added that he was no "amateur Don Juan" seeking some seamy "amourette"; he was "as unromantic . . . as a gatepost." What he proposed was much more serious than sex—friendship, "a matter that should never be approached frivolously, but soberly and in the fear of God." Assuring her he felt sure she did not need another lover in her life, Johnson proposed trying to navigate "the gulf that separates the sexes and speaking honestly across it" in hopes of making "a friend of the first order." Only twice in his life, Johnson claimed, had he experienced this powerful recognition of a kindred soul, who was "essentially simple, honest and very fine . . . and commanded my admiration and affection ever since." But both times the objects of his emotions had been men. "In fact, what gets my goat," Johnson complained, "is that you are a woman. Had you been a man, I should have said without hesitation that here is another friend to swear at, and laugh at, and bedevil, and worry and love with all my heart. But a woman—good God, it isn't done."[22]

Other men had similar dilemmas. English professor Howard Mumford Jones wrote Pinckney a thoughtful letter about her future in literature and thanked her for her hospitality during a trip to Charleston but fumbled at the end for the proper closing to would convey his affection. In frustration, the usually eloquent Jones resorted to "and O hell—you're a good egg." DuBose Heyward, who kept up his correspondence and his love for Pinckney after his marriage and move from Charleston, also struggled for the proper tone. That she had an androgynous nickname helped. A letter in which he reflected on their "extraordinary friendship" over the years began "Dear Old Jo."[23]

In between her house renovations and entertaining, Pinckney had started work on a second book of poems. She wrote Harriet Monroe in May 1931 that "After a long period in which the flesh was more than willing but the spirit non-productive, I am back in the writing vein again and getting another book ready."[24] She had about twenty-three poems, some quite long, for her second volume, "Twelve Sang the Clock: New Poems." The title has the ring of familiarity. Amy Lowell's last book, *What's O'Clock* (1925) had garnered a posthumous Pulitzer Prize for the Brookline poet. In June 1931, Pinckney's "Yolanda's Garden" ran in the coveted top-center column, always reserved for a particularly well-wrought poem, of Canby's *Saturday Review of Literature*. In the poem, Queen Yolanda waits: "What clouds those rounded mirrors with discontent? / Is it a fear of dying or a fear of loving?" Later that month, Pinckney nearly lost her life.

Returning home with friends from a late-night party on Edisto Island, Pinckney was in the back seat when the driver sideswiped a passing car on the Savannah Highway and sent them crashing into a ditch. Only Josephine was seriously hurt. Her face was a mosaic of shards from a broken window; blood rushed from a lacerated vein in her neck that was sliced almost from ear to ear. In a piece of almost unbelievably good fortune, an off-duty taxi driver and his wife arrived on the scene. They quickly got Pinckney into their car; the taxi man sat with her in the back, holding a cloth to her neck wound, and supporting her upright so that she would not drown in her own blood. The man's wife took the wheel and drove "magnificently," like a woman possessed, with foot on the accelerator and hand on the horn. The taxi shook at speeds of nearly eighty miles an hour, shimmying across gravel and black top the six miles to town. In the sort of improbable coincidence that no novelist would attempt, just as the driver came to a screeching halt at the door of Roper Hospital about 1:30 A.M. and leapt out of the car, surgeon Dr. Robert Cathcart, making a late night call on a patient, walked up behind them. A few minutes longer in the back seat of the careening sedan and no surgeon's intervention could have saved her.[25] Her face healed nicely, but her throat was scarred for life.

Regrettably, Pinckney's second volume was never published, although the individual poems appeared in noted journals and magazines. She had matured as an artist, and her poems reflected her improved mastery of rhythm and technique, greater intensity and power, and broader themes. No longer the ingénue, she wrote darker poetry with references to death and suicide reflecting the sober emotions of a woman whose life was not quite the exciting journey it had seemed a decade before. Her courage wavered. Pinckney no longer thrilled to the unexpected knock on the door, but now worried about being alone in her house at night.

As the Great Depression ground down on America, not just the economic firmament but also the literary environment had changed. Gone were the Imagists; not a peep from the Dadaists. The New Poetry had become old hat. John Donne was making a comeback in some quarters, but Pinckney, a Wordsworthian herself, doubted the staying power of this "dryly abstract" seventeenth-century poet the second time around. Poetry lacked excitement, the readers had fled, and Pinckney could find no publisher.[26]

The economic rip tide threatened to sweep away all the advancements of the Charleston Renaissance as culture became a luxury. In 1933, Pinckney made a pilgrimage to the little cabin in the coastal settlement of Legaréville that Heyward and Allen had rented for their parties a decade before. It had disappeared, lost to the relentless rising tides. "The whole place looked entirely different, even the creek seemed to be in a different direction," Pinckney reported to Hervey Allen. "I shed a few wet tears into the dark backward and abysm of Time which seems to have swallowed all trace of us."[27]

The City of Charleston was broke; its workers paid in scrip. In 1931, the Carolina Art Association had six dues-paying members and a yearly income of $2,500. Its director, Robert N. S. Whitelaw, began taking in boarders to stay more or less solvent. Every mail delivery brought resignations from the Poetry Society; in 1933, the *Yearbook* ceased publication. After all his successes, Dubose Heyward was "crippled in the slump in stocks." Nature writer Alexander Sprunt found things so "dark" in the New York magazine game he moaned. "If I sold anything now it would be like getting the first check ever from an editor." Pink slips piled up on Herbert Ravenel Sass's desk.[28]

Pinckney's royalty check from sales of *Sea-Drinking Cities*, "the rewards of genius and verse," totaled one dollar in 1933 when the value of her total assets in property, stocks, and bonds had shriveled by 75 percent. She wrote a note to John Bennett after receiving news that a local "Temple of Mammon at the corner of Broad and State Streets had locked their doors." "I fear that you are feeling, in like case with myself, slightly flattened by the toppling of the pillars. On the Biblical list of moth, rust, thieves, earthquakes, and rumors of war, as reasons for not overloving earthly existence, a cogent argument was missed when bank failures were not included, though the others really seemed enough . . . Well, God send us all a good ending."[29]

Henry Seidel Canby's effervescent faith in progress was so shattered by the

Great Depression that he suffered a psychological breakdown in 1930, then retreated to the safe nostalgic realm of the first American Renaissance to write about Thoreau and Whitman, but Pinckney reached down and found an untapped well of strength. She approached her new situation with philosophy. "I find living in reduced circumstances is not really so bad," she wrote Laura Bragg, "except for the feeling that I can't have my friends as freely. This and the distress of unemployment, and having little to give those who are hard hit are the bad features." "Pleasant quiet things," listening to the radio or the Victrola, filled her life with "social diversions having shrunk to a thin stream." To her friends' amazement, Pinckney began gardening in earnest. "My psyche feels so trimmed and squared and weeded," she told Prentiss Taylor. "My biceps are a sight to behold." And, of course, in those quiet moments, she found much more time for writing and reflection.[30] Rather than crush her spirit, the Great Depression actually forced Pinckney to plumb the depths of her talent as a serious writer.

On the positive side, as her ability to make charitable contributions declined, and with her parents gone and her brother in Richmond, Pinckney began to enjoy some freedom from the Code and the heavy weight of family duty. Her generation of the "clan" began breaking up with "lots of splits and quarrels" as fortunes declined. She picked and chose among her relatives. "I have family feeling of a sort, but am not close to my immediate family unless I like them," Pinckney confided to her diary and admitted acting "snobbish" toward those relatives who were not in her social circle.[31]

Pinckney transferred her affections and loyalty to a "family" of her own creation. The "irreplaceable" person in Pinckney's life remained Victoria Rutledge. At the end of the busy day, they could still "bask in the old contentment in each other." Rutledge resented the new housekeeper that Pinckney brought in to help her out, Lula Pencel Moore. Moore, who had first come to work in the Pinckney household as a young girl, now had a family and lived in her own home. Moore laid out clear guidelines that defined her relationship with Pinckney. She did not "live-in." She did not like to be referred to as a "servant." She saw herself as the "help," which indicated accurately her independence. Moore did not receive "wages" but pocketed her weekly "change." Moore was also very free with commentary on her employer, especially the fact that she was not very "bussinessfied."[32]

"Loo-la, Loo-laaa," was a familiar refrain that rang through 36 Chalmers Street when Pinckney entertained in her second-floor drawing room. Moore would sprint from the first floor kitchen to receive her instructions from Pinckney, who leaned over the highly polished mahogany railing to request fresh ice for cocktails or more shrimp paste and crackers. Pinckney's habit of command made some northern guests uncomfortable.[33] Still accustomed to being quickly obeyed from a lifetime of privilege and not yet faced with the full blown economic realities of the depression, she often took for granted the goodwill of her staff. Only years later did Pinckney fully appreciate all that Moore had quietly done for her, her willingness to work so hard, "to rub floors, and scrub, and try to economize for me—to stay late in the evening" when she gave her parties. A strict churchgoer, Moore did, however, strongly disapprove of liquor. Moore remembered and would recite with brutal accuracy all the missteps of Pinckney's guests who often had some difficulty navigating the narrow spiral steps when going home. Moore had high expectations of behavior from Pinckney's friends and did little to hide her disappointment at inappropriate behavior among the upper crust. Toward the end of one dinner party where the wine had flowed freely, the talk began to get a little loose while Lula was clearing the last course. One guest started to tell an off-color joke. "Wait, wait" warned another, "there is a lady present." The entire table fell silent, eyes downturned, until Moore, with great dignity, left the room.[34]

A generation younger than Rutledge, Moore possessed the "new style" approach to life fully reflecting what Pinckney called the "bourgeois propaganda" preached by the black ministers to their city congregations during the 1920s. Moore eschewed the turbans and gingham frocks of her elders for a neat black dress with well-starched apron, conducted herself in a formal manner, and took great pride in her work ethic. Moore took only the absolute minimum amount of time from her job when she gave birth to her babies. Being single-minded in her determination to have her children receive the best education available, she sent them to Catholic parochial school where they had a better chance than in the badly neglected segregated public schools. Moore expected her older children to take some responsibility to help out the younger ones, and they did. Their good report cards always found their way to 36 Chalmers and Pinckney's approving eye.[35]

Ironically, as Pinckney and her associates became increasingly interested in preserving the traditional Gullah language, Lula worked conscientiously to rid her speech of the old patois. Pinckney noticed that Lula began cultivating a "Yankee accent" as the number of northern visitors to Chalmers Streets increased during the 1930s, and she began interjecting such foreign pronunciations such as "Tooosday" into her everyday speech. Moore could also do a very convincing imitation of Miss Jo's own refined voice with its clipped and precise intonations. She unrelentingly chastised her own friends for their sloppy old-fashioned country talk and expressed only disdain for the spirituals that Victoria Rutledge sang with such energy in the kitchen. Sometimes Pinckney could hardly work as Lula raised her voice singing the gospel favorite "The Old Rugged Cross" to overpower Rutledge's

"Duh Blood Pit ee Maark on Me."[36] About this time, Pinckney also dropped Gullah references and themes in her poetry.

Moore became legendary for her defense of Pinckney's privacy and guarded it fiercely against bridge-playing ladies who planned their days around lunch. Knowing Pinckney's natural sociability and the ease with which she was often distracted from her writing schedule, Lula's deep voice could be gruff, even frightening, to callers, when she insisted they could not speak with Pinckney between 9:30 A.M. and 2 P.M., the hours she spent alone in her third floor study. Over the years, the three women of 36 Chalmers Street shared such a close bond that Pinckney played with the idea of writing a story about the "close interweavings of our lives—An Autobiography for Three" that would describe the daily interaction of the races in Charleston.[37]

At 36 Chalmers Street, Pinckney wove together her old childhood friends with an eclectic, "half-nutty" circle of interesting people she had met during her travels and winter residents from the North; the "otherworldly moneyed eccentricity" mingled easily with the Low Country aristocracy. This grouping of the "deliberately chosen" provided Pinckney with intellectual stimulation, pleasant diversions, travel companions, honest criticism, and the devotion often longed for, but not always realized, in a family. Through her frequent entertaining and keeping open house for distinguished visitors, she encouraged the friends she had made in a variety of venues to become friends themselves and, thus, enjoyed a net of supportive connections almost as dense as her Pinckney cousinage.[38]

Her friends also provided her with invaluable "research" into human nature for her future novels. When her girlhood friends had married and started their families, Pinckney observed them closely. Always a good listener, her natural reticence gave her intimates the feeling that she would take their secrets to the grave. Over the years, she watched from a remove as her friends played out the human drama. She saw the emotional neglect of children and the struggles of wives to strike a balance between marriage and aspiration. She observed their casual flirtations, was privy to confessions of adultery, and learned to spot those men "who liked gentlemen."[39]

Although appearing the quintessential Charleston "insider" in her social life, Pinckney often felt detached and alone in her emotional life. In her own mind, at least, she believed that her distinguished lineage, her standing as a literary figure, and her own reserved personality had combined to separate her from others. Some advantages definitely accrued from her reputation as "special," but still she could not help but "fret" about her alienation. "My chief line of connection with people," she wrote in her notebook, "is through being the sympathetic confidante . . . There's very little I can do for them—I know so few of the answers—except to be an *ear,* a safety valve. *But* I can give them *affection* and sympathy when they are in a state of frustration and insecurity. Of course, their 'expressions' dump wonderful material into my lap. I've never been able to use it directly, but no doubt I use it in my estimates of character and motive."[40]

Three women members of Pinckney's chosen "family"—Harriet Porcher (Stoney) Simons, Emily Sinkler Roosevelt, and Caroline Sinkler Lockwood—had been friends of her youth, schoolgirls on plantation house parties who matured into exceptional, well-read political activists with notably liberal political leanings and deep concern with public affairs. Simons, wife of architect Albert Simons, had, like Pinckney, descended from a line of highly intelligent, articulate and often blunt-spoken women. The nineteenth-century conservative ideologue, dramatist, and poet Louisa Susannah McCord was her ancestor. Her mother, Louisa Stoney (dubbed "the Woman" by her daughters) was the leader of a "ring" of ladies who ruled Charleston society. An outspoken advocate for women's rights, birth control, child welfare, and later civil rights, Harriet Simons and her husband were among the several couples (including young Thomas R. Waring Jr. and his wife Clelia) who helped anchor and stabilize Pinckney's life. Simons, "a Charlestonian by birth and inheritance," shared her view of the world. Affection for the city and for the South, Simons recalled, was "one of the controlling emotions of my life."[41] In consultation and cooperation with the Simons over the course of their long friendship, Pinckney practiced the "Charleston tradition," a last dutiful remnant of the old aristocratic code. Whenever a community need came to their attention, they would quietly recruit their friends, pool resources, and attempt to resolve it as a "private venture." Their projects ranged from saving some of the most important buildings in Charleston to underwriting the education of promising "native talent," black and white.[42]

Pinckney also maintained close connections with other childhood friends, two sisters who married outside of the Charleston circle. Emily Sinkler and Caroline Sinkler were born on Belvidere Plantation near Pinopolis, South Carolina. Their father was Charles Wharton Sinkler, brother of Elizabeth Sinkler Coxe and the fabulous Caroline "Aunt Cad" Sinkler of Philadelphia. Elizabeth Sinkler Coxe had introduced her niece Emily to the world beyond Belvidere Plantation and often took her on winter trips to Egypt. Elizabeth's son, Eckley Brinton Coxe, was a passionate collector of Egyptian antiquities. Sinkler ultimately made a proper match with the wealthy Philadelphia businessman, Nicholas Roosevelt, a cousin of the Hyde Park branch whose conservative politics had much more in common with those of his distant connection at Sagamore Hill. The Roosevelts bought Gippy Plantation, a working farm near the Sinkler family home in Pinopolis, in 1927. At Gippy, they gave lavish entertainments and sponsored "Jousting Tournaments," reminiscent of the Old South tilting contests. Earning the reputation as a doyenne of "gracious living," Emily Sinkler Roosevelt retained enough of the plantation girl about her to pad about Gippy in her bare feet. She served as chairwoman of the Democratic Women's national campaign committee in 1932 and the next year walked a picket line with women factory workers seeking a living wage.[43]

Emily Roosevelt's sister Caroline Sinkler ("Carrie" or Cad Jr.) was the baby of the Sinkler family. Her mother, Anne Porcher Sinkler, forbade her marriage to one of Pinckney's former beaux, Dunbar Lockwood of Boston, and held her on the plantation with the powerful emotional adhesive that only southern mothers know how to apply. When her mother died in 1920, Carrie was free to wed. The Lockwoods ultimately settled in Harvard, Massachusetts, with Josephine Pinckney as a frequent visitor while on her New England jaunts.[44]

To add spice to the mix, Dunbar Lockwood's sister Grace, Pinckney's chum since their days at the Munoz sisters' "Pinelands" camp in New Hampshire, married ultraconservative financier Archibald Bulloch Roosevelt, son of the former president and his Georgia-born wife, in 1917. Grace became a tireless anti-prohibition advocate. This Roosevelt couple also made regular trips to Charleston, often enjoying Pinckney's hospitality at 36 Chalmers Street, where they seldom failed to ignite a controversy when talk turned to politics, as it usually did. Before a visit with Archie and Grace Roosevelt, Harriet Simons wrote her husband, "I pray I fill my mouth with food and not with hot words."[45]

In the dining room of 36 Chalmers, Pinckney oversaw and promoted a trend that was occurring in similar venues across the nation; the reunion of the national elite who once dined and danced together in fashionable watering holes at Virginia spas. As Democratic politics squeezed the old ruling classes of both North and South out of power, they found common cause, or at least comfort, with old adversaries. During the 1920s and into the 1930s, wealthy northerners drifted back into the southern orbit; only this time the Yankees now owned the great plantations. In their twilight years, the American aristocracy chose to let bygones be bygones in the wake of other enemies and clustered together.

The rise of the Franklin D. Roosevelt "menace" encouraged a sympathy between the northern industrial capitalists and the old Low Country gentry. Consider the proposition that the enemy of my enemy is my friend. Add to that the fact that most of the northerners were usually agreeable, sometimes clever, and almost universally well-informed about ducks and quail. Political coalitions have been founded on less. Doubting the Democratic Party's candidate was like having to admit that God was dead, but conservatives such as Tom Waring's brother-in-law and local newspaper editor William Watts Ball felt like political orphans, and they looked expectantly in every political newcomer's face for an alternative to FDR. "Drinks parties" at Josephine Pinckney's house often took on the tone of a gathering of Whigs in 1850, the political party that had been expansive enough to accommodate southern planters, New York merchants, and Massachusetts mill owners. As happened in all political coalitions, some moved to the left and others moved to the right, but at 36 Chalmers, a good time was had by all.

The first wave of northerners converging on Charleston after the Civil War was a group of civilians following in the shadow of the Federal army of occupation and popularly denigrated as "carpetbaggers" because they toted their few possessions in cloth satchels. Much of the mythology about the carpetbaggers' determination to take advantage of a prostrate South has been discredited, but many did come to make a profit. The second wave, children of the North's industrial aristocracy, came to play. Discovering the salubrious winter weather, northerners began buying up inexpensive plantation lands and enjoying themselves like children, shooting over baited fields, building golf courses, and organizing horse shows to display their fine hunters. Much of the region's cultural renaissance in the 1920s may have been inspired by Charlestonians, but it was underwritten by the contributions of these northern birds of passage. When Josephine Pinckney was elected a trustee of the Charleston Museum in 1928, taking on her father's old position, she was put in charge of soliciting out-of-town prospects and found a willingness to contribute from everyone she asked.

Many northerners of more recent wealth who gathered at 36 Chalmers Street, however, praised Franklin Roosevelt. Marjorie Nott Morawetz, accompanied by her husband Victor, glided gracefully onto the Charleston scene in 1929 in search of a warm climate to improve her much older husband's health. She had the unique ability to be dignified and fun at the same time. Descended from a family of distinguished educators and lawyers (one grandfather was Mark Hopkins, famous president of Williams College; the other, Eliphalet Nott, headed Union College in Schenectady for sixty years), Morawetz had dabbled in romantic, left-wing politics. She worked in settlement houses uplifting the urban downtrodden and agitated for equal suffrage. During this period, she shared a free-spirited romance with Max Eastman and helped edit his early works. "I loved Marjorie as Spinoza loved God," Eastman later recollected, "with an intellectual love."[46]

The Morawetzes had only been married for five years when they arrived in Charleston and became among the most generous patrons of the city. Highly cultured and European-educated, Victor Morawetz possessed one of the most brilliant legal minds in the country. After graduating early from Harvard and writing his first legal text at twenty-three, he had become enormously wealthy in his capacity as counsel to both Andrew Carnegie and J. P. Morgan and as counsel and chairman of the board of the Atchison, Topeka, and Santa Fe Railroad. Morawetz and her husband fell in love with Charleston and its people. They restored Fenwick Hall, a romantic ruin on Johns Island along the banks of the Stono River and helped save many other endangered properties in the city.[47] They also preserved the crumbling Pink House, a tiny seventeenth-century tavern at 17 Chalmers Street, a block from Pinckney's home, where they held parties. Pinckney became fast friends with the Morawetzes and enjoyed meeting their frequent guests at Fenwick Hall who ranged from Sara Delano Roosevelt and Woodrow Wilson's adviser Colonel House to British actor George Arliss and his wife Florence. One Easter, the Morawetzes brought Milton Berle, as the "whiskered catch," to Pinckney's annual cocktail buffet.[48]

The Morawetzes were particularly supportive of the Society for the Preservation of Spirituals and played an important role in making it perhaps the best known aspect of the Charleston Renaissance. They helped organize a northern tour for the singers of Spirituals Society, who were advertised by New York's Thursday Evening Club as survivors of a "vanishing civilization."[49] After this concert the Morawetzes hosted a dinner at the apartment that included Corrine Roosevelt Robinson, sister of Theodore Roosevelt. She observed that the Charlestonians had many of the qualities of her Georgia-born mother and displayed "that enchanting breeding that the old Southern families have to an extent that is rare anywhere else."[50] When the Spirituals Society decided in 1933 they would like to give a "complimentary concert" at the White House, Marjorie Morawetz was asked to contact Eleanor Roosevelt. She assured the First Lady that the singers were not blackface minstrels but descendants of "the most sacrosanct first families who wear lovely costumes, preserve the old songs, never take money for themselves and are so really good beside being charming." In fact, she and her husband both believed "they are a group of people who for *many* reasons you might like to meet."[51]

The only thing the Morawetzes asked of Charleston for all their good works was to join the St. Cecilia Society. Victor was blackballed (probably over rumors of Jewish heritage) by the Low Country "elite" whose only real remaining power was the power to exclude. The Society for the Preservation of Spirituals, actually the more select of the two associations, invited him and his wife to become "honorary members."[52]

The northern colony generally elevated the tone of social life and intellectual life in Charleston, a community famously resistant to new ideas. In 1933, Pinckney ventured that as "the sea of culture is beginning to rise," Charlestonians were becoming "quite art minded." She wrote Prentiss Taylor that Robert N. S. Whitelaw had arranged for a traveling exhibit of reproductions from the collection of the Museum of Modern Art to come to the Gibbes Art Gallery the next year. When it was installed, eight hundred curious Charlestonians passed through the gallery and left with their minds broadened a bit if not changed. Charles Fraser's minia-tures, Pinckney thought, were secretly still Charleston's passion. In 1936, Solomon Guggenheim, who owned a mansion on the Battery, offered to let the Gibbes stage the public premiere of his collection of "non-objective art." In order to create the proper setting, Guggenheim also made a substantial gift to redecorate the gal-lery and provide new lighting. Pinckney predicted Kandinsky and Klee would "set Charleston on its ear." Viewers tilted their heads this way and that, wondering if what they had just seen was indeed art, just as they had wondered earlier if the work of Carl Sandburg and Robert Frost was indeed poetry.[53]

After a visiting lecturer had panned the modern exhibit from MoMA, a tall elegant woman in her sixties approached the podium and berated him for his philistine views. Sophisticated New Yorker Alice Kydd Carmalt Huntington had joined Charleston's winter colony at Marjorie Morawetz's suggestion. She become another major supporter of the arts in the city, as well as a close friend of Pinck-ney's. Warm, kindly, and thoughtful of others, the widowed Huntington, whose husband had been a distinguished professor at Columbia University, filled a moth-erly space in Pinckney's life. Huntington became quickly known for her generos-ity, not only to cultural groups but also to cash-strapped Charlestonians.[54]

Over the years, Pinckney's friendship with the Massachusetts artist Bay Wig-glesworth also deepened. Her embarrassing episode with Bay's brother-in-law, Dick Wigglesworth, receded into the past. His career as an earnest, but scarcely electric, representative of his Massachusetts district in the U.S. House of Repre-sentatives ground along unremarkably. Bay had developed her talent for painting to the point where her work was achieving critical attention. Life with the card-playing, golfing set that summered around the family place at Manchester-by-the-Sea bored her to death, mainly because she could beat all comers, but she loved the briny coast around Gloucester to the north. Pinckney visited Bay every Sep-tember when she could no longer stand the Low Country humidity. They delighted in packing a picnic and heading into the countryside (without the Wigglesworth children). At a scenic spot, Wigglesworth would pull out her paints and Pinckney, her latest sheaf of poems. While Bay tried to capture the beauty of the spot, Jo would read her poems out loud. Sharing the desire to seize all the sweet things in life, they always had their coffee and dessert first.[55]

Opposite in almost every way to Pinckney's other friends was sophisticated novelist Grace Zaring Stone who rocked downtown Charleston in 1931 when she breezed into Tradd Street's Brewton Inn. Titian-haired with "incandescent" beauty, Stone had opted to stay behind in Charleston with her daughter Eleanor when her husband Captain Ellis Spencer Stone, a career naval officer, shipped out for sea duty. Heads turned when she began attending meetings of the Poetry Society. Besides her good looks, which proved almost fatally attractive to men, Stone possessed the glamour of a published author. She also had a movie contract for her second novel, *The Bitter Tea of General Yen* (1930), which drew from her years living in China. DuBose Heyward joined a steady stream of local gentlemen who felt that neighborliness demanded that they call on "Miss Gray-ace" with some regularity to check on the well-being of this lone woman. Pinckney's close friend Sam Stoney fell particularly hard for the exotic outsider. Full of amusing anecdotes from her travels and a gold mine of literary gossip, Stone admitted she "preyed on the kindness of Charleston" and spent the winter as a popular guest.[56]

A year younger than Pinckney, Stone's early upbringing could scarcely have been more different. Motherless since birth, Grace was passed around among relatives. At one point, she fell under the care of an actress who kept her in a thespians' boarding house and even got her a part in a play that ran for a year. Grace was sent to a New York convent school after that and later studied music and dance in Paris.

With the exception of Pinckney, who often perversely enjoyed bucking popular opinion in Charleston, Stone found few friends among the women of the city who resented her casual flirtations, open sensuality, and total freedom from the Code. Susan Smythe Bennett bluntly asserted "everyone will be better off" when she leaves town. "Our Gracie" was the frequent topic of local gossip. Rumors flew around town that she was as familiar with cocaine as with whiskey. Whenever "Miss Gray-ece" was around, wives fixed hawk's eyes on their husbands, lest she vamp them away, and with good cause. Stone always wedged out the competition for the most attractive man in the room. Telling Pinckney about a visit to a mutual acquaintance, Grace related that all her hostess's friends were interesting and "one of them developed into quite an exciting beau for me—which is always satisfactory."[57]

Stone evoked jealousy wherever she went, and she especially loved to gossip to Pinckney about the various catfights among women authors. When editor Maxwell Aley gave a party in her honor, she reported to Pinckney, Virginia novelist Isa Glenn went around "all evening saying that she saw no reason to make a fuss over me as I was quite clearly—shall I say it—a bitch." Despite Glenn's organization of a "cabal supposed to make me have a bad time, I knew nothing of it, never remembered which one she was," and thoroughly enjoyed herself. When Isabel Paterson, lethal critic at the *New York Herald-Tribune,* later held a party for Stone, she invited only men. "And that was quite all right with me," Stone added, "which may prove Isa Glenn to have been right."[58]

Stone left Charleston in 1932 for California when her husband was reassigned. She made Pinckney envious with a note written while basking on Coronado beach: "Hollywood has engaged a thousand Chinese laundrymen for my film and they held a contest to decide which of thirty possible actors had the most sex appeal for the general."[59]

For her part, Pinckney shared with the worldly Stone tales of her own "flings" in Europe and New York, a side of her life she hid from her Charleston friends. Chiding Pinckney for passing up the casual attentions of an army officer they encountered on their travels, Stone wrote, "Tell me, by the way, how you managed to resist that attractive Major Young! You are the best resister. I wish I were more like you in that, as in many ways." At heart, both Pinckney and Stone were bound by a lust for fame that surpassed any passion they had for the male conquests they made along the way.[60]

One of Pinckney's pet peeves was the smug superiority of married people and their assumption that unmarried women simply withered alone without companionship of the conjugal variety. Pinckney found numbers of men anxious for her company well into her middle age. Of course, she had to analyze all her relationships. When the husband of a relative starting making advances toward her, she scrutinized her feelings toward him. "It is probably that his hostilities and aggressiveness arouses a kind of sexual timidity in me something I've felt several times with strange men who made advances," she wrote in her journal. "Anyway, I mustn't fight his egotisms, but remember to build him up [because he] sounds like a man with a bad sexual conflict who has to prove his virility." Although he had not yet made any overt passes at her, "I think he'd liked to"; "I may resist him out of snobbishness." She later returned to her notebook and penciled in "He did—and I *did.*"[61]

Grace Stone, well-connected, well-known and often controversial, became deeply involved in the politics of publishing. She was a partisan of Irita Van Doren and her book section of the *Herald-Tribune* while Pinckney carried the flag for Henry Seidel Canby and the *Saturday Review.* Stone felt Canby was "consistently snooty to me" and "unjustly so as I believe." Stone had little patience with long discussions about the democratic imperatives to uplift the American mind or of the ethereal pleasures of the well-crafted line. Stone had a hard, practical edge; writing was a business. She had started writing novels to subsidize the active social life she and her husband, a young naval officer, led when they were first married and posted in Washington. Stone had no artistic pretensions. She wrote ripping good tales for popular magazines that paid well. Nor did she shy away from provocative themes. The *Saturday Evening Post* turned down one story she wrote as "immoral and censorable," but a women's magazine picked it up. "What the American businessman can't stand, his wife can!" she wryly observed.[62]

Stone, innocent or indifferent to the importance of being "a Pinckney," resented Josephine's expectation of deference. Pinckney never learned, nor tried to learn, the simplest kitchen skill, and when she made extended visits to the Stones, which she did in Europe and in Mexico, she would sit purse lipped with impatient leg swinging until someone dashed to the kitchen to make her coffee. Stone, who struggled to make ends meet in the early years, also resented Pinckney's pinchpenny ways. She "eats for two, drinks and smokes the same" without ever offering to pay for anything or even sending more than a card at Christmas, Grace Stone complained. She wondered if someone ordinarily so "full of sensitiveness and of humor and intelligence" might be using money in revenge because she in turn resented Stone's "acting the femme fatale, the devoted mother, the successful writer."[63]

But Stone maintained close ties with the Charleston author because, as she wrote early in their friendship, "I enjoy you more than nearly anyone I know," and she wrote early in their friendship, "You will have me on your hands for life more or less from now on. I don't know what you can do about it, but of course if it seems too bad you could commit suicide." In the end, Grace Stone summed up the feelings of Pinckney's ersatz family, that even though she was a poor correspondent, often imperious, and sometimes neglectful, "we are all agreed we love you."[64]

# 8

# Speaking for the South

In 1930, Pinckney's career again intersected with that of Donald Davidson when she reluctantly agreed to make her first foray into expository writing. Howard Mumford Jones, her friend from Chapel Hill, invited them both to participate in a symposium on the South. With a working title of "Civilization Below the Potomac," William T. Couch of the University of North Carolina Press envisioned a volume roughly constructed along the lines of Harold Stearns's *Civilization in the United States: An Inquiry by Thirty Americans* (1927) in which representatives of the younger generation of artists, intellectuals, and activists would comment on a wide range of subjects from politics to religion. He wanted a public expression of the modern temper as manifest in the South (the states of the old Confederacy) since World War I.[1]

Pinckney immediately regretted her decision. She found she was the only woman among fourteen participants, and she bristled at her assigned topic, "the southern social scene," an unchallenging task that evoked images of brides' luncheons and bridge clubs. Subverting Jones's intent by taking the social science approach rather than the teacakes and white gloves definition, Pinckney hurled herself into a flurry of extensive research on southern society. She considered her essay a continuation of her quest for truth about the South that engaged her as a poet. Of course, she consulted Davidson as "one of the few people I know in the South from whom I can expect a detached point of view." He was dragging his heels on his own chapter on trends in southern literature. His professional career was not going very well either, and he worried that he was much too "skeptical" and "pessimistic" about the direction of the South and southern writers for the optimistic book Jones imagined. He was frankly "scared" by the responsibility of making definitive statements about the controversial and tendentious issue of southern culture.[2]

Consumed with the "inexhaustible topic of the South," Pinckney fired off a series of questions about southern society to Davidson that revealed her own uncertainty about the region's inherent distinctiveness. She speculated with a bold iconoclasm that "much of what we think of as Southern," such as the "clannishness" of family groups or the cultivation of manners and personal relationships, were merely throwbacks to the nineteenth century, "habits left over from a lei-surely, horse drawn society." She even ventured that "southern" might merely be a synonym for "unprogressiveness." If so, she extrapolated, the days of southern distinctiveness were doomed by the modern tide of development and industry poised to engulf the region. Over the years, she had watched the regional charm of New England destroyed and wondered if the South was next.[3]

For all their mutual admiration, Pinckney and Davidson actually talked past each other when speaking of the South. Pinckney, a well-traveled cosmopolite, saw the South as a multifaceted jewel with some conspicuous flaws. Davidson was turning inward, and in his search for an intellectual home began to imagine a South of an organic, almost mystical, unity, a prelapsarian paradise corrupted by industrialism. Technology had robbed Tennessee's tall men of their power.[4] In contrast to Pinckney, who developed a skeptical, probing modern sensibil-ity as she matured and traveled, Davidson had submerged his own ambivalence about the South in a romantic haze. He had begun constructing his concept of southern nationalism by imagining southerners as a distinct ethnic group imper-vious to change. "The South is pretty much the same everywhere, in spite of local diversities. It is just more so, here; and less so, there," he wrote Pinckney.[5] Lying beneath the talk of a different civilization, however, was his yearning shared by many southern traditionalists for a moral community bound by a common faith. Thinking he was perpetuating the southern tradition, Davidson had actually begun generating a new mythology for the modern age, since so much of the past had already faded away.

Pinckney saw something different when she surveyed the southern past and present. Unafraid to ask difficult questions about the aristocratic tradition, she was among the first to acknowledge that the quality of life that southerners enjoyed, their famous "hospitality," was made possible by large corps of black domestic help. Despite their leisure, wealthy southerners displayed a stunning lack of inter-est in philosophical and ethical speculation. Why was it, she asked Davidson, that "the South's contributions to human knowledge appear so small," and "why [do] we never promulgate new ideas ourselves?" After the brilliant founding generation and a few great minds, such as that of John C. Calhoun, in the antebellum years, the South had produced no original thinkers. "We have no equivalents that I know of to Emerson, John Dewey, or even Walter Lippmann. These men may be on the wrong track; their philosophies will go out of fashion, come back in, or possibly be outmoded, but at least they are working on the problems that beset humanity, and are trying by the method of trial and error—the only method we have, appar-ently—to comprehend our direction and to draw some conclusions that may guide us in the future." As far as Pinckney could fathom, all that really remained in the South of the aristocratic past was its deep-rooted conservatism.[6]

Davidson countered that southern conservatism was "a good thing." "Stability," he insisted, "is preferable to insufferable inconstancy." Why not be "cautious about accepting new ideas that tomorrow will have to be swapped and junked for other new ideas?" Although no longer a churchman himself, he defended the South's "militant Fundamentalism" as a counter to the watered-down religion in which traditional faith had been edged out by all the various "isms": "progressivism, which has all along linked up with transcendentalism, idealism, industrialism, efficiency—they all go together. Emerson, John Brown, Whitman, Wendell Phillips, Rockefeller, and Harry Emerson Fosdick are all spiritual brethren, in the same line of descent."[7]

Davidson admitted he was "raving" and confided to Pinckney: "The truth is, I am so full of stuff about the South that I am in danger of becoming a public menace. I have just finished and sent off to Harpers the manuscript of a book by twelve Southerners . . . which takes a pretty strong stand, rather conservative than otherwise, in favor of the Southern tradition as we understand it. It is not a symposium so much as a concordance [with all the essays leaning] in a single direction."[8]

Reflecting on the regionalist approach popular at Chapel Hill, Davidson admitted that "we are all rather definitely opposed to the North Carolina trend, though not, of course, without sundry admirations here and there, and much friendship." Never developing a plantation aristocracy to slow down the state's adoption of new modes of thought, North Carolina moved much more quickly into the modern age than the neighboring bastions of conservatism of Virginia and South Carolina. During the 1920s, the Tar Heel state enjoyed a reputation as the most progressive of the southern states, with good schools, well paved highways, an equitable tax system, and more or less honest politicians. And yet North Carolina produced no poets.[9] The tone at the University of North Carolina was set by the regionalists, students of the new discipline of sociology, who doubted the uniqueness of southern culture. Led by Howard Odom and later Rupert Vance, the regionalists measured the progress of southerners on every quality of life issue from health to literacy, from bathrooms to radios, and found them at the bottom of every index. Where the Charlestonians had seen a renaissance, and the Fugitives an opportunity, the regionalists saw a crisis, a South plagued with poverty, disease, and racism. Their solution—to accelerate the industrialization of the region—made Davidson apoplectic.

In the summer of 1930, Pinckney retreated from the heated fray to contemplate the southern social scene from the vantage of the cool hills of West Cornwall,

Connecticut. She framed her essay, "Bulwarks against Change" as a response to the question, "Can the South's deep provincialism survive the invasion of new people and new ideas?" In rejecting the term "social scene" as too static, she asked her readers to imagine the South not as a tableau fixed in time but as a fast moving river. "Industrialism," she observed, "having gained momentum slowly in other sections, has carried away the dam erected by Mason and Dixon, those famous engineers, and pours in full freshet upon the southerner slumbering beneath his live-oak tree. Whether he rides the waves or [is] ignominiously rolled along the bottom is yet to appear, but his movement is certain to be lively."[10]

Pinckney, who understood history as a succession of generations, dramatized the particular swiftness of change in the South by pointing out the great varieties of experience that have shaped its people. The plantation-born possessed a much different outlook on the world than those growing up during the Great War, whose viewpoint differs greatly from the next wave, "the corn-liquor generation," raised in the shadow of prohibition, whose main interests in life seemed to be "speed, and the sports page."[11] Speed, the change in the rhythms of life, Pinckney surmised, presented perhaps the most serious challenge to traditional southern life. Even in southern towns, people adapted more or less the same patterns as those in the country. For the southerner who embraced a "rather ritualistic attitude" toward the dinner table, a leisurely dinner in the middle of the day was one of the most important institutions of everyday life. The three o'clock dinner, often amended to the two o'clock dinner during the work week, was a lingering remnant of Charleston's West Indian influences.

Many of the founding Carolina families had gained their first plantation experience in Antigua or Barbados before coming to Carolina. During their Caribbean interlude, English planters learned the wisdom of adjusting the rhythms of their labors to the intensity of the sun that burned brightest in the hours after noon. Clinging to a tradition that had little practical justification in the nine-to-five workday of industrial America was, Pinckney understood, a symbolic "bulwark against change," subtle resistance to the tyranny of the time clock. Pinckney related the story of the misguided bank manager in "a certain southern city" who violated Old South tradition in search of New South efficiency. When he proposed instituting a lunch room in the bank basement serving cold sandwiches so that employees did not have to take time to go home for okra soup and shrimp pie, there was a general mutiny. Pinckney predicted that with declining leisure time becoming a fact of modern life, "the eighteenth century will have increasingly hard going in the twentieth," even in Charleston.[12]

The changing role of women in the modern world similarly presented a challenge to the old way of life in the South. The forces of modernism "tended to level the differences, not only between the sections, but between the sexes also." The landscape of the business districts in southern cities changed markedly with the introduction of the female secretary after World War I, high-stepping with no gloves, no hat. Southern women suffer from the two messages that they have received in their lives. One, from their mothers and the older generation, says be "a lady," attractive and pleasing to men; the other, from modern pressures, encourages them to assert their equality and worth through a career and competing with men.[13]

Resistance to change found its most potent expression in politics. Conservatism, Pinckney grants in a nod to Davidson, has a place in a time of national turmoil, such as the dislocations of the Great Depression. But economic conservatism, the unwillingness to provide an environment congenial to industry, only continues the circle of poverty forged by the Civil War. Once-proud country families have been unable to climb out of their impoverishment through farming. Embarrassed by their circumstances in comparison with northern city dwellers, the southern farmers are susceptible to the "inferiority complexes of poverty" and defeat, producing an "exaggerated sensitiveness to criticism." However, Pinckney added, because of their volubility and love of talk, southerners enjoy remarkable freedom from the other "complexes" that haunt the lives of northerners, and this perhaps explains their lack of "deep thinking in the intellectual realm or in the realm of philosophy and pure thought." Southerners did not probe deeply into the nature of their own society because they uncritically loved "the land that bred them."[14]

Pinckney believed that in 1930 the world was witnessing "the last stand of the Thin Gray Line." Clearly the line was buckling, "but will it break under the new invasion" of people and ideas, she was not sure. One thing she did believe wholeheartedly. The "Union, one and indivisible, is a solid fact of American life," and "for every difference, North and South, there is a similarity."[15]

When Pinckney arrived home from New England in September, she found a thick packet from Nashville waiting for her. In late August, Davidson had put together a "long screed, or series of screeds, for her consisting of carbon copies of this, that, and the other—the whole composing a kind of prospectus of our book" and a "statement of principles." He sought her "critical advice." "You will probably be aghast to discover how ridiculous we are about to make ourselves before the public," Davidson warned Pinckney. But he held out the possibility that the Agrarians still might get "the last laugh ourselves, sometime, somehow." Admitting the impracticality of many of their proposals, Davidson hoped that these substantial essays on a wide range of topics finally would change the reputation of the South as anti-intellectual.[16]

Remembering the Vanderbilt contingent's insistence on finding the universal in literature, Pinckney was amazed to learn they had regrouped under new colors and taken up the cause of the South. The Fugitives had come down (at least part way) from their ivory tower and hammered out a romantic form of agrarianism. Although Tate and Davidson liked to compare themselves to General Lee at Gettysburg bringing the war to the North, Pinckney thought their fate more likely to be that of General Pickett. The "Twelve Southerners" made an emotional, headlong, foolhardy, direct charge, with fixed pens against the forces of Americanism—industrialization, liberalism, capitalism. The great disorganized mass of papers landing on Pinckney's doorstep was the genesis of one of the most original and provocative statements coming out of the modern south, *I'll Take My Stand*. The Agrarians, some former Fugitives, joined in a common cri de coeur that "life should determine economics and not economics life."[17]

Pinckney surveyed Davidson's "collected works" with interest and sympathy, but her natural skepticism intruded. She confessed, "I am less hopeful than you." Although she too connected "all social ills to the avalanche of industrialism," she explained, "I can't, at present, see what we can do about it, since it is not at all the South's problem, but the world's problem, or rather the problem of the times. I agree with you, however, that it doesn't do [to] sit under it,—it is only that, having jumped up, I don't know which way to go. But your group will doubtless work something out; you are plainly destined to provide the leadership which the South needs, and at least one South Carolinian will enlist under your banner."[18]

Davidson in reply admitted, "Perhaps we are not quite as hopeful as our arguments might suggest. We have no notion that we—or others who might be more able and influential than we are—can stop the avalanche, offhand. But we do hope to get the atmosphere clarified somewhat, to draw people out of their holes and get them to declare themselves, even to stiffen the resistance of Southern folks to some degree, . . . It makes us feel good to have you on our side, and I hope you'll find the book, when it appears, not too foolish and not too unworthy of the cause we are devoted to."[19]

With the former competition with the Charleston poets now faded away, Davidson and other remaining Fugitives thought of Pinckney as a compatriot. John Crowe Ransom judged the time he spent at 21 King Street with her during a lecture stop at the Poetry Society in 1928, as "my pleasantest recollection of Charleston" of both the "literary and personal" nature. In 1932, Allen Tate included her (and no other Charleston writer) with the Nashville poets in the "galaxy of stars" of southern letters who shared "feelings for nature and the humane life." Fugitive poet Merrill Moore sent Pinckney a new book of his poems with the assurance that "it carries considerable feeling about the debt we owe you for your continued friendliness and interest."[20]

Davidson invited Pinckney to join him in Richmond in November 1930 for his debate with Stringfellow Barr on the questions raised by *I'll Take My Stand*. Barr was a professor of English at the University of Virginia and an editor of the *Virginia Quarterly Review*. He thought she might relish "the fray and (I hope) to give us a little much-needed support, bind up our wounds, etc." With friendship on both sides, she declined and laid low in Charleston, but the audience of nearly 3,500 that filled the Richmond City Auditorium included Ellen Glasgow, Henry Seidel Canby, James Branch Cabell, and Henry Mencken.[21]

After her initial reservations, Pinckney found the finished version of *I'll Take My Stand* "enthralling." She expressed her fervent hope to Davidson "that you will be the foundation stone of a newer South." Genuinely interested in the issues the Agrarians raised, she wrote her editor Eugene Saxton at Harper Brothers, conveying her interest in the Agrarians' efforts and offering to help promote their book. Saxton agreed with her opinion that "they are up against a pretty tough proposition," but added, "I like the spirit of the attack."[22]

Pinckney did offer one recommendation "along practical lines" for Davidson's consideration. She believed industrialization to be a global, rather than a regional, problem and could see the similarities between the struggles of the South and Ireland, as both fought for their economic and cultural identity. She suggested the Agrarians contact Irish journalist and poet George William Russell, also known as A.E.; "We need all the help we can get."[23] A theosophist, mystic, and visionary, A.E. was not a dreamy theoretician but a saint who helped launch a war. He had inveighed his young protégés, Padraic Colum and James Stephens, to fight alongside working men of the unions in Dublin in 1913 and designed the flag, "The Plough and the Stars," carried by James Connolly's ill-fated citizen army during the Easter Rebellion of 1916. A.E. was also a writer of powerful political prose, a skill honed when first an editor of *Irish Homestead* and then the *Irish Statesman*, a liberal weekly paper backed by sympathetic Americans. Brought to politics by the plight of Ireland's poverty-stricken farmers, he advocated farm cooperatives and worked out a combination of economic and political democracy in his book *National Being* (1916), which sold ten thousand copies in the United States in the 1930s. A.E. found Americans "very depressed here about both agriculture and urban industry, and [would] listen eagerly to any solution to their problem."[24]

While in New York early in 1930, Pinckney had met A.E. and was fascinated by the towering bear-like poet whose brown clothes looked like they had been tossed on with a pitchfork. Kind eyes illuminated a face otherwise full of undisciplined whiskers. His whole being radiated good will.[25] Pinckney had discussed the ideas of the Nashville Agrarians with the Irishman, who seemed interested. A.E. was, after all, practicing what the Agrarians preached. He advocated replacing the "root, hog, or die" capitalist approach with the cooperative ideal that would make the Irish economy both more efficient and more humane. Pinckney and A.E. talked of how the economic agricultural reform and poetry might somehow be merged, and she invited him to speak to the Poetry Society in Charleston.[26]

A.E. arrived in Charleston in the spring of 1931. He addressed the Poetry Society on the importance of dreams to poets and told the fascinated crowd in his mesmerizing voice about the fairies, angels, and cherubim who advised him. He chanted some of his best known poems from heart as he always did, swinging hypnotically from syllable to syllable.[27] Pinckney took the Irish poet for the Low Country tour. He thought Middleton Place looked "like the gardens of a great king." A.E. had not expected to like the South because of its history of slavery, but he felt very much at home. He preferred the southern philosophy of "let us then lie down and idle" to the New Englander Henry Wadsworth Longfellow's "Let us be up and doing." He agreed with Pinckney that the South was quite obviously caught in a web of economic circumstance and destitution not so very unlike that of Ireland. A.E. wrote in his *Memoirs* that the South had gone "to pieces after the slaves were freed . . . There are great numbers of rich places, some going to ruin, others are bought up by the Northern inhabitants and kept in good order. The Northern victor inherits the civilization of the Southern rural aristocracy. I understand the Confederate point of view now as I never did before, and I rather like the Southern passion for a rural life and culture as against the machine civilisation of the New England industrialists. They are such nice human beings these Southern folk."[28]

Eager to have her voice included in the second great debate about the South, Pinckney grew impatient while her essay gathered dust at the University of North Carolina Press. Few of the other authors had been as conscientious as Pinckney. The promised articles dribbled in. Howard Mumford Jones lost interest. He and Couch clashed over the purpose and direction of the symposium, as well as over the quality of several of the essays. When Jones took a position at the University of Michigan, Couch assumed control of the project and began a thorough revision, more or less going back to square one. He tossed out some essays (keeping Pinckney's) and invited more writers to participate. Several years would pass before the revised volume was published.

Another project quickly claimed Pinckney's attention. Herbert Ravenel Sass, noting the increased national interest in the South, proposed that the Society for the Preservation of Spirituals compile a collection of essays, poetry and songs as a fundraiser for the relief and improved medical care of the "old time negroes." Pinckney joined over forty Charlestonians in producing this "labor of love," *The Carolina Low-Country*.[29] By 1930, she had helped transcribe almost 120 spirituals; fifty spirituals, most published for the first time, were included in the book, as were essays by Sass, DuBose Heyward, Tom Waring, and Sam Stoney.[30]

Pinckney also gave the society permission to reprint her prizewinning poem from 1927, "Island Boy," about the country joys of a white boy finally free to join the play of black children during summer vacation.

> The beach—the beach! Round his wet legs the water swirling
> Curls under—rasps—curls under, scuffles the shelly sand;
> Moon-washed and wave-washed, endless the coast appears;
> He races whirling foam, light as gull-shadows whirling
> Races with whish of wind enormous in his ears.

When Major Alfred Huger approached H. S. Lathan of Macmillan Press about publishing *The Carolina Low-Country*, he explained that Charlestonians had given their time to honor the history of a special place and as "a memorial to other days." He quickly assured the New York editor that northern readers would find no "harsh note in the book. We have gone beyond that here."[31]

Pinckney was intrigued in January 1931 by a cryptic note from DuBose Heyward. Fresh from a meeting in Charlottesville, Virginia, he wrote: "Something really big and interesting is in the air. It's for next fall, and you're to be in on it." Heyward had just participated in a meeting called by Professor James Southall Wilson, a Poe scholar at the University of Virginia, to discuss the possibility of bringing together about thirty of the leading southern authors. The university's president, Edward A. Alderman, an editor of the old *Library of Southern Literature* series, shared Wilson's contagious enthusiasm. So did Ellen Glasgow. According to Heyward, the committee did not have anything too serious in mind, more like a big house party than a seminar.[32]

An invitation to the first annual Southern Writers' Conference in Charlottesville followed Pinckney all over New England and finally caught up with when she stopped in the Berkshires for a music festival. She accepted the committee's invitation immediately. "Not for pearls and platinum would I miss such a delightful gathering as this promises to be," Pinckney responded to Professor James Southall Wilson.[33]

One thing had not changed in the decade since the beginning of the southern literary revival; the hotly contested debate over who could speak for the South. The invitation list of more than thirty authors suggested how spacious a realm "southern literature" had become. Authors in attendance ranged from the brooding William Faulkner, who had been receiving praise for his violent novel *Sanctuary,* to the frumpy Alice Hagan Rice, author of the much more popular *Mrs. Wiggs and the Cabbage Patch.* Heyward had proposed expanding the list to include historians such as William E. Dodd, "an ardent and unreconstructed Southerner" who "has done fine missionary work for us among the Yankees [at the University of Chicago]" and whose biography of Woodrow Wilson was "more important than most of our novels." The final list also included Ulrich B. Phillips, the Georgia-born specialist in southern history based at the University of Wisconsin who preached a New South gospel of "progress."[34]

The invitation committee fell into a terrible muddle in the case of literary couples. Bridge and tea were planned for spouses, meaning wives. When DuBose Heyward saw that his wife, Dorothy, an author and playwright as well as his collaborator, was not on the list, he brought this fact to the attention of Wilson. Heyward hastened to add, "If you need her place for someone else at the official meetings, she would be delighted, I am sure, not to attend." When Paul Green raised the issue of inviting Allen Tate's wife, Carolyn Gordon (who had recently published her novel *Penhally*), the committee agreed to send her a belated bid to join them. Tate tut-tutted and responded that Gordon "understands perfectly" why she was not originally invited, and he encouraged the group not to give her a second thought.[35]

As the date for the meeting approached, Pinckney drove south as far as Richmond where she met up with Emily Clark Balch, former editor of *The Reviewer,* who now lived with her husband in Philadelphia. They rode together to Charlottesville chatting the whole way about the current field of southern authors. After hearing so much about Allen Tate from Donald Davidson, Pinckney finally met him and Carolyn Gordon for the first time. She was also introduced to Sherwood Anderson, who remembered her as quite charming and southern in her manner, "very lovely, really." Despite her illustrious ancestry, Pinckney struck the New Orleans writer as "one of the nicest, simplest persons" at the conference. He thought Heyward, who was frequently at her side, gentle, but "a bit too soft."[36]

Henry Seidel Canby had invited Pinckney to do an article on the "Southern Writers' Congress," so she studied the interaction of the authors with particular attention. Characteristically, she took a light tone as she described the complicated program of discussions, seminars, cocktails, tours, and dinners. Ellen Glasgow set the tone with her introductory lecture in which she essentially threw her notes away. Instead she lobbed the first stone of a two-day "donney-brook," according to Pinckney's account, by making incendiary remarks about the distinctions between fictional truth and "real truth." Glasgow also pressed the audience to remember they were "not only Southern writers, but world writers," who should undertake universal rather than parochial themes. What southern writers had to offer literature was "the diversity which is life, not the standardization which is death."37

When the group gathered for discussions in Madison Hall, Pinckney observed, there were no "appointed leaders, yet the talk led through the mazy and dangerous stream of ideas with a result that was not serious, yet not frivolous, but something in between, or rather, around the two, for both were included." The writers fell upon the abundant liquid Virginia hospitality in a way that released their inhibitions, but not so much, she assured her readers, that the event collapsed into "merely another wild party." In casual conversations, they "rubbed shoulders and theories." In meetings, ideas were tossed up, then "snatched up, worried, torn, and revamped all over the countryside between times."38

In a nod to the individualistic nature of the southern artist, the committee had stipulated that all events were optional. Of course, Pinckney observed, "Everybody went to everything." Even William Faulkner, who relentlessly wore an aviator's cap to give the false impression he had just piloted himself in, showed up at the Farmington Country Club for social hours. The one attractive feature of the event for Faulkner was the chance to see for the first time the campus he had fantasized about as the fount of the aristocratic tradition. He had even sent some young denizens of Yoknapatawpha County (including Bayard Sartoris II) to the University of Virginia. After a long evening with some fraternity boys and a jar of corn liquor, Faulkner walked unsteadily into a party on the second night. Pinckney, chatting with a group in the rotunda of the club, caught sight of him and darted over with several friends in her wake to meet this new star in the southern firmament. When Faulkner saw this pack coming for him, he fell violently ill, puking up a day's worth of rotgut, which flowed ominously in the direction of Pinckney's pumps.39

Going into the belly of the beast, the breeding ground of "high caste Brahmins," made the "over-the-mountain men" of Nashville a bit queasy as well. Actually, the invitation committee resisted including any of the Fugitives, especially in their new incarnation as Agrarians. Since the publication of *I'll Take My Stand* the year before, Donald Davidson particularly had ruffled more than a few feathers in the Old Dominion. Heyward, however, insisted the Fugitive poets had played a major role in the early southern renaissance and he wanted at least John Crowe Ransom invited. Davidson and Tate were ultimately added to the list as well. Then, to Heyward's chagrin, two months passed with no reply from Nashville. The "Gods of our Near-West Olympus appear to be high-hatting us," he wrote Wilson. It "looks as though Southern authorship would have to stagger on toward the light without a single Fugitive, Agrarian, Neo-Confederate or 'what have you,' to serve as its guiding star."[40]

Ultimately, Tate and Davidson agreed to come to Charlottesville with big plans about causing arguments and having their say. Despite his bravado in the safety of his office, Davidson arrived in town swathed in self-doubt, painfully aware of his ill-fitting department store suit and rough-edged manners. Davidson cringed at the thought of embarrassing himself and confided "for your private ear" to Wilson "that my modest experience has familiarized me with hotels rather than country clubs—doubtless I would prefer the hotel as a normal and ordinary choice."[41]

Davidson regained his confidence when the discussions began. During one meeting, Paul Green delivered a soliloquy about the loneliness of the writing life. He then shifted gears to plug the Chapel Hill position on industrialism in the South. Green argued that the creative mind was so powerful it could withstand all real and imagined threats from the Machine Age. At that moment, Donald Davidson leapt to his feet "to take his stand against the wheels and the crank-shafts," as Pinckney phrased it.[42] Davidson caused quite a stir. The casual after-dinner discussions focusing around Stringfellow Barr, Ellen Glasgow, and Sherwood Anderson were notably, and probably deliberately, mild, "a real thaw-out, fun, going it hot & heavy, good-natured raillery and good talk."[43]

Writers who had "hated each other's books" ended up liking each other, Emily Clark Balch observed.[44] Donald Davidson and Allen Tate sat down with the "two old snobs" Ellen Glasgow and James Branch Cabell and their fellow Virginian Mary Johnston and found they had a great many pleasant things to discuss. Tate and Harriet Monroe even had a moment to make up after ten years of bad blood over the "Southern Number."[45] Allen Tate, humbled a bit by life, and Harriet Monroe, mellowed a bit by age, called a truce after a decade of snippy guerilla warfare. He suggested to her that the time had come for a second "Southern Number" of *Poetry* that would evaluate the progress of the Southern Literary Renaissance. She agreed. Tate set to work. The obvious fact that poetry in the South was clearly in decline did not faze Tate. "The point of such a number is political," he confided to Robert Penn Warren, "though of course we mustn't confess that to our hostess."[46]

By 1932, events seemed to have come full circle. The literary renaissance that had been inspired in part by the final collapse of the old southern economic system after World War I began to change course with the Great Depression. Now, Allen Tate argued, the South and the nation have together fallen into the abyss as "we are confronted with the breakdown of the new industrialism." As expected, Tate weighted the second "southern number" with Fugitive poets. Davidson complained of difficulty reclaiming "my lost poetic self." Tate planned to assert that southern literature constituted a separate genre in American letters. You know I dearly love Miss Glasgow," Tate wrote Pinckney, "admire her extremely, but I thought what she said about being 'universal' was a half-truth that, taken in the wrong way, as I believe she took it herself, is quite false, and dangerous."[47]

Tate requested submissions from the best of the Charleston poets from the 1920s. Hervey Allen no longer posed as a southern writer. Heyward had left poetry far behind, but Pinckney expressed her eagerness to participate. Pleasantly impressed with Pinckney in Charlottesville, Tate invited her to visit him and his wife in Clarksville, Tennessee. Finding Charlottesville the western-most limit of her interest in the South, Pinckney declined but offered to give him "a little refined advertising" in the *Saturday Review,* noting that Henry Canby had asked her to contribute "a sort of newsletter" on trends in southern literature.[48]

Tate accepted two of the three poems, "A Fig for Selene" and "An Old Man Remembers." She pressed him about why he rejected the third, "Bitter Burial," assuring him she wanted the truth; "manners" do not forbid honesty. She wondered if he had a negative reaction to her phrase, "leap like a fish." If the reference to the fish "startles you," she asked, "I am anxious to know why. Did you feel that there was a phallic suggestion about it?" Her purpose in putting a fish in the pond was to add "something elemental." "I don't object to a faintly phallic tinge; it is unavoidable; but I don't want to be thought, in this instance anyhow," Pinckney explained forthrightly, "to have deliberately sought a phallic symbol."[49]

Pinckney had her opportunity to comment on Tate's work when he submitted his new collection for the Poetry Society's Caroline Sinkler Prize. She was particularly struck and somewhat confounded by "Ode to the Confederate Dead." "Your poems have a lovely clarity—not always of meaning, I must confess, but of feeling, a matter of sound and precision," she wrote. "I suppose 'Ode to the Confederate Dead' baffles me, which may be obtuseness on my part, though your foreword indicates that it baffles you a bit too." "The power of a poem to bedevil its author is limitless. My admiration, however, is not impaired by these considerations, nor my response to the delicate overtones audible above the lines." Some months later, she wrote with the news that the judge, Emily Clark Balch, had awarded him the prize of one hundred dollars.[50]

In July 1932, Pinckney added the MacDowell Colony to her New England itinerary. Merely a visitor a decade earlier, she now earned a place based on her own achievements. As she moved her books and typewriter into Star Studio, reminders of the past, of Allen and Heyward, surrounded her. The colony rested on a gentle plateau covered by several hundred acres of farm fields, orchards, and wooded hollows thick with pine and hemlock spread. The ridge offered an inspiring view of Monadnock Mountain. Within walking distance stood the little town of Peterborough near the little Nubanusit River. During his tenure at MacDowell, Thornton Wilder had traversed the area and drew heavily on local landmarks and local characters for his poignant 1938 hit *Our Town*.

Pinckney craved surcease from the bustle of Charleston society, but she found all the wooded quiet of the colony a little too quiet. Social life had toned down dramatically from the early 1920s. The "girl-poets" had all grown up, gotten older, gained weight, and gone gray. Pinckney did find one colonist to her particular liking, a sweet-faced, self-possessed young artist in his mid-twenties named Prentiss Taylor. They shared a caustic wit and skill at anagrams. After two weeks, he declared her "a very good friend," such "a very delightful and civilized person." Neither took the Peterborough scene terribly seriously (this was Taylor's fourth summer there), and they frequently broke ranks. One night they sneaked out of the rarefied atmosphere for the middlebrow pleasure of a Jimmy Cagney film, *Winner Take All*.[51]

Before Taylor and Pinckney parted in Peterborough, they made a pact to meet in New York. Taylor lived on Bank Street and moved in the artistic circles associated with the Harlem Renaissance. He had collaborated with Langston Hughes in establishing the Golden Stair Press and publishing the broadside "The Negro Mother and other Dramatic Recitations." Through Hughes, Taylor found his way to the elegantly decorated West Side apartment of novelist and critic Carl Van Vechten, who had become entranced by the exotica of Harlem during the 1920s. For his generous patronage and shrewd promotion of African American artists, "Carlo" was often called the "godfather" of the Harlem Renaissance. Van Vechten accepted the honor but said he remembered little of the 1920s, having been drunk for most of the decade. Pinckney first met the flamboyant Van Vechten through Joseph Hergesheimer. Taylor reintroduced them, much to Pinckney's regret. The following Christmas, Van Vechten sent her a "fascinating Christmas card," which she never acknowledged. "If I had been a nice girl, instead of being me," she confessed to Taylor. "I would have written him a graceful note saying how pleasant it was to be remembered." "You might when you see him," Pinckney instructed Prentiss, "tell him that I am dumbly grateful."[52]

Pinckney dashed home from New Hampshire to help Heyward prepare for the second annual Southern Writers' Conference in Charleston. The mood in the nation was grim in October 1932. The depression showed no signs of easing, and the country waited to see if it would be Herbert Hoover or Franklin D. Roosevelt who would lead them. Writing to Pinckney from his new post in Michigan, Howard Mumford Jones predicted the "downfall of Chapel Hill as a center of sweetness and light." He saw a "gorgeous opportunity for South Carolina to snatch the torch before Vanderbilt sweeps it—can't you persuade Reid Smith and Yates Snowden that Columbia [home of the University of South Carolina] ought to become a light amid the darkness?"[53] Little did Jones realize that in late 1932, the state of South Carolina suffered such poverty that scarcely a flickering match could be lit in any public institution in the cause of poetry.

When the invitations to the Charleston House Party went out, acceptances slowly wafted in. A trip to Charleston for most writers represented an unjustifiable expense. The 1932 House Party highlighted the various dimensions of the Charleston Renaissance, a cultural revival with many facets. It was strictly a community, rather than an academic event, with more women playing key roles in planning and organization than in Charlottesville. After ten years, the Poetry Society's appeal to the "word using community" had generated broad (though not very deep) interest in writing and literature. The Junior League's Scribblers Club, for example, organized receptions and lunches.

The Society for the Preservation of Spirituals sponsored a party for the authors in the eighteenth-century Heyward-Washington House. Two local institutions, the Charleston Museum and the Society for the Preservation of Old Dwellings, had recently scraped together enough money to purchase (but not pay for) the notable building where Washington spent a week. In 1932, what would become Charleston's first house museum was still almost bare. In a scenario reminiscent of depression-era movies such as *Alice Adams,* when a family struggles to fix up their tumbled-down house for the inspection of a wealthy suitor, Pinckney had her friends plunder their own homes for rugs, tables, chairs, paintings, to make the place presentable, to the discriminating eye of the New York press whom Heyward had invited. They worked like Trojans cutting vases of flowers from their gardens and polishing their silver candelabras. The second floor had no electricity and was illuminated that evening by flickering candles. Pinckney and Heyward were all smiles and nervous geniality acting as the hosts. Sam Stoney told a Gullah sermon, and the Spirituals Society sang "Lonesome Road." The party was, from the Charlestonians' perspective, a disaster; "dreadful" was Harriet P. Simons's reaction. Whether the "back-biting" quotient exceeded by too great a degree the "back-slapping," or whether the distinguished visitors condescended to the local amateurs, or whether the organizers simply tried too hard, no one could say. But it was "a frost," an experience one Charleston man hoped he would live long enough to forget.[54]

None of the published accounts betrayed the tension at the meeting. Columnist Fanny Butcher, who accompanied Julia Peterkin to the conference, remembered the weekend as a time of pure delight—"No organizing, no 'purposes,' no discussion of what is wrong with life and literature or how it could be bettered marred two gay, happy days of charming companionship under a sun which beamed its blessings in a spot of fragrant time-toned enchantment." Davidson, who suspected that Heyward and Pinckney had "judiciously oiled the wheels" to prevent a flare up of the fighting of Charlottesville, confided to Tate who was in Paris, "I must say that I felt rather alone at the Charleston gathering," feeling as he had in Virginia, shut out by "a strangely exclusive air."[55] Yet he thanked Pinckney for all she had done to make his family welcome and asked to see her most recent poems; "I feel a deep desire to hold on, as long as possible, to the full flavor and grace of those few days in Charleston. I would like to read your verses and keep remembering."[56]

Don Adams of the *New York Times* and novelist Laurence Stallings joked that all the southern writers at the conference really cared about was "corn liquor a year in char," old houses, and southern culture "before the War." One afternoon, they slipped away from the official sessions to stroll the tree-lined streets of Charleston and to discover the city for themselves. As they passed run-down tenements, neat single houses, and gated mansions, all needing paint, they remarked to each other how much ancient beauty still remained. Having made an "art" of poverty for so long, Charleston seemed one of the few places that appeared unchanged even as the depression deepened. They noted the poetry of the setting as they debated why it was that writers from the South had produced such "marvelous stuff," the best American writing for more than a decade. This dark year of 1932 was proving to be perhaps the most fruitful for American literature of any Adams could remember. Talking as they walked, they vainly sought the single strand than gave southern writers a common identity.[57]

At one point during their tour that had taken them down the main shopping district on King Street, Stallings and Adams paused in front of the display window of Legerton's Book Store. In honor of the writers' meeting, the window was filled chockablock with books by Charleston authors. Even though Stallings kept up with regional literature, the sheer number of volumes all related to the Carolina Low Country nevertheless astounded him. The expected names of Pinckney, Heyward, and Bennett adorned handsome editions, but his surprise came from the score of books by local folk who felt compelled to write, who wanted themselves to bear witness to the southern experience. Still, even Charleston authors defied easy generalization. The only unifying factor these two New Yorkers could deduce was "a deep affection for the sights and sounds and wind and waters of the country from which they sprang."[58]

For Josephine Pinckney and DuBose Heyward, working closely together again renewed their deep affection. Despite all the burdensome organizational work involved, sponsoring the Southern Writers' Conference brought back the old excitement of the early Poetry Society days, of their early ambitions, before life and the world got so complicated. That Christmas, so many years after Camilla Pinckney had poisoned his hopes, in the full flush of his fame, after a productive marriage and a beautiful child, Heyward sent Pinckney a special greeting: "I cannot let the season pass by without letting you know that I love you just as deeply as I did when you were a proud beauty living in a palace with four floors and an elevator."[59]

In early summer 1933, Pinckney encouraged the struggling Prentiss Taylor to leave New York for Charleston where the living was easy. When Taylor arrived in early May, he was stunned by the unique beauty of the town. To Carl Van Vechten, he gushed that "the decay is too, too divine"—a "land that would make your camera lose its mind." Taylor was entranced by this "historical and inter-related Paradise."[60]

Pinckney arranged for Taylor to stay in Marjorie Morawetz's tiny pre-Revolutionary structure at 17 Chalmers Street locally known as "the Pink House." Living happily, albeit in a haze of "Flit and citronella" as he battled the city's invincible cockroaches, Taylor fell comfortably into the rhythm of Charleston life. Pinckney, however, was the only intellectually simulating friend he had met, his "only star." To his diary, Taylor confided that his time in Charleston was some of the "most agreeable" living he had ever enjoyed; "I haven't been so content in years." He was fascinated by the denizens of Horlbeck Alley and Short Street; charmed by the Jenkins Orphanage Band. He slipped into a service at the Macedonia AME Church as the preacher proclaimed, "Jedus see we climb the rough side ob de mountains." Taylor made sketches and stored memories of this moment of high drama that would find expression when he returned to New York. His attempts at photographing the blacks of Charleston were less successful since his subjects were "camera shy" and disliked his "puttin' that ting on them."[61]

By the end of August 1933, Pinckney was packing to leave for the MacDowell Colony once again. She invited Prentiss Taylor to stay at 36 Chalmers in her absence and take care of her beloved cocker spaniel, Peter. Back in Peterborough, Pinckney worked in a desultory way on her poetry. A constant drippy rain beat on the window of the Cheney Studio where she was staying. She was bored. The weather prevented her from taking the long walks she loved. None of the other colonists could compare with Taylor for entertainment, or even challenge her at word games. She vowed never to return.[62]

The real trouble was not the weather. She had convinced Sam Stoney to come with her to Peterborough and probably imagined the fun of being these two southern aristocrats, sitting around the fire telling Gullah stories with Stoney as Hervey had done with DuBose a decade earlier. On the day they arrived, amid all the whispering, nodding, and discreet pointing among the artists, writers, and musicians, Pinckney nudged Stoney to check out a mannishly dressed poet she knew to be Frances Frost. Pinckney whispered a précis to Stoney, outlining the "controversial character" of this diminutive divorcée. The two women circled circumspectly, looking "at each other like strange cats." The second night, in the congenial mist of alcohol, singing of "crazy songs," and general hilarity, Stoney began to warm up to Frost, who now looked more vulnerable than decadent as she struggled to play a large guitar. She responded to his intense dark-eyed gaze. After a week of "merrymaking" with Frost, during which Stoney was, of course, utterly lost to Pinckney, the couple decided to marry.[63]

Stoney asked Pinckney to stand up with him as an official witness, and Frost asked writer Chard Smith. This posed an awkward situation given the tradition of best man and maid of honor, so, Pinckney wrote to Prentiss Taylor, "We exchanged functions." She pulled together an ersatz bouquet of juniper and white berries for the bride. During the brief ceremony, as the prickly bouquet was being passed back and forth with the exchange of rings, Frost stuck Pinckney "quite hard." Pinckney, completely undone that she was losing another one of her devoted Charleston male friends to a MacDowell "vamp," returned the favor with a very discreet jab of evergreen. At the moment when the bride usually tosses the bouquet aloft with great delicacy to her hopeful bridesmaids, Frost "heaved" her bouquet inelegantly and beaned Pinckney hard. When Pinckney surveyed the astonishing events of the week, all the Charleston wordsmith could find to say was, "Well, I swan."[64]

Stoney's two sisters, Harriet P. Simons and Louisa Popham, came up to MacDowell for the ceremony. Simons surveyed the assorted band of writers, artists, and musicians and quipped, "Most of the colonists looked as if their parents did not understand them." She thought Frost "not pretty or prepossessing looking in any way, . . . not sophisticated nor polished, but experienced and toughened by life." In ironic contrast to the indomitable Charleston ladies who filled Stoney's life, the hard-boiled Vermont poet was emotionally needy, a romantic underneath the edginess, looking for a strong arm to lean upon. Unburdened by expectations of gentility, she could be a great deal of fun, swearing like a sailor and drinking Stoney under the table. She was also dead broke.[65]

How much Pinckney knew about Frost at the time of Stoney's marriage and how much she shared with him initially is unclear, but once the romance began, Pinckney was constrained from telling Sam the details of Frost's antics that she picked up from MacDowell Colony gossips. After leaving Middlebury College under a cloud (probably pregnant), then marrying and having two children, she left her husband and children to pursue would-be writer Irving Fineman, with whom she had started a very public affair (sleeping together in the sheep pasture) at the colony. After Frost filed for divorce, the caddish Fineman refused to marry her. What Pinckney probably did not know was that Fineman was also carrying on a romantic relationship with the much older South Carolina author Julia Peterkin.[66]

This later news confirmed what Pinckney and her crowd already thought; Peterkin was no lady. A distant, unacknowledged relative of Sam Stoney, Peterkin often tried to play the southern aristocrat and plantation owner for the northern audience, but the Charleston writers thought of her more as a farmer's wife who actually put her hands in dirt and never accepted her into their fold.[67] Peterkin, who won the Pulitzer Prize for her 1929 novel *Scarlet Sister Mary,* had made her reputation chronicling the lives of the blacks living on her farm where she lived with her husband in Fort Motte. The dialect she used to tell her stories was her own version of the daily vernacular she used directing her workers, not the precise Gullah of Sam Stoney and others of the Charleston school. Over the years, Peterkin's work grew darker and played to modern salaciousness and racial essentialism, as she struggled with personal demons of her own.[68]

Even if Stoney's friends had been willing to overlook Frost's past, no one who wished him well could be sanguine about Frost's drinking, which turned out to be much worse than convivial boozing. After their marriage, Stoney and Frost took off for Soufriére in St. Lucia where they hoped to work uninterrupted, Sam on the early history of South Carolina and Frances finishing her long poem "Woman of This Earth" (1934) and beginning a novel.[69] When the couple returned to the Carolina Low Country in 1934, they also entered fully into the cultural life of the city. Pinckney began to see Frost, who had won the Katherine Lee Bates poetry prize given by the New England Poetry Club in 1933 and the Shelley Memorial Award in 1934, as a rival.

When *Culture in the South* was finally published in 1934, Pinckney found the volume "depressing." Davidson gallantly, and truthfully, praised Pinckney's essay and assured her, "It's one of the best in the book. I enjoyed it and admired it tremendously. I bank on it to do a world of good in a world that needs good." Donald Davidson considered Pinckney's essay in the category of "excellent ones," one of the few that might be called "literature." Still smoldering because he was not asked to contribute, Allen Tate wrote an inflamed review designed to "smite the wicked and reward the faithful," but he spared Pinckney and even praised her for "shrewd and sensitive observation."[70]

Although neither *Culture in the South* nor *I'll Take My Stand* enjoyed widespread popularity when first published, over time both have gained recognition as important contributions in the debate over modern southern identity. Pinckney won national attention for her insights in "Bulwarks against Change." A review essay in the *New York Times* book section by Dorothy Scarborough, "The South: Her Level of Culture" began with a summary of Pinckney's analysis: "The section that was before the Civil War considered the aristocrat of the nation, now is called (by Josephine Pinckney) the poor relation of the other regions. By nature conservative, reluctant to change, the South, since the Civil War, has experienced violent changes, from wealth to poverty, from power to defeat, from ownership of slaves to temporary (during the Reconstruction's vicious policies) political helplessness, while the former slaves held office and controlled the courts . . . The young generation coming on feels the pull of tradition against the push of modern business life, uncertain which way to turn."[71]

A number of reviewers positioned *Culture in the South* against *I'll Take My Stand* as representing two competing views of the future of the South between industrialism and agriculture. Because Couch transformed the North Carolina symposium into a liberal response to the conservative Agrarian position, William S. Knickerbocker of the *Sewanee Review,* deemed *Culture in the South* "a fighting book." The dispute surrounded the question of whether the old Confederacy should finally capitulate and adopt the American creed of capitalism and industrialism, or if twentieth century southerners should try to hold on to their unique agrarian ethic derived from a civilization based on subsistence farming. The Agrarians, Knickerbocker charged, were "gunning" for the progressive southerners, such as Broadus Mitchell, who advocated industrial development as the salvation of the undeveloped South. The twelve southerners used an "esoteric dialect," a cunning, intricate, and profound language of their own, to make their case. Knickerbocker found that the only liberals in the Couch book who could interpret the "Agrarian vocabulary" were Josephine Pinckney and Clarence E. Cason. He also mentioned Pinckney's essay as one of the three with "very high literary value."[72]

Pinckney's name among the essayists in *Culture in the South* piqued the curiosity of those who had known her as a poet. Her former editor at Harper Brothers, Eugene F. Saxton, anxious to recoup his investment in her, wrote of his hope that "this is a visible sign of your return to manuscriptual occupation. It's time we had another book from you."[73]

# 9

## Farewell to First Love

"As a means of helping the [poetry] pot to boil" once again, Pinckney wrote "They Shall Return as Strangers," an allegory about southerners losing touch with their land which was accepted by the *Virginia Quarterly Review* in April 1934. Pinckney's story was her contribution to the on-going discussion about the impact of industrialization on the South and its people. Pinckney rejects the Agrarian's romanticism about life on the land and substitutes the wise Sea Island Gullah for the noble yeomen. Drawing on the experience of her own ancestors, she also corrects the widespread assumption that southern planters were enemies of capitalism. The great planters labored over their ground with "a hoe in one hand and a bunch of high-grade bonds in the other," she observes.[1]

Pinckney sets her narrative in the 1930s and begins the action with her protagonist, young Henry Fairfield, scion of an old Low Country family, hunched over his typewriter (the typist having become synonymous with alienated modern man), alone in a cubicle at the Richbourg Radiator Company. He has come to New York to escape the languishing South, intent on "grabbing success by the throat." He stops to mull an interesting letter from a developer who wants to buy April Island, the last of his family's ancestral holdings, to stock with exotic animals for a hunting preserve and tourist attraction. Since he has never even seen this property, left to him by an uncle, he takes some vacation time to return to the Carolina coast. This journey to the sea islands takes him back in time to a place without clocks, cars, schedules, a cash economy, or competition. He cannot even communicate with the Gullah-speaking locals, ancestors of the slaves who once cultivated the valuable sea island cotton. After a few draws of local corn whiskey at lunch time, the young man fantasizes about returning to this island, giving up the rat race, perhaps becoming a poet. But as the hot sun rises in the sky, he is sobered by the realization that unlike his forefathers, he has no other source of income as hedge against the boll weevil or decline in the market. Plantation life could never be recreated anyway because that "personal compact" between master and slave had been forever broken in "a new and free world" (556).

Slowly Fairfield understands that through his neglect (he had never even bothered to collect the paltry rents from his black tenants), he has forfeited his spiritual right to the land. Land demands to be tilled "not agriculturally, but humanly" and bedewed with "his thought, his love, and his duty." Fully a creature of the modern world, he has become a stranger to his own past. The real owners, he finally understands, were the small colony of blacks, ancestors of the slaves who worked that land, who really comprised "the genius of the place" (546). Fairfield had momentarily let the "egotism of the blood" fool him into believing that "the accomplishments of his distinguished family had somehow been mystically dowered to him" (544). Returning to his nine-to-five life seems his only choice. April Island was "a place of pure magic" reserved for the giants of the earth. And he is a typist, not a king (557).

Pinckney had been in an introspective mood when she wrote her story. April Island is a thinly veiled surrogate for Pinckney Island, General Cotesworth Pinckney's favorite home in Port Royal Sound, near Hilton Head. The property had been in her family since the days of Eliza Lucas Pinckney. When the relative who inherited the island was forced to sell during the Great Depression, Pinckney's own depleted finances prevented her from keeping the island and its unproductive acres in the family, although she managed to hold on to Eldorado and her brother to Fairfield. As in the story, General Pinckney's mansion house with its library and collection of scientific instruments had indeed washed out to sea decades before, a fitting metaphor for the end of the Age of the Pinckneys and of the South as a center of liberal thought.

As Pinckney had hoped, "They Shall Return as Strangers" piqued the interest of publishers. Clifton Fadiman of Simon and Schuster inquired if she was working on a novel. Her answer was yes. Earlier, Pinckney had admitted to Allen Tate, "I have momentarily abandoned poetry and am floundering about in this too wide savannah of a novel, which won't come out the way I want . . . If it ever gets done, I shall return suing for forgiveness to my first love."[2]

A combination of many factors—the changing nature of poetry and the decline of its popularity, the temptation of profits from best-selling historical novels (especially those promoted by the book clubs), the changing perspective on the world that comes with age, the impact of disappointment and disillusion on youthful inspiration—had already sent most of Pinckney's friends from the early days "withering" into fiction, as she described it. In 1932, DuBose Heyward completed *Peter Ashley*, a historical novel of the Civil War era. The next year, Herbert Ravenel Sass published his own story of the war in the Low Country, *Look Back to Glory*. Hervey Allen, who had moved to Bermuda, wrote his last book of poems, *New Legends*, in 1929 and produced the mother of all historical novels, *Anthony Adverse*, in 1933. This romantic epic of the Napoleonic era exceeded eight hundred pages and through shrewd marketing sold almost two million copies. This blockbuster hit, possibly the biggest novel since *Ben-Hur*, not only made Allen's reputation but also assured the viability of Farrar and Rinehart during the uncertain days of the depression. Farrar's faith in the young poets of Charleston a decade earlier was confirmed. Allen attributed the amazing success of *Anthony Adverse* to a change in the popular mood: "People are tired of incomplete and inadequately phrased experiences, of shallow books about abnormal people and neurotic experiences with which they have no general sympathy, . . . phrased in constipated staccato style."[3]

With his bonanza, Allen set up the life he had always wanted, one that protected him as much as possible from the modern world. He invited Pinckney to his new estate on the Maryland shore where he had established himself as the master of "Bonfield Manor." Given her background, he wrote, she would "thoroughly understand" the exclusive world in which he now moved. "Not that you aren't pretty good at understanding any neighborhoods, anywhere," he added.[4] Allen also had a Florida winter compound, "The Glades," at Coconut Grove near Miami.

Anxious to capitalize on the popular passion for historical fiction, Pinckney cast about for a southern hero uncompromised by plantation slavery or secession. While doing research at the Charleston Library Society, she picked up the tracks of her ancestor Dr. Henry Woodward, reputedly the first Carolina settler, and transformed his remarkable story into her first novel, *Hilton Head* (1941). When Pinckney spoke of her first efforts at novel writing, she sounded offhand and often made jokes about this "doctor in moccasins," but *Hilton Head* is a major work of research, a serious study of the economic and political origins of South Carolina. Pinckney also presents an understanding view of the various tribes of Indians who lived along the Carolina coast, emphasizing their sophisticated social organization and contributions to the establishment of the colony.

Born in 1643 in Virginia, Henry Woodward—physician, linguist, explorer, diplomat—is also credited with introducing rice cultivation to the Low Country with some seeds from Madagascar. Dashing and difficult, educated and entrepreneurial, adventurous and audacious, fallible and feckless, Woodward proved a man complicated by human frailties, but extraordinary events elevated him to near-greatness. Woodward studied medicine at Surgeon's Hall in London until he lit out at nineteen to seek his fortune in Barbados. Finding no ready employment and rebuffed by Mary Godfrey, the daughter of a wealthy merchant, he signed on to an exploratory expedition led by Robert Sandford, an agent of Anthony Ashley Cooper and the other Lords Proprietors of lands called Carolina. Sandford had accompanied William Hilton on a reconnaissance run two years before as the Barbadians sought new areas for expansion and for trade to benefit their patrons. The

French and Spanish had earlier made inroads near the present day towns of Beaufort and Hilton Head. The Orista (Edisto) and the Escamacu Indians claimed this area as their sphere of influence, but competition was relentless among the coastal tribes. Warring chiefs tried to cultivate alliances with the various European groups for protection. When the cacique Nisquesalla asked Sandford to take his nephew back with him to learn the language and ways of the English, Henry Woodward surprised himself by volunteering to stay behind and similarly immerse himself in the culture of the Escamacu.[5] The Escamacu proved excellent hosts, providing him with bed, board, and a willing young woman, Tu-que, to care for him.

The drama of young Woodward standing on the shore at the edge of the virgin forest, alone among the natives as he watched his mates sail for home, sparked Pinckney's imagination. In contrast to poetry, a lonely task dependent on inspiration and demanding exhausting precision of language, Pinckney found historical research strangely liberating and was dogged in her quest for authenticity. Woodward's story turned out to be more complex than Pinckney had imagined. Once the Spanish in St. Augustine learned of an Englishman striking deals with the native tribes in 1667, they kidnapped him and held him until English privateer, Captain Robert Searle, came to his rescue in 1668. Woodward then sailed with Searle, serving as ship's surgeon until they wrecked on the island of Nevis in 1669. Eventually, Woodward returned to the Port Royal area where the first English settlement was planned. Word of the raids of the warring Westoes encouraged the settlers to go northward where they settled on a bluff at Albemarle Point and called their new home Charles Town. The two rivers that flowed together to make the broad harbor nearby they named the Ashley and the Cooper.[6]

Pinckney wanted Woodward to settle down with his wife and children and become a political leader of the colony experimenting with a limited self-government; instead he was constantly running off to the territory beyond. He negotiated a peace with the Westoes in 1674, which provided security to the fledgling colony and opened up the west to Charleston traders. By the time of his death in 1686, Woodward had helped extend the westward range of the Charleston traders deep into the Indian lands almost to the Mississippi River. Pinckney has Woodward dream of the future for Carolina as "an English possession much like Barbados, only superior, thriving on its great resources and with a liberal Whiggish sort of aristocracy founded on trade."(261) Pinckney subtly slipped in editorial comments about the folly of utopias and the futility of eliminating the "profit motive" that reflected her growing unhappiness with the leftward veer of Franklin Roosevelt's New Deal.[7]

At a critical juncture during her research into the life of Henry Woodward, past the point of no return actually, she also had to face the fact that she "had been a bit rash in choosing such an active and versatile gentleman." His time aboard a privateer in the Caribbean also proved "inconvenient" because of her total ignorance about life aboard a square-rigger. And then, describing the native tribes, all of which had characteristics of their own, posed an insurmountable quandary because of the lack of written evidence. She mined the travel accounts of John Lawson, Benjamin Hawkins, and others, all much after Woodward's day, counting on the fact that "fashion changed very little in the wilderness." Pinckney exhaustively researched the material history of seventeenth-century Carolina to create an authentic setting and studied the earliest English novels, such as *Moll Flanders* (1722) and *Roderick Random* (1748), and plays by William Congreve for guidance in reproducing seventeenth-century speech and idiom. Fearful of anachronism, she had to do extra inquiry in seventeenth-century medicine. In the end, Pinckney became impatient with the trouble-prone Woodward, who refused to conform to her idea of a hero. Pinckney disliked Woodward's "flamboyance," especially his wanderlust and unwillingness to stay home and care for his family after Mary Godfrey agreed to be his wife.[8]

Pinckney developed a theory of historical fiction influenced by Joseph Hergesheimer that "elaborated" on the "spare skeleton" unearthed by her research. She did not fabricate events and based her novel on the public record "as far as it goes with only such minor trimming as raw history needs to give it the shape of a novel." All of the major characters who populate *Hilton Head* were "real" inasmuch as they existed in the historical past, but their personalities were for the most part "a long guess" on Pinckney's part. A conscientious writer of historical fiction, Pinckney argued, "borrows light-fingeredly from other sources—from letters, diaries, wills of the period, and from human nature as he knows it—and adapts his plunder to his plot"(vii). The author who writes from history, she believed, is really only the middle-man conveying to readers "the exuberant melodrama that fills the pigeonhole, the tin box, the hair trunk that have preserved for us the color of early America" (viii). "Trying to reconstruct the lives of men and women who lived in the remote past is like a treasure-hunt and a detective story with the most exciting features of both."[9]

Rummaging in the collection of the Gibbes Art Gallery, she found a yellowed map marking the exact location of Woodward's home at the headwaters of Abapoola Creek. Sam Stoney proved a never-ending source of information about seventeenth-century life in the West Indies and the complex linkages between England, Barbados, and the Carolina Low Country. Langdon Cheves, a lawyer and gentleman historian, guided Pinckney's quest to understand the seventeenth-century mind, loaning her his copy of Noel Sainsbury's magisterial *Calendar of State Papers, Colonial Series, America and West Indies, 1669–1674* (1889), which would provide the intellectual scaffolding for her novel. Cheves also suggested she consult the papers of the First Earl of Shaftsbury, Lord Anthony Ashley Cooper. As one of the original Lords Proprietors of the new colony of Carolina, Shaftsbury had seized upon his unique opportunity to turn the Enlightenment's cherished dreams of a more perfect world into a reality. His secretary, philosopher John Locke, crafted the "Fundamental Constitutions" for governance of the New World that echoed many of the idealistic hopes of the time when England was torn by the rivalries of Crown and Covenanters. Cheves had painstakingly edited and annotated transcripts from the British Public Record Office for the South Carolina Historical Society.[10]

Pinckney's long-distance task of research in the archives of Seville was complicated by the Spanish Civil War. When she finally tracked down copies of the documents she needed about Woodward's captivity in the Library of Congress, she found they were in archaic seventeenth-century Spanish, which entailed a long search for a translator. Just as despair began to creep upon her, DuBose and Dorothy Heyward returned to Charleston during the winter of 1934. Much to Pinckney's delight, the Heywards bought a rustic cottage on Folly Beach, about twelve miles south of town, where DuBose planned to write the libretto for an operatic interpretation of *Porgy* at George Gershwin's suggestion. Pinckney found having her old friends nearby "a perfect joy" and spent many weekends with them at "Follywood," as they called their getaway financed by DuBose's screenwriting projects. Heyward congratulated Pinckney on taking up the challenge of fiction writing. "You confirm a conviction of mine that with but a very few great exceptions," he wrote, "poetry is an evolutionary phase and leads to the broader scope of prose." He warned her that a historical novel was a slow, often tedious process (his took five years).[11]

The old friends picked up where they had left off "in the old days." Heyward even assumed the presidency of the Poetry Society again. The basic creaky machinery was still running, thanks to Pinckney who had stayed with it in a "gallant" way, but few young people seemed interested enough to help out anymore. To fill a breach in the program list, Heyward, Pinckney, and John Bennett even "jumpted through the hoops" at a Poetry Society meeting, the first time they had "twinkled" together since Hervey Allen left Charleston ten years before. Frances Frost also gave a program.[12]

At some point in early 1934, perhaps during one of their beach walks or over a late night drink, Heyward and Pinckney decided to collaborate on the Woodward novel. Pinckney had planned to take her novel to Eugene F. Saxton, her patient editor at Harper Brothers, but Heyward charged ahead and approached Farrar in April. To Pinckney's irritation, Farrar began spreading rumors "quite prematurely" about a Heyward-Pinckney collaboration that began attracting a great deal of attention in the publishing world.[13] Heyward's assumption of dominance probably spurred the row that threatened their long friendship. No one knows exactly why, but loud voices rose out of her study, where they worked together, piercing the quiet of 36 Chalmers Street. The pedestal was still too narrow for them both. What might be called "creative differences" rapidly wormed their way into the working sessions. Heyward may have pulled creative rank, or he may have been too preoccupied with his other writing projects. Pinckney did complain to Hervey Allen that Heyward had spent the entire winter "with his head buried in sand," leaving the Poetry Society (and presumably *Hilton Head* ) to survive only through "the guidance of the Holy Spirit."[14]

Whatever unpleasantness lingered between Heyward and Pinckney after their blowup burned itself out quickly. In October 1935, Pinckney laid aside her manuscript to attend a command performance in New York. After months of preparation and a successful run in Boston, Heyward's "shy slim novel" was about to make its Broadway debut as the folk opera *Porgy and Bess*. Few things on earth could have prevented Pinckney from packing up her jewels and furs and attending this gala premiere.[15]

The ambience in the Alvin Theatre on the evening of October 10 was pure magic. The packed house overflowed with the beautiful, rich, and famous. *Porgy and Bess* attracted one of the most distinguished audiences in several years. Everywhere Pinckney cast her eyes, she recognized celebrities. Film stars Katharine Hepburn, Joan Crawford, Franchot Tone, and the famous theater couple, Helen Hayes and Charles MacArthur waited for the curtain, as did two stars of the Harlem Renaissance, Josephine Baker and Paul Robeson. Here, under the bright lights, Church Street's "Cabbage Row" was transformed into Catfish Row. The lyrics of Heyward's haunting "Summertime" filled the theater. When the curtain fell, Pinckney and the others waited for that fraction of a second that always seemed a lifetime. The applause went on for a half hour.[16]

Pinckney then dashed with the Heywards to the Park Avenue apartment of publishing mogul Condé Nast. Just as in the movies, talented friends of George Gershwin took turns entertaining the crowd until almost dawn when the first editions with their make-or-break reviews hit the newsstands. Whiskey flowed freely during the vigil. When it came, the news was not good. Heyward permanently soured on Gotham, but Pinckney became increasingly certain that destiny meant her for the bright lights.[17]

While in New York, Pinckney signed a contract with Farrar and Rinehart for

*Hilton Head.* She had been gaining in confidence as she approached her fortieth birthday, enjoying the solid satisfaction of recognition for her work in southern letters, though nothing, of course, like the fame she craved. In December 1934, Pinckney was inducted as an honorary member of Phi Beta Kappa at the College of William and Mary, home of the first chapter, and where Captain Tom's nephew, John Stewart Bryan, was then the president. She read her long poem "Romantic Mr. Swallow" and spoke briefly about her inspiration for the story of the tavern keeper who, unable to stand his hectoring mercenary wife or accept the crude commercialism of the eighteenth century, took his own life in a swamp near a heron rookery:

> To leave the husk of the world and seek like these
> An element not earth,—with no disease
> Of clocks and commerce. Rising like a king
> He passed into the pool. The silver breeze
> His garments held rose in a bubbly ring
> And signed away, . . . the last trump of his wayfaring.[18]

Back in Charleston, Tom Waring was popping his vest buttons with pride, strutting around the office of the Poetry Society exclaiming how Pinckney's "literary integrity," her concentration on the worthwhile instead of the fashionable, had finally "won out."[19]

In 1936, when the *Virginia Quarterly Review* accepted Pinckney's essay "The Marchant of London and the Treacherous Don," about the seventeenth-century competition between England and Spain, editor Lambert Davis congratulated her on her versatility, noting she had become "one of our two 'four letter men': contributors who had published stories, essays, poetry and book reviews. There is only one other person who has made such varied contributions, Robert Penn Warren."[20] After Gerald W. Johnson read her essay, he wrote a note of encouragement: "I don't mean to deprecate Faulkner, Erskine, Wolfe, and—sh-h-h! don't quote me—Julia Peterkin; their work is important and, I believe, necessary. But they are the forerunners of the fine Southern literature, not the thing itself. Someone is destined to build on the foundation they have laid; why not you?"[21]

Pinckney had seen Johnson the year before when they both received honorary degrees from the College of Charleston at the time of its 150th anniversary celebration in May 1935. Pinckney was one of three women among the twenty recipients; author Julia Peterkin and local librarian Ellen Fitzsimmons were the others. Pinckney gave a party for the distinguished group at 36 Chalmers Street that included Bernard Baruch, Mayor Burnett Maybank, and Senator James Byrnes. Johnson found her still alluring, ever the smiling gracious hostess, but that evening he caught her in a fleeting, unguarded moment and glimpsed what he believed was "an incomprehensively lonely person."[22]

Since their last meeting, Pinckney had suffered a staggering double loss. In August 1934, her brother Cotesworth had drowned from a massive heart attack while swimming alone at Virginia Beach. In his will, Pinckney had asked to be buried alongside his mother, Mary Stewart Pinckney, at the family's Emmanuel Episcopal Church near Brook Hill. "Brother" re-entered the circle of his long dead brothers and sisters whose little stones ringed that of their mother. Josephine now stood quite alone. When friends offered condolences, Pinckney thanked them politely and acknowledged her loss but remained closed and uncommunicative about her feelings. "That was a bad chapter," she responded to Prentiss Taylor's expression of sympathy, in a way that did not invite further inquiry.[23]

A few months later, word had reached Pinckney in New England that Victoria Rutledge was near death. Rutledge held on to life by the narrowest thread until Pinckney arrived at her bedside, then slowly gave up the ghost. "You can well imagine how bereft I feel," Pinckney wrote Laura Bragg, allowing herself more open grief than with her brother. "I can't remember a time when she was not a fixed part of my background . . . My feeling for her had profound roots . . . The house seems unbearably quiet without her frequently annoying bustle in the kitchen. A complete devotion and loyalty like hers is a terrible loss."[24]

And then, in the spring of 1935, about the time of her dinner with Johnson, Tom Waring was dying. Never robust after a heart attack he suffered in New York during 1932, he managed to maintain an intense interest in the world around him. Sharing Pinckney's excitement about the *Hilton Head* project, he had been helping her with research. During the summer of 1934, when Pinckney took a break to visit Grace Stone in Taxco, Mexico, Waring wrote her long missives with clockwork regularity. In a fit of curiosity over who could be sending such fat letters, the Stone's teenaged daughter Eleanor opened Miss Jo's mail. The girl was amazed to read professions of love, in the most vivid detail, written on foolscap by the editor who interspersed words of passion with tidbits of new information about Henry Woodward. Waring died on June 1, 1935. When John Bennett asked Pinckney to write a resolution about Waring for the Poetry Society, she begged off, claiming that the flu had thrust her into "the blackest depths of physical and mental depression." "Nor," she added, "would I be adequate if I were well."[25]

Waring had lived a life described as "sweetly brave" and was perhaps the only newspaper editor in the country whose coworkers thought his most notable virtue was tenderness.[26] Without Waring, Pinckney felt fearfully, terribly alone. DuBose Heyward had warned her years before that settling for a romance with a married man was having "half-a-loaf, where you should have so much." Heyward feared she would miss her chance for "complete fulfillment" because he had played the "dog in the manger," coming in and out of her life, enjoying "our extraordinary friendship" at the same time he had a marriage and family of his own. And yet, he closed by leaving the door open: "I am just where I have always been with you as friend, confidante [sic], and any other old thing that you would like to have me be."[27]

After Tom Waring's death, Pinckney had pulled out some old Carolina Art Association stationery (with Waring's name, as president, still on the letterhead). Ever thrifty, she used these sheets for scratch paper. At this crucial point in her life, she issued some instructions to herself:

> Organize my emotions.
> It is later than I think.
> Remember T. and his pride in me.
> Remember Grace and Clare—if they can do it so can I.
> I must get on to other and better books.
> I must think more widely and more deeply.
> I must invent ways of meeting my problems of construction.
> I must find time to read.
> I must get on with my book. I must keep it central in my emotions.[28]

Pinckney pressed on with *Hilton Head* for seven more years. By Christmas 1939, the research was complete, the narrative constructed; now only the last revisions, the excising of redundancy, the sharpening of a phrase, the perfecting of the word choice remained. Her old nemesis, John Bennett, who always had whispered behind her back that Pinckney was a lightweight and a wealthy dilettante, believed she had, at last, shed "the damson plum bloom" of the dabbler. Submitting herself to "the professional grind of rehashing a book to meet a publisher's liking" had caused her to "very nearly" graduate "from the haughty ranks of amateur authorship and politesse."[29]

In celebration of Pinckney's success, Dr. Francis Stewart and his wife Kate sent a suckling pig to 36 Chalmers Street for Christmas dinner which was, as Sam Stoney recalled, "as big as a hound." With great fanfare, two serving men in high white hats brought in the succulent pig warmed by an enormous tray of hot coals underneath it. They then proceeded to skillfully carve the roast in delectable slices, producing quite a "sensation." Sam came to dinner alone. In 1937, he and Frost had a terrible "bust-up," largely due to her heavy drinking.[30]

Henry Canby urged the Book-of-the-Month committee to select Pinckney's manuscript, "a distinguished historical novel," as one of their choices for 1940, even though their docket was "clogged" with efforts to reproduce the success of *Anthony Adverse*. He particularly praised Pinckney for the sensitivity with which she rendered the first Carolinians and her descriptions of the wild, fresh earth, the primordial forest explored by Woodward. He had a hard sell and ultimately failed to sway the judges. Pinckney was partly to blame for ignoring his advice to excise all the treaties and other details of the early experiment in government, but she felt that Carolina's contributions to the republic were the heart of her work and refused to make concessions for the popular reader. "Every one liked it," Canby assured her. "They judged the writing 'distinguished,' but thought (I didn't), that it was a little too slow and quiet in movement to catch the attention of many readers, at a time when so many historical novels are being published."[31]

When the critical reviews came in, most agreed about the exceptional quality of Pinckney's writing, the "unexpected turns of phrase, wry and subtle humor, sagacious observations, and colorful descriptive passages." Gerald W. Johnson deemed Pinckney's historical narrative "art" more than fiction. He praised Pinckney's poetic style that tended away from the lush and melodic toward the "finely chiseled" and even "austere." The beauty of the book, Johnson thought, comes from its "lucidity and gem-like quality of catching and reflecting light until it seems luminous." The *New York Times* gave Pinckney lead billing over Carson McCullers's *Reflections in a Golden Eye* (considered by the reviewer as too self-consciously "grotesque"). Pinckney won praise for resisting the popular vogue for "brisk and realistic" prose and for writing instead in the subtle style of the poet, "making words say more than they actually mean." The *Times* review also extolled Pinckney's research and shrewd observation, noting that one reading was insufficient to mine all the riches of *Hilton Head*. Unfortunately many put *Hilton Head* down before giving it a fair chance.[32]

When *Hilton Head* reached the bookstores in January 1941, Pinckney returned to the list of goals that she drafted after Tom Waring's death. On the entry assuring herself that if Grace Stone could be a novelist, she could too, she went back and penciled in "(I did!!)."

## 10

# *Willkie and War*

Pinckney fell out of love with Henry Woodward early in their relationship. He disappointed her. She wanted a hero, a leader, a mouthpiece for her various ideas about politics and government. In *Hilton Head* she had hoped to make the point that America had aristocratic as well as democratic origins, that the founders were both realists and utopians. After two terms of Roosevelt's New Deal, she had had her fill of social experiments and the common man. As it happened, fate delivered her up another hero in the flesh, this one an "economic royalist."

Indiana Democrat Wendell Willkie first came to Pinckney's attention when editor William Watts Ball began giving him play in the *Charleston News and Courier*. Disgusted with the New Deal that only gave southern states the leftovers of national largesse and distrustful of Roosevelt's grab for power in a third term, Ball had begun agitating for a conservative revolution around 1937. He joined a growing number who wanted to declare South Carolina "independent" from the national Democratic Party and its platform. The state was ripe for change; only no leader was in sight.[1]

Then Willkie came into view. A broad-shouldered veteran of World War I, Willkie began his career as a country lawyer and worked his way up to wealth and power as president of a giant utilities-holding company, Commonwealth and Southern Corporation. With interests in the Charleston power company, Willkie became a regular visitor to the city. Bored with business talk at the end of the day, Willkie often stopped by Ball's office for a chat. He would settle in a chair, put up his feet on Ball's desk, and engage in lively, wide-ranging conversations with the opinionated editor. By 1939, Willkie had left the business world a very wealthy man, moved with his wife from Indiana to New York, and become affiliated with a Wall Street law firm. He soon changed his party affiliation from Democrat to Republican and began planning his campaign for the presidential nomination.[2]

Pinckney's interest in Willkie was piqued when Ball explained his new friend's interest in literature. In fact, Willkie wanted to meet the writers of Charleston. Since Ball's wife (a sister of Laura Witte Waring) never went out into society, he asked Pinckney to help him organize a party. Willkie was paying, so the sky was the limit. Rather than the local academic writers, Willkie wanted an evening with the "light literati," including Pinckney, John Bennett, Herbert Ravenel Sass, the Heywards, Beatrice Ravenel, and Sam Stoney. Ball also invited his daughter Katherine and son-in-law Clements Ripley, both writers as well.[3]

After years of grinding away on *Hilton Head* and being restrained by her own diminished personal resources, Pinckney was thrilled to plan a spectacular spread and send the bill to a New York millionaire. Happy days might, indeed, be here again. Since Charlestonians had not yet adopted the habit of "eating out," Pinckney thought propriety demanded that the hometown crowd should host this distinguished guest at 36 Chalmers Street, but Willkie insisted and she acquiesced. Pinckney hired some elegant rooms at 6 Gibbes Street where she set the scene with cocktails, caviar, and candlelight. In February 1940, with the exception of the Sasses and Beatrice Ravenel, who had family emergencies, all the "alleged" literary circle was assembled for the evening—for the last time, as it turned out. Willkie brought along editor Irita Van Doren, recently divorced from her historian husband. He also invited Lambert Davis, who had left the *Virginia Quarterly Review* for a position with the Indianapolis-based Bobbs-Merrill publishing company.[4]

Willkie's well-muscled mass dominated the head of the table. On his right was Pinckney, so perfectly in her element. To his left, competing for his attention, sat Julia Peterkin. At the other end of the table, W. W. Ball held forth, "running on all six." Everyone was on his best, most agreeable, behavior. The conversation centered on the current work of the assembled authors. DuBose Heyward, now back in Charleston full time, had hit a wall with his own writing, but found a wonderful situation mentoring talented young writers as the resident playwright at the Dock Street Theatre, a position funded by the Rockefeller Foundation. Dorothy spent her days deep in research for a play about the 1821 Denmark Vesey rebellion, called "Set My People Free." John Bennett went on at great length about all the many besieging daily interruptions (forty years worth actually) that had prevented him from finishing his book *Madame Margot*. At last, he announced, he was staggering along on "the last quarter mile." Susan Smythe Bennett spoke to all who would listen about her genealogy research and her proposed tourist guide to Charleston. Pinckney, of course, told about finishing *Hilton Head*, the difficult process of revision, and her fears about the critical reception of her long novel. Only Josephine's aging cousin, Archibald Rutledge of Hampton Plantation, feeling superannuated and out of place, projected a somber withdrawn countenance, his frail wife silent as the proverbial oyster. Despite his many achievements in the world of law and business, and the interest swirling about him in political circles, Willkie took the greatest pleasure in telling his guests about a review he had recently written of Lord David Cecil's *The Young Melbourne*. With childlike delight, he explained that his essay would soon appear in the book review section of the *New York Herald-Tribune* edited by Van Doren. The dinner ended with more conversation punctuated by the passing of coffee and brandy and lighting of cigarettes. Willkie thoroughly enjoyed this mellow interlude from the other, less genteel smoke-filled rooms in which he had been spending his time.[5]

Pinckney fell hard for the considerable charms of this "amiable tornado" who blew in and out of the quiet town so quickly. Willkie, a prodigious reader and perhaps the only person to ever sit down and systematically peruse every volume of the *Dictionary of American Biography* from cover to cover, had come to Charleston prepared with a detailed, almost encyclopedic, knowledge of the Pinckney family. The image of Willkie captured in his photographs suggests a hulking bozo, oversized farm boy sort of figure. His dark circled eyes, heavy jowls, and wide girth make his playboy reputation hard to fathom, but he possessed the "well-organized bulkiness of a healthy bear, and singularly brilliant eyes." Apparently his boundless vitality, almost a palpable heat—and later, the widespread belief that he was going to be the next president of the United States—made him irresistible to many women. After author Rebecca West met Willkie briefly in England, she wrote Van Doren to congratulate her on her catch: "He has everything, and I still feel the better for having warmed my hands at that fire." When Willkie left the Democratic Party to make his presidential bid in 1940, he became the first Republican in anyone's memory with sex appeal. Democrats believed he was a political gigolo out to seduce the American people.[6]

Willkie mailed Pinckney a packet of his various writings stating his political positions. Josephine replied with "a slug of Pinckneyana." She included an extract from Alexander Garden's *Anecdotes of the American Revolution* describing General Thomas Pinckney's approach to a mutiny among one of his regiments. He walked "right into their midst with no thought to his own danger, and with one blow of his sabre, cut down their ringleader," pivoted and left the survivors suing loudly for mercy and forgiveness." "If you should observe the trait of 'walk-in-and-cut-'em-down' cropping out in any of [General Pinckney's] descendants," she chided Willkie, "don't say you didn't have fair warning."[7]

Pinckney had fair warning as well. She could not have missed Irita Van Doren's proprietary beam when she looked at Willkie; their open affair was the talk of New York. Van Doren had opened the door of her charmed circle of intellectuals to Willkie, inviting him to her rustic home tucked in the hills around West Cornwall, Connecticut. The star-struck Willkie became a regular visitor. He met her friends, including Carl Sandburg, Sinclair Lewis, Dorothy Thompson, Stephen Vincent Benét, and of course the Canbys. After leaving the utility business, Wendell Willkie thrashed about, restless with no outlets for his capacious energy. He recklessly chased after women, all sorts of women, from secretaries to movie stars. To stave off boredom, he engaged in these affairs (many one-night stands actually) in indiscreet, daredevil fashion, taking "careless and stupid" chances that made his advisers blanch. Roosevelt adviser Harold Ickes noted, "Willkie likes to play with a lot of women and is quite catholic in his tastes."[8]

During the ten years of Willkie's ascent, having a fling with the "barefoot boy of Wall Street" (FDR's formulation) was a rite of passage for many ambitious, talented women at home and abroad. Mary McCarthy, another author given the rush by Willkie, wrote a short story satirizing the modus operandi of a Midwestern businessman with literary interests. "The Man in the Brooks Brothers Shirt" begins on a train with a female writer for a Leftist intellectual journal trying to ignore the gaze of a lurking figure, whose face looked like "a middle-aged baby, or like a young pig, or something out of a seed catalogue," dressed in a well-tailored suit and an expensive monogrammed shirt. Finally, he makes his move, asking her questions in his "soft and furry" flat Midwestern voice, and seeming absolutely captivated by every extraordinary thing she said. Suddenly she feels "beautiful and gay and clever, and worldly and innocent, serious and frivolous, . . . bad and really good, all mixed up together" as these "multiple personalities all bloomed on the stalk of her ego." Perhaps she had been mistaken and this was "a frustrated man of sensibility," a Sherwood Anderson–type character, with a wife who was a member of the Book-of-the-Month Club and didn't understand him. The suspected Rotarian turns out to be a steel magnate and begins to wear her down. One thing leads to another. They go to his roomette for a drink. She starts to believe she could open the door of his soul. Ultimately, the inevitable happens. Then there is talk of love, of divorce from the mousy wife, of their marriage together, a marriage of minds. At the same time that his raw potential draws her in, his innate vulgarity repulses her. Just as her interest is waning, his correspondence begins to take the form of dictated letters in correct business English typed by his secretary. He has the nerve to cast his calf eyes on some other woman of interest.[9]

Willkie's philandering became embedded in popular culture with the film *State of Union,* with Spencer Tracy playing a womanizing business tycoon turned politician and Katherine Hepburn (miscast) as his estranged but still loyal little wife who decides to be a good sport and play the role of the adoring spouse on the campaign trail. Only in the Hollywood version of the story does fidelity overcome all odds. New Yorkers frequently saw the "plain vanilla" Edith Wilkie walking aimlessly through the Metropolitan Museum all alone.[10]

During May 1940, Pinckney followed political events even more closely than usual during Willkie's whirlwind political campaign that lasted only forty-eight days. Once Henry and Clare Booth Luce, who had a home north of Charleston, decided Willkie could beat the prim Thomas E. Dewey in the Republican primary, they marketed him like toothpaste through their media empire that included *Time, Life, Look,* and *Fortune.* Petitions even circulated in the streets of Charleston advocating Willkie as the Independent Democrat's presidential nominee. Immediately after his nomination, Willkie showed surprising strength in South Carolina: "the most astonishing political manifestation since 1876," wrote W. W. Ball.[11]

But the events of the summer merged into the blur of grief to Pinckney. On June 16, 1940, just before the Republican convention, she received the shocking, almost stupefying, news of the death of DuBose Heyward. He had suffered a heart attack while in the North Carolina mountains and was buried under the oaks of St. Phillip's Church Cemetery on the morning of June 28, 1940. His old friends turned out. Pinckney, Hervey Allen, Albert and Harriet Simons, John and Susan Bennett, Sam Stoney all huddled together, competing for bits of shade in the blazing summer sun.[12]

Dorothy Heyward looked ashen and frail at the funeral, a mere wisp really. Pinckney transferred much of her affection for DuBose to his wife and child, ten-year-old Jennifer. DuBose Heyward had been adamant that his daughter should maintain her Low Country roots and hoped Pinckney would raise his child if somehow both of her ailing parents died. Although Pinckney had agreed with alacrity, Dorothy thought that in her "heart of hearts—her subconscious maybe," she might actually be "appalled" if Jennifer showed up on her door suitcase in hand. After Dorothy moved her base to New York City, Pinckney agreed to tend DuBose's grave, making sure there were poinsettias at Christmas and lilies at Easter. She also kept close accounts of her expenses so that Dorothy could reimburse her.[13]

Wendell Willkie further endeared himself to Pinckney and her friends by sending a contribution to the memorial fund established in Heyward's name at the Dock Street Theatre. After Willkie's convention victory in Philadelphia, Robert N. S. Whitelaw of the Carolina Art Association who also oversaw the Dock Street Theatre sent Willkie a telegram: "Remembering your interest in us, we wish you to know that we have followed your nomination with interest and offer our sincere congratulations."[14]

Pinckney spent much of the summer with Alice Huntington in what may be described as the enemy camp. The Franklin Roosevelts had helped Huntington find a place to rent in Barrytown, New York, near Eleanor's haven at Val-kill. Pinckney found the household in disarray when she first arrived. Huntington was on the phone to Adolf Berle, an assistant secretary of state. Her daughter had been arrested in Paris when the city fell to the Nazis. "We have been chugging back and forth to Hyde Park while Mrs. R. stirred up the State Department which has obtained Elizabeth's provisional release," Pinckney wrote Hervey Allen. "We don't know what 'provisional' means but at least it is something to have her out of the jug."[15]

Pinckney and Huntington, of course, wrangled incessantly about the election. When she returned home to Charleston in the fall, Pinckney embraced the Independent Democrat position and enlisted in Willkie's "electric light brigade." On Election Day 1940, Pinckney had been disappointed, but not surprised, at Willkie's defeat. In South Carolina, the "barefoot boy" charmed 1,727 voters out of 95,000. He did carry, however, three precincts in the city of Charleston. Nationwide, he won the most votes ever tallied by a losing candidate. In December, Willkie flew into Charleston on a private plane to have a postmortem of his campaign with the Luces at Mepkin Plantation. Edith Willkie and journalist Russell Davenport accompanied him. The next day, Edith went ahead to Hobe Sound, Florida, to begin a long recuperative vacation. Willkie lingered behind in Charleston.[16] When he left, packed into his suitcase for seaside reading was an advance copy of *Hilton Head*.

The holiday mail at 36 Chalmers Street was finally thinning out just after New Year's Day 1941 when a telegram arrived from Hobe Sound. This was the gift Josephine Pinckney had been hoping for. It read: "The novel is wonderful and everything OK. Wendell." Four days later, Western Union rang again with a wire from New York: "That sentence on bottom of page 230 and top of page 231. I reread it this morning. It still makes me mad and it again will make me mad if I reread it a year from now. I hope in later edition it is deleted. Nobody but a feminist, a southern lady and a Pinckney could have written it. I stayed up until half past four this morning and finished the book. It is magnificent. As I told you. I knew you were good, but I never knew how good. Affectionately. Wendell."[17]

Pinckney was transported with pleasure. "Fancy taking it all in one dose like that!" she responded. "The celebrated Willkie vitality must be even better than I've heard tell." She knew he had been inundated with mail (thirty thousand letters in the first five days after his defeat) urging him to run again for president in 1944.[18]

Willkie penetrated Pinckney's usual sangfroid with his unexpected words of praise. "Your comments on the book made me so happy I almost wept," she confessed. "If you meant half of what you said," she continued, "those years of hard work have now brought me success, since I have pleased the audience whose opinion I value most. You won't be able to imagine what a thrill your words brought me nor how you have bolstered me up to face the queasy time just ahead for me and H[ilton]. H[ead]. I send you my love and thanks."[19]

Typically, Pinckney's mellow mood evaporated rather quickly. She soon picked up her pen to respond to Willkie's complaint. The offending passage from *Hilton Head* comes when Henry Woodward is sulking dejectedly on his surgeon's chest. He had decided to remain behind in 1670 while the crew of the *Carolina* sails northward in search of a likely place for a settlement. He ponders why he has lost the affections of two women, the rich merchant's daughter in Barbados and the once devoted Indian maiden Tu-que given to him by the Westoes in Carolina. "Painfully, he plumbed his mind and finally wrought up an idea—a quite simple idea that he had heretofore overlooked; in his pursuit of new coasts, new towns, of knowledge and money, he had never given himself wholly to either woman, and they had rewarded his half-measures—sensible women—by taking their wares to other markets" (230–31).

Pinckney reminded Willkie, that the objectionable words reflect Henry Woodward's sentiments, not her own. The ripening of Woodward's "callow and half-hearted" feelings for his wife Mary was an important part of the story. "Hell," she retorted, "of course they were sensible [women] . . . sensibleness is not one of the most admirable human qualities. Personally, I am inclined to belittle it, not being very sensible myself." She warns him also not to "fall into the egregious error of confusing me with Mary—actually she's a triumph of objective creation; I'd probably have waited for him, like a ninny." She added tartly, "you are really a ridiculous, vestigial remainder of the Victorian period." Then she goes to the heart of the matter. "Maybe your heated defence of Woodward comes from the circumstance that you also are only half- to three-quarter-hearted in matters related to that explosive organ. You lawyers are cautious fellows and totally unlike us poets who say what we feel without hedging."[20]

At this juncture, just as Pinckney was pounding her typewriter, getting up a real head of steam, her telephone rang. It was Willkie. His voice lush with excitement, he told her he was going to England to see the war first hand. She fell silent, "floored" by his news. Throughout the holiday season, Pinckney, like most Americans, had been riveted to radios following reports of the Battle of Britain, of the horrific bombing of London by the German Luftwaffe. This could be Armageddon, Roosevelt had warned, the end of western civilization. Knowing her unenthusiastic response had disappointed him, she later apologized: "My heart and mind are too full for a letter. More at some other time, perhaps."[21]

Pinckney, ever the Anglophile, had raged at Roosevelt's neutrality during the moment of Britain's great trial. She signed on to the international "Author's Manifesto" circulated by the PEN organization urging "all aid and at once, whatever that may have to mean, to the embattled isles, whose language, which is also ours, is the only tool by which we live and think."[22]

After Pearl Harbor, Pinckney joined the thousands of South Carolina volunteers watching the skies for enemy planes. "I am practically in the Army now," she explained to Willkie. She rose at the crack of dawn ("the greatest sacrifice my country could ask of me") and reported to the Charleston Information and Filter Center on Hayne Street affiliated with the Third Interceptor Command. In the afternoons, she performed civil defense work. Both jobs she found "utterly fascinating." Not only had she learned about enemy airplanes, which she could now identify on sight, but the total involvement of the community in the war effort put her in contact with "people that I never knew before . . . In spite of the catastrophes in the papers, I must confess to getting a horrid enjoyment out of the war so far."[23] Her first close-up exposure to all the mix of classes in Charleston began her thinking about situations for her next novel.

Pinckney also lent her pen to the war effort. She wrote two scripts for patriotic radio programs aired under the auspices of the Dock Street Theatre. Each ran about fifteen minutes. In one play, Pinckney has the ghosts of Confederate seaman lost in 1863 in the "Little David" (an experimental "submersible" invented by Charlestonian St. Julien Ravenel) return to save Charleston once again. Only this time, Germans, not Yankees, lurked just outside the harbor trying to find the channel.[24]

Given no role to play in the war effort by Roosevelt, Willkie assumed the part of the loyal opposition. He warned the Republicans not to try to make political hay over the costs of this crusade; "this death struggle of democracy against totalitarianism is the most tremendous thing in history." In the fall of 1942, Wendell Willkie left the country on a whirlwind trip around the world, drinking vodka with Stalin and having an audience with Madame Chiang Kai-shek. Pinckney followed his progress closely, clipping news articles and listening to his radio addresses. Whenever she heard his voice crackling over the wires, she always felt a "little twist of the heart." When he returned in October, he found a telegram from Pinckney. "So happy you are back safe, a swell job and love and congratulations. Jo."[25]

Pinckney anticipated Willkie's much-publicized "Report to the People" about his trip "with excitement and impatience" and offered some advice. She thought his title sounded too populist, too much like the Henry Wallace's "Common Man."

All four major networks carried Willkie's talk on October 26, 1942. More than thirty-six million Americans tuned in, many imagining they were listening to their next president. "Our thinking and planning in the future must be global," Willkie asserted. Defeating the Axis was only one war aim. The other must be for America to take the lead in liberating the world to assure peace in the future. Pinckney nearly "burst a blood vessel" when he spelled out his vision of the postwar world, demanding the liberation of all British colonies but remaining silent about the future of Poland and other Eastern European nations under the boot of Stalin. "Personally, I am very democratic, so I believe in fair and equal treatment for all the oppressors," she wrote in a blistering letter. "The truth is, Wendell," she continued, "that we have first to decide on our own war aims. . . . announcements that our hearts bleed for the subject peoples is going to sound phony unless we are ready to bleed, and bleed out loud, for the Poles, the Letts, the Syrians and what have you, and the call for a declaration of post-war policy is equally fake if we haven't got what it takes to ask Stalin for his along with the rest."[26]

Pinckney was upset because she knew what was coming next. Willkie's speech was not just about postwar Europe. Willkie had begun listening sympathetically to African Americans when they appealed to him about their virtual disenfranchisement in the Jim Crow South. Willkie's overnight reincarnation as a social liberal left Pinckney "somewhat breathless." The Charleston radio station WCSC stopped broadcasting his speeches. Even W. W. Ball, his "former gauleiter" seldom published his name anymore. "God knows how many indiscretions you've committed that I don't know about," she wrote Willkie. "What makes me maddest of all is that no matter how mad I get with you I still care so much what you do. I can't seem to control my unruly feelings—you know . . . I still expect a hell of a lot out of you—good judgment and tough-mindedness and a steady eye on where you are going, and I'm going to keep after you until you deliver. So now you know what to expect of me—love and brickbats. Not a bad regimen; it may land you in the Presidency of the New World Order. It wouldn't be surprising."[27]

Willkie scarcely had time to digest this diatribe when the next evening Pinckney fired off another midnight "lecture" in a long telegram warning to him about taking a position against the poll tax, a hot button issue among southerners. "I beg you to consider carefully before pitching into the current mess over it. The passage of this bill will not increase the vote in the South appreciably and the idiotic controversy is devastating to the efforts of southerners who are trying to get for the [Negroes] the right to vote in the primaries. The best thing you could do for the Negro is to keep build[ing] up two parties in the South and this cause will not be served by your joining in the political claptrap dished out by the professional liberals." Willkie later retorted that her limited ideas of social change only revealed how "a southern aristocrat can become fearful when she allows her notion of aristocratic paternalistic liberalism to be tested by real liberalism."[28]

In 1943, Willkie's *One World,* a summary of his internationalist philosophy, was published and became an overnight hit, selling a million copies in seven weeks, two million by the end of the year. He advocated uniting the diverse peoples of the world in the human struggle for freedom and justice in some international forum, along the lines the United Nations later took.[29]

Despite their obvious differences, Willkie asked her not to abandon him. She assured him, "I've invested too much faith in you during the last three years to give up my stake without a struggle. If I really lost my faith in you, I'd give up the world, retire to a hermitage—not so much because of my personal feeling for you (as you may hastily assume) but because of what it has meant to me, and to all the others who voted for you, to find a leader, a spokesman with idealism which was not the phony idealism of the New Deal, a champion of a point of view that seemed about to go down before the mush-headed philosophy and the intellectual dishonesty of the Administration." "Perhaps you never realized—and perhaps its just as well—how much your leadership means to me, how much hope it gives me in the daily struggle to make some sense of this cock-eyed world," Pinckney confessed. "I want you for a leader, and I mean to have you. So."[30]

During January 1943, Willkie and Pinckney seized the chance for one of their rare meetings in New York. After she returned home, she wrote him that "the war has landed practically in our laps" when a British air-craft carrier was torpedoed at the mouth of the Charleston Harbor. "Altogether life seems full of incident," she wrote Willkie. "If this keeps up, I'll be too busy plotting plane flights to write you lecturing letters. But this wasn't meant to be all lecture. It is meant to say, how are you, and a lot of other things. It was lovely to see you again."[31]

In the spring, Pinckney resolved that she would rent out 36 Chalmers Street and move to New York where she could work undisturbed on the new novel that was beginning to take shape in her mind, and, of course, be closer to Willkie. Pinckney ultimately leased a small cozy spot, an apartment in a three-story townhouse at 154 East 61st Street that would not have been out of place in Charleston. The winds of winter blizzard swirled outside, but an old coal furnace kept her "workshop" warm, and she made excellent progress with her story about Charleston on the eve of World War II. "I haven't enjoyed myself as much in years," she wrote Emily Sinkler Roosevelt as she described her busy schedule of operas, concerts, and art exhibitions.[32]

Pinckney also loved reconnecting with old friends in New York, but the talk was no longer about writing and literature. Over drinks and dinner, she found herself embroiled in "bouts, jousts, tourneys, dog-fights and cutting scrapes" about politics. Pinckney was amazed at the level of anti-British sentiment that still flourished among liberals. Her visits to long time friends Padraic and Molly Colum inevitably ended with fighting about the war. "The goddamn Irish!" she complained to Hervey Allen. "They can't get over their grudge against England."[33]

Of course, part of the attraction of New York was Willkie. Pinckney had made little effort to conceal their relationship. On one occasion when she was staying with Carrie Lockwood in Massachusetts, the telephone rang very late at night. The next morning, Lockwood's daughter, Sidney, wanted to know who had called at such an hour. Lockwood told her it was Wendell Willkie calling Jo; he was her lover. Pinckney invited him to spend a weekend at the Highlands with Nicholas and Emily Roosevelt. She also admitted that Willkie gave her stock tips. When a bank stock he recommended lost value, he offered to take it "off her hands" at her original purchase.[34]

For those highly invested in Willkie's career, such as Henry and Clare Booth Luce, Pinckney was just one more unnecessary distraction. The two had become something of an "item" in New York. In 1943, Willkie decided to throw his hat in the ring against Roosevelt, who gave every indication of running for a fourth term. When Pinckney learned that Willkie was coming for a quick strategy meeting at the Luce's Mepkin Plantation in November, she wrote Clare inviting them all to dinner. Clare Booth Luce, who broached no competition, timed her note to arrive after Willkie had left for the train station. Her message said that Willkie had just been too tired to come into the city. What Luce did not know was that Willkie, so familiar with the machinations of women's minds, had lied about the train schedule and left many hours early, giving him plenty of time to spend at 36 Chalmers Street before returning to New York.[35]

Someone, probably Pinckney herself, leaked the story to the New York press for a bit of revenge. The *New York Post*'s Broadway gossip columnist Leonard Lyons picked it up and revealed all the details. According to Lyons, Luce's offending note arrived while Willkie was visiting "his old friend." "Josephine Pinckney read their message, while Willkie was in the room," Lyons reported. "Then the true Southern hostess tore it up, and didn't let Willkie know." The *New Yorker* picked up this tidbit and added "Mum's the word, eh, Josephine?" As soon as Prentiss Taylor read this juicy piece of gossip, he wrote Pinckney for the scoop. She confirmed the facts but said Lyons had one bit wrong. He credited her with too much restraint. My "snobbish Southern-lady-ness which, as you have guessed, would never have torn up the Luce letter had it arrived while Mr. W. was with me."[36]

At some point, Pinckney claimed, her ardor for Willkie melted away. The moment that heralds the end of an affair, the death of passion, is almost always a quiet small thing that usually passes unnoticed except in the recollection; the cigarette ash falling unnoticed on the floor, the feet on the desk, a jarring malapropism. For all his political and intellectual achievements, Willkie never totally overcame the habits that had marked him as a "pretty crude country boy" (with exclamations such as "that's a lot of spinach!") when he first came to New York in 1929. Pinckney's awakening about Willkie occurred in the back seat of a New York City cab. During one of their visits together, their cabby had screeched up to their destination, the impatient Willkie tossed him the fare and lumbered from the back seat out onto the sidewalk waiting for Pinckney to slip over and hop out behind him. Not accustomed to slipping or hopping, Pinckney remained in the car, back straight, eyes ahead, chin up, lips pursed. Miss Pinckney was waiting for her door to be opened. That was the moment when she realized that despite the addition of his name to the New York Social Register in 1936, this Indiana farmer was still no gentleman. Another possible explanation for the end of the affair was Willkie's unwillingness to divorce his wife after the campaign was over. Pinckney had probably overstepped by coming to New York. Irita Van Doren was still very much in the picture, although she and Willkie were more discreet than in the past. Pinckney could seldom produce Willkie on demand when her friends came to visit. "Wendell," she explained to Emily Roosevelt, "has a curious habit of going to Indiana like a horse to the stable."[37]

Willkie failed to excite the nation in 1944 as he had four years earlier. His leftward turn disturbed former supporters. The war had drained internationalism of its appeal. He had failed to pay his dues to the Republican Party by supporting other candidates and failed to win the nomination. In April 1944, Pinckney wrote a consoling note to the man "who would rather be right than president." "You told me once that you would rather be an influence in your time that be elected president," she reminded Willkie. "I remember receiving this with the natural skepticism I have for the pronouncements of politicos, in general and for yours in particular. It now appears that this once I was wrong, and I hereby offer amends. In this country, it's impossible to be a leader in the real sense of the word and be president."[38]

Despite an "avalanche of mail," Willkie answered her "sassy but sweet" note personally. Willkie assured her he wasn't depressed by the Wisconsin primary defeat that ended his second presidential bid. "As a matter of fact, I'm on top of the wave. I fought the kind of a fight I wanted to fight. And I didn't dip my colors in falling. You probably don't realize how much satisfaction there is in that. For you have not had to live amid the crushing pressures of political expediency." He concluded with his hope that they could meet soon, perhaps "before Charleston again becomes an anachronism as it was before touched with the miracle of war prosperity."[39]

Pinckney was back in New York staying with Alice Huntington on Fifth Avenue when Wendell Willkie died early on the morning of October 8, 1944. After years of almost maniacal overwork, hard drinking, overeating, and three packs of Camels a day, he suffered a massive coronary after a series of smaller heart attacks. When Pinckney learned of Willkie's passing, she broke a date with Prentiss Taylor claiming incapacity from a bad cold. She explained her loss in a clinical, matter-of-fact fashion to Taylor, who had been apprised of most of the details of her affair. "Willkie's death depresses me horribly; there seems to be no one to lead his group in the Republican Party at a time when that group needs to throw its weight for all it is worth." Perhaps she joined the crowd of sixty thousand Americans who paid their respects when his body lay in state. Long after the Indiana businessman's death, Pinckney still considered herself "a Willkie-ite," an internationalist, in politics. When she first appeared in *Who's Who* in 1947, she still called herself an Independent Democrat.[40] Although she had admired many of Franklin D. Roosevelt's goals, "his way of going about them usually gave me mild apoplectic seizures."[41]

In January 1945, Pinckney turned fifty years old. Her search for a good New England preparatory school for DuBose Heyward's daughter Jennifer made her realize how rapidly time was passing. After visiting Hervey and Ann Allen at their Maryland estate, Pinckney wrote them that "In a world of rapidly diminishing pleasures, we must hang on to such enjoyments as eating, swimming and wrangling together." The numbers of admiring men had also diminished, not only because of her age but because of the war. Grace Stone commiserated with Pinckney on the scarcity of male diversion but told her, "Don't despair, we'll probably *enjoy* being queer old ladies together."[42]

As the "heavy hand of age" pressed upon her, Pinckney resisted, getting herself a "new tuck-up hair do" to slow down the clock a bit. She had been lying about her birth date for years. When she encountered John Bennett at a meeting of the South Carolina Historical Society, they had a pleasant interchange. The world had been so transformed since those simple days twenty-five years before when they started the Poetry Society, Bennett felt compelled to write her a line. "It was like old times, seeing you again . . . There is something about you that does not change, nor seems to show the shadow of changing, a delicate, perdurable charm, as delightful as a spring morning."[43] Neither one of them knew it at the time, but Pinckney was on the eve of her own rendezvous with destiny.

# 11

# *American Fantasy*

In October 1944, Marshall Best, managing editor of Viking Press, surveyed the stack of mail on his desk with dismay. The stream of authors anxious to publish with this prestigious house seemed to swell every year. A small pale blue envelope of the sort used for social correspondence caught his eye in the mounded drift of white overstuffed packets. Intrigued, he opened it. The upright Best was immediately taken back by the bold message conveyed on fine ladies' stationery. Josephine Pinckney was making an adulterous overture to him at a time when authors and editors enjoyed relationships much more sacred than most modern marriages.

Confessing that her long relationship with Farrar and Rinehart was no longer satisfactory, Pinckney wrote Best of her "secret admiration" for Viking Press and offered him first option on her manuscript. He generally disdained the "pimping and procuring" side of publishing by which editors seduced successful writers away from the competition, but seeing a mature manuscript by a published author as "grist to our mill," Best invited her to submit her work. Years later, Best recollected that his greatest professional rewards had sprung "from the unheralded manuscript which he is the first to recognize," a first or second book that would be the forerunner of an important literary career. The two most vivid examples he could recall involved Elizabeth Maddox Roberts's *The Time of Man* and Josephine Pinckney's *Three O'Clock Dinner*.[1]

In her second novel, Josephine Pinckney flung open the shutters of the cloistered life of Charleston aristocrats, once ascendant but now on the wane. She flooded their wainscoted rooms with sunlight and revealed their well-worn upholstery and mended linen, their vanities and insecurities, their impotence and their inward gaze. Pinckney rendered the superannuated master class with both sympathy and irony, in a way that was clearly a valediction, not a vindication. Her characters had more in common with the bumbling, enervated European aristocracy than with the coarse, ill-mannered industrial "aristocracy" depicted by Henry James and William Dean Howells. In *Three O'Clock Dinner*, Pinckney not only forces the old aristocrats to lock eyes with the vulgar parvenu but to dine with them as well when the only son marries a young woman who is both an affront and a threat to their well-ordered world.

Pinckney had begun outlining *Three O'Clock Dinner* in 1941 when she began her civil defense work during the war. Fascinated by the diverse elements of Charleston she met—the brash, upwardly mobile grandchildren of Irish and German immigrants, the downtown Junior Leaguers, the new breed of high-stepping career girls who went to their secretarial jobs without hats or gloves, middle-class housewives from the Terrace—she wanted to make a statement about class dynamics in Charleston. Pinckney studied the lingo and mannerisms of her coworkers with the same intensity that she had scrutinized the Gullah singers when she was recording their songs.

Pinckney had planned to write a tragic novel about love thwarted by class prejudices along the lines of Christopher Morley's popular *Kitty Foyle* and J. P. Marquand's *The Late George Apley*. The bourgeois Hessenwinkles and the patrician Redcliffs of her story were not exactly the Capulets and the Montagues, nor were their children, Lorena and Tat, exactly Juliet and Romeo, but Pinckney wanted to create a heartrending situation of true love thwarted by outmoded strictures of class and religion. The tragedy ramped away from her, however, and she ended up with a social comedy of manners more on the order of Jane Austen, with the central action and best writing focused on the meeting of immigrants and emigrants over a broad expanse of damask.

*Three O'Clock Dinner* is set in Charleston about 1937. The drama of the two families unfolds as a "pinpoint" against storm clouds of war brewing in Europe and the domestic social changes brought by the New Deal in the South. Pinckney chronicles the final passing of Charleston's depleted aristocracy on the eve of World War II. When she began contemplating this decline in the mid-1920s, she thought that the transformation of the power structure might be the stuff of a great epic novel, but in *Three O'Clock Dinner* only the sadness of lost opportunity lingers. By 1945, the old aristocrats of Charleston had done little to make their passing of very great moment. Readers are no more sorry to see them lose influence than they did the decline of Edith Wharton's spoiled children of America's industrial elite. With her image of the American aristocrat shaped by the Code, Pinckney is absolutely unsparing in her criticism of the failure of the "top drawer" to live up to their responsibilities.

The novel begins with Judith Redcliff, one of Pinckney's best characterizations, embarking on a long, tortured path toward self-realization. The young widow with only "grief as a bedfellow" is tortured by the past. Even after two years, Judith is still obsessed with the tragic death of her husband. With only her small walled garden, the antics of her little dog, and her job at a local charity to occupy her, Judith spends her evenings alone reliving scenes from her childless marriage. Unable to repress Fen's sharp, careless words or condescending gestures, she is forced to admit that their time together was not the idyll she had once imagined but really the story of a hundred little hurts. Always grateful, but never fully understanding why the handsome, charismatic Fen chose her, proper and plain, for his wife, she concludes that given all her inadequacies, he could not possibly have loved her. She agonizes over her thin, angular body and the long difficult hair she tries to tame with old-fashioned hairpins. Her slight limp, a legacy of her struggle with polio the summer before her husband died, completes her self-concept of total undesirability. As she mentally paces the boundaries of her circumscribed life, Judith realizes that she lived a typical "woman's world, clean split as half an apple," divided between the meaningless tasks of her own daily occupation and her real life that only began when her husband came home from work and told her the news from the outside.[2]

The dignified and reserved Judith is jerked out of her morbid preoccupation with the past, by the brash and lusty Lorena Hessenwinkle, whose family lives behind the Redcliffs' sagging antebellum Georgian mansion. Lorena, a woman of indeterminate age who overindulges in henna dye, has a shadowy past and a present that is the subject of much local speculation. Recently she has been seen keeping company with Judith's idealistic and naive brother-in-law Tat, the Redcliffs' only surviving son. During a chance meeting, the effusive Lorena says too much about her friendship with both Redcliff boys and leaves the insecure widow with an unsettling feeling.

Tat is a constant source of worry to his parents. With their two married daughters off in California and seemingly of little interest to Etta and Fenwick Redcliff, Tat is the one hope that their name and values will live on. His mother's favorite, Tat has also been a problem child, always jealous of his older brother. He flunked out of Princeton but is full of high talk about the insights of Karl Marx, the need for government regulation of the economy, and "changing the system." A seeker after absolute Truth, Tat might have been an abolitionist and co-conspirator with the Grimké sisters had he lived in a different time. He describes his work, pumping oil at an independent filling station, as striking a blow against the Rockefeller Standard Oil monopoly and the loss of local economic control. Of course, he challenges the Code and all his parents hold dear, even marriage. Tat is an advocate of free love.

Most painful of all is Tat's disdain for the Redcliff family home. Located in the Wraggsborough section of town, which had grown unfashionable and run-down, the house was admittedly a white elephant. Fen had always planned to continue the family tradition in the Redcliff home, but Tat, a self-declared individualist, argues that Charleston needs "more smokestacks along the waterfront and less crumbly Colonial" (86). The house had actually been inherited by Etta Redcliff, but she signed it over to Wick. He at first thought this an act of trust, but after many years he realized by accepting this house he had given her a bond upon him. Still, even with this knowledge, he remained devoted both to her and their home in the same sort of comfortable unquestioning way. His only real complaint focused on her complacency—and her resistance to having lunch at two o'clock. "In Papa's time," she reminded him almost daily, "we dined at three" (81).

In contrast to the well-modulated, predictable rhythms of life in the Redcliff establishment stood the teeming Hessenwinkle house. Their sheer numbers served as daily reminders to Wick of how tenuous a hold his class had on the city. The Hessenwinkles belonged to an invasion of German and Irish families who swarmed into the stately old "boroughs" on the upper reaches of the Charleston peninsula as their fortunes had improved. Formerly proud mansions were divided into apartments or reduced to sheltering boarders. For Lorena's father, business-man August Hessenwinkle, owning his own home in the borough represented a major step up the social ladder. His German-born father had been a baker who raised his children "over the store." Hessenwinkle's crassly ambitious wife, Vinny, belonged to the Irish Catholic O'Dell family. The Hessenwinkle's marriage repre-sents the merger of the immigrant factions fiercely vying with both the conser-vative, patrician Charleston leaders (still hoping to stave off the democratizing trends of the modern age) and the slightly more progressive "Broad Street Ring" for political and cultural control of the city. By the 1930s, no candidate could win a city election without support of the white working classes. Like the ethnic politi-cal coalitions of Charleston, the marriage of August and Vinny was not always harmonious. August Hessenwinkle, a stolid Lutheran, often felt uncomfortable with the high degree of corruption and sin prevalent in the city, whereas the Irish O'Dells not only accepted but often profited from prostitution, gambling, and the bootlegging "blind tigers" that thrived in the notorious demimonde of prohibition-era Charleston. Vinny prided herself on her active involvement with "the boys" in the democratic process; she spent each Election Day on the phone establishing who on the electoral rolls was dead so the local machine could "vote the grave-yard" (140–41).

Vinny's misguided energy in shady political operations provides a dramatic contrast to the languorous rectitude of the Redcliff men. Wick Redcliff had descended from a long line of men active in the public life of the state and nation but had done little in the way of community service himself. Judith Redcliff who believed the "the top drawer" of society should accept their responsibilities asks

Wick, "Why don't decent people go into politics any more?" "Selfishness and defeatism," he admits, sensitive that he has never taken advantage of the opportunities for local office assured by his prominent name. He had held back, believing in the eighteenth-century idea that the "office should seek the man," but confesses that his principle was also an "alibi." Still, he was interested in politics and deplored the "folly" of the one-party system in the South: "For years I have been clamouring for an Opposition—Republican, Socialist, whatever . . . against the Solid South" (21).

Excited over the possibility of change, Judith Redcliff shows unusual animation and stabs at the air with one finger: "Why don't you start a new party then?" Wick falls back on another alibi, claiming that his historic ties to the Democratic Party prevent him from branching out: "God made me a Southerner, an Episcopalian, and a Democrat . . . in a world of shifting truths these are the principles I like to stand on" (21). In reality, old aristocrats of Wick's generation seemed, like the South's cotton land, sad, exhausted, and drained trying to find an economic niche appropriate to their station. Wick made an erratic living marketing phosphate fertilizers, a product tied to the cotton market. Lucian Redcliff, his half brother, sold real estate. Judith's husband Fen had worked with a local dry-dock and never made enough money to afford her desire to have a baby.

The Redcliffs are shaken when the dreaded telegram from Myrtle Beach arrives announcing Tat has taken Lorena as his wife. Tat's ideology is no match for the seductive powers of Lorena, a girl with a great deal more experience with love (albeit not always free) than the young service-station attendant. Determined to prove herself the equal of Judith, Lorena insists that the price of her favors is a ring.

Etta Redcliff draws strength from the Code and announces the family will close ranks behind Tat and do the right thing. She begins organizing a proper three o'clock Sunday dinner to welcome the newlyweds home. Despite pleas from her husband to consider the working-class habits of the Hessenwinkles, she is firm. "We'll have dinner at three because that is when we have dinner," Etta replies with a hard face, feeling the need to throw herself into the breach and help hold the line of tradition. "The Hessenwinkles can come full or empty as they choose" (133).

As strong willed in her own way as her son, Etta Redcliff wages a one-woman campaign against insidious corporate values boring through the supporting timbers of southern tradition. Southerners had bitterly resisted the implementation of standard time (as opposed to "God's time") that they properly saw as a concession to the railroad schedule. The three o'clock dinner was in fact one of the last vestiges of the old plantation culture. Charleston's seventeenth-century founders, such as Henry Woodward, had come to Carolina from the West Indies. They imported with them the sensible habit of making the most of the cooler morning hours, then having a substantial meal in the afternoon followed by a rest, then resuming work in the cool of the day. At night, they partook of a light supper. Changing the dinner time was another inroad of standardization resisted by the South.

The handwritten invitations on Etta's engraved stationery are personally delivered by the gossipy Lucian who in his excitement over the coming domestic fireworks can hardly restrain himself from asking each person he sees, "Guess who's coming to dinner?" Everyone accepts, including cousin Jane Catesby and her children, Judith, and Aunt Quince, Wick's stepmother. Uninvited, but in attendance, is Harry O'Dell, Lorena's enterprising uncle, who in a foreshadowing of what is to come brings the number around the Redcliff table to an unlucky thirteen.

Pinckney's novel moves into high gear when the old Madeira is passed and the first course is served. Her treatment of the diverse elements of Charleston society toasting one another with the Redcliffs' very fine old claret is masterful. She does a skillful job of circling the table, revealing the thoughts of each character. Departing from the omniscient authorial voice, Pinckney switches points of view, describing the dinner through one pair of eyes, then another. Wick shows himself an old fool as he makes indiscreet, julep-inspired advances toward his buxom new daughter-in-law. Her red and pink taffeta contrasts dramatically with his thin black-draped wife, "half crow and half curate." Even Judith looks pale and diminished in her overrefined homemade flounces. After so many years of standing outside looking in, Vinny Hessenwinkle is clearly disappointed when the reality of the Redcliff home does not match her "fabricated mystery of the unknown" (213). The ill-fitting white muslin summer slipcovers look shabby; the ordinary furniture that anyone could buy on King Street diminishes the well-polished family antiques. The dinner too seems almost an affront, with only a common chicken fricassee and no jellied salad in sight. Aunt Quince sits in uncharacteristic Buddha-like silence.

Tat is also quiet. As he follows the conversation, gloom weighs on him. Lorena, voluble from too much wine, begins speaking as if she expects to one day be the mistress of the Redcliff home. Her mother interjects how the young couple might afford the upkeep by taking in boarders. When Lorena betrays her knowledge of the intimate spaces of the house, all eyes turn to Tat in reproach. He explodes from the table, not in shame but in anger, for he now knows what others suspected. Lorena had been in the house before—not through the front door with Tat but through the back door with Fen.

At this point, the farce turns tragic. In a half-confessing, half-bragging manner, Lorena blurts out her shocking story. Two years earlier, when she was putatively on a visit to an aunt in Detroit, she gave birth to Fen Redcliff's son, conceived while Judith was away having physical therapy and the family was in the mountains. Lorena placed the difficult child with a relative in the country. The true heir to the Redcliff name, as it turns out, has been receiving charity from the Maternal Aid Society where Judith works. Pinckney had hesitated over the introduction of the illegitimate child, knowing that even the mention of adultery and divorce invited outrage among gentle readers, but Henry Seidel Canby urged her on. The surprise of little "Red," he argued, "would be a good way to break the Redcliff pride." He had been circulating drafts of the novel around to his friends and assured her, "I haven't the slightest doubt myself that it's going to be a brilliant and successful novel."[3]

By the conclusion of the story, both the Redcliffs and the Hessenwinkles acknowledge that their worlds have collided, and nothing will ever be the same. Judith Redcliff's pride competes with her compassion, but finally she steps forward and adopts her husband's strong-willed child. She restores "Red" to his rightful place; he brings Judith back to life. Pinckney concludes with the clear message that those who would survive in the modern world must not only accept the new order, however inconvenient and unruly, but also embrace it.

Although not a feminist novelist in the conventional sense, Pinckney moves women to the center stage, probing their hidden strengths and their fierce competitiveness. The lesson Judith Redcliff learns after so many of her illusions are destroyed is that the modern woman "must give up romance, exchange it for wisdom, that barren bedfellow, knowledge of human nature, acceptance of reality." Pinckney tried to replicate life rather than make political statements. She bristled when Marjorie Morawetz interpreted the character of the afflicted, old-fashioned Judith Redcliff as a symbol of a "decadent aristocracy" on the course of ultimate extinction. Pinckney insisted, "I don't think of my characters as social symbols first. I think of them as human types." Southerners, she argued, tend to look at life more personally, never thinking of themselves or others as symbols or as part of an economic trend or social cycle. The northern "liberalité," such as Morawetz, "loves humanity, [is] full of earnest talk about the common good" but sees people only as statistics.[4]

After Marshall Best worked through Pinckney's manuscript, he passed it along to Viking senior editor Pascal Covici. About six weeks after her brazen overture to Best, Covici sent Pinckney a letter of agreement and an advance for five hundred dollars. Delighted at having cash in hand, she replied, "We are mutually embarked on the risky enterprise of getting out a book. We shall certainly agree, or else—like men bobbing about on a raft."[5]

Pinckney could not have picked two better raftmates. Romanian-born "Pat" Covici began his career as a Chicago bookseller and then started his own firm publishing quality books. He enjoyed successes with authors such as Ben Hecht and Charles McArthur, who wrote *The Front Page,* but Covici and his partner went bankrupt during the depression. Covici then took a position with Viking in 1937. One of the authors who came with him, John Steinbeck, gave the press its first Pulitzer Prize novel, *Grapes of Wrath.* Best, a forty-three-year-old Harvard graduate whose grandfather founded the Chicago-based department store Best and Company, had learned his trade with "saintly "publisher Benjamin W. Huebsch, who had introduced James Joyce and D. H. Lawrence to American audiences. Best was "an old fashioned gentleman," and Pinckney felt immediately comfortable with him. Soon she was sipping Best's special bourbon "Orange Blossoms" at his intimate dinner parties (he usually cooked) with his wife and their literary friends. Whenever Pinckney had trouble writing in Charleston, Best found her a retreat near his family's weekend place in Connecticut. She, in turn, introduced his children to the mysteries of turtle hunting in the summer moonlight on Edisto Island.[6]

When Pinckney first visited the Viking offices at 32 East 48th Street near Madison Avenue, the press, in operation since 1925, was approaching the pinnacle of its success. During her long sessions with the Viking editors, she brought up the question of book jackets and recommended her close friend Prentiss Taylor as exactly the right person to capture the feeling of Charleston "in a free and modern way." She wrote Taylor, now living in Washington, D.C., and working as an art therapist with psychiatric patients at St. Elizabeth's Hospital, that "I like the Viking crowd enormously, and find them agreeable to deal with" but "a little tight with money." Although Covici had been "very sweet-mouth" about Taylor's work, he eventually commissioned Robert Halleck who did a rather pedestrian drawing of a Charleston single house.[7]

On April 25, 1945, Pat Covici wrote Josephine the words she had been waiting to hear after months of revisions, "Your last two lines are superb." She also learned some upsetting news. Robert Molloy, a Charleston native working for the *New York Sun* had written a novel from the perspective of his own middle-class Irish Catholic upbringing that was about to be published by Macmillan and Company. *Pride's Way,* a social comedy about two feuding sisters and the tensions that tear at a family on its way up the social ladder, was advertised as a dissection of the "habits and manners of the Charlestonians."[8]

Wanting to present more contrast between her novel and Malloy's, Pinckney decided to make a last minute change in the title. "Three O'Clock Dinner" became "The Laughing Animals," drawn from William Hazlitt's saying "Man is the only animal that laughs or weeps; for he is the only animal that is struck with the difference between what things are, and what they ought to be." She hoped to emphasize "the story, the characters or the philosophical implication, if there are such, rather than the setting." Pinckney's only concern at the time was that the title could be misinterpreted, "for one thing the local gentry will think I'm calling them animals and not like it at all." As the thermometer crept up in Charleston and social engagements and other distractions slackened off, Pinckney continued to brood about the title and made one more eleventh-hour change. "The Laughing Animals" was out and "Three O'Clock Dinner" back in. The editors insisted on retaining the explanatory subtitle: "A Comedy of Manners." Pinckney resisted. The new title sounded "affected, a little pretentious" to her ear. Accommodatingly, Covici agreed to excise the offending phrase from the title page. Pinckney breathed a sigh of relief and felt quite vindicated when Robert Molloy's book came out with the title *Pride's Way: A Comedy of Manners.*[9]

When Pinckney finally relinquished her tortured final draft and Best accepted it, he bundled up her typescript, the only one in existence, tied it with a string and sent it over to his close friend John Beecroft who, as the sole arbiter of the Literary Guild, could act swiftly. His competition, the Book-of-the-Month Club, required a copy for each of the five readers, including Canby, and took at least a month to render a decision. As Best predicted, Beecroft called in a few days with a positive report. On June 11, 1945, Pat Covici placed a long-distance call, a rare event that carried with it the same portent that a telegram did in an earlier century, with news that would change Pinckney's life. With excitement shaking his voice, he told her that the Literary Guild with its thousands of subscribers had selected *Three O'Clock Dinner* as its first choice for October. Pinckney's willingness to write for the middlebrow had paid off.

After she put down the receiver, Pinckney feared that she had been hallucinating. By that evening, after some time had passed and the blood returned to her brain, she still had a "floaty feeling." She could fathom her good luck about the Literary Guild but not the staggering sums involved. She wrote Covici for confirmation "*pronto,*" so she could sort out "how much of my delusion of grandeur is real and how much is a manifestation of the creative imagination." "How rich shall I *plan* to be?" she asked Marshall Best, wanting to know the exact retail price of the book so she could put her sharpened pencil into action. She did not need any money immediately, she assured him; "Its too hot to commit extravagances at the moment." She just wanted to know.[10]

Unknown to either Best or Pinckney, the stealthy Henry Seidel Canby had lobbied the BOMC judges, who owed him a favor after their disappointing decision on *Hilton Head*. The BOMC offered greater prestige as well as a larger readership, and payout. When Canby learned of Josephine's deal with Literary Guild, he passed the news on to BOMC chief Harry Scherman. The excitable Scherman got Best on the phone and "bawled" him out for giving his competitor first chance at a potential best seller.[11] At fifty years old, Josephine still had powerful men fighting over her.

"I had no *idea* of the size of these book clubs," Pinckney wrote to Best after he told her the Literary Guild had more than 800,000 members. "It's sort of appalling. However, I won't waste any tears at this time on the standardization of the American mind etc. The future looks rosy to me, and since I wished myself on the Viking Press, I'm particularly pleased that your faith has been justified by works." All of Charleston noticed Pinckney "blooming with pleasure."[12] Pinckney's old friend from the MacDowell Colony, Chard Smith, wrote a letter of congratulations, expressing confidence that she would wear the "mantle of fame" with humorous glitter. In an interview for the *New York World Telegram,* Pinckney declared "I haven't had such a surprise since I stood on an air jet at Coney Island."[13]

*Three O'Clock Dinner* hit the bookstores with a great deal of Madison Avenue "ballyhoo" on September 21, 1945, and flew off the shelves with "atomic speed."[14] The poor-quality paper and close, space-saving type and delays in distribution served as a reminder that the transition from the wartime economy would take time. On November 11, 1945, *Three O'Clock Dinner* landed on the *New York Times* best-seller list.

Pinckney's life became a blur of interviews and public appearances. Jack Harris, whose usual beat was the racetrack, interviewed Pinckney for *Hobo* magazine in the back of a cab as she raced from one appointment to the next. In just that short time, Harris accurately perceived Pinckney as a person who "was not easily licked." "Her chin is firm, and she holds it up, her eyes—unusually clear and expressive—are the eyes of a woman who will keep fighting against any odds. She reminds you of a brunette Billie Burke." Harris predicted the book would make her rich. When he asked how many people had put "the Touch" on her now that she was famous, Pinckney looked puzzled. "The Touch?" she asked. "What's that?" After he explained, she laughed. "Then she stopped laughing and said with a scowl that Katharine Hepburn would have envied: . . . 'I know about the Touch, because a great many people have tried to put it on me.'"[15]

From her safe haven in New York City, Pinckney anguished about a discussion organized by Emily Sanders at the Charleston County Free Library. Hundreds of local citizens crowded into the cramped spaces of the old I. Jenkins Mikell mansion on Rutledge Avenue, "thick as dogs in a pound," according to Sam Stoney. Latecomers perched on bookcases and desks, clambered on top of file cabinets, used the spiral stairs like bleachers, or stood outside on the piazza listening to the conversation in the dark. Stoney who served as "moderator" (if such a term could ever apply to the opinionated historian) noted the preponderance of Pinckney relatives with their notable inherited features, looking like replicas of the family portraits that lined the walls at 36 Chalmers Street.[16]

Stoney proclaimed *Three O'Clock Dinner* the quintessential Charleston novel. He also had to remind critics in the audience that this was a work of fiction, not history. He summarized the give and take of the evening for his anxious friend waiting in New York: "We fought at Arques last night, without you, but about you. But instead of hanging, you can partly congratulate yourself." A few noses were out of joint, of course. Her spaniel, Peter, Stoney teased was unhappy as being portrayed as the feist dog "Rags." "And he is not the only one of your gentlemen friends," Stoney continued, "who running about grinning at your service finds himself dished up for vulgar consumption."[17]

The most heartfelt objection to *Three O'Clock Dinner* came from the Catholic community. Competing author Robert Molloy accused Josephine of an "unconscious act of snobbery" when she "overloaded the dice in making one of the opposing families so extremely cultivated and articulate and the other [the Catholics] so completely boorish and ignorant." Still, in the end, he conceded that this was not her purpose and that *Three O'Clock Dinner* was, on balance, "a civilized, intelligent, sometimes brilliant picture of what happens in a caste-conscious city."[18]

"Charleston is in quite a stew over the book," Josephine wrote Prentiss Taylor with evident glee. "Everybody's having a field day finding themselves and their relatives in it; the Catholics are still reading me out in meetings—why they find it so offensive, I can't make out—and my scouts bring me daily bulletins of the comments they gather in—outraged, weird, amusing, and luckily many approving ones. But I certainly didn't bargain for such widespread literacy."[19]

A number of Charlestonians in the fall of 1945 received their copies of *Three O'Clock Dinner* while waiting to muster out of the army. An aspiring young writer who had boarded with Alice Ravenel Huger Smith during World War II wrote Pinckney that he hoped to be part of "a virile school of Southern writers . . . which can transcend sectionalism and reach out as you have done to encompass the nations." Albert Simons, stationed at Camp Upton, waited until he achieved "complete exile" in a solitary corner of the bustling post. As he read her words, he later told Josephine, "the vividness of the Charleston scenes filled me with a nostalgia for its sights, sounds, and smells that was almost too poignant to be borne."[20]

In early September, before her flurry of activity promoting *Three O'Clock Din-*

*ner,* Pinckney spent some time with Harriet P. Simons at the Log House, a retreat in North River, New York, where Simons had found relief from her chronic allergies. Accompanying Pinckney was Colonel Ronald V. C. Bodley of the ancient family from whom the Bodleian Library at Oxford derived its name. Pinckney soaked up "large reserves of rest and mountain air to fortify me for the competitive existence of the city" and helped Marshall Best plan her book party scheduled for September 20 at the Ritz-Carlton Hotel in Manhattan. "Although slightly intimidated at the prospect of encountering a group of fierce publishing folk," she wrote Best, "I am not going to pretend that I don't like parties given for me."[21]

Hervey Allen gave Pinckney a "boost" of confidence when his congratulatory telegram arrived at the hotel just as she was leaving for the party. She later responded that it was "great disappointment to me not to have you there, and, of course, I missed DuBose. Our fortunes have been so bound up together over many years that it should have been possible for us to celebrate together. John F[arrar] and Dorothy H[eyward] were there, and that was swell." She invited Allen to stop by the Mayfair for "a drink and one of the good old talks." Allen's wife had fallen into one of her depressions and he could not easily get away but promised that at some point they could have "a bit of a celebration."[22]

On her return trip South in November, Pinckney stopped as usual in Richmond, now so different than during the brief years of *The Reviewer.* Richmond welcomed Pinckney as a conquering heroine. Pinckney made a pilgrimage to One Main Street. She left flowers and a copy of *Three O'Clock Dinner* on Ellen Glasgow's doorstep to honor this pioneer of southern literature. Two days before Glasgow died in 1945, a magazine article cited Ellen Glasgow's response to an inquiry "Books I Have Liked." She named an old classic, Edith Hamilton's *Great Age of Greek Literature,* Joan Bennett's *Virginia Woolf: Her Art as a Novelist,* and Josephine Pinckney's *Three O'Clock Dinner.*[23]

*Three O'Clock Dinner* soon entertained readers in seven different languages. Pinckney won the Southern Authors Award given annually for the most distinguished book on a southern subject, an honor that had earlier been received by Ellen Glasgow and Thomas Wolfe. The American Library Association included *Three O'Clock Dinner* on its list of the "Fifty Most Outstanding Books" of 1945 along with Richard Wright's *Black Boy* and John Steinbeck's *Cannery Row.* Pinckney became widely billed as one of the "most gifted American writers."[24] Viking gave *Three O'Clock Dinner* big spreads in major publications, which often appeared side by side with promotions of Grace Stone's latest novel, *Winter Visitor.*

"What a time to bring home the bacon!" wrote Pinckney's close friend, Clelia Waring. Her whole family cheered Pinckney's "glory." Her coup "was the reward for good, hard sweat and work—I know—and it is wonderful just one time to see virtue get its just due." For the first time since 1932, Pinckney had some extra cash. In 1945, she received $42,500, the next year Viking added $129,730 to her account. But her new wealth worked to separate her from others, much as her old wealth had in her childhood. Pinckney remained uncharacteristically insensitive to the feelings of old Charleston friends struggling to make ends meet while she flaunted her new fur coat, expensive jewelry, and sporty automobile.[25]

In May 1946, Pinckney helped out Prentiss Taylor by buying two of his Mexican drawings and donating them to the Gibbes Art Gallery. Taylor was delighted. He wrote Carl Van Vechten with the news and reminded the Harlem impresario of some earlier advice he had given him to the effect that "it was good for artists to have writers as their friends." "Here's . . . seeing you on that," Taylor added.[26]

Perhaps Pinckney's most gratifying and heartfelt plaudits came from her housekeeper Lula Moore. Moore had run the household at 36 Chalmers Street all during Pinckney's preoccupation with her manuscript, protected her privacy, and when Pinckney traveled she oversaw the care of Peter. Old and infirm, doddering around like a little hippopotamus on four skinny legs, Peter would have perished long ago had Moore not hand fed him delicate morsels and encouraged him to keep up his strength for Miss Jo. When Viking Press accepted *Three O'Clock Dinner*, Pinckney had drawn Moore aside and told her she could never have done it without her help. Moore glowed with happiness when she told her friends about the success of "our book." A national magazine carried a notice about Moore receiving congratulations from her church group on the success of *Three O'Clock Dinner*. After she related the incident to Pinckney, Moore added, "I took a bow for you—real graceful too."[27]

*Three O'Clock Dinner* found an interested audience in Charleston's African American community. Lula Moore wrote Pinckney with pride that "I have heard from many of the Charleston colored readers, [that they] are delighted with your book." Moore's friends particularly appreciated Pinckney's treatment of Bristol and Bekkah, the butler and housekeeper, because she did not have them speaking in dialect or broken English, as other authors had. Moore reported that her friends thought "the words are real[,] for Charleston [blacks] do not speak Gullah and they are blame[d] for it by some writers and they are all very hurted [by that]. They also wanted to know what happened to the little boy." Her final judgment: "Well I am pleased over it all."[28]

Pinckney found the applause of family and friends gratifying; recognition among professional writers, vindicating. Margaret Mitchell enjoyed *Three O'Clock Dinner* so much that she sent it to a French publishing house that was anxious for American novels. Mitchell had savored Pinckney's shrewd observations while she read the book aloud to her ailing husband. "How well you know the Southern people," Mitchell observed. "So often when a writer knows his section so well he is not able to communicate it, but you have done it."[29]

The unexpected success of *Three O'Clock Dinner* made 1945 a time of personal triumph for Josephine Pinckney. At the end of the year, she had been caught up in such a whirlwind of activity, she confessed to Prentiss Taylor, "I didn't know whether I was standing on my hair-do or my platform shoes." At least a dozen agents clamored to represent her, each making "visions of sugar plums" dance through her head. Already dizzy with her celebrity, Pinckney nearly swooned when Pascal Covici dangled one more sugar plum to dream about—Hollywood.[30]

Before *Three O'Clock Dinner* went to press, Metro-Goldwyn-Mayer studio had notified Viking Press that for the third year in a row they planned to offer a prize of $125,000 for the best novel of the year already accepted by an American publisher. The winning press received a $25,000 finder's fee as well. Covici nominated *Three O'Clock Dinner* as Viking's entry but warned Pinckney not to get her hopes up, given the gossamer nature of her prospects. The chances of any film company buying her book, he estimated, were "a thousand to one shot . . . as tenuous as transparent clouds over a full moon." Fortified by Covici's warning, Pinckney was disappointed but not surprised to learn that *Before the Sun Goes Down* had snagged the M-G-M prize. But soon a telegram arrived announcing that on the advice of the judges who thought Pinckney's novel a close runner-up, M-G-M (whose staff was searching for a vehicle for contract player Lana Turner) was prepared to offer her the same price, one of the ten highest fees ever paid for a manuscript.[31]

Pascal Covici wrote with great excitement to John Steinbeck that one of his authors, that Josephine Pinckney, had "caught all the lucky breaks." The validation of her work, first by the Literary Guild and then by M-G-M, catapulted Pinckney to front and center of attention at Viking Press, where her work caused a great deal of "excitement." "When I signed her up," Covici confided to Steinbeck, "I was lucky enough to get 25% of the movie rights and so Viking isn't doing so badly either." Covici had not thought the story line of *Three O'Clock Dinner* very earth-shattering but privately praised Pinckney highly for "good characterization and understanding and a discriminating poetic feeling." As in so many of the fine things that happened in her career, the darting shadow of Henry Seidel Canby can be glimpsed in this piece of good fortune as well. Amy Loveman, Canby's longtime associate at the *Saturday Review* and later at the Book-of-the-Month Club, was one of the M-G-M judges.[32]

News of the Hollywood contract had hit the press before *Three O'Clock Dinner* arrived at bookstores, so Josephine had an audience already primed. She wrote Prentiss Taylor on the day that *Three O'Clock Dinner* went on sale, "I am indeed spinning round in the American Fantasy. I am feeling quite mixed in my mind about it." Her name flashed across the front page of *Variety* along with speculation about when *Three O'Clock Dinner* would be "skedded for lensing." After delays, *Three O'Clock Dinner* was put on the calendar for 1947 along with the stage hit "Annie Get Your Gun" starring Judy Garland and Irving Stone's best seller *Lust for Life*.[33] Everett Riskin was signed as director. Lana Turner was given star billing as Judith.

During the 1940s, the production companies of Hollywood had become like giant maws, insatiable in their desire for scripts with popular appeal. Manuscripts became more widely known as "properties," underscoring Hollywood's interest in profit rather than art. Almost anything in print short of the backs of cereal boxes was fair game and evaluated for marketability: magazines, short stories, articles, plays (those that made it to Broadway, as well as those that languished along the way), radio dramas, and, of course, original film scripts. Competition among the eight leading studios and the fifteen or so independents became fierce. As book clubs gained increased influence over the reading habits of Americans with their clever advertising and marketing, the film companies parlayed this high-powered publicity to their own benefit by snatching up the movie rights to best sellers while they were still in manuscript or galley form. Like everything else in modern America, speed was paramount; twenty thousand "properties" passed through the literary assembly line, not only best sellers but also classics with expired copyrights that might have modern appeal.[34]

In May 1945, veteran Hollywood scriptwriter Leonore Coffee and M-G-M staff photographers arrived in Charleston to soak up some local color. Pinckney walked the "old Hollywood warhorses," Coffee and her husband William Cowan, a director of "B" movies and former assistant to Cecil B. DeMille, around town. Highly regarded in the movie industry and well known as a "script doctor" for her ability to rescue floundering plots, Coffee had begun writing stories and captions for silent movies in 1919. She later wrote scripts for Clark Gable, Joan Crawford, and the Barrymores in the 1930s, Claudette Colbert and Orson Welles in the 1940s.[35]

By the following spring, Coffee had a first draft of the screenplay. She shifted the focus of the action to Judith and away from Lorena because of the prevailing "Hollywood ethic," which discouraged directors from making an immoral character the star. Lorena's adultery and illegitimate child posed enough of a challenge. Having to fit the sultry Lana Turner, who was born to play Lorena, into the role of the lanky, repressed Judith presented an equally difficult casting problem. With

Christmas 1948 as the scheduled release date, rumors flew around town that a Charleston premiere on the order of the Atlanta spectacle for *Gone with the Wind* might be held during the holidays.[36]

Even after three scripts, five casts, and two directors, *Three O'Clock Dinner* never made it to the silver screen. Lana Turner's unreliability caused part of the problem. Turner's tenure at M-G-M had been turbulent. She proved a poor fit for the studio that had a reputation for reverential treatment of its female stars, on stage at least. Despite the best efforts to transform this contract player into a cool, ethereal virgin type (she often was dressed in white), her carnal nature always broke through. Turner had three movies scheduled right in a row, *Green Dolphin Street*, *Three O'Clock Dinner*, and *Cass Timberland* in 1946. During the filming of *Green Dolphin Street* (where she ends up in a nunnery), Turner slipped out of town for a Mexican vacation with her latest infatuation, Tyrone Power. Her adventure disrupted the carefully orchestrated studio timetable.[37]

Coffee's screenplay made all the mistakes Pinckney had tried so hard to avoid. Coffee relied heavily on the local color, and played up the peculiarities of the South. Bristol and Bekkah were given more play but took on the characteristics of stock characters along the lines of Mammy and Pork in *Gone with the Wind*. More interested in box office receipts than an author's intent, Coffee stripped away the irony and complexity from Pinckney's novel, leaving it a very conventional love story set among the oleanders and mansions of the Deep South. Judith loses her limp; Tat, his ideology; Lucian, his cynicism; and August, his nationality, becoming an Austrian "Hessel" at a time when anti-German feeling was still high. Vinny's only corruption is a taste for betting on the horses. Wick affects a "pince-nez." The prickle of class conflict that makes the dinner scene so entertaining was excised. Lorena (with real red hair) is portrayed as an innocent, seduced by the aristocratic Fen, who truly loves Tat. The only drama involves Lorena getting tipsy and spilling her secret. In contrast to Pinckney's lime-tart prose, Coffee's version of *Three O'Clock Dinner* is Hollywood saccharine, concluding with a traditional happy ending: Judith and Lucian Redcliff are destined for marriage, everything's going to be all right.[38]

With plenty of advice from friends whose novels were optioned by Hollywood, Pinckney gracefully abandoned all hopes of influencing Hollywood's interpretation of her story. Her only public remark expressed her hope that the Charleston accents affected by the actors would not be too offensive to the local ear.[39]

About the same time that Pinckney moved into the national literary spotlight with *Three O'Clock Dinner*, she pulled out her notes on family genealogy, the cascade of

Pinckneys, Mottes, Rutledges, and Middletons on one side; Scotts, Lyons, Watkins, Picketts on the other. Rejecting the traditional grids, the "waterfalls" that stuck single women on remote, discontinuous archipelagoes of their own, she fashioned a different sort of chart. Abandoning the schematic of the "pedigree" or family "tree," she reconfigured the names of her ancestors into a series of concentric circles, much like a Buddhist mandala that arranges symbols of deities around a common core.[40] At the center of the Pinckney-Scott universe, she places herself. In this system, rather than being a failure for not carrying on and producing issue, she reconfigures history and appears as the final result, the ultimate realization of the many distinguished generations: Josephine Lyons Scott Pinckney, poet and best-selling author.

# 12

# Great Mischief

As Josephine Pinckney's star ascended in the Viking Press firmament, she felt herself being dragged deeper into the artistic netherworld where literature and commerce merged. She wondered if in her reach for fame she had unwittingly made a Faustian bargain. At least a dozen literary agents hounded her to sign with them. Her Viking editors barraged her with pestering letters urging her to begin another marketable manuscript double-quick. Pascal Covici announced that he expected to have three titles on the Book-of-the-Month Club list in 1947 and that her next book would be one of them. Viking founder Harold A. Guinzburg pressed her to churn out at least a barebones outline to huckster directly to movie producers. "There is nothing to lose, and maybe a good deal to gain, by trying to wangle a little easy money out of Hollywood before the fact," he wrote Pinckney in December 1946.[1]

Pinckney, who had once been accustomed to the reflective tranquility of the poet, had shifted into high gear with the rest of American society after World War II. In record time, she hammered out "the bones and gristly parts" of a story set in Charleston during the 1880s. Taking a holiday from the rational world, Pinckney indulged in a fantasy and spiced her story with magic rather than morality. "The Blue-Eyed Hag" chronicled a young Charleston pharmacist's ill-fated quest to learn the truth about good and evil. His spiritual journey is complicated not only by the conventional tensions between science and faith but also by the animism of Gullah traditions taught him by his nurse Maum Rachel. Drawing from the stories first told her by Victoria Rutledge, Pinckney adds another dimension to the evil forces at work in the world. She torments her protagonist with plat-eyes, hags, witches, and incubi; things that went "bump" in the Low Country night. "Without the assistance of motivations and build-ups, it sounds pretty ham-y . . . Southern-cured by an old recipe," she warned Guinzberg when she mailed him a draft, "but MGM shouldn't boggle over a little of that flavor."[2]

Pinckney's initial plan for her third novel had been a "personal subjective narrative," but she soon dismissed that strategy as "too autobiographical and self-revealing." The "hag story," which became *Great Mischief*, she believed, "will free me of certain complications of *Three O'Clock Dinner*—the names, the correspondence to living people, the applications to myself." The magical nature of the story also lent itself to a poetic treatment, "which is my stuff, my contribution."[3]

Pinckney had been playing around with the idea of a fantasy since 1923 when she wrote a story in her very correct school-girl French as an exercise for Charleston's *Alliance Française*. Her satirical tale set in the early twentieth century blends two Charleston traditions, aristocratic pride in family and Gullah mythology of voodoo and witchcraft.[4] In the mystical world of the Gullah imagination, the wrongs suffered by the poor, oppressed, and downtrodden were righted by magic. With this story of the three Peronneau sisters, the last remnants of an impoverished but distinguished old family, living frugally together, Pinckney first began cultivating her fascination with black magic as a source of female power. The youngest of the three fears she is picking up old maid habits from her domineering sisters and makes a scandalous break for freedom from their suffocating presence. The only place she can afford is in a tiny old building, once a tavern, with tile roof and dormer windows in the heart of a disreputable, dockside neighborhood. As she is enjoying solitude before her fire, bits of mortar fall, followed by puffs of soot. Then, out pops a hag in search of a vulnerable soul to ride. The self-possessed Miss Peronneau naturally asks if the hag is a native Charlestonian, and who her people were. The wraith proudly announces she is a descendant of Landgrave Smith, one of the early founders. On learning they are kin, the hag spares the woman and sits down for a chat. The hag complains how difficult Charlestonians are to deal with. One snobbish woman refused to carry the hag north of Broad Street. The Charleston men, dissipated by high living, were hopeless mounts. Trying to be helpful, Miss Peronneau suggests that the witch try the sober, sturdy French Huguenots of the city and provides her with a roll of the Alliance Française. Excited by the prospect of a new stable, the hag who shed her skin at the witching hour, takes her leave, and slips away through the keyhole, the usual passageway of these menacing spirits.[5]

The popular 1926 novel *Lolly Willowes* also influenced Pinckney. Sylvia Townsend Warner's intriguing tale of an outcast spinster who makes a pact with a handsome devil had been selected by Henry Canby and his panel of judges as the premier selection of the new Book-of-the-Month Club.[6] Over the years, Pinckney had been making notes until the character of Lucy Farr finally materialize in her mind. In *Great Mischief*, Lucy is the poor girl who mastered witchcraft in self-defense again her ignorant, abusive family and became a powerful lieutenant of the Devil as the hag "Sinkinda." Although Pinckney's story is driven by the earnest protagonist Timothy Partridge's search for a workable universal ethic, Lucy gets the best lines.[7]

*Great Mischief* also reflects Pinckney's disquiet over the state of the world in the wake of World War II as she tried to sort out why "the brave efforts of the moralists and reformers . . . [are] constantly defeated by evil." Pinckney sets her tale in 1886, on the eve of much destruction in Charleston by a great earthquake that destroyed many of the old historic houses and psychologically rocked the city to its very core. This is the same earthquake that shattered the chimneys at Pinckney's Eldorado plantation and ultimately caused it to burn. In her story, not only were the foundations of the city's buildings shattered but also many of its beliefs. Woven throughout with Pinckney's signature intricate twists and turn of plot and word play, her story can be read as psychological realism (the story of a man going mad), as fantastic "sheer spun gossamer," or as "sinister heresy." Pinckney also makes the subtle point that the wonders of modern science are almost indistinguishable from magic.[8]

The story begins in an old apothecary shop. On its shelves, ancient nostrums line up with newer potions. The druggist, Timothy Partridge, a bachelor in his thirties who has already begun to dye his hair, is notably credulous for a man of science. Walking through a foggy night, Partridge glimpses a church steeple with its long white flank through the "mother of pearl air" and imagines it might be a giant unicorn. When his spinster sister admonishes him for being sacrilegious and superstitious, Partridge counters that he can "believe in anything."[9]

As his name suggests, the timid Partridge quails before his Pharisee of a sister, Penelope. Her public reputation for selfless charity is soon revealed as self-serving and manipulative. Most of her cases were victims of the Civil War, as indeed all Charlestonians were in some way or another. She quite literally keeps the spirit of the Lost Cause alive in the person of pathetic Mr. Dombie. Rescued by Penelope as she searched among the Confederate dead at Secessionville during Charleston's last stand in 1865, the severely disabled Dombie lives a shadowy half-existence at the Partridge home, like the soulless "zombie" of voodoo tradition. Although the veteran's spirit has gone the way of the Old Confederacy, Penelope sacrifices Timothy's comfort to keep him warm and well fed. Their cousin, Will Golightly chastises the Partridges for living in the past. An advocate of the New South philosophy of "If you can't beat 'em, jine 'em," he has made a great deal of money on Wall Street. Golightly parries his cousins' retorts that he has sold out to money and machines: "I love this Lowcountry of ours and couldn't breathe away from it . . . But you've let defeat suck you dry" (24).

One stormy evening, the unsophisticated Partridge is "beglamoured" by a mysterious cloak-draped young woman, Lucy Farr, who appears in his shop asking for solanum, a powerful drug from the deadly nightshade family which ancients believed could make witches fly. As both scientist and Christian, Partridge initially rejects the idea of witches and the supernatural, but childhood memories of his Gullah nurse Maum Rachel and her stories of spirits roaming the countryside at night, the ghost-dogs, witch-doctors, hags, and hobgoblins waft into his conscious-ness. Disturbed by heretical thoughts, Partridge turns to the Bible. Finding no consolation, he throws the Holy Book into the fire and storms out of the house as it explodes in a blaze of flames. He walks all night and returns home to find his house a heap of smoldering ashes, Penelope and Mr. Dombie burned to crisps. Braced for divine punishment, Partridge is rewarded. Between the insurance and a surprisingly large inheritance left by Mr. Dombie, the poor pharmacist becomes a rich man.

One night, the seductive hag Sinkinda pops out of the drowsing Partridge's fireplace. She is later revealed as the alter-ego of Lucy and Partridge's own anti-conscience who knows and encourages all his darkest thoughts. She leaps on his back, clinging with clammy caterpillar-like fingers and drives him on making an excited whistling noise as the wind rushes between her teeth. Helpless to shake her, "he lurched, fell, and gave in at last to the luxury of defeat" carrying her about the city in his stocking feet (108).

As Partridge vacillates between his hope of Christian salvation in eternity and his present lust for Sinkinda, Lucy Farr offers to introduce Partridge to the "Other One." Transformed by herbs, ointments, and incantations, they fly through the gates of hell into a great auditorium (that looks rather like Radio City Music Hall), alive with deafening screeching and wailing, hollering, and shrieking. Expecting horns or cloven feet, he is surprised when Satan appears in the guise of a well-groomed Charlestonian. When, under close questioning, Partridge inadvertently admits he believes in God, the Devil is unexpectedly pleased: "Unless people believe in some Good they have no sense of guilt in doing wrong and therefore offer me no hold" (193). Of all the mansions of Hell, the exquisite rare book room overseen by Mammon provides Partridge his greatest temptation. A collector of first editions, Mammon enjoyed following their market value as much as the con-tents within. "Knowledge is power," Mammon reminds Partridge offering him the book of evil, *The Damned Art* (207). But just as he is about to open the goatskin cover and lose his soul, a revelation comes to him. Evil is the sum total of all "the senseless brutality, the blood; treacheries and corrupt lusts, cowardices like wharf-rats, all that was finally unacceptable, swam in those dissolute waters" (212). With imps biting and nipping at his ankles, he takes hold of the book of Evil and, like Gideon tearing down the altar of Baal, consigns it to the roaring fire, just as he had done the Holy Bible. Flames engulf the whole room. Panicked, he makes his way through the labyrinth of hell and flees home in Satan's own gig.

Partridge awakes trembling in his own bed, soaked in cold sweat. Had he really burned down Hell or merely dreamed it? An exhausted-looking Lucy confirms his memory. "You burnt up your idea of Hell, that's all. You don't suppose you could deprive others of theirs do you?" (220). When Partridge vows to give up evil and accept God's punishment, Lucy gets bored and leaves him in search of a new recruit for the Master of Darkness.

   On a September night in 1886, Partridge thinks judgment day has come when his house begins to shake and rattle. Panicked, he invokes Sinkinda and pleas for a little more time to see if life holds some great moral lesson he could take away with him. He realizes that if Retribution exists, so must Justice. "The mouth of hell" (the earthquake) swallows "all of his furnishing and belongings," and "his plush pretensions" also disappear into a great crevasse. He feels Sinkinda's weight leave him as he comes to a jarring stop at the fissure. Peering down he can see the hags and the witches flying about. Sinkinda flies off to join them, then turns back, beckoning him—"Ride out." He leaps into the abyss: "it was no harder than jumping off the roof" (247).

On receiving the first third of *Great Mischief,* Marshall Best declared himself, "delighted and enchanted." "For style alone it has given me more pleasure than any other recent book that I could think of, . . . the best prose you ever wrote," but he thought the conclusion too ambiguous. He had hoped she would take the ironic fantasy approach rather than the psychological. "The book is nevertheless entirely publishable," he assured her. "It will do you no discredit and will be loved by a great many readers." If Canby's full-court press to have the Book-of-the Month Club judges put her manuscript directly on their "A" list was successful, Best thought she should "to take the cash and let the credit go."[10]

   In February 1948, an exhausted Pinckney mailed her manuscript off to Viking, and set off for a winter vacation in the West Indies with Canby and his wife. Sam Stoney and Bay Wigglesworth joined their Caribbean cruise to Antigua, Trinidad, Martinique, Barbados, Dominica, and St. Vincent's islands. After two weeks, Pinckney's party settled in "rather ruthlessly" on St. John in the American Virgin Islands for "swimming, loafing, reading and wrangling and all the mixed pleasures of one another's company."[11]

   On the way home, Stoney and Pinckney stopped in Dade County, Florida to visit Hervey Allen at his Coconut Grove estate. The plane ride was bumpy, but the reunion went splendidly reminding both Allen and Pinckney of the innocent happiness of their early days venturing into a life in literature. Pinckney later wrote Allen, "I liked the feeling of being in touch with you again. Somehow life takes up so much time that we succeed in seeing the people we really want to see only by main effort, and I am more and more resolved to pleasure myself in my declining years by enjoying the good friends I am lucky enough to have." Allen wrote John Bennett that only minutes after the "hectic" arrival of his two old friends, the years melted away. "After a little talk I felt I could just walk around the corner and tap on the door at #37 [Legaré Street]."[12] Neither Pinckney nor Bennett would ever see Allen again. He died at Christmas time in 1949 and was buried at Arlington Cemetery.

A copy of *Great Mischief* fresh off the press was waiting for Pinckney on her return to Chalmers Street. The allegorical cover art by Prentiss Taylor delighted her. He had adapted a "gay spirited" unicorn like that which pranced over the pulpit at the chapel at St. James, Goose Creek, and superimposed it over a representation of St. Phillips Church. "Half the commentators," Pinckney wrote Taylor, "think the unicorn is a horse, but they like it just the same." The very "correct" Marshall Best, however, had been "chopfallen" with the overly symbolic dust jacket art, hoping to have "a little sex" on the cover to boost sales.[13]

Best actually had been phoning her constantly until he was "dizzy" from the effort. He had an excellent piece of news. The Book-of-the-Month Club had agreed to take her book. Best believed that Pinckney's month-long sojourn with the head judge had made the critical difference. "For whatever degree you are responsible—and I am sure it is not small—we give you our thanks," he wrote. He added, that judge Clifton Fadiman "implied that Henry's letter determined the decision." In truth, Dorothy Canfield Fisher also had been exceptionally supportive of *Great Mischief*, calling Pinckney's fantasy "as adroitly written as Isak Dinesen's double-talk story, *The Angelic Avengers*." Fisher thought the novel "so realistically done that it seemed like a real sure enough story of witchcraft by some body who did believe in it. It was one of the books that had a lining of another color from the outside, which are always interesting." The Book-of-the-Month Club accolade was even sweeter because the latest novel by her friend and competitor, Grace Stone, did not make the cut. Stone took the news "handsomely," writing Pinckney "a swell letter," her most enthusiastic ever, assuring her that *Great Mischief* "comes off" and was her best book yet.[14]

The team at Viking Press was elated. Although a year later than predicted, Pinckney joined two other Viking authors, her friend Carl Van Doren, and Graham Greene to give the press three authors listed with the Book-of-the-Month Club in one year. With its use of the devil as a character, *Great Mischief* was compared with stories by Goethe and Hawthorne. The recently published *Screwtape Letters* by popular Anglican theologian C. S. Lewis was also on everyone's mind. Nash Burger of the *New York Times* hit on the central failing of *Great Mischief*. Noting that the war had encouraged many authors to take a stand in the clash of darkness against light, "Miss Pinckney, no C. S. Lewis, is never too certain herself as to the nature of good and evil."[15]

Some of her detractors had jealous grudges. Sometime Charleston resident William McFee bragged "with sheer delight" to his friend and Pinckney's literary rival Robert Molloy, "I did her in the eye in the [New York] *Sun* on Monday." Others insinuated that Pinckney had used her charms to sway Canby. In the March 28, 1948, issue, a reviewer from *Time* magazine accused the Book-of-the-Month Club judges of buying the "saleable name" of Josephine Pinckney but not receiving a "satisfactory novel." Alongside the punishing critique was a photo of Pinckney and Canby posed together on the Alcoa line steamer that gives no indication that others were in the party. The review concludes with a quotation from the book in which Timothy Partridge is regretting his abortive relationship with Sinkinda: "If only we could have met under different circumstances! It should have been different, somehow." Her reply: "Ah, my friend, how many star-crossed lovers have uttered that cry!"[16]

As if in divine compensation, the next week Canby's Cornwall neighbor Lewis Gannett (fresh from a winter visit to 36 Chalmers Street) wrote an appraisal of *Great Mischief* for the *New York Herald-Tribune* which Pinckney regarded as "the absolutely perfect review from the writers' standpoint" and that almost compensated for "what the dark backward and abysm of Time spewed forth." "Well," she wrote to Prentiss Taylor, "you have to take the ups with the downs, I always say."[17]

Charleston's Unitarian minister, Horace Westwood, considered *Great Mischief* one of the "Five Significant Books of 1948." During a lecture series, Westwood praised Pinckney's book for expressing "indignation against self-righteousness; against the complacency, the assumption of superior virtue and the patronizing condescension, of those who seek merit by doing good; yet beneath its irony and sometimes biting humor, there is compassion for the frailties to which humanity seems heir, whether they be of the flesh or of the spirit. Also there is sympathetic, psychological understanding of those the author appears to condemn." Westwood concluded that the message of the book is "Goodness is the wisdom of the heart. And the essence of evil is ignorance and the failure to understand."[18]

As promised, Best arrived in Charleston on March 22 to set up a "coming out" party for *Great Mischief*. Pinckney organized the Class A tour of the Low Country to entertain Best. Almost thirty years later, he still remembered his visit to her "delicately mauve" house on Chalmers Street. When he stepped out on the second floor piazza at dusk, his "Northern ear was startled by eloquent song."

Without missing a beat, Pinckney quipped, "Yes, that's my hahed-in [hired-in] mockin' bird." After an elegant dinner at her home, Pinckney took him to the annual concert of the Society for the Preservation of Spirituals in which she sang and kept him up late at a party afterward mingling with her friends dressed in their nineteenth-century finery. During his Low Country marathon, Best ate cooter pie, Awendaw bread, and drank Sam Stoney's special Old Fashioneds made with bourbon and marmalade. Pinckney drove Best all over three counties, from the Roosevelt's Gippy Plantation near Pinopolis, to her family place at Fairfield, to Cat Island with the Phelps family, and finishing with Pierates Cruze in Mount Pleasant overlooking Charleston harbor, home of the Dana Osgoods, "mad collectors," whose butler looked like a diplomat in his cutaway coat.[19]

A film crew from *Life* Magazine came to cover the Viking launching of *Great Mischief*. Staging the event in the greenroom of the Dock Street Theatre, Pinckney displayed her flair for the dramatic. The elegant paneled room was transformed into an old apothecary shop with antique instruments and vials on loan to the Charleston Museum from Schwettmann's Drug Store and G. W. Aimar and Company. Herbs, roots, bats, and newts, basics of the magician's trade, were somehow procured. No proper witch would be without a cat, so Laura Bragg even dug up a stuffed wildcat from the museum's natural history collection. One of Pinckney's friends dressed as a nineteenth-century apothecary and stirred an iron cauldron. Double, double toil and trouble. To her surprise, Pinckney ended up having "a weird sort of good time, appropriately enough."[20]

The next morning the *Life* photographers planned to set off for Eldorado for more background shots with Pinckney, but a driving spring rain flooded the deep rutted roads and aborted their plans. They "dragooned" Pinckney into leading them around town and pointing out her various sources of inspiration, from the model for the Partridge house at the corner of Beaufain Street and Ashley Avenue to Washington Park, scene of the post-earthquake "tent city."[21]

A much more menacing manifestation of evil, the Soviet blockade of Berlin in June 1948, preempted Pinckney's "feature spread" in *Life*. This "world-shattering event" threw all national events into the shadows. Covici warned Pinckney that sales of all novels were plunging from their previous highs and she must be prepared for disappointment on that front as well. As the cold war began heating up, she acknowledged the truth of his warning but added, "I'm so gloomy about the state of the world at the moment that I haven't much gloom left over for book sales." She feared that soon the "fat will be in the fire."[22]

*Great Mischief* failed to entice Hollywood, but two young men formerly connected with the Dock Street Theatre were captivated by Pinckney's story. In 1951, George E. Hamlin Jr., who resigned his position as associate director in 1946 to work with the New Dramatists in New York, and Bill Taylor, a dancer who had studied at the Dock Street Theatre, set out to transform Pinckney's novel into a "musical play." Pinckney was thrilled at the prospect (perhaps already mentally picking out her wardrobe for the Broadway opening). Her story, however, was too complex for the lighthearted fantasy they imagined. Dorothy Heyward and Pinckney both gave advice about music and choreography, but in the end, the musical never materialized.[23]

Harold Guinzberg's pressure on Pinckney to produce a saleable story for Hollywood diverted her from her own personal desire to probe the issue of race in the South. In 1946 her ruminations about good and evil after World War II had focused on the terrible moral dilemma facing southerners who realized the wicked dimensions of segregation but did not know how to unravel this historic and deeply entrenched institution. Two years earlier, Georgia writer Lillian Smith's *Strange Fruit,* a novel of miscegenation and violence, sold three million copies and helped shape the nation's negative postwar attitude toward the South. Pinckney wondered if the instinctive tribal emotions that in part explained Hitler's rise to power might also explain the passions around "the Negro question—the irrational instinct against exogamy." She decided the issue of race was "too controversial at present—people are too irrational on both sides."[24]

Pinckney agreed with Smith's indictment of the old aristocratic class for failing to provide leadership and offer moderate alternatives to the ruthless racism of the region's most radical and violent elements. While she was working on *Great Mischief,* Pinckney became more deeply involved in the issues around racial justice. She feared that Charleston's reputation could be ruined as more and more Americans began to see the South as the nation's number one moral problem.

By 1946, the hopeful Charleston Literary Movement had dimmed into memory. The second wave of southern writers described a much different South. Faulkner's imaginary Yoknapatawpha County, stained by incest, lynching, and rape, eclipsed the image of the moss-draped Carolina Low Country so carefully cultivated by the artists and writers of Charleston. Northern readers confused Faulkner's powerful stories of human passions with actual history. Debauchery replaced honor as the prevailing southern ethic in the northern mind with the popularity of sensational novels, such as *Tobacco Road* written by Georgian Erskine Caldwell. James Agee's stark descriptions of life among the sharecroppers in *Let Us Now Praise Famous Men* exploded the Agrarians' romantic mythology about the ennobling effect of laboring on the soil. Walker Evans' haunting photographs of the faces of poverty and despair that accompanied Agee's text overpowered the ethereal landscapes of Alice Ravenel Huger Smith as visual representations of the spirit of the South. The modernist's jaded vision of "life as it is" ultimately won out over the Charleston writers' assertion that beauty could coexist with imperfection.

Under the influence of Faulkner, the frontier and the hamlet became the controlling images of the South, as the plantation, mansion, and the city receded. In contrast to Donald Davidson's frontier ideal where men stood tall and took slow deadly aim in defense of their God-given freedoms, W. J. Cash, born in a mill village in western South Carolina, put forward a different model in his influential *The Mind of the South* published in 1941. The Cash family were, like Donald Davidson's people, middling folk with no love for the old plantation owners or their former slaves. The germ of Cash's book first appeared in an article for Mencken's *American Mercury* in 1929. Cash adopted the Baltimore sage's acerbic tone throughout his brief career. His central theme concerned the "savage ideal," the southern determination to hold on to their traditional folkways (especially concerning race) through any means necessary, including violence. His models were Faulkner's Sutpens, not the Pinckneys. Charleston, Richmond, Mobile, and New Orleans played no role in his analysis. Not surprisingly, given his early homage to Mencken, his most potent attack was reserved for the southern lady.[25]

After World War II, Charleston was still widely regarded as the spiritual center of the South. When reporters from the national press arrived in the city, they were no longer interested in aristocrats in amber, beautiful gardens, or the preservation of the Gullah language, however; they came to "expose" local inequalities. Peeling paint and unpaved streets once thought charming, now looked decadent.[26]

Pinckney, who always sought to convey a subtle "affirmative regionalism" rather than a "conscious regionalism" in her writing, saw an opportunity to help improve Charleston's public reputation and bolster its economy in 1946.[27] Robert N. S. Whitelaw, director of the Carolina Art Association, approached her about writing an outdoor play along the lines of North Carolina dramatist Paul Green's "The Lost Colony." In 1937, Green's historical drama had put the little town of Manteo, North Carolina, on the tourist map and proved a godsend to the struggling coastal community. Initially, Whitelaw proposed Pinckney do an adaptation, perhaps of a Shakespeare play. Whitelaw painted a grand picture of costumed players on the terraced greensward surrounding the beautiful butterfly lakes at Middleton Plantation. If successful, a pageant would extend the lucrative tourist season beyond the few weeks of exuberant spring into the early summer and benefit not only the town and Carolina Art Association but also her cousins, Heningham and J. J. Pringle Smith, who owned the famous plantation.[28]

Whitelaw also contacted his friend Lincoln Kirstein. The multitalented Kirstein had started out as a poet and edited *Hound and Horn* when the literary magazine moved from Cambridge to New York in 1930.[29] After World War II, he organized New York's Ballet Society. Kirstein liked the concept of an outdoor festival but threw cold water on the idea of Shakespeare-on-the-Ashley, urging Whitelaw to let the location inspire the play. He imagined Middleton Gardens as "a jardin anglaise in which nature has been trimmed consciously" but still has the dominant role. The broad expanses of lawn provided the perfect stage for "spectacular dance interludes," modern interpretations of "eighteenth-century garden dances" with the full development of contemporary ballet to superb music—Hayden, Mozart, even Bach—but the dancers in modern summer ball-garden-party dresses.[30]

Ironically, Middleton Gardens' dramatic beauty made selection more difficult, since any play would have to be the "perfect equivalent" of the natural splendor found there. Kirstein assured the Charlestonians, "I am thinking about it all the time." Kirstein researched some of the historic plays that had been performed in Charleston, hoping to find one that Pinckney could adapt. He first thought that William Ioor's Revolutionary-era play, "The Battle of Eutaw Springs and Evacuation of Charleston," which had been performed in 1807, might be fun, but he concluded it was essentially "just too silly" for a modern audience.[31]

The project began maturing in the imaginations of Pinckney, Whitelaw, and Kirstein (although not in the same way). When Kirstein visited Charleston in mid-December 1946, Whitelaw and Pinckney walked the length and breadth of the plantation with him. As a chill wind whipped across the salt marsh, they tried to envision a lush early summer landscape. In the course of the day, their enthusiasm "ebbed and flowed." Kirstein played the role of "wet-blanket" pointing out the multitude of possible pitfalls involved in outdoor dramas. He had become discouraged when his friend John Houseman declined to direct the production because he was working on Duke Ellington's "Twilight Alley." However, Kirstein did very much enjoy his visit to Charleston and found one of Pinckney's fine linen cocktail napkins in his pocket when he returned to New York as a reminder of her hospitality.[32]

Between Kirstein's charm and Whitelaw's badgering, Pinckney finally agreed to write a new script, a long narrative poem, after she finished *Great Mischief*. Whitelaw cautioned both Kirstein and Dudley that when they discussed this project with Pinckney, they should be very upbeat and reassuring because he knew his old friend needed a great deal of "encouragement to overcome her modesty" and self-doubt.[33]

Savvy about the connection between art and commerce, Whitelaw and Kirstein started cooking up ways to finance their vision of dancers on the lawns of Middleton Place. One plan was to capitalize on Pinckney's celebrity (the film version of *Three O'Clock Dinner* was still on schedule and much in the press) and begin generating interest in this project. Whitelaw and Kirstein plotted a scenario in which shortly after the New Year, when she had planned to consult with her Viking editors, Pinckney would sweep into the Mayfair Hotel (where she was well known), acting "mysterious in a loud way." Under her arm she would carry, with exaggerated stealth, a "portfolio of photographs, maps, diagrams, and a small-scale model of the playing area." Lincoln Kirstein speculated that the film people would be intrigued, "begin to ask questions and express a desire to be cut in. From then on, we will play both ends and the middle, and funds will be forthcoming, here and from Hollywood."[34]

Before Pinckney could do much more than rough out an outline, Whitelaw's "dream" of a pageant that would both elevate Charleston's reputation and increase tourism collapsed. Pinckney's novel *Great Mischief* took a year longer than anticipated. Whitelaw's abrasive brilliance and uninhibited honesty continued to exasperate local art patrons. Conflict between the Dock Street Theatre group and the Carolina Art Association made cooperation almost impossible. Lincoln Kirstein drifted off to other projects. Interest lingered in local quarters about producing a statewide historical pageant, but that project held little appeal for Pinckney.[35]

Pinckney's surviving notes, however, are suggestive of the way she interpreted southern history through the lens of her own family's past. She argued, "The order of the garden made in the wilderness is the symbol of order in government."[36] She posits that the elaborate eighteenth-century garden at Middleton Place symbolizes the high degree of civilization attained by the early Carolina society. She perhaps still remembered the rather vicious comments made by Amy Lowell during her 1922 visit to the Low Country gardens. Unable to resist pricking the pride Charlestonians had in presenting the gorgeous springtime display, Lowell wrote a set of poems about the feral decay of Magnolia Gardens with its unruly azaleas and overgrown camellias all returned to "a state of nature." The smug Bostonian intimated that beneath the thin veneer of Georgian houses and fine manners lay the inherent savagery of the South, the region that through slavery had introduced sin into the American Garden.[37]

The single thematic thread of Pinckney's play emphasized the role of the southerner as American. Her first point was the importance of the Carolina Low Country in the founding of the nation. Pinckney held that John Locke's Fundamental Constitutions, which laid out the rights of settlers within the context of a Carolina aristocracy, deserved the same honor as a founding document of the

American republic as did the Mayflower Compact drawn by the Puritans of Massachusetts Bay. The creation of Middleton Place by Henry Middleton (father-in-law of General Charles Cotesworth Pinckney) out of the dense Low Country jungle bordering the Ashley River predated Monticello, Jefferson's architectural wonder on the edge of the Virginia frontier. Middleton's son Arthur, signer of the Declaration of Independence, was born and died at Middleton Place. At the time the American union was forged, Pinckney points out, the settlement at Charleston had been established for over a hundred years. The Middleton's manor house was destroyed first by the British during the American Revolution then by the Union troops during the southern war for independence.

Pinckney begins her drama with the first cultural contact between the native tribes and the European colonists. In a dance sequence, she has the Indians mock the inappropriate European dress; the French try to teach tribes sarabandes and other dances. Later, African Americans add diversity to Carolina with the establishment of plantations. With the introduction of rice, indigo, tobacco and cotton, the Low Country economy flourished. Pinckney conceived a garden fete to represent the highly sophisticated social life that had evolved among the barons of the Ashley River by the eve of the Civil War. Pinckney imagined that the industrial age would be introduced with a replica of the Best Friend, Charleston's first steam engine, puffing in. The final scene brought Charleston into the modern era. With soil exhausted and markets in decline, cutting timber was the most lucrative occupation after 1900. Pinckney touched on Charleston as "melting pot" with the blending of numerous ethnic groups and suggested the literary renaissance be celebrated with a "procession" of local writers. Restoration of the Dock Street Theatre would symbolize the New Deal era. For the finale, the narrator would assume the role of a broadcaster, the voice of the modern age, speaking from WCSC radio, which began its operation in 1930.

Pinckney skirted lightly over the Civil War, slavery, and emancipation, all elements of Charleston's history that challenged her thesis about the essential harmony between southern values and American values, and the continuity between past and present. In the course of their collaboration, Kirstein expressed his keen interest in having the story of the freedman's journey from slavery to freedom told. Pinckney, raised on stories of the horrors of Reconstruction, demurred. Weighing Kirstein's idea, she wrote in her notebook, "I must insist it should be the way I want it." About this time, Kirstein's interest shifted away from Charleston and back to New York.

In 1946 when Whitelaw still believed that the outdoor drama might work out, he asked attorney John Stuart Dudley to draw up papers for a corporation that would include Josephine Pinckney, Lincoln Kirstein, Thomas R. Waring Jr., J. J. Pringle Smith, Robert N . S. Whitelaw, and Dudley himself as principals in this joint artistic venture. The corporation would commission Pinckney to write the script and she would in turn assign all the rights back to the corporation, whose directors would be authorized to use the income for any civic purpose in Charleston. Pinckney personally donated $2,000 to the Carolina Art Association primarily for "the [Dock Street] theatre's plan of a production in Middleton Place Gardens" with the understanding Whitelaw not come back to her later for another contribution.[38]

When the project collapsed, Whitelaw used Pinckney's contribution to under-write the 1946 theater season, but soon he had another intriguing proposal for her. In 1940, the Carolina Art Association created a Civic Services Committee to address community issues such as off-street parking. Among other things, this committee identified the need for an organization to promote both the preservation and the use of the city's architectural and historic treasures. The fruit of their deliberations was the creation in 1947 of the Historic Charleston Foundation to promote both progress and preservation. Pinckney was one of the twenty founding board members, along with her old friends Marjorie Nott Morawetz, Albert Simons, Sam Stoney, Thomas Waring Jr., Eliza Dunkin Kammerer, and Alice Ravenel Huger Smith. When the foundation first began offering tours of private historic houses as a fund-raising strategy in 1950, she offered to open 36 Chalmers Street to inquisitive tourists. One of the foundation's first projects was a collaboration with the Daughters of the American Revolution to make repairs to the Old Exchange Building (damaged since the 1886 earthquake) that housed the chapter named for Pinckney's great-great grandmother, Rebecca Brewton Motte. In 1955, Pinckney became deeply involved in raising funds for the purchase and restoration of the Nathaniel Russell House, an early-nineteenth-century treasure on Meeting Street, and led the Furnishings and Decoration Committee designated to set up the period rooms.[39]

Pinckney's deep awareness of the issues of race and prejudice as the great post-war challenge in Charleston and in the world at large encouraged her in January 1947 to donate $10,000 to the Medical Society of South Carolina toward the establishment of a free dental clinic serving both blacks and whites. Local black leaders felt free to solicit her for donations, and over the years she did what her finances permitted to promote the advancement of African Americans in Charleston, such as helping pay deserving students' tuition to one of the black colleges in the state, but she always thought the most hopeful route to change lay in politics.[40]

Josephine Pinckney continued to believe that the "top drawer" of America needed to set an example that would launch the nation on a more equitable course, but she knew the limits of paternalism. Pinckney placed her faith in the reintroduction of the two-party system in the South as a first step in addressing some of the most egregious flaws of the region. She collaborated in stealth political agitation with her friend Harriet P. Simons, who believed strongly that whites and blacks were all citizens. "If the South does not provide its own leadership in these matters," Simons asserted, change "will be imposed upon us."[41]

Many white Charlestonians, such as Pinckney and Stoney, still maintained a personal relationship with the older generation of Charleston blacks and thought they had an understanding of the needs of the African American community as a whole. Race relations in the peninsula city were unique in numerous ways. The historical residential patterns of blacks and whites living close to one another had changed little since the days of slavery. Although prejudice and animosity existed, much of the overt hostility was tempered somewhat by the personalism that historically characterized southern social relations. The everyday familiarity and frequent kindnesses that passed between individuals could never compensate for the evil of caste segregation put in place during 1880s, but it did go a long way to erode some of the stereotyping that took place in cities where the races had almost no interaction on the human level. However, the children of the much venerated Old Time Negro had grown up with different expectations and understandings of themselves. As white Charlestonians poured out of the city to the new postwar suburbs across the Ashley River, the black population increased proportionately, gaining a 51 percent majority of the peninsula's population and potentially a new level of power. In 1944, the mostly black Progressive Democratic Party had been organized in the state.

Politics had always competed with poetry for Pinckney's attention. During her correspondence with Wendell Willkie she would often send him a few pages of her thoughts on world and national affairs. "As you know," she wrote Willkie, "I have to air my head every now and then to keep it from catching on fire."[42] When journalist John Gunther interviewed Pinckney for his sprawling *Inside USA* (1947), she gave him a copy of a 1945 article she wrote for *Transatlantic*, a wartime magazine devoted to shoring up the cultural bond between Great Britain and the United States. The South, Gunther observed, was the "problem child of the nation," but South Carolina was the worst of the worst, the poorest and most resistant to change, "a case apart" with its white mill workers "the most poverty blanched and backward folk in America." After his conversation with Pinckney, Gunther was impressed with Charleston's considerable intellectual and social life, an oasis in the desert: "It has never heard of Minneapolis or Akron, of course, and is just coming to recognize Atlanta; but it has a good art gallery and a theatre." Although having lost its polished look long ago, this "gem" among the dross "still retains a cardinal quality of grace, Gunther observed, and he quotes from Pinckney: "Physically the Low Country retains its glamourous air under the scourings and sweepings of industrial change."[43]

Pinckney's *Transatlantic* article laid out her understanding of the state's political past and her expectation for the future. She believed the pivotal political event of the twentieth century in South Carolina was the revolt of the yeoman class after centuries of domination by the planters. During the 1880s, the state government passed from the Redeemers, the patricians who wrestled control away from the Republican Reconstruction governments established after Civil War, into the callused, gnarled hands of men who had once walked behind plows. Pinckney agreed in theory that "native ability should be able to pass readily over the barriers of class." However, she could find no great leader emerging from the "middling classes." Public morality in South Carolina politics during the twentieth century had actually declined with the expansion of the franchise among the white population. In the case of South Carolina, and in much of the South, the "common man" so lionized by the liberal New Dealers was in fact deeply conservative. He is a "dissenter, fundamentalist in religion and puritanical in his code of morals" who supports prohibition, and condemns divorce for any cause. The average voter in South Carolina has been brainwashed to believe "the Republican Party means to elevate the interests of the blacks over the whites" and clings to the Democratic Party. With no second party, liberal voices for social change are silenced. The "lily white" Democratic primary, Pinckney declared, violated the principles of "simple justice."[44]

Pinckney's disciplined mind rejected wishful thinking, quick fixes, and cheap grace regarding the race question. She conceded that widespread "bafflement" reigned about how to attack racism. She did not think that the race problem in South Carolina (or anywhere else) would be cured by some nostrum, a bolt from the sky, the passage of a bill, or enactment of a penalty, but incrementally, one small concession after another, with most compromises coming from the southern whites. She believed that the majority of white southerners were willing to make changes for a more just world, but outside critics had to understand what a strong hold the history of failure and humiliation still had on the psychology of the modern South. Having known "invasion, enemy occupation, and (unlike other sections of the United States) defeat," the southern white will turn "belligerent and stubborn" when criticized and attacked by outsiders. Left alone, Pinckney asserted optimistically, southerners would probably do the right thing.[45]

In 1947, Pinckney's optimism seemed quite unexpectedly justified when the voice of a Charleston aristocrat was once again heard across the land. The message was a surprise. Federal judge Waties Waring, the much younger brother of newspaper editor Thomas R. Waring Sr., issued a decision in *Elmore v. Rice* challenging the constitutionality of the South Carolina Democratic Party primary's excluding blacks. Pinckney applauded his ruling that a political party is not a private club with sole discretion over membership. "I've been so stirred up over politics recently," Josephine confessed to Prentiss Taylor in 1947 that she had let her writing go. "All spring South Carolina had been in a turmoil over the business of having negroes enroll in the Democratic Party. One good result is that the citizens are aroused about politics as never before and since apathy has been one of our worst curses, that is all to the good." Judge Waring's decision "has really forced the politicos to actually enroll negroes at last. It has split the local party high, wide and handsome, to my great delight. Even though I don't like the Dixiecrats [segregationist southern Democrats who broke away from the national party], their defection may be the beginning of establishing two parties in the South and that will be a great gain."[46]

Pinckney and Harriet Porcher Simons met with the black community and with local officials "haranguing, petitioning, etc. to get the election rolls open to all, and having a hell of a good time, especially now that we are winning." "Most of the people I talk to are quite prepared to have the negroes," Pinckney reported to Taylor. "The chief trouble is that the politicians listen to the die-hards and [don't] recognize the change that has taken place."[47]

Ironically, the involvement of Waties Waring probably weakened support for expanded civil rights among the Charleston elite. The judge had violated the Code in 1945 by divorcing Ann Gammel Waring, his wife of many years, then quickly marrying a twice-divorced Yankee woman. Cast out of her home and into a nearby dependency, Annie Waring was soon taken to a hospital in a "pitiful mental state." Waites Waring had been consigned to social purgatory long before his controversial ruling. No one will ever be able to know for certain whether it was the message or the messenger that sent many Charlestonians into a froth. Nor will it be certain whether Waring had indeed had acquired "a passion for justice" (after a lifetime of indifference to black rights) as he claimed or whether he acted (as Pinckney and her friends suspected) in revenge.[48]

Pinckney viewed the Waring scandal with both bemusement and embarrassment. The vocal second Mrs. Waring spoke to Charleston's black YWCA and flailed the local southern whites as a "sick, confused and decadent people . . . full of pride and complacency, introverted, morally weak and low." Honoring her past ties with his brother, Pinckney wrote, "I don't even criticize [Waties Waring] to outsiders.

This makes it difficult to know how to react to his disloyalty. I'm more hurt and sentimental than angry."[49]

Never reconciling with the national Democratic Party after Willkie's defeat in 1940, Pinckney began distancing herself from the local Democrats as well. She attended the National Republican Convention with Emily and Nicholas Roosevelt in 1948. Carrie Sinkler Lockwood came down from Topsfield, Massachusetts, to join them. Uncomfortable with either the northern liberals or the southern conservatives among the Democrats, Pinckney found a happy home within the genteel, old money branch of the Republican Party, just as her ancestors had found a comfortable fit among the Federalists. The Philadelphia gathering was much more to her taste than the explosive Democratic gathering in the same city. She reported to Prentiss Taylor, "we had a high old time seeing people" and discussing the issues in "a perfervid manner." Pinckney also caught her first glimpse of television when she watched Joe Lewis pummel "Jersey Joe" Walcott on the flickering screen. She did not think this new technology boded well for the American mind. Pinckney's crowd, some pulling for Arthur Vandenburg, others for Harold Stassen, were crushed by the nomination of Thomas E. Dewey. "It certainly gives a poor choice in November," she complained, contemplating the three-way race between South Carolina Dixiecrat Strom Thurmond, Democrat Harry Truman, and Dewey. Pinckney had retained her dislike of Dewey since he bumped Wendell Willkie off the Republican ticket in 1944. She still mourned Willkie, or at least she still mourned the political leader she had hoped he would become.[50]

Even after Willkie's death in 1944, Pinckney had continued to weigh and balance the possibility of moving permanently to Manhattan. By December 1948, however, she decided once and for all to stay put in Charleston. When she wrote a New York friend, author Tibor Koeves, of her decision, he fully understood her preference for Charleston over "the metropolitan forest of dirty stones," even though he regretted it. "It seems to me," he wrote, "that there aren't many happy and satisfactory ways of life but among the few, living in one's own cherished house and working there at a metier one likes is very nearly the best."[51]

# 13

## *"Death, My Son and Foe"*

Josephine Pinckney neared the peak of her career as she started work on her fourth novel. She had fans across the country and in Europe eagerly awaiting her next book. All of Charleston was Pinckney's stage. As "leading lady," she played many roles—author, poet, preservationist, hostess to the famous, civic leader, philanthropist, political intriguer. An article in the *Charleston News and Courier* asserted that Pinckney's ability to be all things to all people, and at the same time, write critically acclaimed best sellers "is just another rung in the ascending ladder of the Pinckney legend." Carl Van Vechten observed that Pinckney could also frequently be seen, laughing and lifting a glass along with the other notables, writers, and actors attending Grace Stone's Sunday luncheon parties at George M. Cohan's table at the Plaza Hotel's Oak Room. He placed Josephine Pinckney among the "Literary Ladies" of the day, one of the "Noble Dames," along with Ellen Glasgow, Edna St. Vincent Millay, and Gertrude Stein.[1]

During Pinckney's Caribbean vacation in March 1948, a cast of characters more perverse and sensual than any she had encountered shanghaied her imagination. An idea for a story, "perfect for the movies and book-of-the-month club," began to bedevil her. At the various blue-skied ports of call, she sensed that life in the tropics was much more complex than the happy faces of the tourist guides suggested. The Caribbean, she decided, would provide not only a romantic setting, but it would also be a better venue than refined Charleston to underscore the "dark accents" of her next novel. Taken with the dramatic possibilities of St. John's during her cruise through the Virgin Islands, Pinckney adopted it as the model for her fictitious island of St. Finbar (Charleston's Catholic Cathedral of St. John the Baptist was once called St. Finbar's). She sought to avoid a repeat of the frequent complaints that *Three O'Clock Dinner* had drawn too closely from real life and real people in Charleston. Because again she had pulled the germ of her story from a real situation in Charleston, and a threat of libel might loom, changing the location made legal sense as well.[2]

The craving for commercial fame also bedeviled Pinckney. After "three scripts, five casts, and two directors," Metro-Goldwyn-Mayer had finally cut its losses and abandoned the expensive *Three O'Clock Dinner* film project. Competition with

Grace Stone drove her to seek another Hollywood contract. Stone's *Winter Visitor,* also published in 1945, was circulating throughout the country as a film starring Bette Davis. Pinckney puzzled over the formula for writing a novel that was of interest to Hollywood yet acceptable to the censors. "Shall I deal with evil in this book?" she wrote in her notebook. "Have I avoided it from conventionality—properness, fear of the Charleston Ladies? . . . Can I deal with it by indirection, or must I use 4-letter words?" Pinckney warned herself: "Look out for being pale, lady-like."[3]

Viking editor Pascal Covici cheered the news of another novel from Pinckney, even in its "embryonic" stages. As he contemplated the current state of fiction he presented her with bad news and good news. The bad news was that "the manuscripts I have seen of late are impossible. The young authors are just trying their wings, the middle-aged ones are frustrated and the old ones seem too tired." The positive aspect of this very "depressing" turn of events was that the field appeared wide open for her. "So here," wrote Covici, "is your chance."[4]

The role of the novel in American life had substantially changed from the time that Pinckney first chose a life in literature. Whimsy and humor all but disappeared from novels after World War II, as writers agonized about the blind fury that swept the world. The search for beauty and truth devolved into the hunt for explanations. After the Holocaust and Hiroshima, writers began to doubt whether the flawed human could indeed be "the measure of all things." Postwar novels generally focused on one big idea instead of one person. Even when an individual was the center of the action, the theme usually focused on loneliness and isolation from others.[5]

In April 1949, Pinckney was nursing her new novel through its "uncertain and queasy" stage when her "pleasure loving" nature got the better of her and she bolted off to Europe for a three-month jaunt. She first flew to Istanbul, where Thomas Whittemore of the Byzantine Institute had promised her a special tour of St. Sophia, the domed church built by Emperor Justinian in 532 A.D. Whittemore had led the American team uncovering the Christian mosaic, obscured for five hundred years during which the Turks had used the building as a mosque. The contrast between the intricate scrolling and decorative Islamic art and the "noble simplicity" of the images of the Virgin and the archangel in the apse moved Pinckney deeply. Then, to Greece, the "one country," she later wrote, "that has influenced, permeated, and informed Western thinking, hung over all our childhoods, given us its myths to be our myths, so that our literature and our psychology are dyed with its colors—indeed, Psyche, the soul, is a word we got from the

Greeks." Modern Athens was more nightmare than dream—expensive, crowded, and dominated by the police. Civil strife so deeply affected life there that she planned her sightseeing around the sporadic fighting in the city, guided by advice from the American Mission for Aid to Greece. At her next stop, Rome, she met up with Grace Stone and her husband, Ellis, then sailed home.[6]

Back in Charleston, Pinckney found she no longer had the stamina to work her usual schedule. When the doctor diagnosed breast cancer, the same disease that had killed Eliza Lucas Pinckney in 1797, she was stoic. After a "nasty" operation, her condition became dire. Rife with grief and worry, Lula Moore approached some of Pinckney's closest friends, suggesting that if the worse happened, the funeral be held in Washington Park across from 36 Chalmers Street. No church in the city could possibly hold "the horde of mourners" the loyal Moore expected would come to pay tribute to Miss Jo.[7] But Pinckney rallied, and returned by dint of internal fortitude to her manuscript.

After her extended contemplation of her own mortality, she changed the title of her novel from "Susanna's Folly" to "My Son and Foe" drawn from a line of Dante's *Inferno*, "Death, my son and foe." Her dark, psychological story once again penetrates into the inner dynamics of family life. She made the father, Basil Metallus, a frustrated Greek inventor. His fair-haired wife, so opposite in many ways, is a Scandinavian with the portentous name of Elsinore. Elsi has two sons, the insecure James, from her first marriage, and the handsome but dimwitted Rikki, son of Basil. Trapped on an unproductive plantation, they make up the classically unhappy family, torn by jealousies, old hurts, and, most of all, boredom. Two disrupting elements shatter the brooding equilibrium of the household: Connie, a young Scandinavian girl invited by Elsi in hopes that she might provide a love interest for James, and Kirk McAffee, a mysterious American engineer who travels the world alone avoiding all emotional entanglements as he tries to escape the pain of his wife's death. During a hike around the island, McAffee accidentally comes upon Susanna's Folly, the Metallus's failing sugar plantation, and sets a series of tragic events in motion.

Pinckney constructed her novel like a play; each scene enlarges the scope of the drama. As the story progresses, Elsi Metallus, who had abandoned her first husband and their son for Basil, begins to look at the mysterious Kirk McAfee as a potential lover and a ticket out of her stagnant life on St. Finbar. Kirk is obviously not Elsi's first love interest. Basil accepts the situation philosophically: "We're all three in the mezzo del cammin, the time of life when we must face old age sensibly . . . Still we must keep hold of what little the gods permit us. There are other forms of marriage than the Western romantic kind" (157–59).

McAfee, obsessed with the remembered perfection of his brief marriage, moves through life keeping an emotional distance from all he meets. As an amateur photographer, his way of connecting with people is by taking their photographs unawares. When he later studies the candid shots he gains insights into his subjects' characters, if not their souls. Pinckney gives McAfee an almost supernatural ability to see, but not stop, the brewing tragedy. Each member of the family begins to turn to him for advice, which he foolishly and freely dispenses.

Inevitably, Connie (whom Pinckney once called "Echo") succumbs to the careless seductive charms of the narcissistic Rikki who is only interested in seeing his own reflection in adoring women's eyes. Elsi's sons leave the island in a sailboat together after a violent fight over Connie. Only James returns home. Elsi assumes he has murdered her favorite son. The facts, however, reveal that Rikki was slain by his own hubris. When a sudden storm breaks the boat's mast, the boys postpone their feuding. Cautious James wants to sit tight and wait for help. Confident Rikki believes his own strength can conquer wind and tide, but he is drowned in the roiling whitecaps.

Technically innocent, James is nevertheless consumed with guilt. During the heat of their fight he had revealed the dark family secret. Rikki was a bastard, born before Elsi's divorce from James's father. In retrospect, James believes this knowledge caused his half brother to be so careless with his own life. Predictably, the whole family turns on Kirk for his interference; he had counseled Elsi to let the boys work out their problems by themselves. Blaming himself for enjoying his role as godlike wise man, Kirk muses, "The lars and the lemures, the fates and furies, they're the projections of ourselves and our passions, all right; but when we send them out they come rolling back, oversize, and give us better than we sent" (224). Elsi returns to the arms of Basil.

The survivors try to discern why this calamity happened. Was it the first sin, Elsi's infidelity with Basil so many years ago? Or the last sin, Rikki's seduction of Connie? Basil believes Rikki's flawed character doomed him and dismisses Kirk's struggle to find a cosmic reason for Rikki's death: "You Americans—you can't learn to accept tragedy as the climate of life. In the vast carelessness of God . . . there is no pattern of morals. Unless to endure irremediable ills is a moral" (244). Kirk is not satisfied with Basil's pessimistic philosophy. As he leaves the island, he burns all his photographs taken at Susanna's Folly, and reflects, "Cynicism is an evasion and a bore. However bad the smash-up, you can't help picking about in the wreckage for—not a moral exactly, but an affirmation of sorts—some old beam or post you can drag away and use another time" (250).

In early August 1951, Pinckney finished her final draft feeling "exhausted, but perfectly well." Sam Stoney thought she looked "a bit too thin, but very handsome" as she set off for an extravagant six-week trip to Europe. As requested, Marshall Best forwarded the galleys of "My Son and Foe" to Pinckney in care of the exclusive Connaught Hotel. In England, she toured with the Canbys in a little "u-drive-it." Pinckney saw John Gielgud and Flora Robeson in *A Winter's Tale,* as well as the "full version" of Shaw's *Man and Superman,* with the "Don Juan in Hell" episode included. She also spent some time with Jennifer Heyward, who was in London studying dance.[8]

After stops in Stockholm and Paris, she returned home in time for Christmas and a party in early January 1952 at the Book Basement, given by John Zeigler and Edwin Peacock, celebrating the publication of *My Son and Foe.* But Pinckney's fans who dashed out to buy her latest, planning to curl up with another light melodrama or amusing fantasy, felt betrayed. They wanted romance, not "dark passions." Neither *Ladies Home Journal* nor *Woman's Home Companion* opted to serialize *My Son and Foe.* "Too subtle for them," concluded Marshall Best kindly, and probably "over the heads of the people at *McCall's.*"[9]

Pinckney's complex story challenged even the sophisticated reader. Her close friend, William Raney, an editor at Henry Holt at the time, had to read her novel twice before he felt he understood it. Then, he judged it "a first-rate work" that blended reality and suspense. In contrast to *Three O'Clock Dinner,* which he had considered "a woman's book and an editor's book," he held up *My Son and Foe* as a "grownup's book . . . one for men and women and writers." "Intellectually," he believed, "it is more your type book . . . a lesson and an exercise in writing."[10]

Orville Prescott of the daily *New York Times,* who still identified Pinckney as "one of the most charming and one of the most blue-blooded ladies in Charleston, S.C.," criticized the characters as too programmed, serving only as mouthpieces, even though he conceded that the entire work, written with "careful strokes," was "artfully constructed and quite clever." Lewis Gannett agreed. "The strength of her writing was also its weakness," he observed, in that "the reader is always aware of the author's mind at work; nothing is left to animal accident . . . As in a cross-word puzzle, every square is in its appointed place, deftly interlocked with its neighbors." By being so controlled and measured, Pinckney makes "the emotional tornadoes that are her story seem intellectual rather than elementally overwhelming."[11] As Pinckney feared, she had held on so tightly to her emotions for so long, she could not now let them go.

Although Pinckney had assured Covici and Best that she had regained her "rugged" health and could work as hard as ever, her illness had taken a heavy toll. Not only did she struggle with her concentration, a tidal wave of self-doubt had swept over her. The slack sales of her book, passed over by the book clubs, confirmed her fears. She wrote in her diary: "Apparently I don't understand at *all* the mechanics of suspense, of keeping the readers interest *going*, of making the dramatic live. I keep telling myself to do it, but I don't do it. I am more interested in smart sayings, character-exposition, jocular humour, essay-exposition. . . . I know I should emphasize warmth, suspense, not deceptions and affection, but I don't succeed . . . *Try harder.*"[12]

Pinckney fell into a protracted siege of self-scrutiny. Did she want to keep writing in the current literary atmosphere? What *did* she want: "Money? Popularity? Sucess d'eshine?" "I don't want lots of money. Only some money," she confessed. She let her mind range freely about what sort of book she should write next, "which is my unconscious wish." "I want to write the poetic story," she concluded, one that would probe "the imaginative truth about life; the significant adventures of the soul and the mind . . . Poetry was my early love." She realized that to write the sort of books she admired, like those of Welty and Woolf, one had to throw her heart and soul into the work. With all her other commitments, she knew this was impossible "unless, I sell my house, dispose of my possessions live away from Charleston. Well, I won't do that." But if nothing else, she was an expert on that old city and realized "the lyric and the social comedy are still within my scope."[13]

Pinckney also realized that her own emotional distance from people had blunted her empathy with others, a crucial ingredient for a writer. "I need to know people better. The ivory tower is no good," she concluded. Haunted by her illness, Pinckney understood that if she did not soon learn to "branch out" she would miss the savor of whatever life remained. Trying to put a name to her feeling of disconnectedness, she blamed the Code. Manners, Pinckney conceded, did have a purpose and frequently "they help us over rough places." Whenever Pinckney's friends indulged in their self-consciously correct behavior, though, she found herself struck with an almost irresistible urge "to spit tobacco juice on the carpet." The principle of giving no offense had blocked her emotions, she thought, and robbed her of honest relationships. In fact, her ingrained "fatal desire to please," she believed, was her major character flaw.[14]

In 1953, Pinckney devised a "Credo" for herself in answer to her lifelong koan of "what a Pinckney should do": "Live the best life you can, people will emulate you; . . . avoid pretentiousness," "ego-greed," and "the heady pleasures of righteous indignation." A good sense of humor provides the "best check rein" on too much solemnity. "Feeling is [the] starting point especially the capacity to have feeling for other people—for others, not self." Could she indeed now free herself from the restraining hand of the Code, or did the habits of a lifetime have her "in chains"?

She worried that the "old fears will have so flabbed the muscles of fresh independent thought and action, that I won't be able to avail myself of my freedom." "I must try. I have had more than enough of tact, feeling, and pity." "I have had love, social position, reasonable intelligence, and now I'll have money and fame. I have no family; I could be independent of the world . . . I must have more vigor, naturalness, forth-rightness. I must be willing to hurt people's egos. I must be willing to have enemies."[15]

Emboldened, Pinckney set out to dissect the great shibboleths of her class in her next novel. She turned once again to the familiar territory of social comedy with a family situation at its core: "clannishness, snobbery, loyalty, and the simple pleasures of kinship, its warmth." She flipped to that section of her notebook marked "Scandals" and began to write.[16]

As the winter of 1954 drew to an end, Pinckney had made substantial progress on her fifth novel. Her title *Splendid in Ashes* reflects her fixation with mortality. She drew a line from Sir Thomas Browne's *Hydrotaphia; or Urne-Buriall* (1658): "Man is a noble animal, splendid in ashes, and pompous in the grave." The ironic title set the tone of the book, a satire on twentieth-century Charleston society executed with probing yet gentle wit. The line from Browne reflects not just the fate of Charlestonian John Augustus Grimshawe but also the fate of the class whose fortunes had so preoccupied her over the years.

*Splendid in Ashes* stands as Pinckney's last testament. Her decision to tell, if not all, then a great deal, sprung from the modernist drive for truth-telling and a craving for the final freedom from the Code. The culture of Charleston is reinterpreted through eyes grown weary with pain and mature from understanding. Pinckney made extra work for herself by attempting two tricky, though effective, devices. She went counterclockwise in time, in the manner of *The Magnificent Ambersons*, beginning with Grimshawe's funeral, then ranging back over forty years and the three generations touched by his magic and destructiveness.

At the conclusion, Pinckney returns to the funeral and finishes up with a series of explosive surprises. Pinckney's other ambitious strategy, also used by Booth Tarkington, involved switching narrative voices between "we," the consciousness of Charleston, and two characters, Cissy York and Carlotta Maillet Grimshawe, who each tell their interconnected stories. This book also has overtones of John O'Hara's popular *Ten North Frederick Street*. In Pinckney's novels, family houses have great symbolic power as sources of stability when the world outside is changing too fast. But having to live in a house built for another time can also prove an insuperable burden.

The story begins in 1947. Propelled by the changes after World War II, the modern age is catching up with the Carolina Low Country, so long in desperate flight: "The cement roads snaked farther and farther out into the untrampeled green countryside and launched us Charlestonians (hard-shell as we are) on a social revolution. We suddenly began to hear Time at our backs—it didn't sound like a winged chariot to us but like a ten-ton truck bearing down, its huge tires squealing. The rush flattened out events that would once have seemed mountainous: deaths, marriages, political changes."[17]

But one death in particular has set the town abuzz. The notorious native son John Augustus Grimshawe, who had survived both world wars, has died in New York City: "We had the conviction, now that after the time of death was over, we were all going to live forever" (3). Once the toast of a town thrilled to have one of its citizens in the headlines, Grimshawe is consecutively revealed as a gambler, charmer, philanderer, egoist, iconoclast, charmer, and, ultimately, fraud. His vacillating fortunes become a favorite topic of nattering, nipping and biting conversation of the sort that go on over ladies' afternoon bridge or men's late-night poker at the Carolina Yacht Club's "back bar."

Born in 1880, John Augustus Grimshawe belonged to the last generation with intimate knowledge of the Low Country plantation world. Grimshawe indulges in no nostalgia for the grim days of poverty that had crushed his father and a whole generation. Even when the agricultural economy ticked up a bit, the dispirited older men could not rally; they had "lost the habit of clean paint." When Pinckney picks up Grimshawe's story in 1912, his prospects look no better than his father's. His cotton brokerage has just gone bankrupt, and he must tell his young wife, Carlotta, and their two small children that they are now totally broke. Creditors will be taking everything: beds, family antiques, and paintings, even the prized childhood portrait of an ancestor, the "Little Grandfather." The beloved old house, a nineteenth-century Victorian mansion, cold and drafty (the last outward and visible sign of the Grimshawe's illustrious past) also must go on the block. Carlotta's father, Mr. Maillet, a thrifty old Huguenot, saves the family honor by placing the highest bid but dishonors Augustus by putting the title in Carlotta's name only.[18]

Carlotta remains stoic through adversity. Sharing her father's passion for frugality, she rallies to the challenge of scrimping and saving and takes pride in her ability to make do. Augustus, on the other hand, is restive under his wife's penny-pinching. Even as he works at menial jobs to feed his family, Grimshawe's brain races with one wild get-rich scheme after another. He gets a position that requires him to travel, and he brings home investors "from away." Carlotta begins noticing unexplained deposits in their bank statements. Augustus starts spending money extravagantly. When Thomas York, Carlotta's former beau who had also suffered financial reverses, accuses Grimshawe of violating the code of a gentleman for dodging his debts though the bankruptcy proceedings, a painful breach erupts between the two families who had one time been as close as blood relatives.

Cissy York, Thomas's much younger sister, is particularly saddened by the split. Carlotta and Augustus had made Cissy practically a member of their family when her parents died. Still unmarried after making her debut into society, Cissy begins to see something other than a father in Grimshawe and is attracted to his energy and sophistication. Augustus, impatient with the restrained and proper Carlotta, responds to Cissy's obvious admiration. When they have a private moment together at the Isle of Palms, Cissy affects the sophistication of the flapper and falsely insinuates that she is much more experienced in worldly ways than she truly is. When Augustus expresses concern that all her "warmth and sweetness" is going to waste without a husband, she flippantly replies, "Oh, women don't have to get married these days." Augustus is startled by her modern view that "The old idea . . . that a woman has to marry some dope to find fulfillment is out the window, thank God" (75). His fatherly interest in her transforms rapidly.

As in *Three O'Clock Dinner*, Pinckney sets two women competing with each other for the same man. Cissy York and Carlotta Grimshawe are proxies for the two sides of Pinckney that had been at war all her life. One is the flirt of Pinckney's youth who forms an alliance with a much older married man, a family friend, and the other the repressed aristocrat who realizes, almost too late, the price of propriety.

Cissy and Augustus begin the exciting tactics of deception, meeting at first in dark corners, then having stolen moments together in the backseat of his fancy new car. They soon assume the boldness of those who think they are invisible to others because they are blind to their own misdeeds. Only feeling alive when living on the absolute edge, Grimshawe keeps upping the ante until finally he lures Cissy into the guest room of his home while Carlotta is away. The mood is set by the poetry of Edna St. Vincent Millay that they read together as they bask in the "lovely light" of the brightly burning candle of adultery. Consciously or not, Cissy who has been pressing Grimshawe to make a commitment to her, leaves behind a sign she had been there. Carlotta learns the truth and is devastated.

Cissy, a "typical southerner [with] no capacity for abstract thought," lacks remorse for her act and is very surprised when she learns that Carlotta has forgiven Augustus, conceding her own repressed sexuality might have spawned her husband's infidelity (22). When Cissy learns that the whole Grimshawe family is joining Augustus on a business trip to Paris, she has a hysterical breakdown. On the rebound, she falls for Sam Rawley, the gentle doctor who is brought in to cure her, and they marry. Through Dr. Rawley, an intelligent, wisecracking woman enters the scene. His sister-in-law, Kay Rawley, arrives from Cleveland and comments on Charleston society from an opinionated northerner's perspective. She and Cissy embark on a "neo-Confederate War," which "brightened their friendship as long as they lived" (197).

Augustus scores a business coup in Paris, and his reputation at home is regained, for a very short time. Drawing from a real event that threatened the stability of France's Third Republic in 1934, Pinckney connects Grimshawe to a scandalous utility bond fraud.[19] His firm, Bascom Brothers, "folded with a clap and smell of brimstone and sulphur" (112). As usual, Charleston is quick to judge. Guilty, and worse, is the verdict. A great deal of bourbon, shrimp paste, and artichoke pickle are consumed in this time of crisis, in the same way that tea and biscuits always miraculously appear when the going becomes rough in Victorian novels. Public opinion excommunicates Grimshawe from the glory of being born Charlestonian. Their long, selective memories suddenly recall he had actually been born in Flat Rock, North Carolina, where Charleston families had resorted in the summer for over a century. Over several weeks while the scandal occupies the headlines, the local folk "cut it up, boiled it down, and mumbled the bones," before they finally let it go (112).

Head held high, Carlotta stands by her husband. At the same time, though, she struggles "as was her wont, with the complex moral issues, the degrees of innocence and guilt" (112). In an effort to redeem himself, Grimshawe enlists in the army when America goes to war in 1941 and serves with distinction. Grimshawe then flees the narrow scrutiny of Charleston and the sanctimonious Carlotta for Argentina. After dictator Juan Peron opened the country up to American investors in 1940 to help fund his reform program, the country was ripe for the likes of Grimshawe. With the full knowledge of Peron, the wheeler-dealer Grimshawe forges a "magic circle" of trade, a sort of pyramid scheme, in which "Dollars turned into cars, cars into pesos, pesos into cans of corned beef, and come out dollars again" (301).[20]

While Augustus follows his wanderlust, Carlotta finally acknowledges her rekindled feelings for Thomas York. Having bided his time, York attempts an "honorable seduction." "Love, if it doesn't come off is ridiculous," Carlotta muses after their first awkward encounter (147). And besides, she frets, "I haven't got the right clothes for this—playing the great mistress, for heaven's sake" (151). Carlotta and Thomas ultimately fall into a comfortable relationship with late suppers together and rides in the country, known to all, understood by all, mentioned by none. They seize any pleasure that comes their way; "Don't ask too much of fate;

we aren't meant to have much" (184). Carlotta resolves to divorce John Augustus Grimshawe, whom she learns is appropriately called "Don Juan" south of the border, although she knows that York can never leave his invalid wife.

*Splendid in Ashes* is Pinckney's tribute to middle-aged love and sexuality. She underscores the need to keep human feeling alive in one's heart for a lifetime. The decade between her second novel and her fifth had mellowed and burnished Pinckney's approach to life and love. Whereas the proper Judith Redcliff of *Three O'Clock Dinner* cannot bring herself to accept the loving overtures made by Lucian after her husband's death, the older Carlotta learns from her painful experience. Remembering how she had complained early in her marriage about her "inconsiderate," passionate young husband, Carlotta later reflects that "we were brought up wrong, they confused the senses and sensuality for us!" (151). Thomas York confirms that Charleston is full of "sad old women made that way by poverty, Queen Victoria and chastity" (143).

Preserving her dignity, but freeing herself of the burden of the "ladylike," Carlotta Grimshawe gets a job as an interior decorator and evolves into a modern woman. Her civic activities include the Interracial Relations Commission and intellectual pursuits with the Alliance Française (132). She even takes up smoking. Reluctantly, she sells the old Grimshawe mansion to some wealthy, anonymous Yankee, who turns out to be Augustus. He swoops back into Charleston with fistfuls of money from his Argentinean adventure. He returns the house to splendor and buys his way back into the fold of the elect. Accompanying Grimshawe is an admiring but sulky young Argentinean. When he throws an open house, only Carlotta and his former lover Cissy can resist his invitation. Public opinion is divided over whether the handsome man with the ambiguous name of Anibal (which Charlestonians corrupt into Annabelle) is an illegitimate son or illicit lover, "an Oscar Wilde man" (220).

Despite his success, Grimshawe appears gaunt and lonely. His promising son, John, had died years before during a spinal meningitis epidemic. Augustus is estranged from his unattractive, awkward daughter, Tottie, who inherited his family's beaked nose but none of its charm. She has married a young man from one of the Sea Island families who had brought their country ways into town with them. Grimshawe, who never overcame a stutter when excited, finally approaches Carlotta with a proposition for a resumption of their former life together, this time "a comfortable middle-aged marriage, a c-c-common-sense arrangement" in which she would serve as his hostess and have a separate apartment of her own (308). Carlotta refuses.

Augustus salves his ego by letting himself be flattered by a circling pack of fundraisers from various civic organizations who bite and snap at each other to get proximity to the great man. The museum's director, Jessica Parkhurst, who rolls her R's and presents herself to the unsophisticated Charlestonians as an expert on almost everything, bore a resemblance to Pinckney's neighbor, Laura Bragg, who always cast appraising glances at the Josephine's family heirlooms. Parkhurst, Pinckney writes, is constantly "on the lookout for angels for her pet, the museum, faithfully stalking the least angelic people" (241).

On the day of a large gala for his New York investors, Grimshawe receives word that his financial house of cards in Argentina has collapsed. He is ruined. After the party, he simply returns to his room at the Waldorf, "went to bed and died . . ." (302). At home, Grimshawe's brother, Theodore, whom Pinckney portrays as an idiot savant, observes that Augustus has "absconded into Heaven." As it turns out, he has known all along he was living with cancer, "a mouse in my stomach." At his funeral in Magnolia Cemetery "the Indian-summer haze blued the vistas; nature, not to be outshone by our funeral pomp, deepened all the fall colors . . . Gusts laden with damp blew in from the marshes beyond, and people began to worry about their sinuses; laden also with sand flies which, in a last chance autumn ferocity fell upon us. But we all kept ranks, the British square held; not a fingernail moved under the gluttonous assaults" (277).

The town immediately turns its attention to Grimshawe's will. He has one more surprise, a thunderclap. Except for a few personal gifts, Grimshawe leaves the bulk of his estate, his house, and its contents as a museum dedicated to the memory of his son, John Augustus Grimshawe Jr.[21] The mystery of Anibal, who receives the same amount of money as Tottie, is cleared up as well. His mother had been Grimshawe's mistress, whose child by Grimshawe had died. In the end, instead of preaching a moral tale of just desserts, Pinckney refuses to be judgmental. Thomas York, Grimshawe's severest critic, concedes that Augustus was "as much sinned against as sinning," for he had been a creation of Charleston and its craving for renewed fame and recognition (297).

During the years that Pinckney carefully crafted her epitaph for an era, she faced up to the reality of her own death as well. In the late spring of 1956 her cancer returned. "The pathologists report on my gland was bad," she confided to Dorothy Heyward. "I started in right away to take x-ray treatments and some injections. It was a jolt, needless to say; but the doctors seem fairly cheerful about it. It seems that they have success in arresting this particular type of cancer, so I'll probably be around to plague my friends for quite a while longer . . . It may be years before you get rid of me." She was quick to warn the high-strung Heyward, who herself struggled with delicate health, "don't let this little do of mine depress you."[22]

Marshall Best worried about Pinckney. Instead of the usual flood of fretful queries as she entered the home stretch with her novel, he heard nothing from 36 Chalmers Street. Pinckney's energy had been drained away by a new course of treatments using cobalt, a last-ditch measure with unpredictable side effects. Each morning, she valiantly confronted revisions, the trimming and pruning, clear-cutting actually, of acres of text. But just as she would get going, with her brain racing full tilt, her body would give out. With burns from the radiation pulling tightly as they healed, she had to stop and retreat from chair to sofa until the siege passed. Then the process began again. She simply had no idea when she might stagger across the finish line, she wrote Best with regret. "All I can say is that I want terribly to get it wound up and off my neck, so I'll do the *best* I possibly can . . . Don't lose heart!"23

By August, Pinckney was mailing the last revisions. Thomas Waring Jr. volunteered to drive her to New York to meet with Best and to consult a cancer specialist. Her New York doctor pronounced Pinckney cancer-free, but the radiation treatments clearly had taken their toll. "This big new machine," she wrote Laura Bragg in September, must have caused her latest bout of illness. "The last set of x-rays really did me in." Although weak, she set off to visit her old friends. After a couple of weeks at China Bank, Grace Stone and Eleanor Perenyi's home in Stonington, Connecticut, Pinckney declared that the salt air had worked wonders for her health. However, when she arrived at her next stops, Carrie Lockwood's Topsfield, Massachusetts home and Bay Wigglesworth's in Cambridge, her friends were stricken by her ravaged appearance. Although she admitted to "feeling punk" with "a frightful cough and shortness of breath," Pinckney pressed on with her New England agenda to promote the Historic Charleston Foundation among her wealthy friends and make some fund-raising calls. At a dinner during her stay in the Boston area, she met Andrew Hepburn, the restoration architect whose firm did much of the best work at Williamsburg. While he discoursed upon his latest project, the restoration of the small town of Newcastle, Delaware, Pinckney "plugged" Charleston's advances in preservation.24

Bay Wigglesworth drove Pinckney back to New York for a cocktail party that Viking Press was giving in her honor. Forced joviality strained the atmosphere. Guests made elaborate professions of how fabulous Pinckney looked even as they wondered privately how long she could stand. Grace Stone and Eleanor Perenyi watched surreptitiously over their cocktail glasses for signs she was fading, but Pinckney maintained a magnificent façade. Little lies, Pinckney always believed, provided the foundation for civilized life. The party proved a success inasmuch as Pinckney survived it, but the effort proved too great. She developed pneumonia. Her condition deteriorated so rapidly that Pinckney soon called her niece Frances

Pinckney Breckinridge to accompany her to Doctor's Hospital, believing such a ceremonial event could only be performed by family members.[25]

When Marshall Best learned that Pinckney's condition had become "desperate," he called the hospital on October 3 to get an update. Pinckney surprised him by answering the phone herself. Feigning the stoicism she always admired (even though she now thought it an unfashionable "repression"), she tried to sound upbeat. When Best expressed his concern, she replied with a cheery, "Oh, we'll survive."[26]

For just as a flame often grows white hot before dying out, Pinckney had rallied. She asked "Fancy," as she called Breckinridge, to fetch a pink hair ribbon to discipline her relentlessly unruly hair. A glance in the mirror suggested some wrinkle cream for her face was also in order. Also, she needed some "wrinkies" and "frownies," little tapes advertised in women's magazines that promised when applied overnight to strategic places on the face to smooth furrowed brows and iron out "crows' feet." Pinckney's mind remained clear and ranged widely, ticking off all her responsibilities. She still had some calls to make on behalf of the Historic Charleston Foundation. She rang Lula Moore at home to ask about Peter's replacement, a Welsh Corgi named Cadwallender, and also inquired whether she or her family had any immediate needs of any kind.

Relatives visiting her bedside could see her struggling against confusion. A restless Pinckney began fretting over the whereabouts of Harriott Pinckney's lyre. During the night of October 4, Josephine Pinckney died.[27]

Friends and family regretted that Pinckney passed away alone in her hospital room. They needn't have. Her memory fed her mind until the very end. Sprawled across the crisp hospital sheets laid the typed pages of *Splendid in Ashes,* vivid with the personalities of her characters, composites of old friends and lost loves.[28] She died still correcting, still searching for the right word, still working to make it "click," still telling herself "Try harder."

Pinckney's body was returned to Charleston on the Palmetto Special. Marshall Best drove her new car back to Charleston and arrived in time for the funeral. In fitting symmetry, she took her leave of Charleston from the same church where she had her beginning. Grace Church rang once more with the "noble poetry" of the Episcopal prayer book. Decades later, Best still remembered her internment on a bright October day at Magnolia Cemetery where she had once read her own ode to the Confederate dead, "We the children of the later days . . . " Pinckney would share a large plot with Captain Tom and Camilla. In the midst of the "eloquent words and solemn mourners great and small," a thousand tiny kamikazes attacked beneath skirts and under starched collars. Best was amused at the "fur-tive slapping at mosquitoes," remembering Pinckney had described so precisely this experience in her account of John Augustus Grimshawe's burial in the same cemetery on the banks of Cooper River. "She would have loved it," he thought.[29]

Pinckney's will proved every bit as interesting to Charlestonians as had Grim-shawe's. The *Charleston News and Courier* published the details. Her real estate and some personal items, she passed on to Cotesworth Pinckney's three children, who sold 36 Chalmers Street and Eldorado. She left gifts for her numerous godchildren and great-nieces and nephews, but her principal legatees were the cultural institu-tions of the city of Charleston: the Charleston Library Society, the Carolina Art Association, the Charleston Museum, and the Historic Charleston Foundation. Her family found Harriott Pinckney's lyre safely stored at 36 Chalmers. Pinckney had proved as good a steward of the family treasures as she had of the family reputation.

Although Pinckney often reflected that she had "no one to love," as far as an immediate family went, her death struck her surviving friends very hard. At first, Lady Canby withheld word of Pinckney's passing from her husband. After a series of strokes, Henry Seidel Canby was so fragile that his wife feared "the news of such a catastrophe might carry *him off.*" When she finally told him, he was "very broken up over Jo." Lula Moore was stricken by the loss of Pinckney, but her religious faith gave her solace. Knowing that before Pinckney "closed her eyes," the Moore family's welfare was foremost in her mind comforted her as well. Moore placed a memorial poem to Pinckney in the newspaper on the anniversary of her death, for a "devoted employer and friend" from her "devoted servant and friend." Pinckney bequeathed Moore an annuity and special funds so that she might have a funeral worthy of her faithful life. When Moore died in 1977, the remnants of Pinckney's circle called on her family. They could scarcely speak for their tears, mourning all that Pinckney and Moore and the lavender house at 36 Chalmers Street had meant to their lives and the life of Charleston, and their youthful dreams of a renaissance.[30]

After Pinckney's death, tributes flowed in from many quarters. *Time* magazine noted her passing in its "Milestones" section, and the *New York Times* published a prominent obituary with a photograph. One of the most heartfelt farewells came from architect Albert Simons, whose life had meshed with Pinckney's at so many junctures. They both felt they were the last of a breed working "together in various fields maintaining the cultural resources of this community in an age of the much too common man." "For many of our generation," he wrote, "Charleston will not be quite the same place without her." Simons also wrote a tribute entered into the minutes of the Board of Trustees of the Charleston Museum where she had carried on the work of Captain Tom and General Charles Cotesworth Pinckney: "Whereas born to affluence and a name of historic distinction, she was not content to accept with complacency the honors inherited from the illustrious past, but generously contributed of her means and her talents in furthering the living culture of her beloved City."[31]

In March 1958, the American Scenic and Historic Preservation Society awarded a posthumous Citation of Achievement to Josephine Pinckney "with gratitude for works nobly done in a truly noble spirit" and with "tact and persuasion." In 1959, Pinckney's closest friends restored and furnished one of the bedrooms on the second floor of the historic Nathaniel Russell House in her honor. Bay Wigglesworth contributed a nineteenth-century "bull's eye" mirror that had once hung in the Wigglesworth family home in Manchester and had, no doubt, once held the reflection of Pinckney and Dick Wigglesworth together. Prentiss Taylor donated a selection of his Charleston lithographs to the Gibbes Art Gallery as a memorial because "she did so much to make Charleston familiar to me—one of the homeplaces."[32]

Reviews of *Splendid in Ashes* were tempered by respect after Pinckney's death, but the praise was genuine and well deserved. Larry Winship of the *Boston Globe* believed Pinckney's death particularly tragic because *Splendid in Ashes* contained "some of her best writing." Virginia Kirkus regarded *Splendid in Ashes* as Pinckney's best novel, "the fruit of her experience, her wit, her irony, her gift for mirroring the city that was her background, her skill in portraying its people, her sophistication in interpreting its contradictions." In the *Saturday Review*, Rosemary Benét, sister of Stephen Vincent and William Rose Benét, described John Augustus Grimshawe as "a Charleston version of the late Mike Todd" (one of actress Elizabeth Taylor's many husbands) and praised Pinckney's rare "deft hand" in mixing levity and gravity. In the *New York Herald-Tribune,* Florence Haxton Bullock deemed *Splendid in Ashes* a novel "perfect in its basic design.[33]

Charlestonians split into the two camps over Pinckney's revealing novel: those who disapproved of portraying Charleston as a haven for libertines but read the book anyway, and those who refused to read it, knowing in advance they would not like it. Former Charlestonian Mary Martin Hendricks's review for a Pittsfield, Massachusetts, newspaper noted that the reasons for Pinckney's lack of audience in Charleston are "many and complex." Marshall Best hypothesized that Charlestonians resented the novel's "recognizable ironies." A letter to the editor of the *Charleston News and Courier* chastised Charlestonians for turning their back on a book describing the "provincialism of Charleston's upper crust" at the same time that they were so eager to read about the secrets of that narrow-minded New England town Peyton Place. Local bookstores could scarcely keep Grace Metalious's satire on their shelves.[34]

Pinckney died before she could finish her final revisions of *Splendid in Ashes*. Marshall Best, to whom the burden fell, likely thought that Josephine, like Augustus Grimshawe, had "absconded into heaven," leaving all the cleaning up to him. The Pinckney family authorized Best to put the finishing touches on the manuscript. He essentially wrote the last pages.[35]

Understanding that Pinckney had mined Charleston, past and present, for her characters, Best asked Clelia Waring to vet the text for possible libel. Going beyond her charge, Waring demanded that 50 percent of the "obscenity" come out since Charleston men never used words such as "cutie" and "slut" in front of ladies. "Jo was a fanatic on words and expression," Waring insisted. She suggested that her judgment "must have been affected by those years when death always hovered over her," especially "those last agonizing months when she was doing the revising. There is a great deal of sex in the book, and that is all right, but I feel very strongly that Josie's special style does not bear the weight of vulgarity. The extraordinary charm that Jo had was partly her ability to use profanity in a moment of shock or surprise and her manner of using it removed it entirely from the realm of the real profane. This is not true in the book." On one point, Waring was adamant. She wanted Blowing Rock, North Carolina, substituted as Grimshawe's birthplace instead of the beloved Flat Rock. Unwilling to take on this local battle, Best acquiesced.[36]

Against Best's explicit instructions, Waring shared the manuscript with two women also very close to Pinckney. Unfortunately, one them spread rumors up and down the Atlantic seacoast that *Splendid in Ashes* was a novel "full of filthiness and sex and is the work of a degenerate mind in the last stages of decay." When this buzz reached Best, he chastised Waring for breaking his confidence, adding "This is so utterly preposterous that it would make me sick if it were not so funny . . . You fell into the trap of thinking it was Josie rather than one of her characters who is using the language . . . Women! Women!"[37] In the end, though, he placated Waring by excising the offending words.

Dr. Morris M. Pinckney thanked Best for all his kindness and help to his aunt, acknowledging that she was unwilling to take advice from almost anyone else. Grace Stone's appreciation of the finished manuscript also pleased Dr. Pinckney enormously. "I hope Jo will enjoy with many chuckles and toothsuckings, the admiration and congratulations of many more of her friends." Admitting some minor shortfalls in its execution, Best concluded that *Splendid in Ashes* ranked as Josephine's "most mature and wise and sensitive book." Critics John Mason Brown and Agnes Allen, two excellent judges, both agreed with Best's analysis. All the editors reading the book in proof at Viking Press applauded Pinckney's curtain call.[38]

Amy Lowell had been right after all. In her greatest test, Josephine Pinckney proved herself "a first class heroine." Faced with a fatal illness, Pinckney yielded to neither despair nor regret. Pinckney's stoic approach to life had not made her cynical, gloomy, or bitter. In fact, it freed her from those traps, allowing her to face life straight-backed, head-high, clear-eyed, and realistically. The ability to see how irony penetrated life fortified her in adversity. During her last illness Pinckney became sardonic at times, but pessimism never conquered her. In her writing, as in her life, suffering took on a redemptive quality. She railed against ignorance, but not against fate, and ultimately learned to venerate the "Roman virtues" of her family. Pinckney cultivated a wry sense of humor as a shield against the inevitable disappointments that haunt those born to high expectations. She finished her life with gallantry, exhibiting a grace in dying equal to her talent for living.[39]

# Notes

| | |
|---|---|
| ALP | Amy Lowell Papers, Houghton Library, Harvard University |
| ASP | Albert Simons Papers, South Carolina Historical Society |
| ATP | Allen Tate Papers, Special Collections, Firestone Library, Princeton University |
| CAA | Carolina Art Association Papers, South Carolina Historical Society |
| DHP | DuBose Heyward Papers, South Carolina Historical Society |
| DKHP | Dorothy Kuhns Heyward Papers, South Carolina Historical Society |
| HAP | Hervey Allen Papers, Special Collections, Hillman Library, University of Pittsburgh |
| HLMP | Henry Louis Mencken Papers, New York Public Library |
| JBP | John Bennett Papers, South Carolina Historical Society |
| JPP | Josephine Pinckney Papers, South Carolina Historical Society |
| LMBP | Laura Mary Bragg Papers, South Carolina Historical Society |
| PSSCP | Poetry Society of South Carolina Papers, Archives, The Citadel |
| Pinckney/Viking | Josephine Pinckney/Viking Press Papers, South Caroliniana Library, University of South Carolina |
| PT/Quiroz | PrentissTaylor Papers, in the possession of Roderick Quiroz |
| PT/Yale | Prentiss Taylor Papers, Beinecke Rare Book and Manuscript Library, Yale University |
| SCHM | *South Carolina Historical Magazine* |
| SCHS | South Carolina Historical Society, Charleston |
| SLTP | Sallie L. Taliaferro Papers, in the General William Booth Taliaferro Papers, Special Collections, Swem Library, College of William and Mary |
| SPSP | Society for the Preservation of Spirituals Papers, South Carolina Historical Society |
| VQR | *Virginia Quarterly Review* |

## NOTES TO PREFACE

1. Thomas Pinckney (1668–ca. 1704) of County Durham, England, first married Grace Bedon in South Carolina in 1692. Before she died, they had a son, Thomas (1696–1733) who was a British army officer. His marriage to Mary Cotesworth, also of County Durham, produced two sons: Josephine's progenitor Charles Pinckney (1699–1758) and William (1704–1766). Each brother had a son who signed the Constitution: Charles's son, General Charles Cotesworth Pinckney and William's Charles Pinckney.

Mabel L. Webber, comp., "The Thomas Pinckney Family of South Carolina," in *South Carolina Genealogies* (Spartanburg, SC: The Reprint Company, 1983), 3:290–91. The other two delegates attending from South Carolina were Pierce Butler, whose wife had Pinckney connections, and John Rutledge, whose brother Edward was an in-law of Charles Cotesworth Pinckney. George C. Rogers Jr., *Charleston in the Age of the Pinckneys* (Norman: University of Oklahoma Press, 1969), 128.

2. Hervey Allen to Marjorie E. Peale, 2 January 1940, in Marjorie E. Peale, "Charleston as a Literary Center, 1920–1933" (M.A. thesis, Duke University, 1941), 201; Frank Durham, *DuBose Heyward: The Man Who Wrote Porgy* (Columbia: University of South Carolina Press, 1954), 24–25; Emily Clark, "Hervey Allen," *Saturday Review of Literature,* 9 December 1933, 323.

3. Hervey Allen to Harriet Monroe, draft letter [1922], HAP.

4. [Thomas R. Waring Jr.], editorial, *Charleston News and Courier,* 6 October 1957.

5. Josephine Pinckney to Prentiss Taylor, n.d., PT/Quiroz.

### NOTES TO INTRODUCTION

1. Josephine Pinckney, notebook [1945], JPP. Pinckney is quoting from Thomas Browne's *Hydriotaphia, Urne-Burial; or, A Discourse of the Sephulchrall Urnes lately found in Norfolk* (1658).

2. *The Viking Log,* 9 October 1945; William Du Bois, "Pluff Mud, Oleanders and Drains," *New York Times Book Review,* 28 September 1945, 5, 28; Pascal Covici to Josephine Pinckney, 20 June 1945, 16 November 1945; Josephine Pinckney to Pascal Covici, 7 June 1945, Pinckney/Viking; "Miss Pinckney Wins Southern Authors Award," *Charleston News and Courier,* 7 January 1946; "Pinckney Novel Among Year 50 Most Outstanding Books," *Charleston News and Courier,* 3 February 1946.

3. Marshall A. Best to Herbert P. Shippey, 16 October 1975, Pinckney/Viking.

4. Michael North, *Reading 1922: A Return to the Scene of the Modern* (New York: Oxford University Press, 1999), 63-64. North refers to this reaction to change as "cultural astigmatism." Anthony Harrigan, "A Great Generation of Charleston Writers," [ca. October 1957], clipping, JPP.

5. C. Hugh Holman, "Detached Laughter in the South," in *Comic Relief: Humor in Contemporary American Literature,* ed. Sarah B. Cohen (Urbana: University of Illinois Press, 1978), 91.

6. Josephine Pinckney, "Bulwarks against Change," in *Culture in the South,* ed. W. T. Couch (Chapel Hill: University of North Carolina Press, 1934), 48.

7. Donald Davidson to Josephine Pinckney, 28 January 1934, JPP; John Crowe Ransom, "Modern with a Southern Accent," *Virginia Quarterly Review* (April 1935): 189, 192, 186.

8. Josephine Pinckney, "The Story behind the Story," *WINGS: Literary Guild Review* (October 1945): 5–6; notebook [1953], JPP.

9. "Notes on the St. Cecilia Society," typescript, JPP.

10. Joseph W. Barnwell, "Captain Thomas Pinckney," *Confederate Veteran* 24 (August 1916): 342. Isabella G. Leland, "Legends of Ghosts, Pirates Still Cling to Fenwick Hall, *Charleston News and Courier,* 16 November 1959. Among the adventurers who sailed to Charleston on the *Loyal Jamaica* was Robert Fenwicke, whose brother John built Fenwick Hall on the Stono River. Josephine Pinckney, "DuBose Heyward," *Dictionary of American Biography, Supplement* 9 (New York: Scribner's, 1971–75): 303.

11. Harriott Rutledge Ravenel, *Eliza Lucas Pinckney* (New York: Scribner's, 1896), 107.

12. The children of General Thomas Pinckney and Elizabeth Motte were Colonel Thomas Pinckney (1780–1842), Charles Cotesworth Pinckney (1789–1865), Elizabeth Brewton Pinckney (d. 1857), Harriet Lucas Pinckney (d. 1824), Mary Pinckney (?), and Rebecca Motte Pinckney (1788–97). Mabel L. Webber, comp., "The Thomas Pinckney Family of South Carolina," in *South Carolina Genealogies* (Spar-

tanburg, SC: The Reprint Company, 1983), 3:300–301. The third daughter of Rebecca Motte, Mary Brewton, married Colonel William Alston and inherited the King Street House that Motte inherited from her brother, Miles Brewton.

13. A. S. Salley Jr. "Col. Miles Brewton and Some of His Descendants" in *South Carolina Genealogies* (Spartanburg, SC: The Reprint Company, 1983), 1:150–51.

14. Frances Leigh Williams, *A Founding Family: The Pinckneys of South Carolina* (New York: Harcourt, Brace, Jovanovich, 1978), 55, 136–37; "Fairfield," National Register of Historic Places Inventory —Nomination Form, in Fairfield file, SCHS. In 1785, Eliza Lucas Pinckney also moved to the Santee District to live with her widowed daughter, Harriott Pinckney Horry, at Hampton Plantation. Charles Cotesworth Pinckney married Sallie Middleton in 1773. Her father, Henry Middleton, possessed eight hundred slaves who manned twenty plantations, including Middleton Place on the Ashley River, where he had overseen the construction of magnificent gardens.

15. Harriette Kershaw Leiding, *Historic Houses of Charleston* (Philadelphia: Lippincott, 1921), 103–4. "Cousin Lizzie Huger's Recollections, 1879," Huger (Webber) file, SCHS. When Governor Thomas Pinckney accepted his general's commission in 1812, Rebecca Motte changed her will. Instead of leaving Eldorado directly to Pinckney, she gave a life interest to her daughter Frances. If Governor Pinckney survived his wife, he would then inherit Eldorado. If not, then the children of his first wife Elizabeth would inherit. Frances and Thomas Pinckney died within months of each other, leaving a long detailed joint will. Will of Rebecca Motte, Charleston County Wills, Book 33C (1807–1818), 1005–9. Will of General Thomas Pinckney and Frances Motte Middleton Pinckney, 23 May 1823, Book 38B (1826–1834); Will of Frances Motte Middleton Pinckney, Book 43B (1839–1845), 598–601.

16. Josephine Pinckney, "They Shall Return as Strangers," *VQR* (October 1934): 548.

17. Bertram Wyatt-Brown, *The House of Percy: Honor, Melancholy, and Imagination in a Southern Family* (New York: Oxford University Press, 1994), 10–11; Josephine Pinckney, "Notes on Family," JPP.

18. Dixon Wecter, *The Saga of American Society: A Record of Social Aspiration 1607–1937* (New York: Charles Scribner's Sons, 1937), 72–73.

19. Anne Baker Leland Bridges and Roy Williams III, *St. James Santee Plantation Parish: History and Records, 1685–1925* (Spartanburg, SC: The Reprint Company, 1997), 332–33; Archibald Rutledge, *My Colonel and His Lady* (Indianapolis: Bobbs-Merrill, 1937), 39–40. Rutledge's grandmother was Captain Tom's sister, Caroline Pinckney Seabrook.

20. "Miss Jane Wightman's House," typescript in posession of Elise Pinckney, 2.

21. Josephine Pinckney, "Meditations," notebook [ca. 1953], JPP.

22. Wyatt-Brown, *House of Percy*, 11–12.

23. Josephine Pinckney, as quoted in "Rich Brothers Southern Book Exhibition" [Atlanta], unidentified clipping [ca. 1928], Caroline Sinkler Lockwood scrapbook, in possession of Sidney Lockwood Tynan.

24. A. Edward Newton to Josephine Pinckney, 31 January 1928, 9 March 1928, JPP. Karen Horney's (1885-1952) books include *The Neurotic Personality* (1937), *Self-Analysis* (1942), and *Inner Conflicts* (1945).

25. Pinckney, "Bulwarks against Change," 41.

26. Josephine Pinckney to Prentiss Taylor, 8 March 1933, PT/Yale.

27. For one example, see Louis D. Rubin Jr., "The Southern Muse: Two Poetry Societies," in *The Curious Death of the Novel: Essays in American Literature* (Baton Rouge: Louisiana State University Press, 1967), 220–21.

28. [Henry Seidel Canby], "Timely and Timeless," *Saturday Review of Literature*, 2 August 1924, 1.

29. Dorothy Heyward to Rebecca West, 21 July 1951; Dorothy Kuhns Heyward to Rumer Godden, n.d., DKHP.

NOTES TO CHAPTER 1

1. Grace Episcopal Church (Charleston, SC), Parish Register, 1846–1971, 19 March 1895, Charleston County Public Library, microfiche.

2. "Birthplace of Josephine Pinckney," *Charleston News and Courier*, 24 December 1945. Captain Pinckney rented 29 Legaré Street from his cousin Robert Withers Memminger. The house was built by the Reverend Paul Trapier Gervais about 1835.

3. Will of Thomas Pinckney, 1915, microfilm, Charleston County Probate Office.

4. Recent scholarship has shown this furniture, once believed to be in the Vernis-Martin style (the French attempt at Chinese lacquering), is actually of English origin and manufacture. Maurie D. McInnis *The Pursuit of Refinement: Charlestonians Abroad, 1740–1860,* in collaboration with Angela D. Mack (Columbia: University of South Carolina Press, 1999), 253.

5. Captain Thomas Pinckney to "Hat" [Harriott Horry Rutledge Ravenel], 16 August 1911, Harriott Horry Rutledge Ravenel Papers, SCHS.

6. As quoted in Michael O'Brien, "Politics, Romanticism, and Hugh Legaré: 'The Fondness of Disappointed Love,'" in *Intellectual Life in Antebellum Charleston,* ed. Michael O'Brien and David Moltke-Hansen (Knoxville: University of Tennessee Press, 1986), 149.

7. Josephine Pinckney, "Bulwarks Against Change," in *Culture in the South,* ed. W. T. Couch (Chapel Hill: University of North Carolina Press, 1934), 41–42.

8. Will of Rebecca Motte, Charleston County Wills, Book 33C (1807–1818), 1005–9. Governor Pinckney and his second wife, Frances, had two children together, Edward Rutledge (1800–1832) and Mary (b. 1804). Edward was slated to inherit Eldorado, but both he and his sister predeceased their parents. Frances Motte Middleton Pinckney survived the governor by four months. In the end, Governor Pinckney's eldest son from his first marriage, Colonel Thomas Pinckney, inherited Fairfield, where he had been living for many years. Cotesworth Pinckney received Eldorado, the house and all its furnishings and with its high lands and 178 acres of the more valuable tidal swamps. Along with Eldorado came a stake in Cedar Island, a seaside retreat.

9. Phoebe Caroline Elliott was also the sister of William Elliott III, a classmate of Cotesworth Pinckney at Harvard. Pinckney graduated in 1808. Lawrence S. Rowland, Alexander Moore, and George C. Rogers Jr., *History of Beaufort County, South Carolina* (Columbia, SC: University of South Carolina Press, 1996), 1:403–5. Their children were Charles Cotesworth (1812–1898), Caroline (1816–1892), Maria (1821–1858), Thomas (1828–1915), and Mary Elliott (1833–1912). Mabel L. Webber, comp., "The Thomas Pinckney Family of South Carolina," in *South Carolina Genealogies* (Spartanburg, SC: The Reprint Company, 1983), 3:300.

10. Caroline Elliott Pinckney to Thomas Pinckney, 3 December 1846, in Pinckney Family Scrapbook, JPP. Caroline Pinckney's family, the Elliotts, was also touched by a similar change in heart. Her nephew, Stephen Elliott gave up the law for the Episcopal priesthood and became the Bishop of Georgia.

11. Joseph W. Barnwell, "Captain Thomas Pinckney," *Confederate Veteran* 24 (August 1916): 342; Petrona Royall McIver, "Minutes of the Parish History Club of Christ Church Parish," 31 July 1928, as quoted in Anne Baker Leland Bridges and Roy Williams III, *St. James Santee Plantation Parish* (Spartanburg, SC: The Reprint Company, 1997), 215.

12. Thomas Pinckney, "My Reminiscences of the War and Reconstruction Times" [ca. 1903], galley proofs, Alderman Library, Special Collections, University of Virginia; Frances Wallace Taylor, Catherine Taylor Matthews, and J. Tracy Power, eds., *The Leverett Letters: Correspondence of a South Carolina Family, 1851–1868* (Columbia: University of South Carolina Press, 2000), 491; Mary Pinckney to "Mrs. Lucas," 13 June [1864], in Pinckney Scrapbook, JPP.

13. Myrta Lockett Avary, *Dixie after the War* (1906; reprint, New York: Negro Universities Press, 1969), 341–42; Caroline Pinckney Seabrook to Mary Maxcy Leverett, 1 July 1865, in *Leverett Letters*, 398.

14. *Richmond Whig*, 22 April 1870; "Brook Hill" Virginia Historic Landmarks Commission: Survey Form, file no. 30-83.

15. J. C. Hemphill, "Thomas Pinckney," *Men of Mark in South Carolina; Ideals of American Life: A Collection of Leading Men in the State*, vol. 3 (Washington, DC: Men of Mark, 1907–9), 303.

16. The children of Captain Thomas Pinckney and Mary Stewart Pinckney were Amanda (27 January 1871–14 November 1875), Thomas (26 October 1872–28 October 1881), John Stewart (22 October 1874–9 July 1875), Charles Cotesworth Pinckney (16 December 1875–20 August 1934), Lucy (18 June 1877–12 July 1877), and Caroline (4 May 1879–23 July 1879). "Pinckney Genealogy," typescript, Pinckney Family Scrapbook, JPP.

17. Barnwell, "Captain Thomas Pinckney," 342–343; Avary, *Dixie After the War*, 348; Rev. C. C. Pinckney to "Ria," 6 January 1887, Charles Cotesworth Pinckney Papers, in Pinckney-Means Family Papers, SCHS.

18. *In Memoriam: Mary Stewart Pinckney* (Richmond: Whittet and Shepperson, 1889), 3.

19. Mary Lyons to Sallie L. Taliaferro, 13 March 1891, SLTP; Lise Rutledge Ravenel to Willie Childs, 5 June 1892, Lise Ravenel Childs Papers, SCHS.

20. *Richmond Dispatch*, 9 May 1862; "Scott Family," in Stella Pickett Hardy, *Colonial Families the Southern States of America* (Baltimore: Southern Book Co., 1958), 454–55; Horace Edwin Hayden, *Virginia Genealogies* (Baltimore: Genealogical Publishing Co., 1979), 589–92.

21. James Lyons first married Heningham Watkins of Goochland and then Imogen Bradfute Penn. The children from his first marriage were Josephine (m. William B. Stanard), Heningham (m. Robert Eden Scott), Sally (m. William Booth Taliaferro), Mary Power (m. Ferdinand C. Hutter), Judge William Henry, Dr. Peter, Edward Carrington, and James.

22. John S. Wise, *The End of an Era* (Boston: Houghton Mifflin, 1899), 69.

23. Unidentified clipping, Keith Family Papers, Virginia Historical Society.

24. Josephine Pinckney, Misc. Notes, JPP.

25. Elizabeth Burden, interview, 9 June 2002; Judge James Keith, interview, 21 October 1999.

26. John A. C. Keith, *J. A. C. Keith Remembers* (n.p., 1970), 95.

27. In 1831, Robert Eden Scott married Elizabeth Taylor (1815–1834) and had one son Robert Taylor (1834–1897). He later married Ann Morson (1816–1846) with whom he had five children: Eliza Gawain (b. 1839) Ann Morson (1841–1915), Susan (b. 1843), John (1845–1883), Robert Eden (1846–1847). His third wife was Heningham Watkins Lyons (1827–1886). Their children were Heningham (b. 1850), Camilla (1854–1928), Lucy (1856–1861), Robert Eden (b. 1858), Josephine (b. 1861), Imogene (1862–1956).

28. U.S. War Department, *The War of the Rebellion: A Compilation of the Official Records of the Union and Confederate Armies*, Series 1, Part 1: *Reports* (Washington, DC: Government Printing Office, 1885), 12:652.

29. Exhibit B: "Testimony of Robert Taylor Scott; Response of Robert Taylor Scott to Bill of Com-

plaint Exhibited in the Circuit Court of the City of Richmond by Heningham W. Scott against himself and others" (filed 16 June 1868), *Scott v. Scott*, September Term 1882, [Chancery Court, Warrenton, Fauquier County, Virginia]; "Dear Joe," Warrenton, 21 November 1862, as quoted in Joseph Arthur Jeffries, *Fauquier County, Virginia 1840–1919*, comp. Helen Jeffries Klitch (San Antonio, TX: Phil Bates Associates, 1989), 157; Heningham Lyons Scott to Sallie Lyons Taliaferro, 15 August 1854, December 10, 1858, SLTP; Mary Boykin Chesnut, *Mary Chesnut's Civil War*, ed. C. Vann Woodward (New Haven: Yale University Press, 1981), 544; Heningham Lyons Scott to Sallie Lyons Taliaferro, [ca. 1868], SLTP.

30. *Mary Chesnut's Civil War*, 544; Heningham Lyons Scott to Sallie Lyons Taliaferro, [ca. 1868], SLTP.

31. Heningham Lyons Scott to Fanny Carter Scott, 13 October 1885, Robert Taylor Scott Papers, in Keith Family Papers.

32. Heningham Lyons Scott to Sallie Lyons Taliaferro, 20–29 December 1870, SLTP.

33. Heningham Lyons Scott to Sallie Lyons Taliaferro, [ca. 1868], SLTP.

34. Bridges and Williams, *St. James Santee*, 311–16.

NOTES TO CHAPTER 2

1. Josephine Pinckney to Heningham Ellet, 7 January 1903, Heningham Ellet Smith Papers, Middleton Place Archives, Charleston, SC.

2. Jack Leland, "O'Donnell's Folly: A Handsome House," *Charleston Evening Post*, 21 January 1969.

3. Will of Captain Thomas Pinckney, 1915, microfilm, Charleston County Probate Office.

4. Robin Elisabeth Datel, "Southern Regionalism and Historic Preservation in Charleston, South Carolina, 1920–1940," *Journal of Historical Geography* 16, no. 2 (1990): 198–99; John Gunther, *Inside USA* (New York: Harper and Brothers, 1947), 724.

5. Louisa Cheves Smythe Stoney to Louisa McCord Stoney, 20 November 1915, Stoney/Popham Papers, SCHS.

6. Josephine Pinckney, "The Story Behind the Story," *WINGS: Literary Guild Review* (October 1945): 5.

7. Josephine Pinckney, *Splendid in Ashes* (New York: Viking, 1958), 224.

8. John Bennett to "Dear Daughter," 18 January 1925, JBP; Mrs. Edward Holden, interview by telephone, 17 January 2000.

9. *U.S. Census*, 1910; Schuyler Livingston Parsons, *Untold Friendships* (Boston: Houghton Mifflin, 1955), 153; Josephine Pinckney, "Autobiography for Three," JPP.

10. Pinckney, "Autobiography for Three."

11. Ibid.

12. Ibid.

13. Josephine Pinckney, *Call Back Yesterday: The First Twenty-Five Years of Ashley Hall* (Charleston, SC: Quinn Press, 1934), 8.

14. Pie Pinckney Friendly, interview, 11 June 2002.

15. Alice R. Huger Smith and D. E. Huger Smith, *The Dwelling Houses of Charleston, South Carolina* (New York: Diadem Books, 1917), 40; Myrta Lockett Avary, *Dixie after the War* (1906; reprint, New York: Negro Universities Press, 1969), 341–42.

16. C. C. Pinckney, *Life of General Thomas Pinckney* (Boston, 1895); Harriott Horry Ravenel, *Eliza Pinckney* (New York: Charles Scribner's Sons, 1896); Patience Pennington [Elizabeth Waites Allston Pringle], *A Woman Rice Planter* (New York: Macmillan, 1914). Archibald Rutledge (1883–1973) wrote twenty volumes of poetry and forty-five of prose.

17. Henry H. Carter, "Early History of the Santee Club" [1934], photocopy, SCHS, 10.

18. Virginius Dabney, *Richmond: The Story of a City* (Garden City, NY: Doubleday, 1976), 318–19.

19. Pie Friendly, interview.

20. Emily Clark, "Richmond," *The Reviewer* (October 1922): 623–31; Dabney, *Richmond*, 292–93.

21. James Fox, *Five Sisters* (New York: Simon and Schuster, 2000), 49–50.

22. Ibid., 19; Judge James Keith, interview, 21 October 1999.

23. Fox, *Five Sisters*, 50; Josephine Pinckney to "Caroline," n.d., JPP.

24. Francis Brenner, interview, 23 March 1999.

25. Henry A. M. Smith, introduction for Captain Thomas Pinckney's Civil War memoirs, typescript, SCHS; Joseph W. Barnwell, "Capt. Thomas Pinckney," *Confederate Veteran* 24 (August 1916): 344.

26. John A. C. Keith, *J. A. C. Keith Remembers* (n.p., 1970), 96.

27. *The College of Charleston Magazine* (June 1919): 202.

28. Harlan Greene, *Mr. Skylark* (Athens: University of Georgia Press, 2001), 140, Sidney Lockwood Tynan to Barbara L. Bellows, e-mail, 16 April 2001; Willie Irvine Shelby, "At Home with the Heywards," *Charlotte Observer*, n.d., clipping in Caroline S. Lockwood scrapbook, possession of Sidney L. Tynan. For more on Heyward's early life, see Harlan Greene, "Charleston Childhood: The First Years of DuBose Heyward," *SCHM* 82 (1982): 154–67.

29. Josephine Pinckney, "DuBose Heyward," *Dictionary of American Biography*, Supplements 1–2: *To 1940* (New York: Council of Learned Societies, 1944–58), 9; Shelby, "At Home with the Heywards"; DuBose Heyward to Josephine Pinckney, [October] 1915, JPP.

30. DuBose Heyward to Josephine Pinckney, [ca. 10 October 1915], JPP; Josephine Pinckney and DuBose Heyward, "To C.S.S. and F.H.H.," 30 May 1915, JPP.

31. DuBose Heyward to Josephine Pinckney, 6 January [1916], JPP; DuBose Heyward to Josephine Pinckney, [ca. 10 October 1915] 1915, JPP; "In Memoriam: John Douglas Matthew, 1885–1916," Brotherhood of Sir Galahad Lodge of Sorrow, Woodland, 8 April 1916, DHP.

32. Gordon Miller to Josephine Pinckney, [ca. 1916], JPP.

33. John Bennett to Susan Smythe Bennett, 20 August 1917, JBP.

34. John Bennett to Susan Smythe Bennett, 18 June 1917, JBP.

35. Heningham Lyons Scott to Sallie Lyons Taliaferro, 10 December 1858, SLTP.

36. Harry Hervey, *The Damned Don't Cry* (New York: Sun Dial Press, 1942), 236, 282, 215, 309, 311. Hervey even used the nickname that many Charlestonians called Mrs. Pinckney behind her back: "Camilla the Gorilla."

37. "Women May Study at Local College," *Charleston News and Courier*, 12 July 1918; Pinckney's "The Cost of a Chance" appeared in the *College of Charleston Magazine* (April 1919): 111–15.

NOTES TO CHAPTER 3

1. Louise Anderson Allen, *A Bluestocking in Charleston: The Life and Career of Laura Bragg* (Columbia: University of South Carolina Press, 2001), 37, 67; Nancy Milford, *Savage Beauty: The Life of Edna St. Vincent Millay* (New York: Random House, 2001), 160.

2. Nina Miller, *Making Love Modern* (New York: Oxford University Press, 1999), 16–17; Milford, *Savage Beauty*, 160.

3. As quoted in Milford, *Savage Beauty*, 248, 291.

4. Josephine Pinckney, "Ode for Memorial Day," May 1927, draft, JPP.

5. Susan S. Bennett to Hervey Allen, 26 May 1924, HAP; Hervey Allen File, MS 30-4, SCHS; J. Bryan III, "Hervey Allen—a Copious Fellow," *New York Herald-Tribune*, 26 November 1933. Allen was

born in Pittsburgh in 1889. He attended the Naval Academy at Annapolis but was honorably discharged after an athletic injury. He graduated from the University of Pittsburgh in 1915 with a degree in economics. He then joined the National Guard and was sent to Texas to patrol the border during the Pancho Villa uprising. While in Texas, he began to write poetry and published a book of poems, *Ballads of the Border* (El Paso, 1916), heavily influenced by Rudyard Kipling's work. He was sent to France in 1917 and returned to America after the peace in 1918.

6. The unpredictable Lowell had taken a shine to the boylike, ingratiating Allen and was largely responsible for the publication of his powerful war poem, "Blindman," in the *North American Review.* Allen soon learned that while Lowell enjoyed mentoring young poets (mostly men, such as Malcolm Cowley, Louis Untermeyer, and e. e. cummings) and fiercely taking up their cause with publishers, she also rode roughshod over them, expecting them to be at her beck and call (even doing garden work while she criticized their poetry).

7. W. H. Allen to DuBose Heyward, 12 December 1921, DHP; Amy Lowell to Hervey Allen, 11 September 1923, ALP; Margaret Widdemer, *Golden Friends I Had* (Garden City, NY: Doubleday, 1964), 89; Hervey Allen, "We," in *Wampum and Gold* (New Haven: Yale University Press, 1921), 68–69. Typical of Allen's approach to life was his admonition to Padraic Colum that "it is better to be shooting at the moon even if the arrows come back and strike you in the eye than to throw pebbles at daisies all your life." Hervey Allen to Padraic Colum, 1 October 1923, Padraic Colum Papers, Henry W. and Albert A. Berg Collection of English and American Literature, New York Public Library.

8. Josephine Pinckney, "Charleston's Poetry Society," *Sewanee Review* (January 1930), 54; Pinckney to Hervey Allen, [1921], JPP. Allen's recommendations included Lowes's *Convention and Revolt,* J. Berg Esenwein, *The Art of Versification,* and Pope's "Essay on Criticism." Poetry Society of South Carolina, Study Group minutes, 21 March 1922, 12 April 1922 microform.

9. Hervey Allen to Amy Lowell, 2 January 1923, ALP; Emily Clark, "Hervey Allen," *Saturday Review of Literature* (9 December 1933): 1.

10. Miller, *Making Love Modern,* 16–17; Hervey Allen to John Farrar, 16 November 1944, HAP.

11. Christine Stansell, *American Moderns: Bohemian New York and the Creation of a New Century* (New York: Metropolitan Books, 2000), 31. Allen's excessive show of masculinity, however, worried Bennett. His bawdy barracks language and preoccupation with libertine poets, such as Lord Byron and Oscar Wilde, also made Bennett uneasy about him or at least concerned about how others might perceive him. James Wallace Irvin, "Cowboy (Hervey) Allen of Charleston," *Literary Digest,* 11 August 1934, 8–9; John Bennett to Van Withal, 4–5 April 1922, JBP.

12. Susan Smythe Bennett to John Bennett, 8 January [1923]; John Bennett to "Dear Heart," 10 August 1921; John Bennett to Susan Smythe Bennett, 12 September 1921; John Bennett to DuBose Heyward, 23 August 1920, JBP.

13. Hervey Allen to Marjorie E. Peale, 2 January 1940, cited in Peale, "Charleston as a Literary Center, 1920–1933" (M.A. thesis, Duke University, 1941), 202; Beatrice Ravenel to Hervey Allen, 14 January 1926, HAP.

14. John Bennett to Yates Snowden, 14 December 1920, in *Two Scholarly Friends: Yates Snowden-John Bennett Correspondence, 1902–1932,* ed. Mary Crow Anderson (Columbia: University of South Carolina, 1993), 159; Poetry Society of South Carolina, *Yearbook* (October 1926): 5; Study Group minutes, 4 February 1924, 13 December 1922, 19 November 1923, PSSCP; Pinckney, "Poetry Society," 54.

15. Laura M. Bragg to Caroline Sinkler, February 4, 1921, Director's Correspondence, Charleston Museum.

16. Editorial, *Charleston News and Courier,* 17 October 1921. Southern literary publications varied a

great deal in quality. They included *The Lyric* (Norfolk), *The Reviewer* (Richmond), *The Fugitive* (Nashville), *Sewanee Review* (Tennessee), *All's Well* (Fayetteville, Arkansas), *The Nomad* (Birmingham), and *Southern Literary Magazine* (Atlanta), plus four general literary magazines.

17. Russell Lynes, "Highbrow, Middlebrow, Lowbrow," *Harper's Magazine* (1949): 26.

18. DuBose Heyward to Hervey Allen, [1923], DHP; Amy Lowell to Hervey Allen, 11 September 1923, ALP. Millay agreed to come, but her honorarium was too high. She did come to Charleston in 1934.

19. John Bennett to Yates Snowden, 14 December 1920, in Anderson, *Two Scholarly Friends*, 159.

20. Widdemer, *Golden Friends*, 40; Josephine Pinckney to Laura M. Bragg, 2 September [1921], LMBP; Gibbes Art Gallery, Visitors Book, Gibbes Museum of Art Archives, Charleston, SC; Amy Helene Kirschke, "Elizabeth O'Neill Verner and the Southern States Art League," in *Mirror of Time: Elizabeth O'Neill Verner's Charleston*, ed. Lynn Robertson Meyers (Columbia: McKissick Museum, University of South Carolina, 1983), 31.

21. Widdemer, *Golden Friends*, 40; Harriet Monroe, "Southern Shrines," *Poetry Magazine* 18 (1921): 92 and 19 (1922): 32.

22. *Poetry* 18 (1921): 194–95; Josephine Pinckney to Laura M. Bragg, 2 September [1921], LMBP. The poems were "In the Barn," "Strange," "The Outcast," and "Swamp Lilies." "In the Barn" won the first Caroline Sinkler Award given by the Poetry Society in 1921. The Caroline Sinkler Award went to members of the Poetry Society who had never received payment for a poem. Pinckney's enthusiasm was tempered when she learned that DuBose Heyward's popular "Gamesters All," about a police shooting of a black man caught in an illegal craps game was also included. She expressed her concern to Laura Bragg that "In the Barn" was "chosen because of subject rather than execution" (ibid.).

23. Hervey Allen to Harriet Monroe, draft, [ca. 1922]; 1 December 1921, HAP; Harriet Monroe, *Poetry* 19 (1922): 32. In their introduction to the "Southern Number," Allen and Heyward argued that they pressed for recognition of a southern school of literature "not by a provincial pride, but by the renascence of poetry throughout America; and being so moved by this spirit, [young southerners] claim to be of it."

24. Harriet Monroe to Hervey Allen, 28 November 1921, HAP.

25. Emma Smith [quoting Pinckney] to Sophie Cheves, 24 October [1921], Cheves Papers, SCHS; Hervey Allen to Josephine Pinckney, n.d., JPP.

26. Josephine Pinckney to Hervey Allen, 7 August 1921 [postcard], 11 September 1921, HAP.

27. Josephine Pinckney to Laura M. Bragg, 2 September [1921], LMBP.

28. Josephine Pinckney to Hervey Allen, 7 August 1921, 11 September 1921, HAP.

29. Ibid.

30. Josephine Pinckney to Laura M. Bragg, 2 September [1921], LMBP; Josephine Pinckney to Hervey Allen, n.d. [1921], JPP.

31. Josephine Pinckney to Laura M. Bragg, 2 September [1921], LMBP; Pinckney to Hervey Allen, n.d., HAP.

32. Josephine Pinckney to Miss Buckingham, Secretary, Radcliffe College, [1921], Radcliffe College Archives; C. T. Copeland to Josephine Pinckney, 25 June 1921, JPP.

33. Stansell, *American Moderns*, 57, 249n, 354n.

34. Ibid., 174; Stearns, as quoted in Michael North, *Reading 1922* (New York: Oxford University Press, 1999), 186, 174; Joseph Hergesheimer, "The Feminine Nuisance in American Literature," *The Yale Review*, n.s., 10 (1921): 716, 718, 722, 723, 725.

35. Josephine Pinckney to Hervey Allen, 10 January [1922], HAP; Josephine Pinckney to Laura M.

Bragg, 23 January [1922] LMBP. Pinckney's final grades were English 5, B+; English 72, D–; English 35a, D; transcript, Radcliffe College Archives.

36. Judge James Keith, interview, 21 October 1999; "Richard Bowditch Wigglesworth, 1891–1960," *Current Biography*, ed. Charles Moritz (New York: H. W. Wilson, 1959), 483–85.

37. *North Shore Blue Book and Social Register* (Boston: Hyde Publishing Co., 1928); "Richard Bowditch Wigglesworth," 483–85; "Richard B. Wigglesworth Dead: Ambassador to Canada Was 69," *New York Times*, 23 October 1960, 88; Sinclair Weeks, *Richard Bowditch Wigglesworth: Way-Stations of a Fruitful Life* (privately printed, 1964).

38. Josephine Pinckney to Laura M. Bragg, 23 January [1922], LMBP; Josephine Pinckney to Hervey Allen, 11 January 1922, HAP.

39. Josephine Pinckney to Hervey Allen, 10 January 1921, HAP; John Bennett to Susan Bennett, 3 September 1921, JBP; Josephine Pinckney to Hervey Allen, 2 October [1921], HAP.

40. S. Foster Damon, *Amy Lowell: A Chronicle with Extracts from Her Correspondence* (Boston: Houghton Mifflin, 1935), 594–95.

41. Josephine Pinckney to Hervey Allen, 10 January 1921, HAP.

42. Hervey Allen to Amy Lowell, 15 January 1922, ALP.

43. C. David Heymann, *American Aristocracy: The Lives and Times of James Russell, Amy, and Robert Lowell* (New York: Dodd, Mead, 1980), 161; "Amy Lowell," *Dictionary of Literary Biography*, vol. 140: *American Book-Collectors and Bibliographers, First Series*, ed. Joseph Rosenbaum (Detroit: Gale, 1994), 141–46. Pinckney became acquainted with the "book collecting game" through its master, A. Edward Newton. A. Edward Newton to Josephine Pinckney, 31 January 1928, JPP.

44. Damon, *Amy Lowell*, 214.

45. Louis Untermeyer, *From Another World: The Autobiography of Louis Untermeyer* (New York: Harcourt, Brace, 1939), 101–2.

46. Heymann, *American Aristocracy*, 172.

47. Ibid.

48. Hervey Allen to Padraic Colum, [1922], Colum Papers. While the American envoy to the Court of St. James, General Thomas Pinckney served as a special ambassador to Spain while he negotiated the Pinckney Treaty. Rutherford B. Hayes appointed James Russell Lowell, Amy Lowell's uncle, minister to the court of Spain and then to the Court of Saint James.

49. Damon, *Amy Lowell*, 410; Heymann, *American Aristocracy*, 33–34.

50. Damon, *Amy Lowell*, 596; Heymann, *American Aristocracy*, 160.

51. Heymann, *American Aristocracy*, 161; Damon, *Amy Lowell*, 350.

52.Alfred Kreymborg, *Our Singing Strength: An Outline of American Poetry* (New York: Coward-McCann, 1929), 356. Richard Addlington dismissed Lowell "as a society woman, who would never have been heard of as a writer if she hadn't been a Lowell"; as quoted in Richard Benvenuto, *Amy Lowell* (Boston: Twayne, 1985), 49.

53. Amy Lowell to Hervey Allen, 11 September 1923, ALP. In 1923, Lowell thought that the young poets had only made "a minor utterance" compared to the old guard of Edwin Arlington Robinson, Robert Frost, Vachel Lindsay, and Carl Sandburg. She ranked Elinor Wylie and Edna St. Vincent Millay most highly for real achievement. Among men, "there seems to be nobody to take up the cloak falling from the shoulders of old poets." Only Hervey Allen struck her as having "a broad vision." She ranked him number one among all the young for his potential. Lowell recommended *Carolina Chansons* as the best example of his work but was quick to explain that his contribution was much superior to that of his collaborator DuBose Heyward. Amy Lowell to Mrs. Becker, 7 July 1923, Lowell Correspondence, Berg Collection, New York Public Library.

54. Joseph E. Garland, *Eastern Point: A Nautical, Rustical, and More or Less Sociable Chronicle of Gloucester's Outer Shield and Inner Sanctum, 1606–1990* (Beverly, MA: Commonwealth Editions, 1990), 182.

55. Ibid., 296, 294; Harlan Greene, *Mr. Skylark* (Athens: University of Georgia Press, 2001), 288n30; Thomas Fleming, preface to *Lady Baltimore,* by Owen Wister (Nashville: J. S. Sanders, 1992), xx.

56. Garland, *Eastern Point,* 175, 289, 296, 317.

57. Josephine Pinckney to Laura M. Bragg, 12 August 1922, LMBP.

58. Dorothy Heyward, "Autobiography," Chapter 2, mss., DKHP.

59. Josephine Pinckney to Laura M. Bragg, 12 August 1922, LMBP.

60. Hervey Allen to Amy Lowell, 2 January 1923, ALP; Hervey Allen to Padraic Colum, 20 April 1922, Colum Papers; Hervey Allen to Harriet Monroe, 25 March 1923, *Poetry* Papers, University of Chicago Library.

### NOTES TO CHAPTER 4

1. Josephine Pinckney to Amy Lowell, 20 January 1923, ALP; Susan Smythe Bennett to John Bennett, 8 January [1923], JBP; Poetry Society of America, *Bulletin* (February 1923): 2.

2. Poetry Society of America, *Bulletin* (February 1923): 2; Josephine Pinckney to Amy Lowell, 20 January 1923, ALP.

3. As quoted in Poetry Society of America, *Bulletin* (February 1923): 2.

4. Hervey Allen to Harriet Monroe, 1 April 1922, *Poetry* Papers, University of Chicago Library; Stork, "Comment," *Contemporary Verse* (April 1922, December 1922): n.p. Stork, who would become president of the Poetry Society of America, visited Charleston in March 1922 to speak to the Poetry Society. Poetry Society of South Carolina, *Yearbook* (1922): 11–12.

5. Clipping from the *Worcester Telegram* in JBP.

6. Thomas L. Connelly and Barbara L. Bellows, *God and General Longstreet: Essays on the Lost Cause and the Southern Mind* (Baton Rouge: Louisiana State University Press, 1982), 35–36, 43.

7. Ann Douglas, *Terrible Honesty: Mongrel Manhattan in the 1920s* (New York: Farrar, Straus, Giroux, 1995), 33; Herbert Ravenel Sass to Thomas R. Waring Sr., 16 October 1933, Herbert Ravenel Sass Papers, SCHS.

8. W. L. George, "Hail Columbia Megalopsis," *Harper's* 142 (April 1921): 630.

9. Robin Elisabeth Datel, "Southern Regionalism and Historic Preservation in Charleston, South Carolina, 1920–1940," *Journal of Historical Geography* 16, no. 2 (1990): 197.

10. Janice A. Radway, *A Feeling for Books: The Book-of-the-Month Club, Literary Taste, and Middle-Class Desire* (Chapel Hill: University of North Carolina Press, 1997), 179, 205; Hervey Allen to Padraic Colum, 25 September 1921, Colum Papers.

11. See Stephanie E. Yuhl, *A Golden Haze of Memory: The Making of Historic Charleston* (Chapel Hill: University of North Carolina Press, 2005), 7–12.

12. Josephine Pinckney to A. H. Hepburn, n.d. [carbon copy], Sass Papers.

13. Francis Butler Simkins, "A Flag of Optimism," *The State* (Columbia, SC), 10 February 1924, clipping, JPP.

14. DuBose Heyward and Hervey Allen, "Poetry South," *Poetry* 20 (April 1922): 35–36; Allen Tate to Donald Davidson, 29 June 1923, in *The Literary Correspondence of Donald Davidson and Allen Tate,* ed. John Tyree Fain and Thomas Daniel Young (Athens: University of Georgia Press, 1974), 79.

15. Allen Tate to Donald Davidson, 12 December 1929, in Fain and Young, *Literary Correspondence,* 243–44. Allen Tate, "Last Days of a Charming Lady," *Nation,* 28 October 1925, 485–86; [Donald David-

son], "South Carolina Poets," *Nashville Tennessean,* 10 February 1924; Donald Davidson, "The Southern Poet and His Tradition," *Poetry* 40 (1932): 95; Davidson, *Southern Writers in the Modern World* (Athens: University of Georgia Press, 1958), 5.

16. As quoted in Poetry Society of South Carolina, *Yearbook* (October 1925): 8.

17. Thomas A. Underwood, *Allen Tate: Orphan of the South* (Princeton: Princeton University Press, 2000), 3–5; Daniel J. Singal, *The War Within: From Victorian to Modernist Thought in the South, 1919–1945* (Chapel Hill: University of North Carolina Press, 1982), 233.

18. J[osephine] P[inckney], "A Group of Southern Poets," a review of *Fugitives,* unidentified clipping, *Charleston Evening Post,* [ca. 1928], JPP. Never able to resist a delicious irony, Josephine points out the "remarkable circumstance" of the exclusive highbrow *Fugitive* magazine "financed by certain businessmen of Nashville and the Nashville Retailers' Association." "All honor to a community," Josephine concluded, "that can produce men who write poetry, men who read it, and men who believe in their writers to the extent of subsidizing them."

19. Tate, "Last Days of a Charming Lady," 485–86; Allen Tate to Donald Davidson, 29 June 1923, in Fain and Young, *Literary Correspondence,* 78.

20. Donald Davidson to Allen Tate, 4 March 1927, 192–93; Allen Tate to Donald Davidson, 29 June 1923 in Fain and Young, *Literary Correspondence,* 78; Donald Davidson to Howard Mumford Jones, 18 December 1929, as quoted in Mark Royden Winchell, *Where No Flag Flies: Donald Davidson and the Southern Resistance* (Columbia: University of Missouri Press, 2000), 283.

21. Donald Davidson to Allen Tate, November 1925, in Fain and Young, *Literary Correspondence,* 79.

22. Gerald W. Johnson to DuBose Heyward, 5 December 1923, PSSCP; Gerald W. Johnson to Josephine Pinckney, 6 April 1936, JPP.

23. John Crowe Ransom to Josephine Pinckney, December 17, [1928], JPP.

24. Richard Morgan Kain, *Dublin in the Age of William Butler Yeats and James Joyce* (Norman: University of Oklahoma Press, 1962), 74.

25. Ibid., 74; Gregory A. Schirmer, "Padraic Colum," *Dictionary of Literary Biography,* vol. 19: *British Poets, 1880–1914,* ed. Donald E. Stanford (Detroit: Gale, 1983), 85. Colum took Allen and Heyward's *Carolina Chansons* to Macmillan and encouraged the press to publish the Carolina poets.

26. Padraic Colum, Poetry Society of South Carolina, *Yearbook* (October 1921): 19.

27. Josephine Pinckney to Amy Lowell, January 20, 1923 [1924], ALP; Josephine Pinckney to Hervey Allen, [13 May 1922], HAP; Poetry Society of South Carolina, *Yearbook* (October 1923): 17, 12; "Poetry Society to Present Play," unidentified clipping, Drama Committee file, PSSCP; Josephine Pinckney to Laura Bragg, 31 May 1924, LMBP. Other Irish literary figures addressed Poetry Society audiences including James Stephens and A.E. "James Stephens to Address Body," *Charleston News and Courier,* 23 April 1925.

28. Kain, *Dublin,* 11, 12, 14; Josephine Pinckney, "Bulwarks against Change," in *Culture in the South,* ed. W. T. Couch (Chapel Hill: University of North Carolina Press, 1934), 43.

29. Pinckney, "Bulwarks against Change," 25.

30. Gerald W. Johnson, "The Congo, Mr. Mencken," *The Reviewer* 3 (July 1923): 890; Percy H. Whaley to Robert Latham, 30 March 1927, Robert Latham Papers, SCHS; Kain, *Dublin,* 11, 14.

31. Michael North, *Reading 1922* (New York: Oxford University Press, 1999), 59–60. A contrary view was put forward by Russian Imagist poet John Cournos in his 1922 novel, *Babel.* He argued that diversity and internationalism touted in modern literature of the 1920s as a global shift toward greater self-expression and celebration of difference was little more than another grand illusion. The search

for the universal, Couros believed, only forces artists to settle for the lowest common denominator—primitivism in art, jazz in music, and Dadaism in poetry. North, *Reading 1922*, 59–61.

32. Louisa Susannah McCord, review of *Uncle Tom's Cabin, Southern Quarterly Review* (January 1853): 107; Harlan Greene, *Mr. Skylark* (Athens: University of Georgia Press, 2001), 71–73.

33. Babette Deutsch, "A Southern Voice," *New York Herald-Tribune Books*, 5 February 1928.

34. Samuel Galliard Stoney and Gertrude Mathews Shelby, *Black Genesis: A Chronicle* (New York: Macmillan, 1930), iii.

35. Ambrose E. Gonzales, *The Black Border: Gullah Stories of the Carolina Coast* (Columbia, SC: The State, 1922), 9, 11.

36. John Crowe Ransom to Josephine Pinckney, 17 December [1928], JPP.

37. "Lonesome Grabeya'ad," appeared in Poetry Society of South Carolina, *Yearbook* (1922): 47–48. Over time the Spirituals Society started cracking down on the free use of songs they had transcribed. In 1929, DuBose Heyward contributed eighty-seven dollars to the Spirituals Society, his royalties from the sale of the *Porgy* program, which included the words to two spirituals. The opera, *Porgy and Bess*, incorporated "Come out duh Wilderness" and "Lebe you een hans of Kind Sabier"; James Hutchisson, *DuBose Heyward: A Charleston Gentleman and the World of Porgy and Bess* (Jackson: University Press of Mississippi, 2000), 68; Minutes, 25 May 1929, 6 February 1939, SPSP.

38. Josephine Pinckney, "Street Cries of Charleston," *Town and Country*, 1 March 1936, 63.

39. Josephine Pinckney to Herbert P. Small, 21 February 1931, Pinckney/Viking; Pinckney, "Street Cries," 86.

40. Poetry Society of South Carolina, *Yearbook* (November 1922): 8.

41. Mrs. William Elliott Hutson to Edwina Kellenberger, 30 July 1930, SPSP; Anthony H. Harrigan Jr. to Barbara L. Bellows, 20 March 2000. Initially, the name was the Society for the Preservation of Negro Spirituals, but it was changed during the first year.

42. M. A. DeWolfe Howe, "The Song of Charleston," *Atlantic Monthly* (July 1930): 108–10.

43. DuBose Heyward, introduction to Stoney and Shelby, *Black Genesis*, ix; Anthony H. Harrigan Jr. to Barbara L. Bellows, 23 February 1999.

44. Augustine T. Smythe, "Preface" [introductory remarks made prior to a Society for the Preservation of Spirituals concert in the 1950s], SPSP.

45. Ibid.

46. Alfred Huger to Florence Gerald, 26 July 1930, SPSP.

47. Anthony H. Harrigan to Barbara L. Bellows, 30 March 2000; North, *Reading 1922*, 27–28. As early as 1918, some Charlestonians were discussing the possibility of recording the Gullah songs; Harriet P. Simons to Albert Simons, April 21, 1918, ASP.

48. North, *Reading 1922*, 64. The analogy between the anthropologist and the artifact was made by North.

49. Howe, "Song of Charleston," 110.

50. Minutes, 4 May 1927, 2 October 1929, 29 January 1930, 23 March 1930, 12 December 1938, SPSP. Pinckney reported in 1932 that a "Good old couple," Rose and Stepney Gibbs, were suffering all alone on Fairfield Plantation. Drawing from her own purse and the Spirituals Society's charity fund, she worked out a plan to get them regular groceries. "Rose and Stepney Gibbs, Fairfield Plantation," Charity Records, SPSP.

51. Douglas, *Terrible Honesty*, 283; Josephine Pinckney, *Splendid in Ashes* (New York: Viking, 1958), 138; Alfred Huger to Louis T. Parker [president of the Society for the Preservation of Spirituals], 15 April 1936, SPSP.

244 | Notes to Pages 72–77

52. Jane Judge, "Old Spirituals Sung at Theatre," *Savannah Morning News,* 17 February 1924, clipping, SPSP.

53. Unidentified newspaper clipping, Caroline Rutledge Scrapbook; Minutes, 23 November 1926; *The Savannah Press,* 23 February 1924, clipping, Smythe Scrapbook, all in SPSP.

54. "Music Society Condemns 'Debauch' of Spirituals," unidentified clipping in the Caroline Rutledge Scrapbook, SPSP.

55. Minutes, 21 February 1924, SPSP; Elizabeth O'Neill Verner, "Spirituals of the Low Country," *Charleston News and Courier,* 11 January 1925.

56. Laura (Riding) Jackson, *The Laura (Riding) Jackson Reader,* ed. Elizabeth Friedman (New York: Persea, 2005), 254; "John" [Grimball] to Josephine Pinckney, [ca. 1927], JPP.

57. Harriet P. Simons to Louisa Stoney Popham, 27 March 1927, SPSP.

58. Minutes, 16 February 1924, 12 March 1924, SPSP.

59. Smythe, "Preface." For examples of songs by the Spirituals Society, as well as by African American congregations and cries by street hucksters, see Society for the Preservation of Spirituals, *Spirituals Society Field Recordings, 1936–39,* audio CD (Charleston, 2004).

60. Howe, "Song of Charleston," 111.

61. Edgar Lee Masters to Josephine Pinckney, 19 January 1943. The spiritual is dated January 20, 1927, JPP. The research Masters did in Charleston found expression in *The New World* (New York: Appleton,1937). By coincidence, the Poetry Society sponsored a one-man show by Dan Reed of the Columbia Stage Society during Masters's visit which dramatized selections from *Spoon River Anthology.* At the conclusion of Reed's performance, the retiring Masters stepped up to the podium at the High School of Charleston Auditorium and delivered "a bully performance" of his own. Poetry Society of South Carolina, *Yearbook* (October 1927): 10; Susan S. Bennett to Hervey Allen, 23 January 1927, HAP.

62. Harriet P. Simons to Louisa Stoney Popham, [April 1933], Stoney/Popham Family Papers, SCHS.

63. Hurston, "Spirituals and Neo-spirituals," as quoted in Douglas, *Terrible Honesty,* 332; Minutes, 14 May 1923, SPSP. In 1928, a rule banned practicing for concerts in private homes because the host for the evening invariably invited friends for a preview, which, in the opinion of some members, made the Society appear "common"; Minutes, 24 October 1928, SPSP.

64. Walter Damrosch to Marjorie Morawetz, 14 January 1930, SPSP. Damrosch belonged to a well-known musical family. He had a distinguished career that included directing the orchestra at the Metropolitan Opera, frequent appearances at the New York Philharmonic, and forming his own company. In 1928, Damrosch served as the host of a weekly music appreciation radio program designed to bring culture to the masses.

65. Phillip Hewitt-Myring, "Whole World of Art Richer by Spirituals' Preservation," *Charleston News and Courier,* 6 April 1928. Some exceptions were made to the policy that only songs verified as sung in the Low Country were made. In 1926, for example, a Columbia performance included "Come out of the Wilderness," a spiritual written by noted Gullah expert and local resident Ambrose Gonzales.

NOTES TO CHAPTER 5

1. Kenney J. Williams, "William Stanley Braithwaite," in *Dictionary of Literary Biography,* vol. 50: *Afro-American Writers before the Harlem Renaissance,* ed. Trudier Harris and Thadious M. Davis (Detroit: Gale, 1986), 7–18.

2. Margaret Widdemer, *Golden Friends I Had* (Garden City, NY: Doubleday, 1964), 36; press release, *The Literary Lantern*, 9 September 1923, PSSCP. Leitch's first book, *The Wagon and the Star*, was published in 1923. Hibbard, a professor of English at the University of North Carolina in Chapel Hill, published his column under the pseudonym of Telfair Jr. In 1928, Hibbard compiled *The Lyric South: An Anthology of Recent Poetry from the South* (New York: Macmillan, 1928). He dated the "Southern revival" as beginning in 1915, and he only included those who had a book published by a commercial press; ibid., xiv. *The Literary Lantern* was based on Kenelm Digby's "Lobby" in *The Literary Review.* Press release, *The Literary Lantern*, 2 September 1923, PSSCP.

3. Hervey Allen to Louisa Stoney, Stoney Family Papers, SCHS; Josephine Pinckney to Amy Lowell, 20 January 1923 [1924], ALP.

4. DuBose Heyward to Josephine Pinckney, n.d., JPP; Josephine Pinckney to Laura M. Bragg, n.d., LMBP.

5. Kuhns had no close relatives in the United States. The Heyward family could not afford much of a wedding in Charleston. When Heyward's sister Jane married Edward Register some years earlier, her ceremony consisted of a "ragged procession" down the beach from the Heyward cottage "Tranquility" to the church decorated by friends with their garden lilies, and back again where the bride was toasted with fruit juice. Willie Irvine Shelby, "At Home with the Heywards," [ca. 1932], unidentified clipping, Lockwood Scrapbook.

6. Josephine Pinckney to DuBose Heyward, 21 September 1923, DHP; Josephine Pinckney to Hervey Allen, 24 September 1923, HAP.

7. Josephine Pinckney to Hervey Allen, 24 September 1923, HAP.

8. Amy Lowell to Hervey Allen, 11 September 1923, ALP; Josephine Pinckney to Hervey Allen, 24 September 1923, HAP.

9. Susan Goodman, *Ellen Glasgow: A Biography* (Baltimore: Johns Hopkins University Press, 1998), 161.

10. Emily Clark to Henry L. Mencken, 19 May, 26 May 1921, HLMP.

11. Mary Johnston, "Richmond and Writing," *The Reviewer* 1 (15 February 1921): 10–11.

12. Emily Clark to Henry L. Mencken, 19 May 1921, HLMP.

13. In 1921, Cotesworth Pinckney had two offerings published—one poem reflecting on a piece of crockery that had seen better days: "Jug Not That Ye Be Not Jugged," *The Reviewer*, 16 May 1921, 205–6; the other an admiring review of the *Cycle of [Charles Francis] Adams Letters, 1861–1865*, "Charles Francis Adams," ibid., 172–74.

14. Henry L. Mencken, "Violets in the Sahara," *Baltimore Evening Sun*, 15 May 1922, clipping in HLMP; Emily Clark to Henry Mencken, 26 May 1921, HLMP.

15. Joseph Hergesheimer to Henry L. Mencken, 11 November 1921, HLMP.

16. Julia Peterkin to Henry L. Mencken, 20 November 1924, as quoted in Susan Millar Williams, *A Devil and a Good Woman Too: The Lives of Julia Peterkin* (Athens: University of Georgia Press, 1997), 83.

17. Emily Clark to Henry Mencken, 15 April 1924; Joseph Hergesheimer to Henry L. Mencken, 18 October 1921, both in HLMP; "Joseph Hergesheimer," in *Dictionary of Literary Biography*, vol. 9: *American Novelists, 1910–1945*, ed. James J. Martine (Detroit: Gale, 1981), 126.

18. Joseph Hergesheimer to Josephine Pinckney, 11 January 1924, JPP; Victor E. Gimmestad, *Joseph Hergesheimer* (Boston: Twayne, 1984), 55.

19. Joseph Hergesheimer to Josephine Pinckney, 23 February 1924, 26 February 1924, JPP.

20. Emily Clark to Henry L. Mencken, 15 April 1924, HLMP.

21. Joseph Hergesheimer to Josephine Pinckney, 21 April 1924, JPP.

22. Mencken, "Obituary of Joseph Hergesheimer," unidentified clipping, HLMP; Louise Anderson Allen, *A Bluestocking in Charleston* (Columbia: University of South Carolina Press, 2001), 90; Joseph Hergesheimer to Josephine Pinckney, 16 May 1924, JPP.

23. Hutchisson, *DuBose Heyward,* 50–52.

24. Josephine Pinckney to Hervey Allen, 23 May [1924], HAP.

25. Ibid.

26. Susan Smythe Bennett to Hervey Allen, 26 May 1924, 9 June 1924, HAP.

27. Josephine Pinckney to Amy Lowell, 5 June 1924; Hervey Allen to Amy Lowell, 3 January 1924, both in ALP; Amy Lowell to Josephine Pinckney, 21 June 1924, JPP.

28. Hutchisson, *DuBose Heyward,* 50–52; Josephine Pinckney to Amy Lowell, 5 June 1924, ALP.

29. Joseph Hergesheimer to Josephine Pinckney, 30 June 1924, JPP; Josephine Pinckney to Laura M. Bragg, [1924], LMBP; Carl Van Vechten, "How I Remember Joseph Hergesheimer," *Yale University Gazette* 22 (January 1948): 89; Allen Nevins, as quoted in Ralph Engleman, "Henry Seidel Canby," *Dictionary of Literary Biography,* vol. 91: *American Magazine Journalists, 1900–1960, First Series,* ed. Sam G. Riley (Detroit: Gale, 1990), 39–46; Amy Lowell to Hervey Allen, 27 May 1924, HAP.

30. Amy Lowell to Josephine Pinckney, 21 January 1925; Josephine Pinckney to Amy Lowell, 10 August 1924, JPP; Sara Teasdale to Amy Lowell, 27 January 1924, as quoted in S. Foster Damon, *Amy Lowell* (Boston: Houghton Mifflin, 1935), 648–49.

31. Josephine Pinckney to Amy Lowell, 10 August 1924, ALP; Josephine Pinckney to Laura M. Bragg, 13 August 1924, LMBP.

32. Josephine Pinckney to Amy Lowell, 7 October 1924, ALP.

33. Josephine Pinckney to Amy Lowell, 10 August 1924, ALP; Josephine Pinckney to Laura M. Bragg, 13 August 1924, LMBP; Josephine Pinckney to Amy Lowell, 16 September 1924, ALP.

34. Josephine Pinckney to Laura M. Bragg, 13 August 1924, LMBP.

35. Josephine Pinckney to Amy Lowell, 16 September 1924, ALP.

36. Ibid.

37. Josephine Pinckney to Amy Lowell, 7 October 1924, ALP.

38. Ibid. In 1930, Wigglesworth married Florence Booth. Two years earlier, he had been elected to the U.S. Congress from the Cambridge district. He served for thirty "unobtrusive" years before being appointed to America's ambassador to Canada. *New York Times,* 23 October 1960; Sinclair Weeks, *Richard Bowditch Wigglesworth: Way-Stations of a Fruitful Life* (n.p.: n.p., 1964), 38, 42–44, 50.

39. Josephine Pinckney to Hervey Allen, 27 November 1924, HAP; Josephine Pinckney to Amy Lowell, 21 December, 1924, ALP; John Bennett to DuBose Heyward, 29 November 1924, Correspondence, PSSCP.

40. H. L. Mencken, *My Life as Author and Editor* (Reprint, New York: Knopf, 1992), 402–3.

41. Josephine Pinckney to Amy Lowell, 21 December 1924, ALP; John Farrar to Josephine Pinckney, 22 January 1925, JPP; Harlan Greene, *Mr. Skylark* (Athens: University of Georgia Press, 2001), 200.

42. Josephine Pinckney to Hervey Allen, 22 November 1924, HAP.

NOTES TO CHAPTER 6

1. Josephine Pinckney to Hervey Allen, 4 March 1925, HAP.

2. Ibid.

3. Josephine Pinckney to Hervey Allen, 11 April 1925, HAP.

4. Josephine Pinckney to Hervey Allen, 27 January [1926], HAP.

5. Hervey Allen, "The Passing of Amy Lowell," *Bookman* 61 (July 1925): 519; Josephine Pinckney to Amy Lowell, 3 April 1925, ALP.

6. Pinckney to Lowell, 3 April 1925.

7. Ibid.

8. Josephine Pinckney to Amy Lowell, 3 April 1925, ALP; Margaret Widdemer, *Golden Friends I Had* (Garden City, NY: Doubleday, 1964), 132.

9. Josephine Pinckney to Hervey Allen, 11 April 1925, HAP.

10. Josephine Pinckney to Hervey Allen, 7 December 1925, HAP.

11. Josephine Pinckney to Hervey Allen, 22 November 1924, HAP.

12. [John Farrar], "The Literary Spotlight: Henry Seidel Canby," *Bookman* 60 (September 1924): 66–70.

13. Henry Seidel Canby, "Adventures in Starting a Literary Magazine," *Saturday Review Treasury,* ed. John Haverstick (New York: Simon and Schuster, 1957), 302–3; Krutch, "Introduction," ibid., xx–xxi.

14. Canby, "Adventures," 301.

15. Henry Seidel Canby, *American Memoir* (Boston: Houghton Mifflin, 1947), 377–79; Richard Kruger, *The Paper: The Life and Death of the New York Herald Tribune* (New York: Knopf, 1986), 286. Van Doren was supported by Helen Reid, the wife of *Herald Tribune* publisher Ogden Reid, who was a lifelong feminist and also hired Dorothy Thompson. Irita and Carl Van Doren divorced in 1936. Steve Neal, *Dark Horse: A Biography of Wendell Willkie* (New York: Doubleday, 1984), 39–40.

16. Joan Shelley Rubin, *The Making of the Middlebrow Culture* (Chapel Hill: University of North Carolina Press, 1992), 118n54, 111n41.

17. Josephine Pinckney to Hervey Allen, n.d., HAP; O. B. Keeler, "Charleston Poet Writes of the Land She Knows Best: Miss Pinckney Refuses to Succumb to Eccentricity," unidentified clipping [1928], Carolina Sinkler Lockwood Scrapbook, in possession of Sidney Lockwood Tynan.

18. Janice A. Radway, *A Feeling for Books: The Book-of-the-Month Club, Literary Taste, and Middle-Class Desire* (Chapel Hill: University of North Carolina Press, 1997), 177; Norman Cousins, in Haverstick, *Saturday Review Treasury,* 3, 4.

19. Nina Miller, *Making Love Modern* (New York: Oxford University Press, 1999), 88.

20. Canby, *American Memoir,* 378, 379.

21. Schuyler Livingston Parsons, *Untold Friendships* (Boston: Houghton Mifflin, 1955), 182.

22. Eric "Tuppy" Gugler to Josephine Pinckney, n.d., JPP.

23. Ann Douglas, *Terrible Honesty: Mongrel Manhattan in the 1920s* (New York: Farrar, Straus, Giroux, 1995), 27, 5; Dorothy Dane, "*Porgy* Best Southern Book in Decade, Says Dr. Canby," *Charleston News and Courier,* 15 March 1927; Ellen Glasgow, "An Experiment in the South," in *Ellen Glasgow's Reasonable Doubts: A Collection of Her Writings,* ed. Julius Rowan Raper (Baton Rouge: Louisiana State University Press, 1988), 84, 86–87.

24. Miller, *Making Love Modern,* 6, 9.

25. A reprint appeared in the *Charleston News and Courier,* 5 May 1929; Marion Ponsby Canby, "Messenger," Poetry Society of South Carolina, *Yearbook* (1929): 41; Henry Seidel Canby, Review of *Carolina Lowcountry, Saturday Review of Literature,* 21 November 1931, n.p.

26. Hervey Allen to Marjorie E. Peale, 2 January 1940, in Peale, "Charleston as a Literary Center, 1920–1933" (M.A. thesis, Duke University, 1941), 202; Rubin, *Middlebrow Culture,* 116–117.

27. Donald Davidson, "The Artist as Southerner," *Saturday Review of Literature,* 15 May 1926, 781–83; Donald Davidson to Allen Tate, 9 May 1927, in *The Literary Correspondence of Donald Davidson and*

*Allen Tate*, ed. John Tyree Fain and Thomas Daniel Young (Athens: University of Georgia Press, 1974), 193; Donald Davidson to Josephine Pinckney, 12 July 1930, JPP.

28. [Josephine Pinckney], "Foreword," Poetry Society of South Carolina, *Yearbook* (October 1926): 6–7; Donald Davidson to Helen Williman, 15 December 1926, PSSCP.

29. DuBose Heyward to Hervey Allen, [June 1923], DHP; Josephine Pinckney to Donald Davidson, 7 June 1923, Donald Davidson Collection, Special Collections, University Archives, Vanderbilt University. Heyward and the inner circle of the Poetry Society kept the dilemma between censorship and community standards quiet and agreed to publish a special bibelot, separate from the yearbook, with the winning poems. The special edition would only be sent to out-of-town subscribers.

30. Donald Davidson to Joan B. Williman, 24 April 1927; Joan B. Williman to Donald Davidson, 1 June 1927, PSSCP.

31. Peter Dzwonkoski, "Harper and Brothers," *Dictionary of Literary Biography*, vol. 49: *American Literary Publishing Houses, 1638–1899, Part 1: A–M* (Detroit: Gale, 1986), 46.

32. Josephine Pinckney to Hervey Allen, 23 May 1927, HAP.

33. Ibid.

34. Josephine Pinckney to Hervey Allen, 7 June 1927, HAP; Eugene F. Saxton to Josephine Pinckney, 8 June 1927, JPP; Josephine Pinckney to Hervey Allen, 13 June 1927, telegram, HAP; Helen Williman to Donald Davidson, 27 June 1927, PSSCP; Josephine Pinckney to Hervey Allen, 20 June 1927, HAP.

35. Poetry Society of South Carolina, "Retrospect," *Yearbook* (1927–28): 13.

36. Donald Davidson to Josephine Pinckney, 12 July 1930, 6 November 1927; Merrill Moore to Josephine Pinckney, 18 September 1929, JPP.

37. Josephine Pinckney to Donald Davidson, 17 November [1927], Davidson Papers; Donald Davidson to Josephine Pinckney, 6 November 1927, JPP.

38. Eugene Saxton to Josephine Pinckney, 9 December 1927, JPP.

39. [Josephine Pinckney], "Foreword," Poetry Society of South Carolina, *Yearbook* (1926): 6–7.

40. Anne Baker Leland Bridges and Roy Williams III, *St. James Santee Plantation Parish* (Spartanburg, SC: The Reprint Company, 1997), 242.

41. Edward Guerrant Lilly, ed., *Historic Churches of Charleston, South Carolina*, comp. by Clifford Legerton (Charleston: John Huguley, 1966), 12–13.

42. "The Misses Poar Drive to Church" was first published in *The Reviewer* (April 1923).

43. Harriet Monroe, "Young Charleston," *Poetry* 32(June 1928): 162–65.

44. "A Review by George Armstrong Wauchope . . . of Josephine Pinckney's 'Sea-Drinking Cities,'" *Charleston News and Courier*, 19 February 1928, clipping, JPP.

45. Percy Hutchison, review of *Sea-Drinking Cities*, *New York Times Book Review*, 8 April 1928; Babette Deutsch, "A Southern Voice," *New York Herald-Tribune Books*, 5 February 1928.

46. "Rich's Book Exposition," unidentified clipping, Caroline Sinkler Lockwood Scrapbook.

47. Donald Davidson, "Josephine Pinckney: *Sea-Drinking Cities* (15 January 1928)," in *The Spyglass: Views and Reviews, 1924–1930*, ed. John Tyree Fain (Nashville: Vanderbilt University Press, 1963), 111–13. Allen Tate to Donald Davidson, 25 April 1928, in Fain and Young, *Literary Correspondence*, 213.

48. Donald Davidson, "Josephine Pinckney's Poetry Glows with Sunny Luxuriance of Imagery from Nature and the Life about Her," *Charleston Evening Post*, 30 September 1928, clipping, JPP.

49. Howard Mumford Jones to Josephine Pinckney, 3 February 1928, JPP.

50. Joseph Hergesheimer to Henry L. Mencken, 3 January 1928; Henry L. Mencken to Joseph Hergesheimer, 4 January [1928, incorrectly marked 1932 on ms.], HLMP; Van Vechten, "Hergesheimer," 89.

51. Joseph Hergesheimer to Josephine Pinckney, 3 February 1928, JPP.

52. John Bennett to Family, 15 January 1928, JBP.

53. DuBose Heyward to Josephine Pinckney, 2 June 1928, JPP.

54. Eugene F. Saxton to Josephine Pinckney, 28 April 1928, JPP. The initial press run had been 775 books, which ultimately sold out. Headley Coxe, "The Charleston Poetic Renascence, 1920–1930" (Ph. D. diss., University of Pennsylvania, 1958), 165.

55. Thomas R. Waring to Hervey Allen, 19 July 1923, PSSCP; Thomas R. Waring to Alfred Kreymborg, 1 January 1928, Thomas R. Waring Sr. Papers, SCHS. Christine Stansell, *American Moderns* (New York: Metropolitan Books, 2000), 82–83; Kreymborg, *Our Singing Strength: An Outline of American Poetry* (New York: Coward-McCann, 1929), 563.

56. Alfred Kreymborg to Thomas R. Waring, 30 March 1928, Waring Papers.

57. Stanhope Sams, "Sea-drinking Cities," *Columbia State*, 29 January 1928, clipping, JPP.

58. C. Cotesworth Pinckney to Josephine Pinckney, 1 March 1927, 29 March 1927, Pinckney file, Archive, Charleston Museum. The final cost was $1,298. Emma Richardson to Laura Bragg, 1 August 1928, ibid; John Bennett to John Bennett Jr., 15 April 1928, JBP.

59. Bill from Minot and Reynolds for consultation and lab work, 1 November 1928 in Mitchell and Horlbeck Law Firm Papers, SCHS; A. W. Curry to Camilla S. Pinckney, 17 July 1928, Mitchell and Horlbeck Papers.

60. John A. C. Keith, *J. A. C. Keith Remembers* (n.p., 1970), 96; *Charleston Evening Post,* 12 October 1928. At the time of her death, Camilla Pinckney was the chairman of the Associated Members of the Carolina Art Association and a member of the Governing Board.

NOTES TO CHAPTER 7

1. Josephine Pinckney to Hervey Allen, 18 August [1929], HAP. Captain Tom had actually bequeathed the Pinckney home to Josephine and her brother, giving his wife a life interest. In 1937, the Pinckneys sold the house to a relative, Lois Hazelhurst Middleton Baker. "Mrs. F. R. Baker Buys Pinckney Residence," *Charleston News and Courier,* 22 July 1937.

2. Josephine Pinckney to Hervey Allen, 18 August [1929], HAP.

3. Josephine Pinckney to Julian Mitchell Jr., 11 July 1929, Mitchell and Horlbeck Papers; Josephine Pinckney to Hervey Allen, 18 August [1929], HAP.

4. Pinckney to Allen, 18 August [1929], HAP.

5. Alice C. Rice, "Josephine Pinckney Works on New Volume of Poetry," *Charleston News and Courier,* 25 February 1931.

6. Minute Book, Society for the Preservation of Old Dwellings, 21 April 1920, 5 May 1920, Society for the Preservation of Old Dwellings Papers, SCHS. Neither Pinckney nor any of the organizers of the Poetry Society were among the founders of the SPOD, although eventually Pinckney, Bennett, and Heyward later joined.

7. Pinckney to Allen, 18 August [1929], HAP.

8. Rice, "Pinckney Works on New Volume."

9. Ibid.; Robert R. Weyeneth, *Historic Preservation for a Living City: Historic Charleston Foundation, 1947–1997* (Columbia: University of South Carolina Press, 2000), 11.

10. Eleanor Stone Perenyi, interview, 12 March 1999. Pinckney's travel notebook is in JPP.

11. Josephine Pinckney, notes on writing poetry [ca. 1930s], JPP.

12. Another of Laura Waring's sisters, Fay Witte Ball, who married W. W. Ball, Tom Waring's coun-

terpart on the *Charleston News and Courier,* became a virtual recluse, only leaving her house to attend the theater. John D. Stark, *Damned Upcountryman: William Watts Ball; A Study in American Conservatism* (Durham, NC: Duke University Press, 1968), 141.

13. Editorial, *Charleston News and Courier,* 2 June 1935; Thomas R. Waring to Hervey Allen, 19 July 1923, 29 September 1926, PSSCP.

14. Warrington Dawson to "Miss Connie," 8 January 1928, JPP; Eleanor Stone Perenyi Interview, 12 March 1999.

15. Susan Smythe Bennett to Hervey Allen, 17 February 1929; Josephine Pinckney to Hervey Allen, 18 August [1929], HAP.

16. Rice, "Pinckney Works on New Volume"; "Lady with a Lavender House Writes Poetry, Tends Garden and 'Contemplates' a Novel," *Charleston News and Courier,* 22 January 1939.

17. Rice, "Pinckney Works on New Volume"; *Worcester Sunday Telegram,* 27 March 1938, clipping, JBP.

18. Barbara Trigg Brown, "Two Houses in the Old Charleston Manner," *Arts and Decoration* 51 (November 1939): 19; Florence Thompson Howe, "The Charleston Home of Josephine Pinckney," *Antiques* (May 1946): 307, clippings in JPP.

19. Carl Van Vechten to Josephine Pinckney, 27 February 1934; Harold Nicholson to Josephine Pinckney, 19 February 1933, JPP.

20. Robert Hillyer to Josephine Pinckney, n.d., JPP.

21. John Bennett to Susan Smythe Bennett, 18 April 1925; Gerald W. Johnson to Dubose Heyward, 5 December 1923, PSSCP; Gerald W. Johnson to Josephine Pinckney, 26 October 1932, JPP.

22. Gerald W. Johnson to Josephine Pinckney, 17 May 1935, JPP.

23. Howard Mumford Jones to Josephine Pinckney, 27 January 1939; Dubose Heyward to Josephine Pinckney, n.d., JPP.

24. Josephine Pinckney to Harriet Monroe, 20 June 1931, Harriet Monroe, *Poetry* Papers, University of Chicago. Monroe asked to use "Phyllis and the Philosopher," "Peggy Considers Her Grandmother," and "In the Barn"; Harriet Monroe to Josephine Pinckney, 9 May 1931, JPP.

25. Langdon Cheves to Anne C. Read, draft, 29 June 1931, Langdon Cheves Papers, SCHS; "Miss Pinckney Better," *Charleston News and Courier,* 29 June 1931; John Bennett to "Family," 7 July 1931, JBP.

26. Josephine Pinckney to Hervey Allen, 18 August 1929, HAP.

27. Josephine Pinckney to Hervey Allen, 26 February 1934, HAP.

28. Robert N. S. Whitelaw to Clare Booth Luce, 21 January 1941, CAA; Whitelaw to Laura M. Bragg, 26 December 26, 1931, LMBP; Dubose Heyward to Hervey Allen, 10 August 1930, HAP; Alexander Sprunt to DuBose Heyward, 23 November 1932, JPP; John Bennett to his family, 20 May 1934, JBP.

29. Josephine Pinckney to Laura Bragg, 30 January 1933, LMBP; Josephine Pinckney to John Bennett, 19 March 1933, JBP. In 1929, just before the stock market crash, Pinckney had drawn a new will. After her mother's death, she possessed three significant pieces of property, 21 King Street, 36 Chalmers Street, and her family plantation Eldorado. Her liquid assets in stocks and bonds probably totaled over $125,000. Draft of Pinckney will, JPP.

30. Joan Shelley Rubin *The Making of the Middlebrow Culture* (Chapel Hill: University of North Carolina Press, 1992), 123; Josephine Pinckney to Laura Bragg, 30 January 1933, LMBP; Josephine Pinckney to Prentiss Taylor, 8 March 1933, PT/Yale.

31. Josephine Pinckney, notebook, [1953], JPP.

32. Pinckney, "Autobiography for Three"; Grace Stone to Josephine Pinckney, n.d., all in JPP.

33. Perenyi, interview.

34. Pinckney, "Autobiography for Three"; Serena Simons Leonhardt, interview, 15 February 2000.

35. Amelia Moore Taylor, interview, 20 April 2000.

36. Pinckney, "Autobiography for Three."

37. Leonhardt, interview; Pinckney, "Autobiography for Three."

38. Pinckney, notebook, [1953]; Marshall Best, "Notes on Charleston Trip," JPP/Viking Papers.

39. Pinckney, notebook, [1953].

40. Josephine Pinckney, notebook, [1953], JPP.

41. Harriet Simons to Albert Simons, 21 April 1918; Harriet P. Simons, misc. typescript giving information about the Charleston Urban League and race relations in Charleston [ca. 1945], ASP.

42. Ibid.; Albert Simons to Josephine Pinckney 12 January 1954; Josephine Pinckney to Albert Simons, 25 January 1954, ASP.

43. Anne Sinkler Whaley Leclercq, interview, 2 May 2002; *New York Times*, 30 May 1933; "Mistress of Gippy Plantation in Picket Line of Girl Strikers," unidentified article, Caroline Sinkler Lockwood Scrapbook, in possession of Sidney Lockwood Tynan.

44. Sidney Lockwood Tynan, interview, 17 April 2001.

45. Harriet Simons to Albert Simons, [ca. March 1934], ASP.

46. Max Eastman, *Enjoyment of Living* (New York: Harper and Co., 1948), 235. Their letters are among Max Eastman's papers at Indiana University's Lilly Library but are restricted.

47. "Victor Morawetz, Retired Attorney," *New York Times*, 19 May 1938; "Mrs. Victor Morawetz," *New York Times*, 4 January 1957; "Marjorie Nott Morawetz," *Charleston News and Courier*, 5 January 1957. In addition to the preservation and restoration of several notable properties in the city including the Haig house at 30 Meeting Street and the Smythe house at 14-16 Legaré Street, Morawetz's benefices to Charleston include the land on which the municipal golf course was built and the bordering avenue of magnolias along Maybank Highway, $1 million to the South Carolina Medical Society, a wing for Roper Hospital for the treatment of black patients with contagious diseases, contributions to the Maternal Welfare Clinic, and much of Seabrook Island to the Episcopal Church with the understanding that its natural beauty be maintained.

48. Prentiss Taylor to Wade White, Easter Sunday 1934, PT/Quiroz.

49. M. A. DeWolfe Howe, "The Song of Charleston," *Atlantic Monthly* (July 1930): 110.

50. Corrine Roosevelt Robinson to Marjorie Morawetz, n.d., Morawetz Scrapbook, SPSP; Harriet Stoney Simons to Louisa Stoney Popham, [June 1929], Stoney/Popham Family Papers, SCHS.

51. Marjorie N. Morawetz to Eleanor Roosevelt, [ca. May] 1933, ERP.

52. Society for the Preservation of Spirituals, Minutes, 10 December 1934, SPSP.

53. Josephine Pinckney to Prentiss Taylor, 3 February 1934, 21 December 1935, PT/Quiroz; Harriet S. Bee and Michelle Elligott, ed., *Art in Our Time: A Chronicle of the Museum of Modern Art* (New York: Museum of Modern Art, 2004), 40.

54. Josephine Pinckney to Prentiss Taylor, 1 February 1934, PT/Quiroz; *Charleston News and Courier*, 28 April 1941; *New York Times*, 6 January 1927. Before his death in 1927, Dr. George Huntington had been regarded as the foremost anatomist as the modern era, adapting the theories of evolution into the study of the human body.

55. Mrs. Edward Holden, interview, 17 February 2000.

56. Grace Stone to Josephine Pinckney, 20 July 1932, JPP; Carl Van Vechten, "Some 'Literary Ladies' I Have Known," *Yale University Library Gazette* 26 (January 1952): 109. Stone's first novel was *The Heaven and Earth of Donna Elena* (1929). Her later books were *The Almond Tree* (1931), *The Cold Journey* (1934), and, under the pseudonym Ethel Vance, *Escape* (1939), *Reprisal* (1940), and *Winter Meeting* (1945).

57. Susan Smythe Bennett to Hervey Allen, 7 August 1934, HAP; Harriet P. Simons to Albert Simons, [ca. 1934], ASP; Grace Stone to Josephine Pinckney, [ca.1934], JPP.

58. Grace Stone to Josephine Pinckney, [ca. 1932], JPP.

59. Harriet P. Simons to Louisa P. Popham, 7 January [1933], Stoney/Popham Papers; Grace Stone to Josephine Pinckney, 20 July 1932, JPP. Stone's thirteen-year-old daughter disliked California intensely, so Stone put her on the train back to Charleston alone, where she was greeted by Pinckney who had arranged for her to stay with Herbert Ravenel Sass's family; Perenyi, interview.

60. Grace Stone to Josephine Pinckney, [ca.1933], JPP.

61. Perenyi, interview; Pinckney, notebook, July 1954, JPP.

62. Grace Stone to Josephine Pinckney, n.d., JPP; Pie Pinckney Friendly, interview, 11 June 2002.

63. Perenyi, interview; Grace Stone, notebook [1934], Stone Papers.

64. Grace Stone to Josephine Pinckney, [1934]; Grace Stone to Josephine Pinckney, 6 August [n.d.], JPP.

### NOTES TO CHAPTER 8

1. Daniel J. Singal, *The War Within* (Chapel Hill: University of North Carolina Press, 1982), 281.

2. Josephine Pinckney to Donald Davidson, 29 June 1930, 13 August 1930, Donald Davidson Papers, Special Collections, Vanderbilt University Library; Donald Davidson to Josephine Pinckney, 12 July 1930, 20 October 1930, JPP.

3. Josephine Pinckney to Donald Davidson, 23 July 1930; Josephine Pinckney to Donald Davidson, 22 June 1930, Davidson Papers.

4. Louis Rubin, "Fugitives as Agrarians," in *William Elliott Shoots a Bear* (Baton Rouge: Louisiana State University, 1978), 154.

5. Donald Davidson to Josephine Pinckney, 12 July 1930, JPP.

6. Josephine Pinckney to Donald Davidson, 23 July 1930, JPP.

7. Davidson to Pinckney, 12 July 1930, JPP.

8. Ibid.

9. Pinckney to Davidson, 23 July 1930; Donald Davidson to Josephine Pinckney, 21 August 1930, JPP; Francis Butler Simkins, "A Flag of Optimism," *The State* (Columbia), 10 February 1924.

10. Josephine Pinckney, "Bulwarks against Change," in *Culture in the South*, ed. W. T. Couch (Chapel Hill: University of North Carolina Press, 1934), 40.

11. Ibid.

12. Ibid., 47.

13. Ibid., 44.

14. Ibid.

15. Ibid., 45, 47.

16. Davidson to Pinckney, 12 July 1930 and 21 August 1930.

17. Donald Davidson, *Southern Writers in the Modern World* (Athens: University of Georgia Press, 1958), 57. The twelve Southerners who wrote essays for *I'll Take My Stand: The South and the Agrarian Tradition* were John Crowe Ransom, Donald Davidson, Frank Lawrence Owsley, John Gould Fletcher, Lyle H. Lanier, Allen Tate, Herman Clarence Nixon, Andrew Nelson Lytle, Robert Penn Warren, John Donald Wade, Henry Blue Kline, and Stark Young.

18. Josephine Pinckney to Donald Davidson, 6 October 1930, Davidson Papers.

19. Ibid.

20. John Crowe Ransom to Josephine Pinckney, 17 December [1928], JPP; Allen Tate, "Poetry in the South," *Lyric* 40 (Winter 1932): 14. Tate thought she belonged to this group who were "first Southern and second universal"; ibid. Merrill Moore to Josephine Pinckney, 13 April 1935, JPP.

21. Donald Davidson to Josephine Pinckney, 20 October 1930, JPP; Mark Royden Winchell, *Where No Flag Flies* (Columbia: University of Missouri Press, 2000), 140.

22. Josephine Pinckney to Donald Davidson [ca. late December 1930], Davidson Papers; Eugene F. Saxton to Josephine Pinckney, 22 December 1930, JPP.

23. Davidson welcomed her suggestion and pressed his publisher to send A.E. an advance copy of *I'll Take My Stand*. Actually the Fugitives had met A.E. years before when he visited his old friend and one of their members, Sidney Hirsch. Davidson speculated the Irishman had long forgotten his visit to Tennessee, for "Like the old Greek heroes, A.E. walks surrounded with a cloud, thrown over him by the gods" Davidson to Pinckney, 20 October 1930, Davidson Papers.

24. [John Eglinton], *A Memoir of A.E.: George William Russell* (London: Macmillan, 1937), 209.

25. Pinckney probably met George William Russell (1867–1935) through Henry Seidel Canby, a frequent traveler in the British Isles in search of new writing talent. In 1918, he went on a mission for the United States government to report on the state of the Irish rebellion, a time when many fugitives from the British were still in hiding. He reported enjoying some of the most brilliant conversation he had ever encountered and likely spent time with A.E.'s circle on Rathgar Street. Henry Seidel Canby, *American Memoir* (Boston: Houghton Mifflin, 1947), 371.

26. Pinckney to Davidson, 6 October 1930, Davidson Papers.

27. Josephine Pinckney to Elfrida Barrow, 21 November 1930, PSSCP; Poetry Society of South Carolina, *Yearbook* (October 1931): 8–9; Colum, "A.E.," *Irish Literary Portraits*, 198.

28. Josephine Pinckney to Elfrida Barrow, 21 November 1930, Poetry Society of South Carolina Papers; Poetry Society of South Carolina, *Yearbook* (October 1931): 8–9; Padraic Colum, "A.E.," *Irish Literary Portraits*, ed. W. R. Rogers (London: British Broadcast Corporation, 1972), 198; [Eglinton], *Memoir of A.E.*, 209, 213, 228.

29. Minutes, 14 March 1929, SPSP.

30. Alfred Huger to H. S. Lathan, 10 January 1931, SPSP.

31. Ibid.

32. DuBose Heyward to Josephine Pinckney, 26 January [1931], DHP; Edward A. Alderman to James Southall Wilson, 27 January 1931, James Southall Wilson/Southern Writers' Conference Papers, Special Collections, University of Virginia.

33. Josephine Pinckney to James Southall Wilson, 23 September 1931, Wilson/Southern Writers' Conference Papers.

34. DuBose Heyward to James Southall Wilson, 29 January 1931, ibid.; Singal, *The War Within*, 38–39. The initial convoluted selection process quickly broke down. Heyward suggested just inviting all the Virginia nominees, all the committee, and the truly distinguished to be balanced with some young talent up to thirty. In future years, some could be dropped and others added. Dubose Heyward to James Southall Wilson, 30 June 1931, Wilson/Southern Writers' Conference Papers.

35. Heyward to Wilson, 30 June 1931; Paul Green to James Southall Wilson, 4 October 1931; Allen Tate to Wilson, n.d., Wilson/Southern Writers' Conference Papers.

36. Emily Clark, "A Weekend at Mr. Jefferson's University," *New York Herald-Tribune*, 8 November 1931; Josephine Pinckney to James Southall Wilson, 20 October 1931, Wilson/Southern Writers' Conference Papers; Howard Mumford Jones and Walter B. Rideout, eds., *Letters of Sherwood Anderson* (Boston: Little, Brown, 1953), 251–53.

37. Quoted in Donald Davidson, "A Meeting of Southern Writers," *Bookman* 68 (November 1931): 495.

38. Josephine Pinckney, "Southern Writers' Congress," *Saturday Review of Literature*, 7 November 1931, 266.

39. Joseph Leo Blotner, *Faulkner: A Biography* (New York: Random House, 1984), 713. Blotner quotes from his interview with Paul Green in 1968, n.103.

40. DuBose Heyward to James Southall Wilson, [ca. 20 January 1931], 10 March 1931, Wilson/Southern Writers' Conference Papers.

41. Donald Davidson to James Southall Wilson, 5 September 1931, Wilson/Southern Writers' Conference Papers.

42. Pinckney, "Southern Writers' Congress," 266.

43. Jones and Rideout, *Letters of Sherwood Anderson,* 253.

44. Clark, "A Weekend at Mr. Jefferson's University."

45. Allen Tate to James Southall Wilson, 29 October 1931, Wilson/Southern Writers' Conference Papers; Jones and Rideout, *Letters of Sherwood Anderson,* 252.

46. Allen Tate to Robert Penn Warren, 19 January 1932, as quoted in Thomas A. Underwood, *Allen Tate: Orphan of the South* (Princeton: Princeton University Press, 2000), 183.

47. Tate, "Poetry in the South," 14; Donald Davidson to Allen Tate, 21 January 1932, in Fain and Young, *Literary Correspondence,* 267; Allen Tate to Josephine Pinckney, 16 January 1932; 23 January 1932; 21 April 1932, JPP; Josephine Pinckney to Allen Tate, 2 March 1932, ATP.

48. Allen Tate to Donald Davidson, 15 January 1932, in Fain and Young, *Literary Correspondence,* 266; Josephine Pinckney to Allen Tate, 30 March 1932; Josephine Pinckney to Allen Tate, 20 January [1932], ATP.

49. Pinckney to Tate, 30 March [1932], ATP.

50. Josephine Pinckney to Allen Tate, 8 November [1931]; Josephine Pinckney to Allen Tate, 26 May 1932, ATP.

51. Prentiss Taylor to Beatrice Hottel Taylor, 12 September 1932; 24 September 1932, PT/Quiroz; Ingrid Rose, "Introduction," in Ingrid Rose and Roderick S. Quiroz, *The Lithographs of Prentiss Taylor: A Catalogue Raisonné* (Bronx, NY: Fordham University Press, 1996), 1; Prentiss Taylor to Carl Van Vechten, 19 September 1932, Carl Van Vechten Papers, Beinecke Rare Book and Manuscript Library, Yale University.

52. Rose and Quiroz, *Lithographs of Prentiss Taylor,* 53; "Prentiss Taylor," *The Washington Print Club Quarterly* (Winter 1991–92): 2–5; Ann Douglas, *Terrible Honesty: Mongrel Manhattan in the 1920s* (New York: Farrar, Straus, Giroux, 1995) 287–288; Josephine Pinckney to Prentiss Taylor, 8 March 1933, PT/Yale. Taylor also established Winter Wheat Press that specialized in rhyme sheets and broadsides. He illustrated the poetry of Stephen Vincent Benét's sister Laura and work by Rachel Field, who is best known as the author of "All This and Heaven Too."

53. Howard Mumford Jones to Josephine Pinckney, 6 January 1932, JPP.

54. Harriet P. Simons to Louisa Stoney Popham, [October 1932], Stoney-Popham Papers, SCHS; Donald Davidson to Allan Tate, 29 October 1932, in Fain and Young, *Literary Correspondence,* 274.

55. Danny Butcher, "Literary Folk Have a Party in Charleston," *Chicago Tribune,* [September 1932], clipping, JPP; Davidson to Tate, 29 October 1932, in Fain and Young, *Literary Correspondence,* 274.

56. The meeting ended with Professor William S. Knickerbocker making a strong bid to have the next meeting at the University of the South in Sewanee, Tennessee. Davidson, furious at the thought of the elite Episcopal school with its faux Oxford-style buildings as being held up as representative of Tennessee and its frontier tradition, warned Pinckney that if the "sleeping dogs" accept the invitation

to come to Sewanee "then most certainly there will be another battle of Bull Run." Donald Davidson to Josephine Pinckney, 5 November 1932, JPP. Tate, who was in Paris with his wife, Carolyn Gordon, consoled Davidson about his experience in Charleston: "Let us forget these Southern Writers' Conferences . . . This disgusting parade of successful authorship should be ignored if possible—if not ignored, then attacked." Allen Tate to Donald Davidson, 10 December 1932, in Fain and Young, *Literary Correspondence*, 279–80.

57. Davidson to Pinckney, 5 November 1932.

58. Laurence Stallings, "Cahiers de Compagne," *New York Sun*, 27 October 1932.

59. DuBose Heyward to Josephine Pinckney, 24 December 1932, DHP.

60. Josephine Pinckney to Prentiss Taylor, 8 March 1933, 15 April 1933, 21 April 1933, PT/Yale; Prentiss Taylor to Carl Van Vechten, 8, 9 May 1933, postcard, n.d., Van Vechten Papers.

61. Prentiss Taylor, diary, 16 August 1933, PT/Quiroz; Taylor to Carl Van Vechten, 27 May 1933, 19 May 1933, Van Vechten Papers.

62. Prentiss Taylor to Beatrice Hottel Taylor, 24 September 1933, PT/Quiroz; Josephine Pinckney to Prentiss Taylor, 18 September 1933, PT/Quiroz.

63. Pinckney to Taylor, 18 September 1933, PT/Quiroz.

64. Ibid.; Harriet Stoney Simons to Albert Simons, 20 September 1933, Stoney/Popham Family Papers, SCHS. About six months after the wedding, Frost, claiming she was "a sentimental cuss," wrote Pinckney to ask what she had done with the bridal bouquet and also apologized: "I didn't mean to hit you so hard—I'm blind as a bat without my glasses"; Frances Frost to Josephine Pinckney, 19 January 1934, JPP.

65. Harriet Stoney Simons to Albert Simons, 20 September 1933; Susan Millar Williams, *A Devil and a Good Woman Too* (Athens: University of Georgia Press, 1997), 189–90.

66. Williams, *Devil and a Good Woman*, 190.

67. In 1931, when Emily Clark wrote a retrospective about the Southern Renaissance, *Innocence Abroad*, she wrote a chapter on DuBose Heyward with much more attention to his background and family history than she gave to other subjects. She believed that his aristocratic heritage defined him as an author. She had included several other authors she believed fit into this same category, almost certainly Josephine Pinckney among them, but her publisher edited out about six lines, fearing that Peterkin would take offense at being struck from the list of southern aristocrats. Emily Clark to Henry L. Mencken, [1929], HLMP.

68. Williams, *Devil and a Good Woman*, 50.

69. Frances Frost to Josephine Pinckney, 2 December [1933], JPP. Typically weaving her friends into one another's lives, and also trying to assist them, Pinckney suggested to Frost that Prentiss Taylor might be just the person to design the dust jacket for her new book. she also offered to pay the artist's fees. *Woman of the Earth*, Pinckney later discovered, Frost had cruelly dedicated to her former lover, Irving Fineman. Josephine Pinckney to Prentiss Taylor, 20 December 1933, PT/Quiroz.

70. Howard Mumford Jones to Josephine Pinckney, 30 January 1931; Josephine Pinckney to Donald Davidson, 20 January 1934; Donald Davidson to Josephine Pinckney, 28 January 1934, JPP; Donald Davidson to Allen Tate, 12 January 1934, in Fain and Young, *Literary Correspondence*, 288–289; Allen Tate, "A View of the Whole South," *The American Review* 2 (November–March 1933–34): 416.

71. Dorothy Scarborough, "The South: Her Level of Culture," *New York Times Book Review* 1 (April 1934), clipping, JPP.

72. William S. Knickerbocker, "Designs for Dixie," *The Commonweal*, 17 August 1945, 384.

73. Eugene F. Saxton to Josephine Pinckney, 22 December 1930, JPP.

NOTES TO CHAPTER 9

1. Josephine Pinckney to Laura Bragg, 30 January 1933, LMBP; Ellery Sedgwick to Josephine Pinckney, 16 March 1934, JPP; Josephine Pinckney, "They Shall Return as Strangers," *VQR* (October 1934), 547.

2. Clifton Fadiman to Josephine Pinckney, 27 September 1934, JPP; Josephine Pinckney to Allen Tate, 8 November [1932], ATP.

3. Josephine Pinckney to Allen Tate, 11 February [1932], ATP; Emily Clark, "Hervey Allen," *Saturday Review of Literature*, 9 December 1933, 323.

4. Hervey Allen to Josephine Pinckney, 23 April 1934, JPP.

5. Lawrence S. Rowland, Alexander Moore, and George C. Rogers Jr., *History of Beaufort County, South Carolina* (Columbia, SC: University of South Carolina Press, 1996), 1:10–11, 60–61, 76n14.

6. Ibid., 1:62–63.

7. Ibid., 1:81. For more on Pinckney's contention that lust for gain was really the midwife of the American republic, see her essay "The Marchant of London and the Treacherous Don," *VQR* 12 (April 1936): 207–19.

8. Josephine Pinckney, radio address on WTMA [Charleston, SC], 1941, ts., JPP.

9. Ibid. Heyward also was influenced by Hergesheimer's method of immersion in the historical sources. See DuBose Heyward, "A New Theory of Historical Fiction," *Publishers Weekly* 13 (1932): 511–12.

10. Pinckney, WTMA radio address; Langdon Cheves to Josephine Pinckney, 26 July 1934, 20 May 1934, JPP; Robert Weir, "Preface to the Reprint," and Charles H. Lesser, "Introduction to the Reprint," *The Shaftsbury Papers* (1897; reprint, Charleston: SCHS, 2000), v–vi; viii–xii. Cheves, a prime mover in the SCHS's revival after the Civil War, labored over the Shaftsbury Papers, which had been transcribed by Noel Sainsbury. Combining a lawyer's love of detail with his remarkable knowledge of the Low Country landscape and history, Cheves's compilation went far beyond the Sainsbury transcripts to include all the other important contemporary documents available. The result was Langdon Cheves, *The Shaftsbury Papers and Other Records relating to Carolina and the First Settlement on the Ashley River* (SCHS, 1898).

11. DuBose Heyward to Josephine Pinckney, 8 September [1932], JPP.

12. Josephine Pinckney to Hervey Allen, 26 February 1934, HAP.

13. Eugene F. Saxton to Josephine Pinckney, 6 March 1934; John Farrar to Josephine Pinckney, 14 April 1934, JPP; Josephine Pinckney to Laura M. Bragg, 12 October [1934], LMBP.

14. Josephine Pinckney to Hervey Allen, 6 May 1935, HAP; Pinckney to Bragg, 12 October [1934].

15. John Farrar, *Chicago Daily Tribune*, n.d., clipping, JPP.

16. Ibid.

17. Ibid.

18. Josephine Pinckney, "Notes for my talk at William and Mary," [December 1934], JPP. "Romantic Mr. Swallow" first appeared in the 1934 Poetry Society of South Carolina *Yearbook*.

19. Joan Williman to Josephine Pinckney, 8 December 1934, JPP.

20. "About a Charleston Author," *Charleston News and Courier*, 23 January 1952; Lambert Davis to Josephine Pinckney, 11 March 1936, JPP. Pinckney wrote a review essay "Jeffers and MacLeish," *VQR* (July 1932): 443–47.

21. Gerald W. Johnson to Josephine Pinckney, 6 April 1936, JPP.

22. Gerald W. Johnson to Josephine Pinckney, 17 May 1935. JPP.

23. Josephine Pinckney to Prentiss Taylor, 6 September [1934], PT/Quiroz. At Pinckney's death,

Fairfield Plantation passed on to his son Thomas with the request that he never let the house pass out of family hands. Will of Charles Cotesworth Pinckney, 1934, Richmond, Probate Office, Book 32, 458–59.

24. Pinckney to Taylor, 6 September [1934].

25. Eleanor Stone Perenyi, interview, 12 March 1999; Josephine Pinckney to John Bennett, 5 June 1935, JBP.

26. "Thomas Richard Waring,"*Charleston News and Courier,* 2 June 1935; "Thomas R. Waring Dies after Long Career as Editor," *Charleston News and Courier,* 1 June, 1935.

27. DuBose Heyward to Josephine Pinckney, n.d., JPP.

28. Miscellaneous notes, JPP.

29. John Bennett to John Bennett Jr., 25 February 1940, JBP.

30. John Bennett to John Bennett Jr., 7 January 1940, JBP. The marriage of Stoney and Frost exploded for several reasons. Frost expected Stoney, who had a kind and magical way with children, to care for her daughter and resentful son while she stayed for long periods in New York promoting her work and renewing her affair with Irving Fineman. Despite her promises, she continued to drink heavily. Frost vacillated about wanting a divorce. Finally, Stoney ended the marriage. Frost returned to New York, finding Fineman in a serious relationship with another woman. Stoney left for Italy where he joined Grace Stone and her daughter. He stood in for Eleanor Stone's absent father when she married Baron Perenyi in Venice in 1937. Harriet P. Simons to Louisa Popham, 8 August 1937, Stoney/Popham Family Papers, SCHS; Susan Millar Williams, *A Devil and a Good Woman Too* (Athens: University of Georgia Press, 1997), 235–37; Perenyi, interview, 12 March 1999; Grace Stone, diary, 20 September 1937, Grace Stone Papers, Boston University.

31. Henry Seidel Canby, draft report on *Hilton Head,* JPP; Henry Seidel Canby to Josephine Pinckney, n.d., JPP.

32. Gerald W. Johnson in *Books,* 23 February 1941, 4; Margaret Wallace in the *New York Times,* 2 March 1941.

### NOTES TO CHAPTER 10

1. William W. Ball to F. Warrington Dawson, 19 May 1939, William Watts Ball Papers, Perkins Library, Duke University.

2. Wendell L. Willkie to William W. Ball, 19 August 1939, Ball Papers; [William W. Ball], "Not a Kneeler," *Charleston News and Courier,* 5 March 1939.

3. William W. Ball to Sara Ball Copeland, 5 October 1939; William W. Ball to Wendell Willkie, 6 November 1939, 13 November 1939, Ball Papers.

4. Ball to Copeland, 5 October 1939, Ball Papers.

5. Ibid.; John Bennett to John Bennett Jr., 25 February 1940, JBP.

6. Josephine Pinckney to Wendell Willkie, 25 February 1940, Irita Van Doren Papers, Library of Congress, 38, 41–42; Rebecca West to Irita Van Doren, [1941], Van Doren Papers; Warren Moscow, *Roosevelt and Willkie* (Englewood Cliffs, NJ: Prentice-Hall, 1968), 51.

7. Josephine Pinckney to Wendell L. Willkie, 7 January [1941], Wendell L. Willkie Papers, Lilly Library, Indiana University.

8.Steve Neal, *Dark Horse: A Biography of Wendell Willkie* (New York: Doubleday, 1984), 38, 39.

9. Mary McCarthy, "Man in the Brooks Brothers Shirt," in *The Company She Keeps* (New York: Simon and Schuster, 1942), 81 89, 95, 133.

10. Neal, *Dark Horse*, 38, 186, 93.

11. W. W. Ball to J. A. Hoyt, 15 July 1940, Ball Papers.

12. Dorothy K. Heyward to "Dear Family," 27 June 1940, DKHP; Greene, *Mr. Skylark*, 244.

13. Heyward to "Dear Family," 27 June 1940; Dorothy Heyward to Uncle Ralph, 21–30 July 1940; Dorothy Heyward to Joseph McGee, 10 July 1940; Josephine Pinckney to Dorothy Heyward, [1941], DKHP.

14. Robert N. S. Whitelaw to Wendell L. Willkie, 28 June 1940, Dock Street file, Carolina Art Association Papers, SCHS.

15. Josephine Pinckney to Hervey Allen, 23 July [1940], HAP. Huntington also had a son from her first marriage to Dr. Churchill Carmalt, Huntington. Churchill Carmalt married a South Carolina girl, Lucy Herndon Kaminer from Gadsden, the daughter of Mr. and Mrs. Harold Glenn Kaminer.

16. "Willkie Here for Visit to Estate of Luce on Cooper," *Charleston News and Courier*, 3 December 1940, clipping in Van Doren Papers.

17. Wendell Willkie to Josephine Pinckney, telegram, 2 January 1941, 6 January 1941, JPP.

18. Josephine Pinckney to Wendell Willkie, 7 January [1941], Willkie Papers; Ellsworth Barnard, *Wendell Willkie: Fighter for Freedom* (Marquette: Northern Michigan University Press, 1966), 269.

19. Pinckney to Willkie, 7 January [1941], Wilkie Papers.

20. Ibid.

21. Barnard, *Wendell Willkie*, 273–75; Neal, *Dark Horse*, 188–89; Pinckney to Willkie, 7 January [1941], Wilkie Papers.

22. "Local Writers Join in Move," *Charleston Evening Post*, 26 May 1941, clipping, JPP.

23. Josephine Pinckney to Wendell Willkie, 13 December 1941, Willkie Papers.

24. "Little David," part of the People in Defense program, produced by the Dock Street Theatre for the Charleston Civil Defense Council, typescript, JPP. Pinckney later submitted the plays both dealing with southern topics to Writers' War Board, part of the Office of Civilian Defense. They did not accept them. Frederica Barach to Josephine Pinckney, 5 August 1942, JPP.

25. *New York Times*, 13 February 1942, as quoted in Barnard, *Wendell Willkie*, 343; Josephine Pinckney to Wendell Willkie, 17 November 1942, 14 October 1942 (telegram), Willkie Papers. Willkie was said to have fallen in love "for the first time" with Madame Chiang Kai-Shek, the wife of the leader of Nationalist China. Neal, *Dark Horse*, 255, 257.

26. Josephine Pinckney to Wendell Willkie, 19 October [1942], 17 November 1942, Willkie Papers, as quoted in Neal, *Dark Horse*, 261.

27. Pinckney to Willkie, 17 November 1942.

28. Josephine Pinckney to Wendell Willkie, telegram, 19 November 1942; Wendell L. Willkie to Josephine Pinckney, 11 January 1943, Willkie Papers.

29. Neal, *Dark Horse*, 265–66.

30. Josephine Pinckney to Wendell Willkie, 25 November [1942], Willkie Papers.

31. Josephine Pinckney to Wendell Willkie, 22 January [1943], Willkie Papers.

32. Josephine Pinckney to Prentiss Taylor, 17 May [1943], PT/Yale; Josephine Pinckney to Laura M. Bragg, 28 January [1944], LMBP; Josephine Pinckney to Emily Sinkler Roosevelt, 18 February [1944], in the possession of Anne Sinkler Whaley LeClercq.

33. Josephine Pinckney to Hervey Allen, 26 March 1944, HAP.

34. Sidney Lockwood Tynan, interview, 16–17 April 2001; Josephine Pinckney to Wendell L. Willkie, 5 July [1941], Willkie Papers; Wendell Willkie to Josephine Pinckney, 10 December 1941, Willkie Papers.

35. Neal, *Dark Horse*, 285; *New Yorker*, [ca. December 1943], 53.

36. *New Yorker,* [ca. December 1943], 53; Josephine Pinckney to Prentiss Taylor, 23 January 1944, PT/Yale.

37. Eleanor Stone Perenyi, interview, 12 March 1999; Pinckney to Roosevelt, 18 February [1944].

38. Josephine Pinckney to Wendell L. Willkie, 23 April 1944, Willkie Papers.

39. Wendell L. Willkie to Josephine Pinckney, 1 May 1944, Willkie Papers.

40. Neal, *Dark Horse,* 321–23; Josephine Pinckney to Prentiss Taylor, n.d., PT/Yale.

41. Josephine Pinckney to Pascal Covici, 17 April 1945, JP/Viking.

42. Josephine Pinckney to Hervey Allen, 26 March 1944, 23 July [1940], HAP; Grace Stone to Josephine Pinckney, [1943], JPP.

43. Josephine Pinckney to Prentiss Taylor, 30 June 1944, PT/Yale; John Bennett to Josephine Pinckney, 11 January 1945, JBP.

NOTES TO CHAPTER 11

1. Josephine Pinckney to Marshall A. Best, 6 October 1944, Pinckney/Viking; Malcolm Cowley, "Remarks by Malcolm Cowley on the Occasion of a Gathering in Remembrance on April 14, 1982 at the Century Association," *Marshall A. Best, 1901–1982* (New York: A. Colish, 1982), 9; Marshall A. Best, Columbia Oral History Interview, Butler Library, Columbia University; Martha Sue Bean, "A History and Profile of the Viking Press" (M.A. thesis, University of North Carolina, 1969), 46, quoting from *The Viking Ship* (September 1956): 493–97.

2. Josephine Pinckney, *Three O'Clock Dinner* (New York: Viking, 1945; Columbia; University of South Carolina Press, 2001), 14.

3. Henry Seidel Canby to Josephine Pinckney, 2 May, 24 April 1944, JPP.

4. Josephine Pinckney, notes for *Splendid in Ashes,* 1953, JPP.

5. Pascal Covici to Josephine Pinckney, 27 November 1944; Josephine Pinckney to Pascal Covici, 30 November 1944, JPP.

6. Bean, "History and Profile of the Viking Press," 3; Cowley, "Remarks," 9.

7. Josephine Pinckney to Prentiss Taylor, 11 March, 16 March, 20 June 1945, PT/Yale.

8. Pascal Covici to Josephine Pinckney, 25 April 1945, Pinckney/Viking; Susan Pringle Frost to Robert Molloy, 16 June 1945, Robert Molloy Papers, South Caroliniana Library, University of South Carolina.

9. Josephine Pinckney to Pascal Covici, 28 May 1945, 4 June 1945, 17 June 1945, Pinckney/Viking. Pinckney's change of mind might have been inspired by the increasing complaints of Charlestonians, such as Susan Pringle Frost who wrote to Robert Molloy, "I am a bit fed up on Charleston being played up by the writers, perhaps to make money, perhaps to exploit their views. The writers on Charleston speak as if we were a lot of subjects from the zoo, orangutans or some other animal from the jungles, and of our beautiful city as if it were living in the time of the flood and the Ark . . ." Susan Frost to Robert Molloy, 16 June 1945, Molloy Papers.

10. Best, interview, 210; Josephine Pinckney to Marshall Best, 7 July 1945, Pinckney/Viking.

11. Best, interview, 210.

12. Pinckney to Best, 7 July 1945, Pinckney/Viking; John Bennett to "Nanny," 8 June 1945, JBP. Pinckney received about thirty-five cents for every $2.50 book sold under five thousand copies; then the sum was reduced somewhat. Marshall A. Best to Josephine Pinckney, 13 July 1945, Pinckney/Viking.

13. Chard Smith to Josephine Pinckney, 7 October 1945, JPP; Pinckney quoted in Henry Hansen, "The First Reader," *New York World-Telegram,* 14 September 1945.

14. *The Viking Log,* 9 October 1945, clipping in JPP.

15. Jack Harris, "A Very Nice Girl," *Hobo News* 6 [1945], clipping in JPP.

16. Samuel G. Stoney to Josephine Pinckney, [October 1945], JPP; "Overflow Crowd Jams Library for Pinckney Novel Discussion," *Charleston News and Courier*, 9 October 1945.

17. Stoney to Josephine Pinckney, [October 1945].

18. Robert Molloy, "On Three O'Clock Dinner," unidentified clipping, [12 July 1945], JPP.

19. Josephine Pinckney to Prentiss Taylor, 21 September 1945, PT/Yale.

20. Harry McIuraill Jr. to Josephine Pinckney, 8 July 1945; Albert Simons to Josephine Pinckney, n.d., JPP.

21. Josephine Pinckney to Marshall A. Best, 8 September 1945, Pinckney/Viking; Harriet P. Williams, interview, 28 February 2003.

22. Josephine Pinckney to Hervey Allen, 24 September 1945; Hervey Allen to Josephine Pinckney, 5 October 5, 1945, both in HAP.

23. Ellen Glasgow to Josephine Pinckney, 28 October 1945, JPP; unidentified clipping, *Three O'Clock Dinner* file, JPP.

24. "Miss Pinckney Wins Southern Authors Award," *Charleston News and Courier*, 7 January 1946; "Pinckney Novel Among Year's 50 Most Outstanding Books," *Charleston News and Courier*, 3 February 1946; Dorothy Mansfield, "*Great Mischief:* A Report," Book-of-the-Month Club promotional flier for *Great Mischief* (New York, 1948), 4.

25. Clelia Waring to Josephine Pinckney, [ca. July 1945], JPP; W. B. LaVenture to Josephine Pinckney, 7 February 1947, Pinckney/Viking.

26. Prentiss Taylor to Carl Van Vechten, 27 May 1946, Carl Van Vechten Papers, Beinecke Rare Book and Manuscript Library, Yale University.

27. Lula Moore to Josephine Pinckney, n.d., *Three O'Clock Dinner* file, JPP.

28. Lula P. Moore to Josephine Pinckney, 15 September 1945, JPP.

29. Margaret Mitchell to Josephine Pinckney, 2 August 1946, JPP.

30. Josephine Pinckney to Prentiss Taylor, 13 December 1945, PT/Yale; Pascal Covici to Josephine Pinckney, 2 December 1946; Josephine Pinckney to Pascal Covici, 17 June 1945, Viking/JPP.

31. Pascal Covici to Josephine Pinckney, 20 June 1945, Viking/JPP; "Important Story Properties Owned by Metro-Goldwyn-Meyer," Metro-Goldwyn-Meyer *Round-Up of 1945*, n.p., 11, from M-G-M File, Margaret Herrick Library, Fairbanks Center for Motion Picture Study, Beverly Hills, CA.

32. Pascal Covici to John Steinbeck, 22 August 1945, in Thomas Fensch, *Steinbeck and Covici: The Story of a Friendship* (Middlebury, VT: Paul Eriksson, 1979), 55; "Third Novel Award Scheduled," *M-G-M Spot News*, 22 October 1945 , clipping from Herrick Library. The other judges were Harry Hansen of Scripps Howard, Sidney Franklin, an M-G-M producer.

33. Josephine Pinckney to Prentiss Taylor, 21 September 1945, PT/Yale; "Third Novel Award"; "Most Pix Based on Novels," *Variety* (Daily), 25 March 1947.

34. "M.G.M. Schedule Lists Array of 'Best Sellers,'" *Los Angeles Times*, 25 March 1947.

35. Josephine Pinckney to Pascal Covici, June 7, 1945, Pinckney/Viking Papers; Thomas Slater, "Leonore J. Coffee," *Dictionary of Literary Biography*, vol. 44: *American Screen Writers, Second Series* (Detroit: Gale, 1986), 91–97.

36. "'Three O'Clock Dinner' Will Not Stray Far from Novel," *Charleston News and Courier*, 15 May 1946; "World Premier of Film May Be Held Here," *Charleston News and Courier*, 20 March 1947.

37. David Thomson, *Bibliographical Directory of Film*, 3rd ed. (New York: Morrow, 1975), 437, 761–62.

38. Leonore Coffee, "Three O'Clock Dinner," screenplay typescript (Culver City, Calif.: Metro-Goldwyn-Mayer Pictures, 19 February 1947), 125, 133.

39. "'Three O'Clock Dinner' Will Not Stray Far."

40. Josephine Pinckney, scrapbook, JPP.

NOTES TO CHAPTER 12

1. Harold K. Guinzberg to Josephine Pinckney, 2 December 1946, Pinckney/Viking.

2. Pascal Covici to Josephine Pinckney, 2 December 1946, Pinckney/Viking; Josephine Pinckney to Harold K. Guinzberg, 10 December 1946, Pinckney/Viking.

3. Notes, *Great Mischief* file, JPP.

4. During the 1920s, black herbalists still sold their nostrums door-to-door among the white community. "Black roots" in tinctures for colds and "gomo" to enhance male virility were most popular. Although most Low Country blacks asserted that voodoo died off with the "old people of rebel days," many could reveal the addresses of "Doctor-niggers" who could make compounds for all purposes. A lively trade also existed in magic devices, such as specially cut cherry branches that could find dimes for its owner or charms to fend off bad juju. Unidentified clipping, 27 December 1928; "Voodooism Has Its Votaries in Charleston; Dark Magic Unearth," unidentified clipping, n.d., JPP.

5. Notes, *Great Mischief* file. The building Pinckney described still stands at the corner of East Bay and Exchange Street and is currently known as The Tavern liquor store.

6. Ibid.

7. A Catholic priest in Brooklyn complained that Pinckney, who possessed a masterful skill with language, had joined other contemporary artists in giving the Devil the best lines. Partridge, the only speaker for Christianity, appears to be a lunatic. In the priest's opinion, she "confuses superstitious belief in witchcraft with orthodox belief in demonology." The reviewer believed that the author knew not what she was doing, but "likes to play with fire . . . Very dangerous, Miss Pinckney." Clipping, *Great Mischief* file, JPP.

8. "Scheme for a Story," [ca. 1946], *Great Mischief* file, JPP; Lewis Gannett, review of *Great Mischief, New York Herald Tribune,* 22 March 1948.

9. Josephine Pinckney, *Great Mischief* (New York: Viking, 1948), 66. All other references will be marked in the text.

10. Marshall A. Best to Josephine Pinckney, 16 July 1947, 24 July 1947; Pascal Covici to Josephine Pinckney, 25 July 1947; Marshall A. Best to Josephine Pinckney, 27 February 1948, Pinckney/Viking.

11. "Two Charleston Authors Return from Caribbean," *Charleston News and Courier,* 7 March 1948; Josephine Pinckney to Hervey Allen, 23 February 1948, HAP.

12. Josephine Pinckney to Hervey Allen, 2 March 1948, 9 March 1948; Hervey Allen to John Bennett, 26 March 1948, HAP.

13. Prentiss Taylor to Carl Van Vechten, 6 August 1933, Carl Van Vechten Papers, Beinecke Rare Book and Manuscript Library, Yale University; Josephine Pinckney to Prentiss Taylor, 9 April 1948, 26 September 1947, PT/Quiroz.

14. Marshall A. Best to Josephine Pinckney, 5 March 1948, Pinckney/Viking; Dorothy Canfield Fisher, interview, "The Book-of-the-Month Club" (Oral History Research Office, Columbia University, 1956), 106; Josephine Pinckney to Marshall A. Best, 18 April 1948, Pinckney/Viking.

15. Nash K. Burger, "Charleston Poet Emerges as Accomplished Novelist," *The State* (Columbia), 28 March 1948.

16. William McFee to Robert Molloy, 31 March 1948, Molloy Papers; "Bewitched Judges," *Time,* 29 March 1948, 109–10.

17. Josephine Pinckney to Prentiss Taylor, 9 April 1948, PT/Quiroz.

18. The Reverend Horace Westwood, "*Great Mischief* in which Miss Josephine Pinckney deals with 'Good and Evil': A sermon preached in the Unitarian Church, Charleston," 23 January 1949," typescript, JPP.

19. Best to Pinckney, 5 March 1948; Marshall Best to Herbert P. Shippey, 6 October 1975, Pinckney/Viking; Marshall Best, notes on Charleston trip [ca. 22 March 1948], Pinckney/Viking.

20. Marshall Best, Columbia Oral History interview, 211; *Charleston News and Courier*, 23 March 1948; Best, notes on Charleston trip; Pinckney to Taylor, 9 April 1948; "Party in Recognition of Latest Novel of Miss Pinckney Held," *Charleston News and Courier*, 23 March 1948.

21. Best, interview, 211.

22. Pinckney to Best, 18 April 1948, Pinckney/Viking.

23. Josephine Pinckney to Dorothy Heyward, 5 August 1951, DKHP; Samuel G. Stoney to Thomas R. Waring, 2 August 1951, Thomas Waring Jr. Papers, SCHS; George E. Hamlin Jr. to Josephine Pinckney, 2 September 1951; Josephine Pinckney to George E. Hamlin, Jr., 24 December 1951, Pinckney/Viking Papers. George E. Hamlin Jr. was the first associate director of the Dock Street Theatre, coming in 1946 from Case Western Reserve Barn Theatre. A navy veteran from Eastover, South Carolina, Bill Taylor belonged to the first class of the Dock Street's unique theatrical school, which offered training in acting, directing, production, and radio. Taylor was accomplished in both tap and modern dance, as well as being a writer of short stories. He aspired to be a director. Nothing ever came of the musical version of *Great Mischief.* "Hamlin Resigns as Director of Dock Street Theatre," *Charleston News and Courier*, 28 April 1951; "Actress's Day Would Balk a Stevedore, But She Does It Without Missing a Cue," *Charleston News and Courier*, 5 December 1948; Betty Vaughn Millar, "Back Stage—On Stage—Up Stage," *South Carolina Magazine* 11 (June 1948): 10, 24.

24. "Scheme for a Story," [ca. 1946], notes in JPP.

25. Bertram Wyatt-Brown, Introduction to W. J. Cash, *The Mind of the South* (New York: Vintage Books, 1991), xiii, xvii.

26. Thomas R. Waring Jr. to Josephine Pinckney, 26 October 1951, Waring Jr. Papers.

27. Josephine Pinckney, notebook, 1953, JPP.

28. Robert N. S. Whitelaw to Lincoln Kirstein, 29 November 1946, CAA/Dock Street Papers, SCHS.

29. Thomas A. Underwood, *Allen Tate: Orphan of the South* (Princeton: Princeton University Press, 2000), 183.

30. Robert N. S. Whitelaw to Lincoln Kirstein, 21 November 1946; Lincoln Kirstein to Robert N. S. Whitelaw, 26 November 1946, CAA/Dock Street Papers.

31. Robert N. S. Whitelaw to Lincoln Kirstein, 1 December 1946; Lincoln Kirstein to Robert Whitelaw, 1 December 1946, CAA/Dock Street Papers.

32. Lincoln Kirstein to Robert Whitelaw, 25 November 1946; Lincoln Kirstein to Robert Whitelaw, 1 January 1947, CAA/Dock Street Papers.

33. Robert N. S. Whitelaw to Lincoln Kirstein, 6 January 1947; Robert N. S. Whitelaw to John Stuart Dudley, 20 January 1947, CAA/Dock Street Papers.

34. Lincoln Kirstein to Robert N. S. Whitelaw, 1 February 1947, CAA/Dock Street Papers.

35. Robert N. S. Whitelaw to Paul Green, 8 March 1949, CAA/Dock Street Papers.

36. "The Garden," notes for historical play at Middleton Gardens, JPP.

37. S. Foster Damon, *Amy Lowell* (Boston: Houghton Mifflin, 1935), 626; Amy Lowell, "Southern Spring," *Poetry* 21 (December 1922): 117–24; Amy Lowell to Harriet Monroe, 16 January 1923, as quoted in Damon, *Amy Lowell,* 597. Lowell's poems stirred a riot of protest from Charleston subscribers to

*Poetry*. She wrote to Allen acknowledging that "I seem to have stirred up a hornet's nest and I am awfully upset about it. They were so hospitable and kind to me in Charleston that I fear any expression of disagreement with the beauty of their cherished garden was almost an act of lese majeste. Needless to say, I would not have committed such an act—and yet that is not quite true. I suppose that I knew at the time that I was committing just that." Amy Lowell to Hervey Allen, 16 January 1923, ALP.

38. Robert N. S. Whitelaw to John Stuart Dudley, 14 December 1946, 20 January 1947; Virginia L. Sterling to Robert N. S. Whitelaw, 6 December 1946, CAA/Dock Street Papers.

39. Robert R. Weyeneth, *Historic Preservation for a Living City* (Columbia: University of South Carolina Press, 2000), 35, 46, 49.

40. *Charleston News and Courier*, 18 January 1947; Minutes of the regular meeting of the Medical Society of South Carolina, 14 January 1947, Waring Library, Medical University of South Carolina; Josephine Pinckney to Dorothy Kuhns Heyward, 7 February [1956], DKHP. Pinckney and Dorothy Heyward cosponsored a young woman attending Claflin College in Orangeburg, South Carolina.

41. Miscellaneous ms., Harriet P. Simons file, ASP.

42. Josephine Pinckney to Wendell Willkie, 25 November [1942], Wendell L. Willkie Papers, Lilly Library, Indiana University.

43. John Gunther, *Inside USA* (New York: Harper and Brothers, 1947), 724–25.

44. Josephine Pinckney, "The Palmetto State," *Transatlantic*, undated clipping, JPP.

45. Ibid.

46. Josephine Pinckney to Prentiss Taylor, 23 July 1948, PT/Quiroz.

47. Ibid.

48. Harriet P. Simons to "Mary," 10 February 1952, ASP; "A Judge Worthy of Honor," *New York Times*, 6 February 1952. At the time of his retirement from the bench in 1952 (at the first moment he could do so at full pay), the *New York Times* hailed Waring and criticized Charlestonians who "ostracized themselves out of his excellent company." Harriet P. Simons wrote to *Times* publisher Arthur Sulzberger with a chronology of Waring's career and personal history, emphasizing his early support of white supremacist "Cotton Ed" Smith for the U.S. Senate and also the fact that he had lived for sixty-five years, holding positions of power in the state and never doing a thing for South Carolina Negroes. Harriet P. Simons to Arthur Sulzberger, 10 February 1952, ASP.

49. *Charleston News and Courier*, 17 January 1950, as quoted in William D. Smyth, "Segregation in Charleston in the 1950s: A Decade of Transition," *SCHM* 92 (1991): 103; Josephine Pinckney, miscellaneous notes on family, JPP.

50. Josephine Pinckney to Marshall A. Best, 11 July 1948, Pinckney/Viking; Josephine Pinckney to Prentiss Taylor, 23 July 1948, PT/Yale; Josephine Pinckney to Marshall A. Best, 19 April 1948, Pinckney/Viking.

51. Tibor Koeves to Josephine Pinckney, 16 January 1949, JPP.

NOTES TO CHAPTER 13

1. Charleston *News and Courier*, [January 1952], clippings, JPP; Carl Van Vechten, "Some 'Literary Ladies' I Have Known," *Yale University Library Gazette* 26 (January 1952): 109.

2. Josephine Pinckney, miscellaneous notes, *My Son and Foe* file, JPP; Beatrice St. Julien Ravenel, "Miss Pinckney's Fourth Novel Appears This Week," *Charleston News and Courier*, 6 January 1952; Mikell Waring, "Want to Write a Book? It Takes Perspicacity," *Richmond Times-Dispatch*, 31 October 1948. Marshall Best implored Pinckney to make sure she was "satisfied in your soul" that "no living

person can identify himself and take offense" at her story. Marshall A. Best to Josephine Pinckney, 3 October 1951, JPP.

3. Josephine Pinckney, miscellaneous notes, *My Son and Foe* file, JPP; Waring, "Want to Write a Book."

4. Pascal Covici to Josephine Pinckney, 23 June 1948, Pinckney/Viking.

5. Tibor Koeves, "Symbols Wearing Pants," *United Nations World* (December 1948), 2–4.

6. Waring, "Want to Write a Book?"; Josephine Pinckney to Marshall A. Best, 29 October 1948, 1 April 1949, Pinckney/Viking; Josephine to Marshall A. Best, 1 April 1949; Josephine Pinckney to Laura M. Bragg, 6 June 1948, LMBP; Josephine Pinckney, "Bird Thou Never Wert," ms., JPP.

7. Pascal Covici to Josephine Pinckney, 21 November 1949, Pinckney/Viking; Dorothy Heyward to Rumer Godden, 16 August [1951], DKHP.

8. Josephine Pinckney to Dorothy Heyward, n.d., DKHP.

9. Josephine Pinckney to Laura M. Bragg, 18 October 1951, LMBP; "Miss Pinckney is Back from European Trip," *Charleston News and Courier,* 11 November 1951; Marshall A. Best to Josephine Pinckney, 7 September 1951, Pinckney/Viking.

10. William Raney to Josephine Pinckney, 8 July 1952, JPP.

11. Orville Prescott, review of *My Son and Foe, New York Times,* 11 January 1952; Lewis Gannett, review of *My Son and Foe, New York Herald-Tribune,* 11 January 1952.

12. Josephine Pinckney to Pascal Covici, 3 May [1951]; Marshall A. Best to Josephine Pinckney, 27 June 1951, Pinckney/Viking; Josephine Pinckney, *Son and Foe,* notes on writing, JPP.

13. Josephine Pinckney, notebook, 1953, JPP.

14. Ibid.

15. Josephine Pinckney, "Credo," notebook, 1953; Josephine Pinckney, notes, *Splendid in Ashes,* 1953, JPP.

16. Josephine Pinckney, "Scandals," notebook, 7 November 1949, JPP.

17. Josephine Pinckney, *Splendid in Ashes* (New York: Viking Press, 1958), 190.

18. Pinckney slipped some of her own belongings into the Grimshawe home, such as her sleigh bed. One of their family treasures, a pastel of Augustus's "little grandfather" in his green velveteen suit and red shoes, actually hung in the living room of 36 Chalmers Street. This was the portrait of five-year-old Cotesworth Pinckney Sr. painted when his father General Thomas was ambassador to the court of St. James.

19. An international adventurer of Russian heritage named Serge Alexandre Stavisky was involved in a scheme in 1933 through which he absconded with $25 million in bonds. The entire justice system of France came under public attack when police complicity with Stavisky was revealed. Stavisky shot himself just as he was about to be apprehended near Chamonix, but public outrage lived on. Riots fueled by further revelations of official involvement brought down the government of two prime ministers.

20. Pinckney's interest in South America had been piqued by her trip to Peru with Dorothy Heyward to view a 1955 revival of *Porgy and Bess* in Lima. In searching for a situation in which Grimshawe's fortune might disappear overnight, Pinckney consulted Macy's Department Store magnate Oswald Knauth, a member of the winter colony in Beaufort. Knauth referred her to Rudolph Groenman, a Dutchman who was the expert on Latin America exchange for the International Monetary Fund. Gordon Williams to Oswald Knauth, 23 February 1955, JPP.

21. The specifics of Grimshawe's will were drawn from those written by Mary Jane Ross, a wealthy Charleston woman with ties to Philadelphia, who died in 1922 leaving a large estate with bequests to many Charleston charities and public institutions. She stipulated however that her family's three-storied

Victorian style home at One Meeting Street be made the Ross Memorial Museum to honor her two dead brothers, and maintained in excellent condition. The exhibits would be comprised exclusively of her extensive collections of family silver, rare books, and other artifacts she had picked up during her vast travels: nothing could be added, nothing deleted. Pinckney had actually been involved in evaluating Ross's embroideries, lace, fabrics, and porcelains. In 1929, the Ross Memorial Museum opened to the public, but in 1935 Roper Hospital of Charleston and the Presbyterian Hospital of Philadelphia brought suit claiming that the collection was too inferior to justify a museum. In November 1943, her will was abrogated and the remnants of her collection were auctioned off, with the proceeds disbursed among to the various institutions with claims on the estate including the Charleston Library Society. Annie M. James, *Ross Memorial Museum* (Charleston: privately printed, 1928); *Charleston News and Courier*, 24 February 1929; 24 November 1940.

22. Josephine Pinckney to Dorothy K. Heyward, 19 March 1956, DKHP.

23. Josephine Pinckney to Marshall A. Best, 14 September, 23 September 1957, JPP.

24. Josephine Pinckney to Laura M. Bragg, 5 September 1957, LMBP; Josephine Pinckney to Marshall A. Best, 31 August 1957, Pinckney/Viking; Eleanor Stone Perenyi, interview, 12 March 1999; Josephine Pinckney to Patti Foos Whitelaw, 27 September [1957], Robert N. S. Whitelaw Papers, SCHS; Charles B. Hosmer Jr., *Preservation Comes of Age: From Williamsburg to the National Trust, 1926–1949* (Charlottesville: University Press of Virginia, 1981), 67–68. Whitelaw experimented with historic methods of brick-making to replicate those used in old Low Country homes.

25. Pinckney to Whitelaw, 27 September [1957]; Perenyi, interview; George W. Williams, interview, 18 March 2003.

26. Marshall A. Best, Columbia Oral History Interview, Butler Library, Columbia University.

27. Isabella Breckinridge, interview, 18 June 2001. Mary Martin Hendricks, review of *Splendid in Ashes*, clipping from *Pittsfield Eagle*, Thomas R. Waring Jr. Papers, SCHS; Amelia Moore Taylor, interview, 20 April 2000; Josephine Pinckney to Patti Foos Whitelaw, n.d., Whitelaw Papers; Breckinridge, interview.

28. Hendricks, review of *Splendid in Ashes*. For example, the name of the character "Thomas York" is a veiled reference to Thomas Richard Waring Sr. Richard of York was prominent in the War of the Roses.

29. Josephine Pinckney, *Splendid in Ashes* (New York: Viking, 1958), 268; Marshall A. Best to Herbert P. Shippey, 16 October 1975, Pinckney/Viking.

30. Marion Canby to Laura Bragg, 20 January 1958, LMBP; "In Memoriam," *Charleston News and Observer*, [October 1958], clipping, DKHP; Taylor, interview.

31. Albert Simons to James Grote Van Derpool, 3 February 1958; Albert Simons to Mrs. Morton Morris Pinckney, 3 February 1958, ASP.

32. "Posthumous Award Given to Josephine Pinckney," [15 March 1958], unidentified clipping, DKHP; Robert R. Weyeneth, *Historic Preservation for a Living City* (Columbia, SC: University of South Carolina Press, 2000), 49; Mrs. Edward Holden, interview, 17 January 2000; Prentiss Taylor to Laura M. Bragg, [Christmas 1957], LMBP; Prentiss Taylor to Helen G. McCormack, 12 February 1958, CAA.

33. Larry Winship to Thomas R. Waring Jr., 25 April 1958, Waring Jr. Papers; "Virginia Kirkus review of *Splendid in Ashes* by Josephine Pinckney, to be published April 14 [1958]," in Pinckney/Viking Papers; *Saturday Review of Literature*, clipping [ca. April 1958]; Florence Haxton Bullock, "Wit Lights the Scene in Miss Pinckney's Last Novel," *New York Herald-Tribune*, [ca. March 1958], JPP.

34. Hendricks, review of *Splendid in Ashes;* Best, interview, 211; Harold Seltzer to the editor, *Charleston News and Courier*, 9 June 1958.

35. Marshall A. Best to Dr. Morris M. Pinckney, 10 October 1958, JPP.

36. Clelia Waring to Best, [ca. 31 January 1958], Pinckney/Viking. A spot called "Grimshawes" actually exists near Flat Rock, North Carolina.

37. Marshall A. Best to Clelia Waring, 29 January 1958, Pinckney/Viking.

38. Dr. Morris M. Pinckney to Marshall A. Best, 31 March 1958; Marshall A. Best to Clelia Waring, 29 January 1958, Pinckney/Viking.

39. Amy Lowell to Hervey Allen, 11 September 1923, ALP; Josephine Pinckney, notebook [1954], JPP.

# Bibliography

CHRONOLOGICAL LISTING OF WORKS BY JOSEPHINE PINCKNEY

"The Cost of a Chance." *College of Charleston Magazine* (April 1919): 111–15.

*Sea-Drinking Cities.* New York: Harper and Brothers, 1927.

"A Group of Southern Poets." Review of *Fugitives: An Anthology of Verse. Charleston Evening Post,* [ca. 1929], clipping, JPP.

Review of Vachel Lindsay, *Johnny Appleseed and Other Poems. Saturday Review of Literature,* 20 April 1929.

Review of *Slave Songs of the United States. Saturday Review of Literature,* 23 May 1929.

"Two Poets." Review of Louis Golding, *Prophet and Fool,* and Alfred Kreymborg, *Manhattan Man. Saturday Review of Literature,* 6 July 1929.

"Charleston's Poetry Society." *Sewanee Review* (January 1930): 50–56.

"Southern Writers' Congress." *Saturday Review of Literature* (7 November 1931), 266.

"Jeffers and MacLeish." *Virginia Quarterly Review* (July 1932): 443–47.

"American Folk Songs." Review of George Pullen Jackson, *White Spirituals of the Southern Uplands. Saturday Review of Literature,* 9 September 1933, 96.

"On Being Poor, Then Rich, Then Poor Again." Review of Katherine Ball Ripley, *Sand Dollars. New York Herald,* 15 October 1933, 5.

"A Charleston Intellectual." Review of Linda Rhea, *Hugh Swinton Legaré: A Charleston Intellectual. New York Herald Tribune Books,* 1 April 1934.

Review of Alice Lide and Margaret Alison Johansen, *Dark Possession. Saturday Review of Literature,* 19 May 1934.

"A 'Furriner' Writes of Life in Alabama." Review of Carl Carmer, *Stars Fell on Alabama. Saturday Review of Literature,* 30 June 1934, 781.

"They Shall Return as Strangers." *Virginia Quarterly Review* (October 1934): 540–57.

"Bulwarks against Change." In *Culture in the South,* edited by W. T. Couch. Chapel Hill: University of North Carolina Press, 1934.

*Call Back Yesterday: The First Twenty-Five Years of Ashley Hall.* Charleston, SC: Quinn Press, 1934.

"Street Cries of Charleston." *Town and Country,* 1 March 1936, 49.

"The Marchant of London and the Treacherous Don." *Virginia Quarterly Review* (April 1936): 207–19.

*Hilton Head.* New York: Farrar and Rinehart, 1941.

*Three O'Clock Dinner.* New York: Viking Press, 1945.

"The Story behind the Story." *Wings: Literary Guild Review* (October 1945): 4–12.

"Palmetto State." *Transatlantic*, [1945], clipping, JPP.

*Great Mischief.* New York: Viking Press, 1948.

Review of Stringfellow Barr, *Citizens of the World. Charleston News and Courier*, 16 November 1952.

*My Son and Foe.* New York: Viking, 1952.

"The Literature of South Carolina." *Charleston News and Courier*, 11 January 1953, 13.

*Splendid in Ashes.* New York: Viking, 1958.

"DuBose Heyward." *Dictionary of American Biography*, Supplement 9, 303. New York: Scribner's, 1971–75.

PRIMARY SOURCES

*Published Materials*

Anderson, Sherwood. *Letters of Sherwood Anderson.* Edited by Howard Mumford Jones in association with Walter B. Rideout. Boston: Little, Brown, 1953.

Avary, Myrta Lockett. *Dixie after the War.* 1906. Reprint, New York: Negro Universities Press, 1969.

Barnwell, Joseph W. "Captain Thomas Pinckney." [An address delivered at the anniversary meeting of Camp Sumter, United Confederate Veterans, Charleston, SC, on 12 April 1916.] *Confederate Veteran* 24 (August 1916): 342.

Bellaman, Henry. "The Literary Highway." *The State*, 26 February 1928.

Bennett, John. "Apothecaries' Hall: A Unique Exhibit of the Charleston Museum." *Contributions from the Charleston Museum* 4 (1923): 15–16.

Brown, Barbara Trigg. "Two Houses in the Old Charleston Manner." *Arts and Decoration*, 51(November 1939): 18–21, 35.

Browne, Thomas. "Dedication to Thomas LeGros of Crostwick Esquire." In *Hydriotaphia, Urne-Burial; or, A Discourse of the Sephulchrall Urnes lately found in Norfolk.* London: Printed for Henry Brome, 1669.

Cabell, James Branch. *Between Friends: Letters of James Branch Cabell and Others.* Edited by Padraic Colum and Margaret Freeman Cabell. New York: Harcourt, Brace, and World, 1962.

Canby, Henry Seidel. "Adventures in Starting a Literary Magazine." In *The Saturday Review Treasury,* edited by John Haverstick, 301–14. New York: Simon and Schuster, 1957.

———. *American Memoir.* Boston: Houghton Mifflin, 1947.

Carroll, Ellen." The Poetry Society: New Charleston Institution a High Moral Force for the Community." *Charleston Sunday News,* 26 December 1920.

Carter, Henry H. *Early History of the Santee Club.* N.p.: n.p., 1934. [Photocopy in SCHS.]

Cash, Wilbur Joseph. *The Mind of the South.* New York: Knopf, 1941.

Chesnut, Mary Boykin. *Mary Chesnut's Civil War.* Edited by C. Vann Woodward. New Haven: Yale University Press, 1981.

Cheves, Langdon. *The Shaftsbury Papers and Other Records Relating to Carolina and the First Settlement on the Ashley River.* 1898. Reprint, Charleston: South Carolina Historical Society, 2000.

Clark, Emily. *Innocence Abroad.* 1931. Reprint, Westport CT: Greenwood Press, 1975.

———. "Richmond." *The Reviewer* (October 1922): 623–31.

Coffee, Leonore. "Three O'Clock Dinner." Screenplay typescript. Culver City, CA: Metro-Goldwyn-Mayer Pictures, 19 February 1947.

Colum, Mary Maguire. *Life and the Dream.* Garden City, NY: Doubleday, 1947.

Colum, Padraic. "A.E." *Irish Literary Portraits,* ed. W. R. Rogers, 186–203. London: British Broadcast Corporation, 1972.

Cowardin, Col. Charles O'B. "A Typical Virginia Matron." *Richmond Times-Dispatch,* 20 October 1899.

Cowley, Malcolm. "Remarks by Malcolm Cowley on the Occasion of a Gathering in Remembrance on April 14, 1982 at the Century Association." In *Marshall A. Best, 1901–1982.* New York: A. Colish, 1982.

Dane, Dorothy. "*Porgy* Best Southern Book in Decade, Says Dr. Canby." *Charleston News and Courier,* 15 March 1927.

Davidson, Donald. "The Artist as Southerner." *Saturday Review of Literature,* 15 May 1926, 781–83.

———. "Josephine Pinckney: *Sea-Drinking Cities.*" In *The Spyglass: Views and Reviews, 1924–1930,* ed. John Tyree Fain, 111–13. Nashville: Vanderbilt University Press, 1963.

———. "Josephine Pinckney's Poetry Glows with Sunny Luxuriance of Imagery from Nature and the Life about Her." *Charleston Evening Post,* 30 September 1928.

———. "A Meeting of Southern Writers." *Bookman* 68 (November 1931): 495.

———. "South Carolina Poets." *Nashville Tennessean,* 10 February 1924.

———. "The Southern Poet and His Tradition." *Poetry* 40 (May 1932): 96.

———. *Southern Writers in the Modern World.* Athens: University of Georgia Press, 1958.

———. *The Tall Men.* Boston: Houghton Mifflin, 1927.

Deutsch, Babette. "A Southern Voice." *New York Herald-Tribune Books,* 5 February 1928.

Eastman, Max. *Enjoyment of Living.* New York: Harper and Co., 1948.

Fain, John Tyree, and Thomas Daniel Young, eds. *The Literary Correspondence of Donald Davidson and Allen Tate.* Athens: University of Georgia Press, 1974.

Fensch, Thomas. *Steinbeck and Covici: The Story of a Friendship.* Middlebury, VT: Paul Eriksson, 1979.

Fisher, Dorothy Canfield. "*Great Mischief:* A Report." Book-of-the-Month Club Promotion Flier for *Great Mischief.* New York, 1948.

Glasgow, Ellen. "An Experiment in the South." In *Ellen Glasgow's Reasonable Doubts: A Collection of Her Writings,* edited by Julius Rowan Raper. Baton Rouge: Louisiana State University Press, 1988.

———. *Letters of Ellen Glasgow.* Compiled and edited by Blair Rouse. New York: Harcourt Brace, 1958.

Gonzales, Ambrose E. *The Black Border: Gullah Stories of the Carolina Coast.* Columbia, SC: The State Company, 1922.

Hemphill, James Calvin, ed. "Thomas Pinckney." In *Men of Mark in South Carolina: A Collection of Biographies Leading Men in the State.* Vol. 3. Washington, DC: Men of Mark, 1907–9.

Hergesheimer, Joseph. "The Feminine Nuisance in American Literature." *The Yale Review,* n.s., 10 (1921): 716–25.

Hervey, Harry. *The Damned Don't Cry.* New York: Sun Dial Press, 1942.

Heyward, DuBose. "A New Theory of Historical Fiction." *Publishers Weekly* 13 (1932): 511–12.

Hibbard, Addison. *The Lyric South: An Anthology of Recent Poetry from the South.* New York: Macmillan, 1928.

Howe, Florence Thompson. "The Charleston Home of Josephine Pinckney." *Antiques* 49 (May 1946): 307–9.

Howe, Mark Anthony DeWolfe. "The Song of Charleston." *Atlantic Monthly* (July 1930): 109–10.

Irvin, James Wallace. "Cow-boy (Hervey) Allen of Charleston." *Literary Digest* (11 August 1934): 20.

James, Annie M. *Ross Memorial Museum.* Charleston: n.p., 1928.

Johnson, Gerald W. "The Congo, Mr. Mencken." *The Reviewer* 3 (July 1923): 890.

Johnston, Mary. "Richmond and Writing." *The Reviewer* 1 (15 February 1921): 10–11.

Judge, Jane. "Old Spirituals Sung at Theatre." *Savannah Morning News,* 17 February 1924.

Keith, John A. C. *J. A. C. Keith Remembers.* N.p.: n.p, 1970.

Knickerbocker, William S. "Designs for Dixie." *The Commonweal* (17 August 1934): 384–85.

Koeves, Tibor. "Symbols Wearing Pants." *United Nations World* (December 1948), 2–4.

Kreymborg, Alfred. *Our Singing Strength: An Outline of American Poetry.* New York: Coward-McCann, 1929.

"The Literary Spotlight: Henry Seidel Canby." *Bookman* 60 (September 1924): 66–70.

Leiding, Harriette Kershaw. *Historic Houses of Charleston.* Philadelphia: Lippincott, 1921.

Leverett Family. *The Leverett Letters: Correspondence of a South Carolina Family, 1851–1868.* Edited by Frances Wallace Taylor, Catherine Taylor Matthews, and J. Tracy Power. Columbia: University of South Carolina Press, 2000.

Lynes, Russell. "Highbrow, Middlebrow, Lowbrow." *Harper's Magazine* (1960): 19–28.

Magee, William Kirkpatrick [John Eglinton]. *A Memoir of AE: George William Russell.* London: Macmillan, 1937.

Mencken, Henry L. *My Life as Author and Editor.* Reprint, New York: Alfred Knopf, 1992.

———. *Prejudices: Second Series.* 1920. Reprint, Octagon Books, 1977.

Monroe, Harriet. "Young Charleston." *Poetry* 32 (June 1928): 162–65.

Pinckney, Eliza Lucas. *The Letterbook of Eliza Lucas Pinckney, 1739–1762.* Edited by Elise Pinckney. Columbia: University of South Carolina Press, 1997.

Poetry Society of South Carolina. *Year Book.* Charleston, 1921–31.

Priestly, J. B. "JH." In *Contemporary American Authors,* edited by J. C. Squire. New York: Holt, 1928.

Pringle, Patience [Elizabeth Waties Allston Pringle]. *A Woman Rice Planter.* New York: Macmillan, 1914.

Ramey, Emily G., and John Gott. *The Years of Anguish: Fauquier County 1861–65.* Collected and compiled for the Civil War Centennial Committee with the editorial assistance of Gertrude Trumbo and John Eisenhard. Warrenton, VA: Civil War Centennial Committee, 1965.

Ravenel, Mrs. St. Julian. *Charleston: The Place and the People.* New York: Macmillan, 1912.

Rice, Alice C. "Josephine Pinckney Works on New Volume of Poetry." *Charleston News and Courier,* 25 February 1931.

Rittenhouse, Jessie B. *My House of Life: An Autobiography.* Boston: Houghton Mifflin, 1934.

Rutledge, Archibald. *My Colonel and His Lady.* Indianapolis: Bobbs Merrill, 1937.

Scarborough, Dorothy. "The South: Her Level of Culture." *New York Times Book Review,* 1 April 1934.

Smith, Alice Ravenel Huger. "Written at Harry's Behest." In *The Charleston Renaissance,* edited by Martha Severens. Spartanburg, SC: Saraland Press, 1998.

Smith, Alice R. Huger, and D. E. Huger Smith. *The Dwelling Houses of Charleston, South Carolina.* New York: Diadem Books, 1917.

Smythe, Augustine T. *The Carolina Low-country.* New York: Macmillan, 1931.

Snowdon, Yates, and John Bennett. *Two Scholarly Friends: Yates Snowdon–John Bennett Correspondence, 1902–1932.* Edited by Mary Crow Anderson. Columbia: University of South Carolina Press, 1993.

Stallings, Laurence. "Cahiers de Compagne." *New York Sun,* 27 October 1932.

Stoney, Samuel Gaillard, and Gertrude Mathews Shelby. *Black Genesis: A Chronicle.* New York: Macmillan, 1930.

Untermeyer, Louis. *From Another World: The Autobiography of Louis Untermeyer.* New York: Harcourt, Brace, 1939.

Tate, Allen. "Last Days of a Charming Lady." *Nation* (28 October 1925): 485–86.

———. "Poetry in the South." *The Lyric* 11 (Winter 1932): 14.

———. "A View of the Whole South." *The American Review* 2 (November–March 1933–34): 416.

"Third Novel Award Scheduled." *M-G-M Spot News,* 22 October 1945.

U.S. War Department. *The War of the Rebellion: A Compilation of the Official Records of the Union and Confederate Armies,* Series I, Part 1: *Reports.* Vol. 12. Washington: Government Printing Office, 1885.

Van Vechten, Carl. "How I Remember Joseph Hergesheimer." *Yale University Library Gazette* 22 (January 1948): 87–92.

———. "Pastiches et Pistaches." *The Reviewer* (January 1924): 98–99.

———. "Some 'Literary Ladies' I Have Known." *Yale University Library Gazette* 26 (January 1952): 97–116.

Warner, Sylvia Townsend. *Lolly Willowes; or, The Loving Huntsman.* New York: Viking Press, 1926.

Wilmer, Richard Hooker. *In Memoriam: Mary Stewart Pinckney.* Richmond: West, Johnston, 1889.

Young, Stark. *A Southern Treasury of Life and Literature.* New York: Charles Scribner's Sons, 1937.

### Manuscripts

Abbeville County (SC) Probate Office. Will Book 4:500.

Allen, Hervey. Papers. Special Collections, Hillman Library, University of Pittsburgh.

Ball, William Watts. Papers. Perkins Library, Duke University.

Bennett, John. Papers. South Carolina Historical Society, Charleston.

Best, Marshall A. Interview typescript. Oral History Research Project, Columbia University.

Bragg, Laura M. Papers. South Carolina Historical Society, Charleston.

Canby, Henry Seidel. Papers. Beinecke Rare Book and Manuscript Library, Yale University.

Carolina Art Association/Dock Street Theatre Papers, South Carolina Historical Society, Charleston.

Charleston County (SC) Probate Office. Wills of Captain Thomas Pinckney (1915), Camilla Pinckney (1928), Josephine Pinckney (1957).

Cheves-Middleton Family. Papers. South Carolina Historical Society, Charleston.

Cheves, Langdon. Papers. South Carolina Historical Society, Charleston.

Davidson, Donald. Papers. Special Collections. Vanderbilt University Library.

Farrar, John. Papers. Beinecke Rare Book and Manuscript Library. Yale University.

Fisher, Dorothy Canfield. Interview. "The Book-of-the-Month Club" (1956). Oral History Research Project. Columbia University.

Gibbes Art Gallery Visitors Book. Gibbes Museum of Art Archives, Charleston, SC.

Grace Episcopal Church (Charleston, SC) Parish Register, 1846–1971. Microfilm. Charleston County Public Library.

Heyward, Dorothy Kuhn. Papers. South Carolina Historical Society, Charleston.

Heyward, DuBose. Papers. South Carolina Historical Society, Charleston.

Keith Family. Papers. Virginia Historical Society, Richmond.

Lockwood, Caroline Sinkler. Scrapbook. In the possession of Sidney Lockwood Tynan.

Lowell, Amy. Papers. Houghton Library, Harvard University.

Lowell Correspondence. Berg Collection, New York Public Library.

Mencken, Henry Louis. Papers. New York Public Library.

Metro-Goldwyn-Mayer (MGM) file. Margaret Herrick Library, Fairbanks Center for Motion Picture Study, Beverly Hills, California.

Mitchell and Horlbeck Law Firm. Papers. South Carolina Historical Society, Charleston.

Molloy, Robert. Papers. South Caroliniana Library, University of South Carolina.

Monroe, Harriet. Personal Papers. University of Chicago Library.

——. *Poetry* Papers. University of Chicago Library.

Peterkin, Julia. Papers. South Carolina Historical Society, Charleston.

——. Director's Correspondence. Charleston Museum Archives.

Pinckney, Charles Cotesworth, Jr. Papers. In Pinckney/Means/Brady Papers, South Carolina Historical Society, Charleston.

Pinckney, Josephine. Papers. South Carolina Historical Society, Charleston.

Pinckney, Thomas. *My Reminiscences of the War and Reconstruction Times.* Galley proofs. Alderman Library, Special Collections, University of Virginia.

Poetry Society of South Carolina. Papers. Archives. The Citadel.

Ravenel, Harriott Horry. Papers. South Carolina Historical Society, Charleston.

Richmond (VA) Chancery Book. Will of Charles Cotesworth Pinckney (1934).

Roosevelt, Eleanor. Papers. Roosevelt Library. Hyde Park, NY.

Roosevelt, Nicholas and Emily S. Correspondence. In the possession of Anne Sinkler Whaley LeClercq.

Sass, Herbert Ravenel. Papers, South Carolina Historical Society, Charleston.

Scott, Robert Taylor. Papers. In Keith Family Papers. Virginia Historical Society, Richmond.

Simons, Albert. Papers. South Carolina Historical Society, Charleston.

Smith, Heningham Ellet. Papers. Middleton Plantation Archives, Charleston, SC.

Society for the Preservation of Spirituals. Papers. South Carolina Historical Society, Charleston.

Stone, Grace. Papers. Howard Gottleib Archival Research Center, Mugar Memorial Library, Boston University.

Stoney Family Papers/Smythe-Stoney-Adger Papers. South Carolina Historical Society, Charleston.

Stoney/Popham Family. Papers. South Carolina Historical Society, Charleston.

Taliaferro, Sallie L. Papers. In the General William Booth Taliaferro Papers. Special Collections, Swem Library, College of William and Mary.

Tate, Allen. Papers. Firestone Library, Princeton University.

Taylor, Prentiss. Papers. Beinecke Rare Book and Manuscript Library, Yale University.

——. Diary. Manuscript in possession of Roderick Quiroz.

U.S. Census, 1860. South Carolina: Saint James Santee.

——, 1910. South Carolina: City of Charleston.

Van Doren, Irita. Papers. Library of Congress.

Van Vechten, Carl. Papers. Beinecke Rare Book and Manuscript Library, Yale University.

Viking Press Papers. Pinckney Correspondence. South Caroliniana Library, University of South Carolina.

*Virginia Quarterly Review* Papers, 1935–1954. Alderman Library, University of Virginia.

Waring, Thomas R., Sr. Papers. South Carolina Historical Society, Charleston.

Waring, Thomas R., Jr. Papers. South Carolina Historical Society, Charleston.

Whitelaw, Robert N. S. Papers. South Carolina Historical Society, Charleston.

Willkie, Wendell L. Papers. Lilly Library, Indiana University.

Wills of Charleston County, SC. WPA typescript in Charleston Public Library. Book 33C (1807–1818); Book 38B (1826–1834); Book 43B (1839–45).

Wilson, James Southall. Papers. Alderman Library. University of Virginia.

———. Southern Writers' Conference Papers. Special Collections, Alderman Library. University of Virginia.

### *Newspapers/Magazines Consulted*

*Charleston Evening Post*

*Charleston News and Courier*

*The College of Charleston Magazine*

*Contemporary Verse*

*The Fugitive* (Nashville)

*Literary Lantern*

*The Lyric* (Norfolk)

*New York Herald-Tribune*

*New York Times*

*Poetry Magazine*

Poetry Society of America, *Bulletin.*

*The Reviewer* (Richmond)

*Richmond Dispatch*

*Richmond Whig*

*Saturday Review of Literature*

*Sewanee Review* (Tennessee)

*Variety*

*Warrenton, Virginia Times-Index*

## Secondary Sources

Allen, Louise Anderson. *A Bluestocking in Charleston: The Life and Career of Laura Bragg.* Columbia: University of South Carolina Press, 2001.

"Amy Lowell." *Dictionary of Literary Biography,* vol. 140: *American Book-Collectors and Bibliographers, First Series,* edited by Joseph Rosenbaum, 141–46. Detroit: Gale, 1994.

Barnard, Ellsworth. *Wendell Willkie: Fighter for Freedom.* Marquette: Northern Michigan University Press, 1966.

Baughman, James L. *Henry R. Luce and the Rise of the American News Media.* Boston: Twayne, 1988.

Bean, Martha Sue. "A History and Profile of the Viking Press." M.A. thesis, University of North Carolina, 1969.

Bellows, Barbara L. "The Lowcountry Lady and the Over-the-Mountain Man: Josephine Pinckney, Donald Davidson, and the Burden of Southern Literature." In *Renaissance in Charleston: Art and Life in the Carolina Low Country, 1900–1940,* edited by James M. Hutchisson and Harlan Greene. Athens: University of Georgia Press, 2003.

Benvenuto, Richard. *Amy Lowell.* Boston: Twayne, 1985.

Blotner, Joseph Leo. *Faulkner: A Biography.* New York: Random House, 1984.

Bowers, Claude G. *Beveridge and the Progressive Era.* New York: Literary Guild, 1932.

Bridges, Anne Baker Leland, and Roy Williams III. *St. James Santee, Plantation Parish: History and Records, 1685–1925.* Spartanburg, SC: The Reprint Company, 1997.

Burt, Nathaniel. *The Perennial Philadelphians: The Anatomy of an American Aristocracy.* Boston: Little, Brown, 1963.

Connelly, Thomas L., and Barbara L. Bellows. *God and General Longstreet: Essays on the Lost Cause and the Southern Mind.* Baton Rouge: Louisiana State University Press, 1982.

Cousins, Norman. *Present Tense.* New York: McGraw-Hill, 1967.

Coxe, Headley M., Jr. "The Charleston Poetic Renascence, 1920–1930." Ph.D. diss., University of Pennsylvania, 1958.

Dabney, Virginius. *Richmond: The Story of a City.* Garden City, NY: Doubleday, 1976.

Damon, S. Foster. *Amy Lowell: A Chronicle with Extracts from Her Correspondence.* Boston: Houghton Mifflin, 1935.

Datel, Robin Elisabeth. "Southern Regionalism and Historic Preservation in Charleston, South Carolina, 1920–1940." *Journal of Historical Geography* 16, no. 2 (1990): 197–215.

Davis, Kenneth S. *FDR: Into the Storm, 1937–1940.* New York: Random House, 1993.

Douglas, Ann. *Terrible Honesty: Mongrel Manhattan in the 1920s.* New York: Farrar, Straus, Giroux, 1995.

Durham, Frank. *DuBose Heyward: The Man Who Wrote Porgy.* Columbia: University of South Carolina Press, 1954.

Fain, John Tyree. "Hergesheimer's Use of Historical Sources." *Journal of Southern History* 18 (November 1952): 497–504.

Fleming, Thomas. "Preface" to *Lady Baltimore,* by Owen Wister. Nashville: J. S. Sanders and Company, 1992.

Fox, James. *Five Sisters.* New York: Simon and Schuster, 2000.

Garland, Joseph E. *Eastern Point: A Nautical, Rustical, and More or Less Sociable Chronicle of Gloucester's Outer Shield and Inner Sanctum, 1606–1990.* Beverly, MA: Commonwealth Editions, 1990.

Gimmestad, Victor E. *Joseph Hergesheimer.* Boston: Twayne, 1984.

Goodman, Susan. *Ellen Glasgow: A Biography.* Baltimore: Johns Hopkins University Press, 1998.

Greene, Harlan. *Mr. Skylark.* Athens: University of Georgia Press, 2001.

Halliwell, Leslie. *The Filmgoers Companion*. Revised and expanded edition. New York: Hill and Wang, 1967.

Hamilton, Elizabeth Verner. "Profile: Josephine Pinckney." *View Magazine* 1 (1986): 21.

Hardy, Stella Pickett. *Colonial Families of the Southern States of America*. Baltimore: Southern Book Co., 1958.

Hayden, Horace Edwin. *Virginia Genealogies: A Genealogy of the Glassell Family of Scotland and Virginia and Also of the Families of Ball, Brown, Bryan, Conway, Daniel, Ewell, Holladay, Lewis, Littlepage, Moncure, Peyton, Robinson, Scott, Taylor, Wallace and others of Virginia and Maryland*. Baltimore: Genealogical Publishing, 1979.

Heymann, C. David. *American Aristocracy: The Lives and Times of James Russell, Amy, and Robert Lowell*. New York: Dodd, Mead, 1980.

Holman, C. Hugh. "Detached Laughter in the South." In *Comic Relief: Humor in Contemporary American Literature*, edited by Sarah B. Cohen. Urbana: University of Illinois Press, 1978.

Hosmer, Charles B., Jr. *Preservation Comes of Age: From Williamsburg to the National Trust, 1926–1949*. Charlottesville: University Press of Virginia, 1981.

Huger, Mary Esther. *Recollections of a Happy Childhood*. Pendleton, SC: Foundation for Historic Restoration, 1976.

Hutchisson, James. *DuBose Heyward: A Charleston Gentleman and the World of Porgy and Bess*. Jackson: University Press of Mississippi, 2000.

Jackson, Laura (Riding). *The Laura (Riding) Jackson Reader*. Edited by Elizabeth Friedman. New York: Persea, 2005.

Jeffries, Joseph Arthur. *Fauquier County, Virginia, 1840–1919*. Compiled by Helen Jeffries Klitch. San Antonio, TX: Phil Bates Associates, 1989.

Kain, Richard Morgan. *Dublin in the Age of William Butler Yeats and James Joyce*. Norman: University of Oklahoma Press, 1962.

Kirkhorn, Michael. "Gerald W. Johnson." *Dictionary of Literary Biography*, vol. 29: *American Newspaper Journalists, 1926–1950*, edited by Perry J. Ashley, 132–38. Detroit: Gale, 1984.

Kruger, Richard. *The Paper: The Life and Death of the New York Herald Tribune*. New York: Knopf, 1986.

Krutch, Joseph Wood. "Introduction." *The Saturday Review Treasury*. New York: Simon and Schuster, 1957.

Leland, Jack. "O'Donnell's Folly: A Handsome House." *Charleston Evening Post*, 21 January 1969.

Lily, Edward Guerrant, ed. *Historic Churches of Charleston, South Carolina*. Clifford Legerton, comp. Charleston: John Huguley, 1966.

McInnis, Maurie D. *The Pursuit of Refinement: Charlestonians Abroad, 1740–1860*. In collaboration with Angela D. Mack. Columbia: University of South Carolina Press, 1999.

Milford, Nancy. *Savage Beauty: The Life of Edna St. Vincent Millay*. New York: Random House, 2001.

Millar, Betty Vaughn. "Back Stage—On Stage—Up Stage." *South Carolina Magazine* 11 (June 1948): 10, 24.

Miller, Nina. *Making Love Modern: The Intimate Public Worlds of New York's Literary Women.* New York: Oxford University Press, 1999.

Morris, Sylvia Jukes. *Rage for Fame: The Ascent of Clare Boothe Luce.* New York: Random House, 1997.

Moscow, Warren. *Roosevelt and Willkie.* Englewood Cliffs, NJ: Prentice-Hall, 1968.

Neal, Steve. *Dark Horse: A Biography of Wendell Willkie.* New York: Doubleday, 1984.

North, Michael. *Reading 1922: A Return to the Scene of the Modern.* New York: Oxford University Press, 1999.

O'Brien, Michael. "Politics, Romanticism, and Hugh S. Legaré: 'The Fondness of Disappointed Love.'" In *Intellectual Life in Antebellum Charleston,* edited by Michael O'Brien and David Moltke-Hansen, 123–51. Knoxville: University of Tennessee Press, 1986.

Olson, Stanley. *Elinor Wylie: A Life Apart.* New York: Dial Press, 1979.

Parsons, Schuyler Livingston. *Untold Friendships.* Boston: Houghton Mifflin, 1955.

Peale, Marjorie E. "Charleston as a Literary Center, 1920–1933." M.A. thesis, Duke University, 1941.

Pinckney, Reverend Charles Cotesworth. *Life of General Thomas Pinckney.* Boston: Houghton and Mifflin, 1895.

"Prentiss Taylor." *Washington Print Club Quarterly* (Winter 1991–92): 2–5.

Radway, Janice A. *A Feeling for Books: The Book-of-the-Month Club, Literary Taste, and Middle-Class Desire.* Chapel Hill: University of North Carolina Press, 1997.

Reniers, Perceval. *The Springs of Virginia.* Chapel Hill: University of North Carolina Press, 1941.

"Richard Bowditch Wigglesworth." *Current Biography.* New York: H. W. Wilson, 1959.

Rogers, George C., Jr. *Charleston in the Age of the Pinckneys.* Norman: University of Oklahoma Press, 1969.

Rose, Ingrid, and Roderick S. Quiroz. *The Lithographs of Prentiss Taylor: A Catalogue Raisonné.* Bronx, NY: Fordham University Press, 1996.

Rowland, Lawrence S., Alexander Moore, and George C. Rogers Jr. *History of Beaufort County, South Carolina,* vol. 1: *1514–1861.* Columbia: University of South Carolina Press, 1996.

Rubin, Joan Shelley. *The Making of the Middlebrow Culture.* Chapel Hill: University of North Carolina Press, 1992.

Rubin, Louis D., Jr. *The Curious Death of the Novel: Essays in American Literature.* Baton Rouge: Louisiana State University Press, 1967.

———. *William Elliott Shoots a Bear.* Baton Rouge: Louisiana State University Press, 1978.

Salley, A. S., Jr. "Col. Miles Brewton and Some of His Descendants." In *South Carolina Genealogy,* vol. 1. Spartanburg, SC: The Reprint Company, 1983.

Scott, Mary Wingfield. *Houses of Old Richmond.* Richmond: Valentine Museum, 1941.

Severens, Martha. *Alice Ravenel Huger Smith: An Artist, a Place, and a Time.* Charleston: Carolina Art Association, 1993.

———. *The Charleston Renaissance.* Spartanburg, SC: Saraland Press, 1998.

Shaffer, Arthur H. "David Ramsey and the Limits of Revolutionary Nationalism." In *Intellec-*

*tual Life in Antebellum Charleston*, edited by Michael O'Brien and David Moltke-Hansen, 47–84. Knoxville: University of Tennessee Press, 1986.

Singal, Daniel Joseph. *The War Within: From Victorian to Modernist Thought in the South, 1919–1945*. Chapel Hill: University of North Carolina Press, 1982.

Slater, Thomas. "Leonore J. Coffee." *Dictionary of Literary Biography*, vol. 44: *American Screen Writers, Second Series*, edited by Randall Clarke, 91–97. Detroit: Gale, 1986.

Smith, Henry A. M. Introduction to Captain Thomas Pinckney's Civil War Memoirs. Typescript. South Carolina Historical Society, Charleston.

Smyth, William D. "Segregation in Charleston in the 1950s: A Decade of Transition." *South Carolina Historical Magazine* 92 (1991): 103.

Stansell, Christine. *American Moderns: Bohemian New York and the Creation of a New Century*. New York: Metropolitan Books, 2000.

Stark, John D. *Damned Upcountryman: William Watts Ball; A Study in American Conservatism*. Durham, NC: Duke University Press, 1968.

Teachout, Terry. *The Skeptic: A Life of H. L. Mencken*. New York: Harper Collins, 2002.

Underwood, Thomas A. *Allen Tate: Orphan of the South*. Princeton: Princeton University Press, 2000.

Way, Rev. William. *History of Grace Church, Charleston*. Charleston: n.p., 1948.

Webber, Mabel L., comp. "The Thomas Pinckney Family of South Carolina." In *South Carolina Genealogies*. Spartanburg, SC: The Reprint Company, 1983.

Wecter, Dixon. *The Saga of American Society: A Record of Social Aspiration 1607–1937*. New York: Charles Scribner's Sons, 1937.

Weir, Robert M. *Colonial South Carolina: A History*. Millwood, NY: KTO Press, 1983.

Weyeneth, Robert R. *Historic Preservation for a Living City: Historic Charleston Foundation, 1947–1997*. Columbia: University of South Carolina Press, 2000.

Widdemer, Margaret. *Golden Friends I Had*. Garden City, NY: Doubleday, 1964.

Williams, Frances Leigh. *A Founding Family: The Pinckneys of South Carolina*. New York: Harcourt, Brace, Jovanovich, 1978.

Williams, Kenney J. "William Stanley Braithwaite." In *Dictionary of Literary Biography*, vol. 50: *Afro-American Writers before the Harlem Renaissance*, edited by Trudier Harris, 7–18. Detroit: Gale, 1986.

Williams, Susan Millar. *A Devil and a Good Woman Too: The Lives of Julia Peterkin*. Athens: University of Georgia Press, 1997.

Wilson, Douglas L., ed. *The Genteel Tradition*. Cambridge: Harvard University Press, 1967.

Wilson, Edmund. *The Shores of Light: A Literary Chronicle of the Twenties and Thirties*. New York: Farrar, Straus, and Young, 1952.

Winchell, Mark Royden. *Where No Flag Flies: Donald Davidson and the Southern Resistance*. Columbia: University of Missouri Press, 2000.

Wyatt-Brown, Bertram. *Honor and Violence in the Old South*. New York: Oxford University Press, 1986.

———. *The House of Percy: Honor, Melancholy, and Imagination in a Southern Family*. New York: Oxford University Press, 1994.

Young, Thomas Daniel, and M. Thomas Inge. *Donald Davidson.* New York: Twayne, 1971.

Zahniser, Marvin R. *Charles Cotesworth Pinckney: Founding Father.* Chapel Hill: Published for the Institute of Early American History and Culture, Williamsburg, by the University of North Carolina Press, 1967.

*Interviews*

Breckinridge, Isabella. Interview with author. Washington, DC, 18 June 2001.

Brenner, Francis. Interview with author. Charleston, SC, 23 March 1999.

Burden, Elizabeth. Telephone interview with author. 9 June 2002.

Friendly, Pie Pinckney. Interview with author. Washington, DC, 11 June 2002.

Holden, Mrs. Edward. Telephone interview with author. 17 January 2000.

Keith, Judge James. Interview with author. Alexandria, VA, 21 October 1999.

LeClercq, Anne Sinkler Whaley. Interview with author. Charleston, SC, 2 May 2002.

Leonhardt, Serena Simons. Interview with author. Charleston, SC, 15 February 2000.

Perenyi, Eleanor Stone. Interview with author. Stonington, CT, 12 March 1999.

Rigney, Harriet Popham McDougal. Interview with author. Charleston, SC, 11 April 2003.

Simons, S. Stoney. Interview with author. Charleston, SC, 7 February 2000.

Taylor, Amelia Moore. Telephone interview with author. 20 April 2000.

Tynan, Sidney Lockwood. E-mail interview with author. 16–17 April 2001.

Williams, George W. Interview with author. Charleston, SC, 18 March 2003.

Williams, Harriet P. Interview with author. Charleston, SC, 28 February 2003, 17 February 2004.

Zeigler, John. Interview with author. Charleston, SC, 18 December 1998.

# Index

JP IN THE INDEX REFERS TO JOSEPHINE
PINCKNEY. PAGE NUMBERS IN ITALIC
REFER TO ILLUSTRATIONS.

*Absalom, Absalom!* (Faulkner), 7

Adams, Don, 147

Addlington, Richard, 240n52

A.E. (George William Russell), 63, 64, *following p.
90*, 138–39, 242n27, 253n23, 253n25

African Americans: churches of, 70; and Democratic Party, 9, 208; dental clinic for, 207;
education of, 9, 71, 122, 207; and Harlem
Renaissance, 75, 98, 145, 159; JP on, 172–73,
202, 207–8; and poll tax, 172; population of,
in Charleston, 208; poverty of rural life of,
71–72; spirituals of, 68–75, 127, 140, 146–47,
201, 244n63, 244n65; and *Three O'Clock Dinner* by JP, 189; and voodoo, 195, 261n4; voting
rights for, 210; Willkie's support of rights of,
172. *See also* Gullah language; Gullah lore;
Race relations

Agee, James, 202–3

Agrarians, 6, 136–39, 142–43, 151–53, 202–3,
252n17, 253n23

Alderman, Edward A., 140

Aley, Maxwell, 129

Allen, Agnes, 229

Allen, Ann Andrews, 101, 176, 188

Allen, (William) Hervey: accusations against,
86–87; approach to life and art by, 40, 238n7;
Bennett's concerns about, 238n11; biography
of, 237–38n5; biography of Poe by, 93; Charleston literary circle of, after World War I,
39–45; child of, 115–16; death and burial
of, 199; departure by, from Charleston for
New York City, 84, 86–87, 158; education of,
40, 45, 55; friendship and correspondence
between JP and, xii, 49, 53, 56, 78–79, 84,
91, 92, 96, 101, 120, 169, 188, 198–99; and
Fugitives, 62; and Heyward's death, 168;
and Heyward's marriage, 78; and Heyward's
*Porgy*, 93; homes of, 40, 84, 155, 176; and JP's
frustration with Heyward, 159; literary and
publishing contacts of, 39–40, 42; and Lowell, 39–40, 49–50, 53, 79, 84–88, 97, 238n6,
240n53, 263n37; Lowell's view of relationship
between JP and, 53, 79, 84–85; at MacDowell Colony, 45, 46, 63, 77–78, 87; marriage of,
101, 188; in New York City, 84; novel by, 154–
55, 163; personality of, 39, 86; photograph of,
*following p. 90*; physical appearance of and
clothing worn by, 40, 46–47; poetry by, 39,
47, 49, 53, 56, 154, 238nn5–6, 240n53; and
Poetry Society of America, 57; and Poetry Society of South Carolina, xi, xii, 41–43, 59; and
*Poetry's* "Southern Number," 44–45, 239n23;
and *Sea-Drinking Cities* by JP, 101; and Stork,
58; as teacher, 39, 46, 87, 93, 101; and *Three
O'Clock Dinner* by JP, 188; and Waring, 114; in
World War I, 40, 238nn5–6

—works: *Anthony Adverse*, 154–55, 163; *Ballads of
the Border*, 238n5; "Blindman," 238n6; *New
Legends*, 154; *Wampum and Old Gold*, 47

Alliance Française, 195

*All's Well*, 239n16

American Library Association, 188

*American Mercury,* 203

American Revolution, 4, 166, 206

Anderson, Sherwood, 80, 90, 141, 167

Andrews (Heyward), Ann. *See* Allen, Ann Andrews

*The Angelic Avengers* (Dinesen), 199

"Annie Get Your Gun," 191

*Anthology of Best Magazine Poetry* (Braithwaite), 44

*Anthony Adverse* (Allen), 154–55, 163

Anti-Semitism, 127

Aristocratic class: and Canby, 96, 98; and Code of honor, 6–8, 37, 38, 121, 124, 181, 210, 217; and JP, 6–8, 9, 12, 14, 21, 30, 37, 59–60, 71, 96, 102; JP's critique of, 133–34; in *Three O'Clock Dinner* by JP, 177–83

Arliss, George and Florence, 127

"Armageddon" (Ransom), 100

Art. *See* Gibbes Art Gallery

Ashley Hall, 28–29

*Atlantic* magazine, 69

*Atlantic Monthly,* 71, 97

Austen, Jane, 3, 33, 178

Author's Manifesto, 171

Automobile accident, 119

Automobiles, 32, 55, 70, 109, 189, 225

*Avalon* (Davidson), 100

Avary, Myrta Lockett, 29

*Babel* (Cournos), 242–43n31

Baker, George Pierce, 48

Baker, Josephine, 159

Baker, Lois Hazelhurst Middleton, 249n1

Balch, Edwin, 93

Balch, Emily Clark. *See* Clark, Emily

*Balisand* (Hergesheimer), 81–82

Ball, Fay Witte, 249–50n12

Ball, William Watts, 126, 164–65, 168, 172, 249–50n12

*Ballads of the Border* (Allen), 238n5

*Baltimore Evening Sun,* 117

Barr, Stringfellow, 138, 143

Barrymores, 191

Baruch, Bernard, 161

Battle of Britain, 170

"The Battle of Eutaw Springs and Evacuation of Charleston" (Ioor), 204

Beaux, Cecilia, 55

Beecroft, John, 185

*Before the Sun Goes Down* (Howard), 190

Belles, southern, 21, 31, 81

*Ben-Hur* (Wallace), 101

Benchley, Robert, 96

Benét, Laura, 254n52

Benét, Rosemary, 227

Benét, Stephen Vincent, 46, 166, 227, 254n52

Benét, William Rose, 94, 227

Bennett, Mrs. Charles, 12

Bennett, John: and Allen's friendship with JP, 199; children's book by, 30; on Chippendale Room at Charleston Museum, 110; and concerns about Allen, 238n11; and Farrar, 89; and Great Depression, 120; and Gullah language, 66; and Heyward's death, 168; and *Hilton Head* by JP, 162; and literary circle of young poets after World War I, 40, 41; on marriage for women, 36; novel by, 165; and Poetry Society of South Carolina, xi, 41–43, 158; and *The Reviewer,* 80; and Society for the Preservation of Old Dwellings (SPOD), 249n6; and Waring's death, 161; and Willkie, 165

Bennett, Susan Smythe (Mrs. John), 41, 66, 84, 115, 129, 165, 168

Berenson, Bernard, xii–xiii, 92

Berkeley, George, 65

Berle, Adolf, 169

Berle, Milton, 127

Best, Marshall A.: in Charleston, 200–201; education of, 89; and *Great Mischief* by JP, 198–201; on JP, 1; and JP's cancer, 223–25; and JP's funeral, 225–26; and *My Son and Foe* by JP, 216; and *Splendid in Ashes,* 227, 228–

29; and *Three O'Clock Dinner* by JP, 177, 183, 185–86, 188

"Bitter Burial" (Pinckney), 144

*The Bitter Tea of General Yen* (Stone), 10, 129

*The Black Border* (Gonzales), 66

*Black Boy* (Wright), 1, 188

Blacks. *See* African Americans; Gullah language; Gullah lore; Race relations

Blease, Cole, 10

"Blindman" (Allen), 238n6

Bobbs-Merrill, 165

Bodenheim, Max, 46, 77

Bodley, Col. Ronald V. C., 188

Book clubs: and Canby, 10, 94, 163, 185–86, 195; and Covici, 194; and *Great Mischief* by JP, 199, 200; and *Hilton Head* by JP, 163; and historical novels, 154; influence of, 191; and Loveman, 190; and *Three O'Clock Dinner* by JP, 1, 185–86

Bonfield Manor, 155

Book collecting, 9, 50–51, 83, 240n43

Book publishing. *See* Publishing industry

Book-of-the-Month Club: and Canby, 10, 94, 163, 185–86, 195; and Covici, 194; and *Great Mischief* by JP, 199, 200; and *Lolly Willowes* by Warner, 195; and Loveman, 190

*Bookman*, 67, 89

Booth, Florence, 246n38

*Boston Evening Transcript*, 77

Bowditch, Nathaniel I., 49

Bragg, Laura M.: and Charleston Museum, 38, 74, 83; and founding of Poetry Society of South Carolina, 41; and Great Depression, 121; interest of, in JP's love life, 48, 56, 87; and JP's cancer, 224; and JP's friendship with Lowell, 86; and JP's grief at Victoria Rutledge's death, 161; and JP's poetry, 44, 239n22; literary circle organized by, 38, 40, 41; and promotion of *Great Mischief* by JP, 201; as treasurer of Poetry Society of South Carolina, 45

Braithwaite, William Stanley, 44, 77–78

Breckinridge, Frances Pinckney, 30, 224–25

Brewton, Miles, 5, 116, 233n12

Brook Hill, 16, 17, 18, 20

Brotherhood of Galahad, 35, 36, 38

Brothers and Sisters Club, 35

Brown, John, 19, 134

Brown, John Mason, 229

Browne, Thomas, 218, 232n1

Browning, Robert, 35

Bryan, John Stewart, 160

Bryan, Joseph, 30

Bryan, William Jennings, 72

Buist, George Lamb, 35, 84

Bullock, Florence Haxton, 227

"Bulwarks against Change" (Pinckney), 135–36, 151–52

Burger, Nash, 199–200

Burnside, Ambrose, 20

Butcher, Fanny, 147

Byrnes, Sen. James, 161

Byron, Lord, 238n11

Cabell, James Branch, 2, 79, 99, 143

Cagney, Jimmy, 145

Caldwell, Erskine, 202

Calhoun, John C., 133

California, 130, 252n59

Canada, 78, 111

Canby, Henry Seidel: and A.E., 253n25; and Agrarians, 138; and Book-of-the-Month Club, 10, 163, 195; in Charleston, 98; Connecticut home of, 85, 94–95; as editor of *Saturday Review of Literature*, 10, 85, 94, 96, 144; and Fugitives, 99; and Great Depression, 120–21; and *Great Mischief* by JP, 200; health problems of, 226; and *Hilton Head* by JP, 163; and JP's death, 226; JP's friendship with, 85, 94–97; Lowell on, 85; and modernism, 95, 96; personality and values of, 94, 95; photograph of, *following p. 90*; physical appearance of, 94; as president of Poetry Society of America 94;

Canby, Henry Seidel (continued)
  psychological breakdown suffered by, 121; and *Sea-Drinking Cities* by JP, 100; and southern literature, 98–99; and Southern Writers' Conference, 141; as speaker at Poetry Society of South Carolina, 85; and Grace Stone, 130; and *Three O'Clock Dinner* by JP, 183, 185, 186, 190; travels by, 101, 198, 216; and Willkie, 166

Canby, Marion "Lady" (Mrs. Henry), 85, 98, 226

*Candida* (Shaw), 64

*Cannery Row* (Steinbeck), 1, 188

Caribbean, 198, 212

Carmalt, Churchill, 258n15

Carnegie, Andrew, 127

Carolina Art Association, 110, 120, 168, 203–5, 207, 226

*Carolina Chansons* (Allen and Heyward), 49, 53, 56, 109, 240n53, 242n25

*The Carolina Low-Country*, 140

Carpetbaggers, 126

Case Western Reserve Barn Theatre, 262n23

Cash, W. J., 203

Cason, Clarence E., 152

Cather, Willa, 67

Catholics, 187, 261n7

Cecil, Lord David, 165–66

*Cerberus*, 28

Cerf, Bennett, 89

Chadbourne, Marc, 117

Charleston, S.C.: A.E. in, 139, 242n27; Allen's home in, 40; architecture of and preservation activities in, 112–13, 114, 124, 127, 207, 224, 227, 251n47; arts and artists in, 44, 128; Best in, 200–201; black population of, 208; Canbys in, 98; Colum in, 63–64; compared with Dublin, 64–65; and Davidson, 3, 101–3; Erskine's tribute to, 57; Farrar in, 89; girls' schools in, 27–28; Great Depression in, 120–21; Gunther on, 208–9; Hergesheimer's visit to, 82–83; history of, 2; Inter-racial Commission in, 9; JP's childhood homes in, 12–13, 23–25, *following p. 90*, 111–12, 234n2, 249n1, 250n29; JP's home on Chalmers Street in, 11, *following p. 90*, 111–13, 115, 116–18, 250n29; Lowell in, 54; Monroe in, 43; Morawetz's contributions to, 126–27, 251n47; northerners in, 125–27; outdoor historical pageant in, 203–7; portrayal of, by writers, 218, 227–28, 259n9; public reputation of, after World War II, 203; and Ransom, 63, 66, 137; reactions to *Three O'Clock Dinner* in, 187; social life focused on courtship and marriage in, 33–34; Southern Writers' Conference in, 146–48; static quality of society of, 3–4; summer in, 111; Taylor in, 148–49; and tourism, 11, 71, 97–98, 203–4, 207; Willkie in, 164–66, 169; and World War II, 171–72. *See also* Pinckney, Josephine; Poetry Society of South Carolina

Charleston County Free Library, 186

*Charleston Evening Post*, 107–8, 113, 114

Charleston Library Society, 28, 65–66, 155, 226

Charleston Renaissance/Charleston Literary Movement: Allen on, 41; Colum on, 63; compared with Harlem Renaissance, 75; compared with Irish literary renaissance, 63–65; and folkways of Low Country, 2, 66–71; and Fugitives, 60–63, 66; and Great Depression, 120; and Gullah language, 66–68, 69; Heyward on, 57; Kreymborg's course on, at New School for Social Research, 109; and modernism, 58–59, 70; Monroe on, 44; and pastoral tradition, 63; and Poetry Society of South Carolina, xi, 42–44, 49; Simkins on, 60; and spirituals, 68–75, 127; and Stork, 58; and Waring, 114. *See also* Poetry Society of South Carolina; and specific authors

*Charleston Mercury*, 28

Charleston Museum, 28, 38, 74, 110, 126, 146, 201, 226, 227

*Charleston News and Courier*, 28, 29, 164, 212, 226, 227–28

Chesnut, Mary Boykin, 20, 28

Cheves, Langdon, 157–58, 256n10

Chiang Kai-shek, Madame, 171, 258n25

*Chicago Daily News,* 108

Civil rights movement, 9

Civil War, 15, 17, 19–20, 28–29, 65, 154, 171, 206

Clark, Emily. 79–82, 88, 93, 141, 143, 144, 255n67

Code of honor, 6–8, 37, 38, 121, 124, 181, 210, 217. *See also* Aristocratic class

Coffee, Leonore, 191–92

Cohan, George M., 212

Colbert, Claudette, 191

College of Charleston, 37, 160

*College of Charleston Magazine,* 37

Colum, Mary (Molly), 63, 174

Colum, Padraic, 46, 63–64, 77, 138, 174, 238n7, 242n25

Columbia University, 33, 57, 84, 95, 99, 128

"The Congo, Mr. Mencken" (Johnson), 81

Congreve, William, 157

Connecticut, 85, 94–95, 134–35

Connolly, James, 138

Conservatism, 125–26, 134, 136

*Contemporary Verse,* 37, 58

Cooper, Sir Anthony Ashley, Earl of Shaftsbury, 2, 155, 158, 256n10

Copeland, Charles T., 47, 48

Cotesworth, Mary, 231n1

Couch, William T., 132, 139, 151, 152

Cournos, John, 242–43n31

Covici, Pascal, 183, 184, 185, 190, 194, 201, 213, 216

Cowan, William, 191

Cowley, Malcolm, 238n6

Coxe, Eckley Brinton, 124

Coxe, Elizabeth Sinkler, 54, 124

Crane, Hart, 80

Crawford, Joan, 159, 191

*Culture in the South,* 3, 151–52

cummings, e. e., 238n6

*Cytherea* (Hergesheimer), 81, 83

Dadaism, 120

*The Damned Don't Cry* (Hervey), 36–37

Damrosch, Walter, 76, 244n64

"Dark Water" (Pinckney), 92

Darwin, Charles, 8, 10, 47

Daughters of the American Revolution, 5, 207

Davenport, Russell, 169

Davidge, Joanna, 55

Davidson, Donald: and Agrarians, 136–38, 142–43, 203, 252n17, 253n23; on artist as southerner, 99; in Charleston, 101–3; as Fugitive, 60–63, 93; and Heyward, 62, 99; JP's friendship with, xii, 100, 101–3; on JP's writing, 3; and localism, 99; and *Poetry's* second "Southern Number," 143–44; review of JP's *Sea-Drinking Cities* by, 107–8; and Southern Writers' Conferences, 141, 143, 147, 254–55n56; and symposium on the South, 132–34

—works: *Avalon,* 100; "Fire on Belmont Street," 100; *Tall Men,* 100, 109

Davis, Bette, 213

Davis, Jefferson, 17

Davis, Lambert, 160, 165

Dawson, Warrington, 115

*Deirdre of the Sorrows* (Synge), 64

Dell, Floyd, 41

DeMille, Cecil B., 191

Democratic Party, 9, 125–26, 164, 166, 208–11

Deutsch, Babette, 66, 106–7

Dewey, John, 100, 133

Dewey, Thomas E., 168, 211

*Diary from Dixie* (Chesnut), 28

Dickinson, Emily, 38

Dictionaries, 65–66

Digby, Kenelm, 245n2

Dinesen, Isak, 3, 199

*Dixie after the War* (Avary), 29

Dixiecrats, 210, 211

Dock Street Theatre: Hamlin and Taylor associated with, 202, 262n23; and Heyward, 165, 168; and outdoor historical pageant, 205–7;

Dock Street Theatre (continued)
and patriotic radio programs during World
War II, 171, 258n24; photograph of, *following
p. 90*; and promotion of *Great Mischief* by JP,
201; and Willkie, 168
Dodd, William E., 141
Donne, John, 120
Doran, George H., 100
Doran Press, 89, 93
*Double-Dealer*, 80, 93
Doyle, Sir Arthur Conan, 100
Driscoll, Louise, 77
Dudley, John Stuart, 204, 206–7
DuMaurier, Daphne, 3
Duse, Eleonora, 86

Earle, James, 13
Earthquakes, 34, 196, 207
East Gloucester, Mass., 54–55, 77–79, 86–88,
110
Eastman, Max, 126
Education: of African Americans, 9, 71, 122, 207;
of girls, 27–28
Eldorado Plantation: fire at, 21–22, 196; history
of, 5, 14, 15, 234n8; as JP's property, 111, 154,
201, 205n29; library of, 29; photograph of,
*following p. 90*
Eliot, T. S., 45–46, 48, 56, 57, 61, 65, 95, 96
Ellington, Duke, 204
Elliott, Caroline Phoebe. *See* Pinckney, Caroline
Phoebe Elliott
Elliott, William, 28
Elliott, William, II, 14
*Elmore v. Rice*, 210
Emerson, Ralph Waldo, 133, 134
England, 45–46, 216
Episcopal Church, 8, 12, 14, 73, 87, 95, 234n10
Erskine, John, 57
Escamacu Indians, 156
Esenwein, J. Berg, 238n8

European travels, xii–xiii, 33, 45–46, 88, 91–93,
101, 113, 131, 213–14, 216
Evans, Walker, 203

Fadiman, Clifton, 154, 199
Fairfield Plantation: history of, 5, 15, 18, 234n8;
house at, 30; and JP, 27, 111, 243n50; and promotion of *Great Mischief* by JP, 201; as prop-
erty of JP's brother Cotesworth, 154; as prop-
erty of Thomas Pinckney (son of Cotesworth
Pinckney), 256n23
Farrar, John: and *Anthony Adverse* by Allen, 155;
on Canby, 94; in Charleston, 89; and *Hil-
ton Head* by JP, 159–60; and party for *Three
O'Clock Dinner*, 188; and *Porgy* by Heyward,
93; and *Sea-Drinking Cities* by JP, 100
Farrar and Rinehart, 100, 155, 159, 177
Faulkner, William, 7, 95, 99, 141, 142, 160, 202,
203
Fenwick Hall, 127, 232n9
Field, Rachel, 254n52
"A Fig for Selene" (Pinckney), 144
Films. *See* Hollywood films; and specific films
and actors
Fineman, Irving, 150, 255n69, 257n30
"Fire on Belmont Street" (Davidson), 100
"First Fig" (Millay), 38
Fisher, Dorothy Canfield, 67, 199
Fitzgerald, F. Scott, 10, 39, 95, 96
Fitzsimmons, Ellen, 160
Fletcher, John Gould, 252n17
Floods, 15–16
Folklore, 8, 26–27, 68, 195
Forbes, W. Cameron, 49
Fosdick, Harry Emerson, 134
France, xiii, 46, 101, 113, 147, 216
Frank, James, 60
Fraser, Charles, 128
Free love. *See* Sexual mores
Freud, Sigmund, 8, 9, 73

Friend, Julius Weiss, 80

*The Front Page* (McArthur), 184

Frost, Frances, 149–51, 158, 163, 255n64, 255n69, 257n30

Frost, Mary, 27

Frost, Rebecca Motte "Rebe," 27

Frost, Robert, 38, 128, 240n53

Frost, Susan Pringle, 112, 259n9

*The Fugitive*, 61, 93, 100, 238–39n16, 242n18

Fugitive poets, 60–63, 66, 93, 99–100, 134, 137, 144, 253n23

Furniture, 13, 23, 234n4, 264n18

Gable, Clark, 191

"Gamesters All" (Heyward), 239n22

Gannett, Lewis, 95, 200, 216

Garden, Alexander, 166

Garland, Judy, 191

George, W. L., 59

George Doran Company, 89, 93

Gershwin, George, 158, 159

Gibbes Art Gallery, 44, 128, 157, 189, 227

Gibbs, Rose and Stepney, 243n50

Gibson, Charles Dana, 31

Gibson Girl, 31, 32

Gielgud, John, 216

Gish, Lillian, 85

Glasgow, Ellen: and Agrarians, 138; award for, 1, 188; correspondence between JP and, xii; death of, 188; as friend of Irita Van Doren, 10; JP compared with, 212; literary ambitions of, 4; novel by, 2; and *The Reviewer*, 79; and Southern Writers' Conference, 140, 142–44; Tate on, 144; and *Three O'Clock Dinner* by JP, 188

Glenn, Isa, 129–30

Godfrey, Mary, 155, 157

Goethe, Johann Wolfgang von, 199

Golden Stair Press, 145

Goldstein, Albert, 80

*Gone with the Wind*, 39, 192

Gonzales, Ambrose E., 66, 244n65

Gordon, Carolyn, 141, 254n56

Gorman, Herbert, 77

*Grapes of Wrath* (Steinbeck), 184

Great Awakening, Second, 14

Great Depression, 120–21, 136, 146

*Great Mischief* (Pinckney): as book club selection, 199, 200; criticisms of, 199–200, 261n7; devil as character in, 199–200, 262n7; dust jacket for, *following p. 90*, 199; Gullah lore in, 8, 194; plan for, 194–95; plot and themes of, 195–98; promotions for, 200, 201; reviews of, 199–200; titles of, 194; writing of, 205

Greece, 213–14

Green, Paul, 93, 141, 143

Greene, Graham, 199

Gregory, Lady Isabella Augusta, 64

Grimball, John B., 115

Groenman, Rudolph, 264n20

Guggenheim, Solomon, 128

Gugler, Eric "Tuppy," 97–98

Guinzburg, Harold A., 194, 202

"Gulla' Lullaby" (Pinckney), 67, 89

Gullah language, 26, 27, 34, 44, 66–68, 69, 122–23

Gullah lore, 8, 26–27, 68, 195

Gullah spirituals, 68–75, 127, 140, 146–47, 201

Gunther, John, 208–9

Habarruk, Ronald Firbanks, 82

"Hag!" (Pinckney), 26–27

Halleck, Robert, 184

Hamilton, Alexander, 5

Hamilton, Edith, 188

Hamlin, George E., Jr., 202, 262n23

*The Harbor* (Pinckney), 63

Harlem Renaissance, 75, 98, 145, 159

Harper Brothers, 100–101, 109, 138, 152, 159

Harris, Jack, 186

Harvard University, 40, 45, 47, 48, 49, 55, 83, 127

Hawthorne, Nathaniel, 199

Hawthorne Inn, 54, 110

Hayes, Helen, 159

Hayes, Rutherford B., 240n48

Hazlitt, William, 185

Hecht, Ben, 184

Hemingway, Ernest, 95

Hendrick, Mary Martin, 227

Hepburn, Andrew, 224

Hepburn, Katharine, 159, 167, 186

Hergesheimer, Joseph: in Charleston, 82–83; on feminization of literature, 48; films from novels by, 83, 85; and historical fiction, 157, 256n9; and JP, 81, 82–83, 85, 88, 108; novels by, 81–83, 85; photograph of, *following p. 90*; and *The Reviewer*, 80–83; and *Sea-Drinking Cities* by JP, 108; travel of, to Bermuda, 108; and Van Vechten, 145; as womanizer, 81, 82–83

Hervey, Harry, 36–37, 237n36

Hewitt-Myring, Phillip, 76

Heyward, Belle, 38, 40

Heyward, Dorothy Kuhns: and accusation against Allen, 87; and adaptation of *Great Mischief* for theater, 202; child of, 168, 176; and death of husband, 168; health problems of, 223; home of, at Folly Beach, 158; and husband's grave, 168; and JP's cancer, 223; marriage of, 78–79, 83–84, 245n5; personality of, 55–56; photograph of, *following p. 90*; physical appearance of, 55; as playwright, 55, 83, 165; return to Charleston by, in 1934, 158; romantic relationship between Heyward and, 55, 78; and Southern Writers' Conference, 141; and *Three O'Clock Dinner* by JP, 188; travels by, 264n20; and Willkie, 165

Heyward, DuBose: and Allen, 39, 87; automobile of, 109; in Brotherhood of Galahad, 35; child of, 168, 176; childhood poverty of, 34; Clark on, 255n67; Davidson on, 99; death of, 168; departure by, from Charleston for North Carolina mountains, 85; and Dock Street Theatre, 165, 168; employment of, in insurance business, 47, 85; family background of, 34; friendship and correspondence between JP and, xii, 37, 118–19, 148, 159, 162; friendships of, 37, 40; and Fugitives, 62; and Great Depression, 120; on Gullah language, 69; Hergesheimer's influence on, 256n9; and *Hilton Head* collaboration with JP, 158–59; home of, at Folly Beach, 158; at MacDowell Colony, 45, 46, 55, 87, 96; marriage of, 78–79, 83–84, 245n5; novels by, 93, 98, 109, 154; personality of, 34, 141; photographs of, *following p. 90*; poetry by, 35, 49, 83, 239n22, 240n53; and Poetry Society of America, 57; and Poetry Society of South Carolina, xi, xii, 41–43, 158, 159; and *Poetry*'s "Southern Number," 44–45, 239n23; and polio, 36; return of, to Charleston in 1934, 158; and *The Reviewer*, 80; romance between Dorothy Kuhns and, 55, 78; romance between JP and, 34–37, 78, 148; and rural poor, 71–72; and Society for the Preservation of Old Dwellings (SPOD), 249n6; on southern literature, 57, 60; and Southern Writers' Conferences, 140, 141, 146–48, 253n34; and Spirituals Society, 68, 71–72, 140, 243n37; and Grace Stone, 129; and Stork, 58; and Willkie, 165; during World War I, 36

—works: "Gamesters All," 239n22; *Mamba's Daughters*, 93, 109; *Peter Ashley*, 154; "Porgo," 89; *Porgy*, 93, 98, 109; *Porgy and Bess*, 158, 159, 243n37, 264n20; *Skylines and Horizons*, 83

Heyward, Jennifer, 168, 176, 216

Hibbard, Addison, 77, 103, 245n2

Hillyer, Robert, 117

Hilton, William, 155

*Hilton Head* (Pinckney): Heyward's collaboration on, 158–59; historical research on Woodward for, 155–58, 164; publishing contract for, 159–60; reviews of, 163; Willkie's response to, 169–70; writing and revising of, 162, 165

Hirsch, Sidney, 253n23

Historic Charleston Foundation, 207, 224, 225, 226

Historical novels, 154–60, 162–63

*Hobo* magazine, 186

Hodges, Joe, 68

Hollywood films: of Hergesheimer's novels, 83, 85; of Grace Stone's novel, 213; *Three O'Clock Dinner* film project, 1, 190–92, 205, 212–13; and Viking Press, 194; Willkie's philandering portrayed in, 167. *See also* specific films and actors

Holmes, Oliver Wendell, 49

Hoover, Herbert, 146

Hopkins, Mark, 126

Horlbeck, Fred, 38

Horney, Karen, 8–9

*Hound and Horn*, 204

House, Colonel, 127

Houseman, John, 204

Hovey, Richard, 107

Howard, Sidney Coe, 39

Howe, M. A. DeWolfe, 69, 71

Howells, William Dean, 177

Huebsch, Benjamin W., 184

Huger, Alfred, 72, 140

Hughes, Langston, 79, 145

Huntington, Alice Kydd Carmalt, 128, 168–69, 176, 258n15

Huntington, Elizabeth, 169

Huntington, Dr. George, 251n54

Hurston, Zora Neale, 75

Hutson, Katherine, 70

Hutson, May Elliott, 69

Huxley, Aldous, 101

*Hydrotaphia* (Browne), 218

Hyer, Helen, 38

Ickes, Harold, 167

"The Idealist" (Pinckney), 56, 81

*I'll Take My Stand*, 137, 138, 151–52, 252n17, 253n23

Imagism, 48, 53, 67, 106, 120

"In the Barn" (Pinckney), 44, 67, 239n22

Indians, 155, 156–57, 206

*The Inferno* (Dante), 214

*Innocence Abroad* (Clark), 255n67

*Inside USA* (Gunther), 208–9

Ioor, William, 204

Ireland, 63–65, 138

"Island Boy" (Pinckney), 100, 140

Istanbul, 213

Italy, 91–93, 214

Jackson, Andrew, 13, 61

James, Henry, 177

James, William, 48

Jefferson, Thomas, 82, 206

Jennings, Edward I. R. "Ned," 74

Johnson, Gerald W., 62–63, 65, 81, 117–18, 160–61, 163

Johnston, Mary, 79–80, 143

Jones, Howard Mumford, 108, 118, 132, 139, 146

Jones, Richard "Bear," 30

Joyce, James, 1, 63, 64–65, 184

Justinian, Emperor, 213

Kaminer, Mr. and Mrs. Harold Glenn, 258n15

Kaminer, Lucy Herndon, 258n15

Kammerer, Eliza Dunkin, 207

Kandinsky, Wassily, 128

Keats, John, 51, 88, 92

Keith, Katherine I., 17

Kipling, Rudyard, 238n5

Kirstein, Lincoln, xiii, 204–7

*Kitty Foyle* (Morley), 178

Klee, Paul, 128

Kline, Henry Blue, 252n17

Knauth, Oswald, 264n20

Knickerbocker, William S., 151, 254n56

Koeves, Tibor, 211

Kolnitz, Helen von, 38

Kreymborg, Alfred, 53, 109

Krutch, Joseph Wood, 95

Kuhns, Dorothy. *See* Heyward, Dorothy Kuhns

Laburnum, 20

*Ladies' Home Journal*, 32

*Lady Baltimore* (Wister), 55

Langhorne, Irene, 31

Language: and dictionaries, 65–66; Gullah language, 26, 27, 34, 44, 66–68, 69, 122–23; and southern literature, 65–68; uniformity of, 65

Lanier, Lyle H., 252n17

Lardner, Ring, 10, 96

Laski, Jesse, 85

*The Late George Apley* (Marquand), 178

Lathan, H. S., 140

Lawrence, D. H., 184

Lee, Robert E., 17, 19, 137

Legaré, Hugh S., 13

Legge, Dorothy, 113

Leitch, Mary Sinton, 46, 77, 245n2

*Let Us Now Praise Famous Men* (Agee), 202–3

Lewis, C. S., 199–200

Lewis, Joe, 211

Lewis, Sinclair, 10, 166

*Life* magazine, 201

*Linda Condon* (Hergesheimer), 81

Lindsay, Vachel, 38, 43, 240n53

Lippmann, Walter, 133

Literary Guild, 1, 185–86, 190

*Literary Lantern*, 77, 245n2

Literary magazines, southern, 43, 61, 79–80, 93–94, 238–39n16, 242n18

Locke, John, 158, 205–6

Lockwood, Caroline Sinkler "Carrie," 9, 54, 124, 125, 174, 211, 224

Lockwood, Dunbar, 125

Lockwood, Sidney, 174

*Lolly Willowes* (Warner), 195

London, 45–46

"Lonesome Grabeya'ad" (Pinckney), 106

Longfellow, Henry Wadsworth, 139

*Look Back to Glory* (Sass), 154

"The Lost Colony" (Green), 203

Loveman, Amy, 190

Lowell, Amy: and Allen, 39–40, 49–50, 53, 79, 84–88, 97, 238n6, 240n53, 263n37; as book collector, 50–51; and Canby, 85; childhood of, 53; cigar smoking by, 51, 92; compared with JP, 52–53; daily routine of, 50; death of, 53, 92; education of, 53; family background of, 52–53, 240n48; and Fugitives, 62; and Heyward, 57, 79, 240n53; home of, 50–51, 116; and Imagism, 48, 53, 67, 106; JP's friendship with, xiii, 49–54, 77, 79, 84–85, 86, 88, 229; Keats biography of, 88, 92; on Millay, 43; personality of, 53; photograph of, *following p. 90;* physical appearance of and clothing worn by, 51; poetry by, 86, 119, 205, 263n37; poets admired by, 53, 240n53; and Pound, 48; and relationship between JP and Allen, 53, 79, 84–85; on slavery and the South, 205; as speaker for Poetry Society of South Carolina, 54

Lowell, Augustus, 50, 52

Lowell, James Russell, 52, 240n48

Lowes, John Livingston, xiii, 47, 238n8

Lowndes, William, 29

Luce, Clare Booth, 168, 169, 174

Luce, Henry, 168, 169, 174

*Lust for Life* (Stone), 191

Lyons, Heningham Watkins, 17, 20, 21, 36, 235n21, 235n27

Lyons, James, 17, 20, 235n21

Lyons, Leonard, 174

Lyons, Peter, 116

*The Lyric,* 238n16

*The Lyric South* (Hibbard), 103, 245n2

Lytle, Andrew Nelson, 252n17

MacArthur, Charles, 159

MacDowell Colony: Allen at, 45, 46, 63, 77–78, 87; Heyward at, 45, 46, 55, 87, 96; JP at, 145, 148–50; Chard Smith at, 149, 186; Taylor at, 145

Macmillan and Company, 184

Macmillan Press, 140

*Madam Margot* (Bennett), 165

Magazines. *See* Literary magazines, southern

*Mamba's Daughters* (Heyward), 93, 109

"The Man in the Brooks Brothers Shirt" (McCarthy), 167

"The Man Who Became a Woman" (Anderson), 90

Manigault, Gabriel, 113

"The Marchant of London and the Treacherous Don" (Pinckney), 160

Marion, Francis, 5

Marquand, J. P., 178

Marx, Karl, 8

Massachusetts. *See* East Gloucester, Mass.

*Master Skylark* (Bennett), 30

Masters, Edgar Lee, 75, 244n61

Maybank, Burnett, 161

McArthur, Charles, 184

McBee, Mary Vardine, 27

McCarthy, Mary, 167

McClure, John, 80

McCord, Louisa Susannah, 65, 124

McCullers, Carson, 163

McFee, William, 200

Mencken, Henry L., 80–82, 88, 89, 108, 138, 203

Metalious, Grace, 228

Metro-Goldwyn-Mayer (M-G-M), 1, 190–92, 212

Mexico, 131

Middleton, Arthur, 206

Middleton, Frances Motte. *See* Pinckney, Frances Motte Middleton

Middleton, Henry, 206

Middleton Place, 203–7, 233n14

Miles, Elizabeth, 38

Millay, Edna St. Vincent: and Harper Brothers, 101; Lowell on, 53, 240n53; persona of, 38–39, 41, 95; Pinckney compared with, 212; poetry by, 38–39, 53; as speaker at Poetry Society of South Carolina, 43, 239nn18–19

Miller, Gordon, 35–36, 78, 101

Miller, Marguerite, 78

Mills, Robert, 113

*The Mind of the South* (Cash), 203

"The Misses Poar Drive to Church" (Pinckney), 104–5, 109

Mitchell, Broadus, 151–52

Mitchell, Margaret, 189–90

Modernism: and antifeminine reaction in literary community, 41, 47–48; and Canby, 95, 96; and changing roles of women, 135–36; and Charleston Renaissance/Charleston Literary Movement, 58–59, 70; of T. S. Eliot, 57, 96; and JP, 8–9, 38–39, 58–59, 96; popular modernism, 96

*Moll Flanders* (Defoe), 157

Molloy, Robert, 184, 185, 187, 200, 259n9

McFee, William, 200

MoMA (Museum of Modern Art), 128

Monroe, Harriet: and Charleston Renaissance, 41, 43–44; compared with Lowell, 40; as editor of *Poetry,* 38, 44–45, 60; and Fugitives, 62; and JP's poetry in *Poetry* magazine, 44, 45; and JP's second book of poetry, 119; and *Poetry's* "Southern Number," 44–45, 60, 103, 143; review of JP's *Sea-Drinking Cities* by, 106; as speaker at Poetry Society of South Carolina, 43; and Tate, 143

Moore, Lula Pencel, 121–23, 189, 214, 225, 226

Moore, Merrill, 61, 100, 138

Morawetz, Marjorie Nott, 126–27, 148, 207

Morawetz, Victor, 126–27, 251*n*47

Morgan, J. P., 127

Morley, Christopher, 94, 178

Morris, Elsie. *See* Pinckney, Elsie Morris

Mosby, John, 19

Motte, Jacob, 5

Motte, Rebecca Brewton, 4, 5, 15, *following p. 90,* 116, 207

Moultrie, William, 5

Mouzon, Harold, *following p. 90*

Movies. *See* Hollywood films; and specific films and actors

*Mrs. Wiggs and the Cabbage Patch* (Rice), 141

Munro, Harold, 45–46

Museum of Modern Art (MoMA), 128

Music. *See* Spirituals

*My Son and Foe* (Pinckney), 212–17

Nashville. *See* Fugitives

Nast, Condé, 159

Nathaniel Russell House, 207, 227

Nathans, Robert, 92

*The Nation,* 95

New Deal. *See* Roosevelt, Franklin D.

New England travels, xiii, 54–55, 77–79, 85, 86–88, 94–95, 110, 125, 134–35, 140, 224

*New Legends* (Allen), 154

New Orleans, La., 80, 93

New School for Social Research, 109

New South, 60, 135. *See also* South

New Women, 17. *See also* Women

New York City: Allen in, 84; and Harlem Renaissance, 75, 98, 145, 159; JP in, 57, 85, 173–76, 211; New School for Social Research in, 109; Poetry Society of America meeting in, 57

*New York Herald-Tribune,* 10, 95, 106–7, 130, 166, 200, 227, 247*n*15

*New York Post,* 94, 174

*New York Sun,* 184, 200

*New York Times,* 106, 147, 151, 163, 186, 199–200, 216, 226, 263*n*48

*New York World Telegram,* 186

*New Yorker,* 94, 174

Newton, A. Edward, 9, 83, 240*n*43

Newton, Caroline, 8–9

Nicholson, Harold, 117

Nixon, Herman Clarence, 252*n*17

*The Nomad,* 239*n*16

North, Michael, 232*n*4, 243*n*48

*North American Review,* 92

Nott, Eliphalet, 126

Novels. *See* Historical novels; and specific authors and titles of novels

"Nuptial" (Pinckney), 37, 58

Oakwood, 16, 19, 20

"Ode to the Confederate Dead" (Tate), 144

O'Hara, John, 218

"An Old Man Remembers" (Pinckney), 144

"The Old Woman" (Pinckney), 104

"On the Shelf" (Pinckney), 105–6

*One World* (Willkie), 173

Orista (Edisto) Indians, 156

Osgood, Dana, 201

Ould, Mary, 21

*Our Singing Strength* (Kreymborg), 109

*Our Town* (Wilder), 145

"The Outcast" (Pinckney), 239*n*22

Owsley, Frank Lawrence, 252*n*17

*Oxford English Dictionary,* 66

Page, Thomas Nelson, 58, 79

Paris, 46, 101, 147

Parker, Dorothy, 96

Pastoral tradition, 63

Paterson, Isabel, 10, 130

Peacock, Edwin, 216

PEN, 171

*Penhally* (Gordon), 141

Perenyi, Baron, 257*n*30

Perenyi, Eleanor Stone, 129, 161, 224, 252*n*59, 257*n*30

*Peter Ashley* (Heyward), 154

Peterkin, Julia, 81, 147, 150, 160, 165, 255n67

Petigru, James Louis, 65

Phi Beta Kappa, 160

Phillips, Ulrich B., 141

Phillips, Wendell, 134

Pickford, Mary, *following p. 90*

Pinckney, Camilla Scott: and accusation against Allen, 86, 87; and appendicitis, 93; birth of daughter of, 18; burial site of, 110; Charleston homes of, 12–13, 23–25, *following p. 90*, 234n2; death and funeral of, 110; and deaths of family and friends of, 161, 168, 176; family background of, 16–21; Hervey's fictional portrayal of, 36–37; and JP's education, 27–28; JP's relationship with, 24–25, 26, 36–37, 115; and Lowell, 50; marriage of, 12, 16; and marriage prospects for JP, 36, 48–49, 88; mourning of, following husband's death, 32–33; nickname of, 237n36; personality of, 16–17, 36–37, 237n36; photograph of, *following p. 90*; in Richmond, 16–21, 31; and Southern States Art League, 44; and summers in New England, 54, 77–79, 86–88, 110; travel by, 28, 33, 45, 88, 91–93, 101

Pinckney, Caroline Phoebe Elliott, 14, 234n9

Pinckney, Chief Justice Charles, 4, 13

Pinckney, General Charles Cotesworth: in American Revolution, 4, 166; daughters of, 13, 28; father-in-law of, 206, 233n14; furniture of, 13; home of, 154; marriage of, 233n14; portrait of, *following p. 90*; as presidential candidate, 5; as signer of Constitution, 4, 231n1; and XYZ affair, 13

Pinckney, Rev. Charles Cotesworth, Jr., 12, 14, 29, 104

Pinckney, Cotesworth (grandfather of JP), 14, 72, *following p. 90*, 234n8, 264n18

Pinckney, Cotesworth (half-brother of JP): childhood and youth of, 15–18; death of, 161; employment of, in Richmond, 30; inheritance of, from father, 154, 249n1; marriage and children of, 30; photograph of, *following p.*

90; poetry by, 80, 245n13; servant of, 30; on stepmother Camilla, 16; travel by, 111; will of, 161, 256n23; as "wit," 30

Pinckney, Eliza Lucas: accomplishments of, 4, 5; biography of, 29; children of, 4; curtains in home of, 13; death of, from breast cancer, 214; at Hampton Plantation, 233n14; JP wearing dress of, 7, *following p. 90*; JP's article on, in *Encyclopedia Britannica*, 5; marriage of, 4; property owned by, 4, 154; tea cup of, in JP's home, 116; writings by, 4, 28

Pinckney, Elizabeth, 5, 233n15

Pinckney, Elsie Morris, 30

Pinckney, Frances Motte Middleton, 5, 233n15

Pinckney, Gustavus Memminger, 29

Pinckney, Harriott, 225, 226

Pinckney, Henry Laurens, 28

Pinckney, Josephine: aging of, 176; and aristocratic class, 6–8, 9, 12, 14, 30, 37, 60, 96–98, 102; in automobile accident, 119; automobile of, 32, 55, 189, 225; birth of, 1, 12; as book collector, 51; and breast cancer, 214, 216–17, 223–25, 229; as Charleston Museum trustee, 110, 126, 227; childhood and youth of, 23–28, 30–37, 53, 67; childhood homes of, 12–13, 23–25, *following p. 90*, 111–12, 234n2, 249n1, 250n29; christening of, 12, 14; and Code of honor, 6–8, 37, 38, 121, 124, 181, 217; commitment of, to writing career, 88–90; death and funeral of, 1, 11, 225–26; depression of, 7, 24, 83–84, 86, 88, 101, 108–9, 161; dogs of, 149, 189, 225; education of, 27–28, 33, 37, 47–49, 53, 240n35; family background of, xi, 4–7, 12–22, 28–30, 52–53, 116, 155–58, 192–93, 231–32n1, 240n48; father's relationship with, 23; finances of, 1, 109, 120, 154, 183, 189, 217, 250n29, 259n12; goals of and "Credo" for, 162, 163, 217–18; and Great Depression, 120–21; and Historic Charleston Foundation, 207, 224, 225; home of, on Chalmers Street, 11, *following p. 90*, 111–13, 115, 116–18, 211, 250n29; honorary degree awarded to,

Pickney, Josephine (continued)

160; honorary Phi Beta Kappa membership awarded to, 160; inheritance of, from father, 22, 154, 249n1; literary background of family of, 28–30; literary circle of, after World War I, 38–41; at MacDowell Colony, 145, 148–50; and modernism, 8–9, 38–39, 58–59, 96; mother's relationship with, 24–25, 26, 36–37, 115; in New York City, 57, 85, 173–76, 211; obituaries and tributes on, 226–27; parents of, 12–21, 23–25, 26, 36–37; personal notebooks of, xiii–xiv, 25; personality of, 1, 8, 31–32, 53, 123–24, 217, 229; photographs and portrait of, *following p. 90*; and Poetry Society of America, 57; and Poetry Society of South Carolina, xi, xii, 41–43, 57, 158, 159; political views of, 9, 164, 171–73, 176, 208–11; popularity of, 10–11; on profit motive, 156, 256n7; property owned by, 154, 226, 250n29; and psychoanalysis, 8–9; public persona of, 11, 97–98, 116; on race relations, 9, 172–73, 202, 207–10; religious views of, 73–74; as reviewer for *Saturday Review*, 99, 111; role of, in Charleston, 212; social life of and entertaining by, 56, 77–78, 79, 84, 85, 88, 92, 113–14, 117–18, 122, 123, 126, 127, 160–66, 212; and Southern Writers' Conferences, 140–43, 146–48; and Spirituals Society, 68–70, 140, 201; and symposium on the South, 132–34, 139, 151–52; and tea-party fiasco, 77–78; will of, 226, 250n29; work schedule of, 123; and World War II, 170–74

—friendships with men and romances of: with Allen, xii, 49, 53, 56, 78–79, 84–85, 91, 92, 96, 101, 120, 169, 188, 198–99; with Canby, 85, 94–97; with Davidson, xii, 100, 101–3; with Heyward, 34–37, 78–79, 118–19, 148, 159, 162; Lowell's view of relationship between Allen and, 53, 79, 84–85; with men generally, 32, 84, 91, 92, 117–19, 130, 145, 148–49; overview, 9–10, 123–31, 255n69;

with Waring, 113–15, 161–62; with Wigglesworth, 48–49, 54, 56, 86–89, 227; with Willkie, 166, 173–76

—travels by: in Canada, 78, 111; in Caribbean, 198, 212; in Europe, xii–xiii, 33, 45–46, 88, 91–93, 101, 113, 131, 213–14, 216; in New England, xiii, 54–55, 85–88, 94–95, 110, 134–35, 140, 224; to New York City, 57, 85, 173–76, 211; to Richmond, 30, 83; in South America, 264n20; to Washington, D.C., 83

—writing by: allegory about South, 153–54; awards and honors for, 1, 44, 100, 160, 188, 239n22; characteristics of, 2–3, 6, 60; essays, 135–36, 151–52, 160; goals for, 217; and Gullah language, 67–69, 122–23; historical fiction, 154–60, 162–63; historical research for, 155, 156–57, 158; and Imagism, 53, 67, 106; novels, 155–65, 169–70, 177–202, 212–17; and outdoor historical pageant in Charleston, 203–7; and pastoral tradition, 63; plays, 171, 258n24; poems, 26–27, 35, 37, 38, 44–45, 46, 53, 56, 58, 63, 67, 74, 79, 80, 81, 92, 144, 160, 239n22; on poetic principle, 67–68; poetry books, 89–90, 93, 103–10, 119–20; rhyming technique, 66; royalty checks from, 109, 120; sales of books, 109, 201, 217, 259n12; short stories, 37, 195. *See also* Poetry Society of South Carolina; and specific works

Pinckney, Maria Henrietta, 28

Pinckney, Mary Stewart, 15–16, 161, 235n16

Pinckney, Dr. Morton Morris, 30, 228

Pinckney, Governor (and General) Thomas: as ambassador to England, 7, 13; death of, 233n15; desk of, 13; Eldorado designed by, 5; as Federalist Party leader, 82; general's commission for, 233n15; library of, 29; mutiny among regiment of, 166; Pinckney Treaty with Spain negotiated by, 240n48; as presidential candidate, 5; will of, 233n15; wives and children of, 232n12, 233n15, 234n8

Pinckney, Thomas (1668–ca. 1704), 4, 231n1

Pinckney, Captain Thomas (1828–1915): birth of, 13; burial site of, 110; Charleston homes of, 12–13, 23–25, *following p. 90,* 234n2; child of, with Camilla Scott, 18; children of, with Mary Stewart, 15–16, 235n16; in Civil War, 15; death of, 22, 32; and death of Mary Stewart, 16; dedication of *Sea-Drinking Cities* to, 109; education of, 14–15; family background of, 12–16; finances of, 25, 30; JP's relationship with, 23; marriage of, to Camilla Scott, 12, 16; marriage of, to Mary Stewart, 15–16; memorial to, at Charleston Museum, 110; narrative by, on Civil War and Reconstruction, 28–29; personality of, 32; photograph of, *following p. 90;* as planter, 15–16; and Virginia writers, 29–30; will of, 22, 249n1

Pinckney, Thomas (JP's nephew), 30, 111, 256n23

Pinckney family, xi, 4–7, 12–22, 28–30, 52–53, 116, 231–32n1, 240n48; homes of, 12–13, 23–25, *following p. 90,* 155–58, 192–93, 226, 234n2. *See also* specific family members

Pinckney Island, 154

Planters and plantations, 73, 125, 126, 135, 153–54, 203–7. *See also* Aristocratic class; Eldorado Plantation; Fairfield Plantation

Poe, Edgar Allan, 93, 140

Poetry. *See* specific poets and titles of poems

*Poetry:* Monroe as editor of, 38, 44–45, 60; Pinckney's poetry published in, 44, 45, 46, 239n22; review of JP's *Sea-Drinking Cities* in, 106; second "Southern Number" of, 143–44; "Southern Number" of, 44–45, 60–61, 103, 143, 239n23

Poetry Society of America, 57, 59, 94, 241n4

Poetry Society of South Carolina: awards presented by, 44, 100, 109, 144, 239n22; Bragg as treasurer of, 45; and Colum, 63–64; decline of, 93, 120; and dilemma between censorship and community standards, 100, 248n29; drama committee of, 64; Folklore Committee of, 68; founding of, xi, 41–43, 57; goals for, in early days of, xii, 41–43; Heyward as president of, 158; JP as treasurer of, 42; meetings of, 42; social gatherings of, 113–14; speakers for, 42, 43–44, 54, 59, 85, 89, 101–3, 137, 139, 158, 241n4, 242n27; *Spoon River Anthology* performance sponsored by, 244n61; Waring as president of, 84, 87, 114

Poetry Society of Virginia, 77

Poll tax, 172

Pope, Alexander, 238n8

Popham, Louisa, 149

"Porgo" (Heyward), 89

*Porgy* (Heyward), 93, 98, 109

*Porgy and Bess* (Heyward and Gershwin), 158, 159, 243n37, 264n20

Pound, Ezra, 38, 48, 61, 95

Poverty, 71–72, 146. *See also* Great Depression

Prescott, Orville, 216

*Pride's Way* (Molloy), 184, 185

Pringle, Elizabeth Allston, 29

Pringle, John Julius, 105

Psychoanalysis, 8–9, 61

Publishing industry, 89, 95, 100–101, 186. *See also* specific publishers

Race relations: Charleston's Inter-racial Commission, 9; JP on, 9, 172–73, 202, 207–10; and tea-party fiasco, 77–78; and Willkie, 172–73. *See also* African Americans

Radcliffe College, 45, 47–49

Radio, 71, 171

Randolph, Harrison, 37

Random House, 89

Raney, William, 216

Ransom, John Crowe: and Agrarians, 252n17; award for, 144; and Charleston, 63, 66, 137; and Fugitives, 60–63, 66, 99, 100, 137; poetry by, 108, 144; and Southern Writers' Conference, 143

Ravenel, Beatrice Witte, 42, 58, 114, 165

Ravenel, Frank, 29

Ravenel, Harriott Horry Rutledge, 5, 29

Ravenel, Lise Rutledge, 16

Ravenel, St. Julien, 171

Reconstruction, 206

Recording machines, 70–71

Reed, Dan, 64, 244*n*61

Reed, Isabelle, 64

*Reflections in a Golden Eye* (McCullers), 163

Regionalism, 58, 59, 67, 134, 203. *See also* Southern literature

Register, Edward, 245*n*5

Register, Jane Heyward, 245*n*5

Reid, Helen, 247*n*15

Reid, Ogden, 247*n*15

"Renascence" (Millay), 38

Republican Party, 164, 166–68, 171, 175, 176, 209, 211

*The Reviewer,* 79–80, 93, 104, 188, 238*n*16

Revolutionary War, 4, 166, 206

Rice, Alice Hagan, 141

Rice, Cale Young, 109

Richmond, Va., 16–21, 30–31, 79–82, 88, 188

Rinehart, Stanley H., 100, 155, 159–60, 177

Rinehart, Ted, 100

Ripley, Clements, 165

Ripley, Katharine Ball, 165

Riskin, Everett, 191

Rives, Lizzie Scott, 18

Roberts, Elizabeth Maddox, 177

Robeson, Flora, 216

Robeson, Paul, 159

Robinson, Corrine Roosevelt, 127

Robinson, Edwin Arlington, 39, 46, 240*n*53

Rockefeller, John D., 134

Rockefeller Foundation, 165

*Roderick Random* (Smollett), 157

Rogers, George C., Sr., *following p. 90*

"Romantic Mr. Swallow" (Pinckney), 160

Roosevelt, Archibald Bulloch, 125

Roosevelt, Eleanor, 127, 168, 169

Roosevelt, Emily Sinkler, 124–25, 174, 175, 211

Roosevelt, Franklin D.: critics of, 125, 164; JP's views of, 156, 176; New Deal of, 156, 164; and presidential election of 1932, 146; and presidential election of 1940, 168; and presidential election of 1944, 174; supporters of, 126; on Willkie's reputation, 167; and World War II, 171

Roosevelt, Grace Lockwood, 125

Roosevelt, Nicholas, 174, 211

Roosevelt, Sara Delano, 127

Roosevelt, Theodore, 127

Ross, Mary Jane, 264–65*n*21

Ross Memorial Museum, 265*n*21

Russell, Ada, 50

Russell, George William. *See* A.E.

Rutledge, Archibald, 7, 29, 165

Rutledge, Caroline, 70, 73

Rutledge, Victoria, 25–27, 67, 111–12, 116, 121, 161, 194

Sainsbury, Noel, 158, 256*n*10

*Sanctuary* (Faulkner), 141

Sandburg, Carl, 38, 42, 128, 166, 240*n*53

Sanders, Emily, 186

Sandford, Robert, 155–56

Santayana, George, 47

Sappho, 86

Sass, Anna Eliza Ravenel, 29

Sass, George Herbert, 29

Sass, Herbert Ravenel: on aristocrats, 60; and *Cerberus,* 28; Eleanor Stone staying with family of, 252*n*59; during Great Depression, 120; historical novel by, 154; as naturalist and writer, 29, 59, 154; on realism, 59; and Society for the Preservation of Spirituals publication, 140; and Willkie, 165

*Saturday Evening Post,* 29, 131

*Saturday Review of Literature,* 10, 85, 94, 96, 99, 111, 119, 130, 144, 190, 227

Saxton, Eugene, 100–101, 103, 109, 138, 152, 158–59

Scarborough, Dorothy, 151

*Scarlet Sister Mary* (Peterkin), 150

Scherman, Harry, 186

Schools. *See* Education

SCHS. *See* South Carolina Historical Society (SCHS)

Scott, Camilla. *See* Pinckney, Camilla Scott

Scott, Fanny, 18, 19

Scott, Heningham Watkins Lyons, 17, 20, 21, 36, 235n21, 235n27

Scott, Imogene, 21

Scott, John, 19

Scott, Robert Eden, 17, 19, 20, 235n27

Scott, Taylor, 18, 19

Scott, Sir Walter, 28, 105

*Screwtape Letters* (Lewis), 199–200

*Sea-Drinking Cities* (Pinckney), 93, 100–101, 103–10, 115, 120, 249n54

Seabrook, Mamie, 22

Sedgwick, Ellery, 97

"Set My People Free" (Dorothy Heyward), 165

*Sewanee Review*, 151, 239n16

Seward, William, 17

Sexual mores, 38, 40–41, 81, 82–83, 95–96, 150

Shaftsbury, Earl of, 2, 155, 158, 256n10

Shaw, George Bernard, 64, 216

Sicily, 91–92

Simkins, Francis Butler, 60

Simms, William Gilmore, 28

Simon and Schuster, 154

Simons, Albert, *following p. 90*, 112–13, 124, 168, 187, 207, 226–27

Simons, Harriet Porcher (Stoney): family background of, 124; friendship between JP and, 9, 124; health problems of, 188; and Heyward's death, 168; and marriage of Sam Stoney, 149; in North River, N.Y., 186; photograph of, *following p. 90*; political views of, 125; and race relations, 208, 210; and Southern Writers' Conference, 146; and Spirituals Society, 71–75; on Waring, 263n48

Singal, Daniel J., 62

Sinkler, Anne Porcher, 125

Sinkler, Caroline Sidney "Aunt Cad," 54–55, 83, 92, 124

Sinkler, Carrie. *See* Lockwood, Caroline Sinkler

Sinkler, Charles Wharton, 124

*Skylines and Horizons* (Heyward), 83

Slavery, 205, 206, 208

*Smart Set*, 81

Smith, Alice Ravenel Huger, 44, 112, 187, 203, 207

Smith, Chard Powers, 95, 149, 186

Smith, "Cotton Ed," 263n48

Smith, D. E. Huger, 112

Smith, Heningham Ellet, 204

Smith, J. J. Pringle, 102, 204, 207

Smith, Lillian, 202

Smith, Reid, 146

Smythe, Augustine T., 74

Snowden, Yates, 43, 146

Society for the Preservation of Old Dwellings (SPOD), 112, 146, 249n6

Society for the Preservation of Spirituals, 68–75, 127, 140, 243n37, 243n41, 243n50, 244n59, 244n63, 244n65; concerts by, 74–76, 127, 146–47, 201, 244n63, 244n65

Society of the Cincinnati, 5, 7

Songs. *See* Spirituals

*Songs of Vagabondia* (Hovey), 107

South: A.E. on, 139; and Agrarians, 6, 136–39, 142–43, 151–52, 153, 202–3, 252n17; Cash on, 203; Code of honor in, 6–8, 37, 38, 121, 124, 181, 210, 217; industrialization in, 153–54; JP on, 132–36, 139–40, 151–52, 208–9; JP's allegory of, 153–54; and Lost Cause, 58, 79; Lowell on, 205; New South, 60, 135, 144; symposium (1930) on, 132–34, 139, 151–52; Tate on, 144; women as southern belles in, 21, 31, 81. *See also* Aristocratic class; Southern literature

South America, 264n20

South Carolina Historical Society (SCHS), 158, 176, 256n10

Southern belles, 21, 31, 81

*Southern Literary Magazine*, 239n16

Southern literature: and Agrarians, 6, 136–39, 142–43, 151–52, 153, 202–3, 252n17; and Canby, 98–99; Clark on, 255n67; compared with Irish writers, 63–65; decline of renaissance in, 93–94; and distinctive features of the South, 59–60; and Fugitives, 60–63, 66, 93, 99–100, 134, 137, 144; and Gullah language, 66–68, 69; Heyward on, 57, 60; and language, 65–68; literary magazines and other publications on, 43, 61, 79–80, 93–94, 238–39n16, 242n18; and Lost Cause, 58, 79; Mencken on, 80; and modernism, 58–59; in 1940s, 202–3; in nineteenth century, 58; and northern critics, 58; *Poetry*'s second "Southern Number," 143–44; *Poetry*'s "Southern Number," 44–45, 60–61, 103, 143, 239n23; Richmond and southern renaissance, 79–82; rivalry for male patrons among southern women writers and editors, 81, 82–83; and Southern Writers' Conference, 140–43, 146–48, 254–55n56; and spirituals, 68–75; and Stork, 58. *See also* Charleston Renaissance/Charleston Literary Movement; and specific authors and titles

Southern States Art League, 44

Southern Writers' Conferences, 140–43, 146–48, 253n34, 254–55n56

Spain, 91, 158

Spanish Civil War, 158

Spencer, Herbert, 47–48

Spirituals, 68–75, 127, 140, 146–47, 201, 244n63, 244n65

Spirituals Society. *See* Society for the Preservation of Spirituals

*Splendid in Ashes* (Pinckney): Charlestonians' reactions to, 227–28; Grimshawe home in, 219, 264n18; plot of, 218–23; reviews of, 227, 229; themes of, 6, 72, 218; writing and revising of, 218, 224, 225

SPOD. *See* Society for the Preservation of Old Dwellings (SPOD)

*Spoon River Anthology* (Masters), 244n61

"Spring Makes Me Wonder" (Pinckney), 45, 103

Sprunt, Alexander, 120

St. Cecilia Society, 40, 69, 127

Stagg, Hunter, 79

Stalin, Joseph, 171, 172

Stallings, Laurence, 147–48

Stassen, Harold, 211

*State of Union*, 167

Stavisky, Serge Alexandre, 264n19

Stearns, Harold E., 48, 132

Stein, Gertrude, 212

Steinbeck, John, 1, 10, 184, 188, 190

Stephens, James, 138, 242n27

Stewart, Annie, 16

Stewart, Dan, 15

Stewart, Francis, 162

Stewart, Kate, 162

Stewart, Lucy, *following p. 90*

Stewart, Mary Amanda. *See* Pinckney, Mary Stewart

Stewart, Mary Williamson, 16

"Still Life" (Pinckney), 74

Stone, Eleanor. *See* Perenyi, Eleanor Stone

Stone, Ellis Spencer, 129, 214

Stone, Grace Zaring: daughter of, 129, 161, 252n59, 257n30; film version of work by, 213; friendship between JP and, 10, 129–31, 224; and *Great Mischief* by JP, 199; in Italy, 214; JP's comparison of self to, 163; marriage of, 129, 131; in Mexico, 161; novels by, 10, 129, 131, 188, 213, 251n56; and relationships with men, 129–30, 176; social life of, 212; and *Splendid in Ashes* by JP, 228

Stone, Irving, 191

Stoney, Frances Frost. *See* Frost, Frances

Stoney, Louisa McCord, 24, 78, 124

Stoney, Samuel Gaillard, Jr.: and Gullah language, 66; and Heyward's death, 168; and Historic Charleston Foundation, 207; historical information from, 157; on JP's health, 216; marriage of, 149–50, 163, 255n64, 257n30;

photograph of, *following p. 90;* and spirituals, 73–74, 140, 146; and Grace Stone, 129; and *Three O'Clock Dinner* by JP, 187; travels by, 198; and Willkie, 165

Stork, Charles, 58, 241n4

Stowe, Harriet Beecher, 28, 65

*Strange Fruit* (Smith), 202

"Strange" (Pinckney), 239n22

*Stygian Freight* (Rice), 109

Sulzberger, Arthur O., 263n48

Sunday, Billy, 72

"Swamp Lilies" (Pinckney), 239n22

Synge, John, 63, 64

Taggart, Lucy, 55

*Tall Men* (Davidson), 100, 109

Tarkington, Booth, 218

Tate, Allen: and Agrarians, 137–38, 252n17; and Charleston Literary Movement, 62; on Davidson's review of *Sea-Drinking Cities,* 107; and *Double-Dealer,* 80; and Fugitives, 61–63, 93, 99, 137; and JP, 137–38, 144, 253n20; and JP's novel writing, 154; and Monroe, 143; in Paris, 147, 254n56; and *Poetry's* second "Southern Number," 143–44; review of *Culture in the South* by, 151; and *The Reviewer,* 81; and Southern Writers' Conferences, 141, 143, 147, 254–55n56

Taylor, Bill, 202, 262n23

Taylor, Prentiss: as artist, 184, 189, 199, 254n52, 255n69; in Charleston, 148–49; and Great Depression, 121; and *Great Mischief* by JP, 199, 200; home of, *following p. 90;* and JP on race relations, 210; and JP on Republican Party, 211; and JP's death, 227; and JP's romance with Willkie, 174, 176; at MacDowell Colony, 145; and modern art, 128; as publisher, 254n52; and *Three O'Clock Dinner* by JP, 184, 187, 190, 191

Teasdale, Sara, 86, 114

Television, 211

Tennyson, Alfred Lord, 27

Theocritus, 91

"They Shall Return as Strangers" (Pinckney), 6, 153–54

*They Stooped to Folly* (Glasgow), 2

Thompson, Basil, 80

Thompson, Dorothy, 166, 247n15

Thoreau, Henry David, 121

*Three Black Pennys* (Hergesheimer), 85

*Three O'Clock Dinner* (Pinckney): African Americans' reactions to, 189; award for, 1, 188; as book club selection, 1, 185–86; Charlestonians' reactions to, 186–87; completion of, 185; criticisms of, 212, 216; dust jacket for, *following p. 90,* 184; film version of, 1, 190–92, 205, 212–13; humor in, 2; plot and themes of, 6, 177–83, 222; promotional activities for, 186, 188; publication of, in Southern Classics series, xi; publishing contract for and earnings from, 1, 183–84, 189, 259n12; readers' reactions to, 169–70, 188–90; success of, 1, 185–86, 188–91; title changes for, 185

Thurber, James, 101

Thurmond, Strom, 211

*Time* magazine, 200, 226

*The Time of Man* (Roberts), 177

Timrod, Henry, 29

*Tobacco Road* (Caldwell), 202

Tone, Franchot, 159

Tourism, 11, 71, 97–98, 203–4, 207

Tracy, Spencer, 167

*Transatlantic* magazine, 208–9

Triplett, Mary, 21

Truman, Harry, 211

Turkey, 213

Turner, Lana, 190, 191–92

"Twelve Sang the Clock: New Poems" (Pinckney), 119–20

*Uncle Tom's Cabin* (Stowe), 28, 65

Underwood, Thomas, 61

Unitarians, 200

University of Chicago, 141

University of Michigan, 139

University of North Carolina, 77, 103, 108, 132, 134, 139, 146

University of South Carolina, 146

University of the South, 254n56

University of Virginia, 138, 140, 142

University of Wisconsin, 141

Untermeyer, Louis, 238n6

Valentine, Mann S., 20

Valentine House, 20–21, *following p. 90*

Van Doren, Carl, 95, 165, 166, 199, 247n15

Van Doren, Irita: divorce of, 247n15; and Glasgow, 10; as literary editor of *New York Herald-Tribune*, 95, 130, 166; physical appearance of, 95; and Grace Stone, 130; and Willkie, 165, 166, 175

Van Doren, Mark, 95

Van Vechten, Carl, 80, 117, 145, 148, 189, 212

Vandenburg, Arthur, 211

Vanderbilt University, 60–63, 102, 103, 146

Verner, Elizabeth O'Neill, 44, 71

Vesey, Denmark, 165

Viking Press: and Covici on state of fiction, 213; and film projects, 194; and *Great Mischief* by JP, 198–201; and *My Son and Foe* by JP, 216; in 1920s generally, 89; pressure on JP by, 194; and *Splendid in Ashes* by JP, 227–29; and *Three O'Clock Dinner* by JP, 1, 177, 183–86, 188–90. *See also* Best, Marshall A.

*Virginia Quarterly Review*, 94, 138, 153, 160, 165

Voodoo, 195, 261n4

Wade, John Donald, 252n17

*The Wagon and Star* (Leitch), 245n2

Walcott, "Jersey Joe," 211

Wallace, Henry, 171

Wallace, Lew, 101

*Wampum and Old Gold* (Allen), 47

Waring, Ann Gammel, 210

Waring, Clelia, 124, 188–89, 228

Waring, Laura Witte, 114, 164, 249n12

Waring, Thomas R., Sr.: contributions of, 114; death of, 161; and *The Carolina Low-Country*, 140; as editor of *Charleston Evening Post*, 59, 107, 113, 114; and *Hilton Head* research with JP, 161; and Historic Charleston Foundation, 207; on JP's literary honors, 160; and outdoor historical pageant, 207; personality of, 161–62; as president of Poetry Society of South Carolina, 84, 87, 114; reference to, in *Splendid in Ashes* by JP, 265n28; romantic relationship between JP and, 113–15, 161–62; and *Sea-Drinking Cities* by JP, 107, 109

Waring, Thomas R., Jr., 124, 224

Waring, Waties, 210–11, 263n48

Warner, Sylvia Townsend, 195

Warren, Robert Penn, 61, 143, 160, 252n17

Washington, George, 5, 7, 19, 146

*The Waste Land* (Eliot), 48, 65

Wauchope, George Armstrong, 106

Way, Rev. William, 87

Webster, Noah, 65

Welles, Orson, 191

Welty, Eudora, 217

West, Rebecca, 1, 166

Westo Indians, 156

Westwood, Horace, 200

Whaley, Percy C., 65

Wharton, Edith, 3, 4

*What's O'Clock* (Lowell), 119

White Sulphur Springs resort, 21, 54

Whitelaw, Robert N. S., 120, 128, 168, 203–7, 265n24

Whitman, Walt, 121, 134

Whitney, Mrs. Harry Payne, 97

Whittemore, Thomas, 213

Widdemer, Margaret, 92

Wigglesworth, Frank, 87

Wigglesworth, George, 49

Wigglesworth, Isabella "Bay," 91–92, 128, 198, 224, 227

Wigglesworth, Mary Dixwell, 49

Wigglesworth, Michael, 48

Wigglesworth, Richard Bowditch ("Dick"): career of, 128, 246n38; education of, 48; family background of, 48–49; JP's relationship with, 48–49, 54, 56, 86–89, 227; marriage of, 246n38; photograph of, *following p. 90*

Wilde, Oscar, 64, 238n11

Wilder, Thornton, 145

Williman, Helen, 101

Willkie, Edith, 167, 169, 175

Willkie, Wendell: book review by, 165–66; career of, 164; in Charleston, 164–66, 169; correspondence between JP and, xii, 166, 208; death of, 176, 211; and Dock Street Theatre, 168; and *Hilton Head* by JP, 169–70; marriage of, 167, 169, 175; *One World* by, 173; photograph of, *following p. 90;* physical appearance of, 166; and presidential election of 1940, 164, 166, 167–68; and presidential election of 1944, 174, 175–76, 211; "Report to the People" radio speech by, 171–72; reputation of, 166, 167, 258n25; romance between JP and, 173–76; as social liberal, 172–73; and World War II, 170–73

Wilson, Edmund, 39

Wilson, James Southall, 140, 141

Wilson, Woodrow, 127, 141

*Winner Take All,* 145

Winship, Larry, 227

*Winter Visitor* (Stone), 188, 213

Winter Wheat Press, 254n52

Wister, Owen, 55, 100

Witte, Beatrice, 29

Wittgenstein, Ludwig, 65

Wolfe, Thomas, 1, 160, 188

"Woman of This Earth" (Frost), 150, 255n69

Women: antifeminine reaction to, in literary community, 41, 47–48; Bennett on marriage for, 36; changing role of, 135–36; and cult of beauty, 81; dual citizenship of, 98; Gibson Girl image of, 31, 32; mixing of marriage and career by, 83–84, 115, 123; New Woman image of, 17; rivalry for male patrons among southern women writers and editors, 81, 82–83; Southern belle image of, 21, 31, 81. *See also* specific women

Woodward, Henry, 155–58, 161, 164, 170

Woolf, Virginia, 188, 217

World War I, 33, 36, 40, 49, 51, 164, 238n6

World War II, 170–74

"Wounded Woman" (Pinckney), 104

Wright, Richard, 1, 188

Wylie, Elinor, 53, 55, 80, 101, 240n53

XYZ affair, 13

Yale University Press, Younger Poets series, 47

*Yearbook of the Poetry of South Carolina,* 43, 99, 100, 120

Yeats, William Butler, 64

Yezierska, Anzia, 95

"Yolanda's Garden" (Pinckney), 119

Young, Stark, 252n17

*The Young Melbourne* (Cecil), 165–66

Zeigler, John, 216

Printed in the USA
CPSIA information can be obtained
at www.ICGtesting.com
CBHW031604190424
7137CB00024B/158/J